The College Board®Technical Handbook
for the
Scholastic Aptitude Test®
and
Achievement Tests

Thomas F. Donlon
Editor

COLLEGE ENTRANCE EXAMINATION BOARD, NEW YORK, 1984

The Admissions Testing Program is sponsored by the College Board, a nonprofit membership organization that provides tests and other educational services for students, schools, and colleges. The membership is composed of more than 2,500 colleges, schools, school systems, and education associations. Representatives of the members serve on the Board of Trustees and advisory councils and committees that consider the programs of the College Board and participate in the determination of its policies and activities.

Copies of this book may be ordered from College Board Publications, Box 886, New York, New York 10101.

The price is $19.95 per copy.

This book was prepared and produced for the College Board by Educational Testing Service (ETS), which develops and administers the tests of the Admissions Testing Program for the College Board.

The College Board and Educational Testing Service are dedicated to the principle of equal opportunity, and their programs, services, and employment policies are guided by that principle.

Library of Congress Catalog Card Number: 83-073742
International Standard Book Number: 0-87447-183-4
Printed in the United States of America

Contents

Chapter I. The Admissions Testing Program: A Historical Overview

Chapter II. Psychometric Methods Used in the Admissions Testing Program

Chapter III. The Scholastic Aptitude Test

Chapter IV. The Test of Standard Written English (TSWE)

Chapter V. The Achievement Tests

Chapter VI. The Student Descriptive Questionnaire, the Summary Reporting Service, and the Student Search Service

Chapter VII. Construct and Content Validity of the SAT

Chapter VIII. Predictive Validity of the ATP Tests

Chapter IX. Descriptive Statistics on College Board Test Takers and Other Reference Groups

Chapter X. Special Studies

Figures and Tables

Chapter IV

Chapter V

Chapter IX

Chapter X

Foreword

Since an earlier edition of this book was published in 1971, tests and their proper usage and role in American society have been subjected to public scrutiny and debate unparalleled in our history. The admissions tests of the College Board—the Scholastic Aptitude Test (SAT), the Test of Standard Written English, and the Achievement Tests—have been at the center of the controversy because they touch the lives of more than one million college-bound high school seniors each year. This book, which describes the technical characteristics and gradual evolution of the tests, the academic and social background of the test takers, and the research findings that testify to the validity of the use of the tests, is intended to help inform the debate and those who use the test results.

The tests have gained a new prominence and role since 1971 as both educators and the public became aware of a decade-long decline in SAT scores of college-bound students. The College Board's Advisory Panel on the Scholastic Aptitude Test Score Decline issued a report, *On Further Examination,* which documented the extent of the decline and offered hypotheses as to its causes. This 1977 report also stimulated several investigations and reports that advocated reform of secondary school education. In the course of these events, the SAT was thrust into a new role, that of the nation's report card. Although scores on a test taken voluntarily by only one-third of all high school graduates cannot be representative of the attainments of all high school graduates, average SAT scores have been used by the public and policy makers for this purpose. Thus, this book will undoubtedly serve somewhat broader purposes than its predecessors in describing the nature and content of the tests and the characteristics of the students taking them.

On behalf of the College Board, I wish to thank all of my many colleagues at Educational Testing Service who contributed to this volume. Thomas F. Donlon deserves special commendation for his skillful work as main author and editor. Gretchen W. Rigol, my colleague at the College Board, merits gratitude for her helpful comments and perceptive suggestions on the draft chapters.

Even as this volume is written, changes in the College Board's testing programs are under consideration. Advanced techniques and theories, made possible largely by the application of electronic technology, give promise of strengthened technical qualities of tests and improved communication about and utilization of test-related information.

ROBERT G. CAMERON
Executive Director, Research and Development
The College Board
December 1984

Preface

This is the second edition of a technical handbook on the admissions tests offered by the College Board. In preparing the first edition of this book, William H. Angoff (1971) noted that it was intended for "the specialist who needs technical information about the Admissions Testing Program." Because the first book was a summary of a considerable number of research and operational studies of the Scholastic Aptitude Test (SAT) and the Achievement Tests, Angoff pointed out that it "assumes a reader fairly well acquainted with the concepts and statistics of educational measurement." Further, he noted the report differed from a number of preceding Board publications in that it was not intended to tell someone how the tests might properly be used in admissions and guidance but, instead, to "provide all the data needed for a comprehensive technical evaluation of the tests."

These general purposes remain valid for this second edition of the book, which is made necessary by a number of changes over the intervening years. The Admissions Testing Program (ATP) of today looks in many respects different from that described in the first handbook. For example, the Student Descriptive Questionnaire (SDQ) was launched in 1971. A second major development was the introduction into the SAT administration of a new test of English language ability, the Test of Standard Written English, in 1974. Each of these developments had a far-reaching impact on the program. In order to make the Test of Standard Written English possible, it was necessary to reorganize the verbal and mathematical sections of the SAT. For the SDQ, the approach to the data collection was a "first" for the Board, in that it was an instrument sent to the student along with the registration materials, completed by the student on his or her own time, and mailed to the ATP with the Registration Form. Thus, it expanded the requirements for matching test-taker information secured at different times, and, as will be seen, it subtly and fundamentally altered the nature of the program. In the years following the SDQ's introduction, the nature of the information "products" of the Board began to shift, with more emphasis on the description of subgroups defined through information provided by the SDQ.

A number of other, lesser changes have also been made. The Admissions Testing Program is, in effect, continually revised to meet changing conditions. The introduction of a new item type, quantitative comparison, into the SAT—and the establishment of Academic Advisory Committees in subject-matter areas, with representation from committees of the Admissions Testing Program—are changes and modifications that have come about since the first report was published. Yet another example is the establishment of an SAT committee of college and high school faculty members, with responsibility for overseeing the development of the test and reviewing all forms of it. The committee's responsibilities include reviewing test specifications and advising the College Board on policy matters relative to the test. In some cases, such changes were known to be in the offing even as the earlier book was written. The SDQ, for example, was being planned and evaluated as the first edition was printed. Much the same situation exists today, giving a contingent quality to any description of the present ATP.

The presentation of the technical side of the testing, however, would be incomplete without some effort to convey the background of the program. Recognizing this, Angoff and Henry S. Dyer, in preparing the introductory chapter of the first edition, included a brief historical summary of the College Board, drawing heavily upon the work of its first historian, Dr. Claude Fuess. This practice is repeated here, and their summary is reprinted with slight modifications. As the account makes clear, this is not the history of a testing agency attempting to market services to colleges; it is the story of an association of colleges joining together for the common purpose of facilitating the transition of students from secondary school to college. The development of the ATP is a process for which decisions are infused with educational, as well as psychometric values, and which requires, for its understanding, not only the interpretation of various correlations between tests and grades, but an appreciation of the fundamental educational purposes of institutions and individuals.

A great many people have contributed to this handbook. Authors, reviewers, and other contributors to specific chapters are acknowledged at the end of each chapter. General administrative direction was provided at Educational Testing Service by Marion G. Epstein and Arthur M. Kroll, as Vice Presidents for the College Board Programs Division. Project administration was provided by a number of program directors, notably June Stern, Richard J. Noeth, and John A. Centra. Valuable reviews were supplied by Professor Robert L. Linn of the University of Illinois, Professor Lloyd Bond of the University of Pittsburgh, and Robert G. Cameron and Gretchen W. Rigol of the College Board. A special debt of gratitude is owed to those who served an editorial function over the period of the writing: Lou H. Kremer, Charlotte A. Kurst, Joan S. Paszamant, and Mary R. Zavada, and to those who handled the text preparation activity: Alice M. Bohmler, Jane E. Harris, Louise W. Hedberg, Linda C. Stroman, Linda L. Thompson, Clara M. Tyler, and Dawn M. Wolkenfeld. As with the earlier book, the staff of the ETS Publications Division provided expert coordination throughout the production of the publication; Eric W. Coolidge served as liaison for the Publications Division.

The book, like its predecessor, should find many applications. Inevitably, however, descriptions of something as dynamic as the Admissions Testing Program can begin to need updating even as they are printed. The seeds of a successor volume have already been cast in the program activity of today.

Thomas F. Donlon
November 1984

CHAPTER I

The Admissions Testing Program: A Historical Overview

The Beginning: Systematizing the Testing

The inception of the College Entrance Examination Board resulted from a resolution adopted at a meeting of the Association of Colleges and Preparatory Schools of the Middle States and Maryland, held in Trenton, New Jersey on December 2, 1899. The move culminated efforts over several years by the association and a number of educators in the East led by Nicholas Murray Butler, President of Columbia University, and Charles W. Eliot, President of Harvard University. The formation of the Board, formally announced on November 17, 1900, was described by the Board's first historian, Claude M. Fuess (1950, p. 3),* as the first organized "attempt to introduce law and order into an educational anarchy which towards the close of the nineteenth century had become exasperating, indeed almost intolerable, to schoolmasters."

At this time there was, in the opinion of the founders of the Board, appallingly little agreement among the colleges about the types of subject-matter preparation and standards of proficiency required of the applicants. One headmaster, for example, complained that for 40 or so boys preparing for college in his school, he had to have more than 20 different classes. The effect of this diversity on the secondary schools was to make the task of preparing their students for college extremely difficult and the task of choosing a college difficult and confusing for the students.

In its attempt to accomplish its purpose and introduce order into the transition from school to college, the College Board established the beginnings of a

system of syllabuses or "course requirements" on which schools and colleges could agree, and which might form the basis of a system of tests offering the badly needed uniformity. The tests would be uniform in subject matter, uniformly administered at uniform times, but held in many places to meet the convenience of the students. They also would be uniformly graded. Tests of this sort were expected to effect savings of time, money, and effort in administering college admissions and to greatly aid the work of the secondary schools by reducing confusion and easing the strain on students. It was also expected that such a system of tests would allow the group of colleges and secondary schools to achieve a set of common goals without asking the colleges to surrender their prerogatives as to the particular tests they required of their applicants or the manner in which they selected their students.

The tests were secondary to the main purpose of the Board at that time, which was to provide a channel of communication between preparatory schools and colleges and to encourage a degree of uniformity in the secondary school curriculum. On the other hand, it is more than likely that these purposes would never have been achieved without the tests, which, upon acceptance by the colleges as a way of setting standards, paved the way for the introduction of uniform curriculums in preparatory schools.

In its first year of operation, the College Board held essay tests in nine subjects: English, French, German, Latin, Greek, history, mathematics, chemistry, and physics. The requirements in each subject were based upon the recommendation of the professional association in each subject-matter area. The content and structure of each test was then determined by a carefully selected committee of examiners, consisting of well-known teachers and scholars in the leading colleges and secondary schools in the East. After extensive preparation, the first tests were finally administered during the week of June 17, 1901, to 973 candidates at 69 testing centers. Thus, although the Board was as yet far from being

---

*In presenting the historical background chapter in the first edition of this handbook, authors William H. Angoff and Henry S. Dyer acknowledged the assistance provided by the content, and, in many instances, the particular phrasing used in Dr. Fuess's excellent overview of the Board's history. They also acknowledged the invaluable information provided by the College Board's Annual Reports.

a national institution—758 of the 973 students were seeking admission to either Columbia or Barnard—it was at least an operation with promising beginnings.

As with the committees of examiners, committees of readers were also chosen with care. These committees, one in each subject, met in the Columbia University Library to grade the papers. A total of 7,889 papers, averaging over 8 papers per student, were read and graded on a percentage-type scale, in which the designations Excellent, Good, Doubtful, Poor, and Very Poor were attached respectively to the ratings 90-100, 75-89, 60-74, 40-59, and below 40. Special attention was given to papers that were originally graded below 60; these were always reread and often discussed at length.

In the second year, Spanish, botany, geography, and drawing were added to the list of test subjects. In 1902, the number of test takers rose to 1,362, a 40 percent increase over the preceding year. Thereafter, growth was regular and continuous. In the course of the first decade, additional colleges became members of the Board, and by 1910, the number of test takers had increased to 3,731.

An important early development was the creation of a Committee of Review for the College Board as a whole. Its main function was to examine the requirements in each subject and arrange with the committees of examiners for modifying the requirements whenever this seemed desirable. It soon became clear that the very fact of the committee's existence had become an important factor in the development of the secondary school curriculum, for it had the effect of moving preparatory schools and colleges toward a badly needed system of uniform standards. However, like the establishment of the Board itself, this change was not universally applauded; many secondary schools and colleges regarded the movement toward uniform standards as a dangerous encroachment on their autonomy. In 1910, therefore, partly in response to this type of pressure, the designations for percentage grades (Excellent, Good, etc.) were dropped, and schools and colleges were left free to attach their own evaluations to the numerical grades.

The Twenties: Introducing the SAT

During the second decade of the Board's existence, the philosophy of admissions tests began to change, gravitating toward the idea of "comprehensive examinations," in which students would not be asked to repeat the facts that they had learned in school but to demonstrate an understanding of the relation of discrete facts to one another, to generalize the facts into working principles, and to apply them to new and unexpected situations. This development—the "New Plan," as it was called—provoked violent objections from the conservatives who insisted that it would be impossible to prepare students for the tests, that it would be difficult to grade the tests, and that tests of this sort would place a premium on superficial cleverness at the expense of scholarship. At the same time, the "New Plan" also tended to discourage attempts to outguess the tests and to predict the particular test questions that would appear in them.

By 1925, the College Board was ready to enter a new era. Stimulated by the World War I Committee for Classification of Personnel in the Army and its work in the testing of "general intelligence," the Board established a commission to investigate the relevance of these new psychological tests to college admissions, and on the commission's recommendation appointed an Advisory Committee of experts, including Carl C. Brigham, Henry T. Moore, and Robert M. Yerkes, to formulate a suitable test development approach. In April 1925, the Board accepted the recommendation that the psychological tests be administered in 1926 and appointed a committee of five with Professor Brigham at its head to prepare and score the tests. Within a short time, the Brigham Committee produced a manual on what they called the "Scholastic Aptitude Test," explicitly distinguishing it from tests of achievement in school subjects but disclaiming any intention to measure "general intelligence" or "general mental alertness." In their preface to the test manual, they included a paragraph expressing a point of view that is still regarded today as highly relevant to the use of test scores (Brigham et al. 1926, pp. 44-45):

"The present state of all efforts of men to measure or in any way estimate the worth of other men, or to evaluate the results of their nurture, or to reckon their potential possibilities does not warrant any certainty of prediction. . . . This additional test now made available through the instrumentality of the College Entrance Examination Board may help to resolve a few perplexing problems, but it should be regarded merely as a supplementary record. To place too great emphasis on test scores is as dangerous as the failure properly to evaluate any score or rank in conjunction with other measures and estimates which it supplements."

The first College Board Scholastic Aptitude Test, a multiple-choice test for the most part, was added to the College Board program and administered on June 23, 1926, to 8,040 students. During the first two years, it consisted of nine subtests: Definitions,

Arithmetical Problems, Classification, Artificial Language, Antonyms, Number Series, Analogies, Logical Inference, and Paragraph Reading. In 1928, these were reduced to seven and a year later to six. In 1929, Dr. Brigham decided that it had become necessary to divide the SAT into two separate sections, one measuring verbal aptitude and the other measuring mathematical aptitude. The decision to report two separate scores was made in order to give differential weight to verbal and mathematical aptitudes in accordance with the nature of the college to which the student was applying, and, in some instances, in accordance with the nature of the curriculum within the college.

The Middle Years: Establishing Standards and Procedures

The early 1930s brought additional changes. The Board moved still further toward developing comprehensive tests in each subject that would call upon a student's ability to integrate material learned from various sources in solving examination problems, rather than merely to recall and reproduce isolated bits of information. It also concentrated on gaining more consistency in its operation. Observations had been made, for example, that the number of students earning passing grades was fluctuating much too widely from one year to another. Because it seemed reasonable to assume that the test-taking populations were more stable than were the difficulties of the tests, the decision was made to fix the proportion passing each test and not allow it to vary from year to year as it had in the past.

The period of the middle 1930s was trying for the Board. The volume of June test takers had dropped over 35 percent from 1931 to 1936, and the Board was under serious criticism by the secondary schools that were chafing under the restrictions imposed on their curriculums. In response to pressures from the schools, the new requirements were broadened to stress general principles and large aspects of the curriculum rather than detailed subject matter.

Technical aspects of test construction also received increasing emphasis. For example, it was felt that the tests should not represent an accidental selection of questions, but a wide variety of areas within each subject, and should yield a score that would adequately reflect the student's ability and training. It was also felt that attention needed to be given to the reliability of the rating process, the methods of formulating the questions, and the production of tests that would continue to have a wholesome influence on the schools.

In 1937, for the first time, an additional administration was instituted—to be held in April, principally for scholarship applicants. In 1938, the April administration was extended to include applicants for admission to college who were not scholarship applicants. From then on, the April administration gained in prominence until in 1940 the number of students taking the SAT in April was larger than the number taking it in June. Because of this increase in the relative size (and importance) of the April administration, it was felt necessary to provide a means of comparing SAT scores on the April and June tests directly. Beginning in June 1941, the scores on every form of the SAT were equated directly to the scores on some preceding form of the SAT, and ultimately and indirectly to the April 1941 form. The group tested in April 1941 thus became the standardization group, defining the continuing scale in terms of which scores on all future forms of the SAT would be expressed.

Also for the first time in April 1937, wholly multiple-choice Achievement Tests were introduced in a move that accelerated the scoring and reporting process, improved test reliability, and permitted the examination of a broader range of subject matter. They were first reported on a scale with a mean of 500 and a standard deviation of 100 (like the scale that had been in use for the SAT since its introduction in 1926) and rescaled each year on the new test-taking group. Two years later, beginning with the April 1939 administration, adjustments were made in the scales for each of the Achievement Tests in accordance with the level and dispersion of the group choosing to take the test, as reflected by the verbal and mathematical sections of the SAT.

With the outbreak of World War II, Harvard, Yale, and Princeton decided as an emergency action to accelerate their program of studies and begin their college year in June or July. This shift made it necessary for their 1942 applicants to take the April Achievement Tests, which were all multiple-choice, instead of sitting for the six-day June Achievement Test program, which in 1941 still consisted of essay tests. It soon became evident that multiple-choice tests were giving admissions officers the information they needed to make their decisions and that the Board should commit itself broadly to the plan that Harvard, Yale, and Princeton had adopted on an emergency basis. This development, intended as a temporary measure in response to the nation's entry into the war, marked the end of the June essay-type tests after continuous use for 41 years.

At the same time, the Board, responding to the needs of the nation at war, developed the V-12 Testing Program for use in the selection of high school graduates for officer candidate training. It also provided tests for the U.S. Armed Forces Institute and the Army Specialized Training Program and involved itself in other operational and advisory capacities to the federal government. Toward the end of the war, in anticipation of the large numbers of veterans who would be seeking postsecondary education, the Board prepared tests for use in the college admission of veterans. It furnished tests for scholarship awards sponsored by the Westinghouse Company, constructed special tests for the Pepsi-Cola Scholarship Program, and assisted in the preparation of qualifying examinations for the Foreign Service, the Military Academy, the Naval Academy, the Coast Guard Academy, and the Bureau of Naval Personnel.

In 1947, the Board having focused its interests and activities on the transition from secondary school to college, turned over its special testing programs, including the military and naval academy tests, to the newly formed Educational Testing Service (ETS) for management. In later years, the service academies dropped their own tests in favor of using the College Board Admissions Testing Program. Special scholarship programs, similar to the Westinghouse and Pepsi-Cola programs of the forties, are managed today on behalf of the College Board by the College Scholarship Service staff at ETS.

The Fifties to the Seventies: Growing and Diversifying

The two-decade span from 1950 to 1970 was a period of astonishing increases in the numbers of people tested by the Board, increases that influenced the nature of the tests and the patterns for their administration. It was fortunate that these two decades were also the years in which the computer came into its own. Without high-speed data processing, the expansion of services to these much larger student populations would have been unthinkable. More complex score reports, more diverse interpretive information, and the integration of descriptive information about the students into the reports were all made possible by the new technology. High schools and colleges that administered Board tests were asked to test more often to accommodate the great increase in test takers. Whereas a single administration had been sufficient in the first years of the Board, and three was the norm in the late 1950s, by 1977 there were six national administrations a year.*

---

*Actually, there are 12 national testing days, because each of the six Saturday administrations is followed by a Sunday administration to accommodate students who cannot test on Saturday for religious reasons.

Further, the internal patterns of the administrations were altered. The two components of the ATP, the SAT and the Achievement Tests, did not grow at the same rate. In the 1950s and 1960s, the typical test day was devoted to both a morning program, the SAT, and an afternoon program, the Achievement Tests. The reduced proportion of students taking Achievement Tests in addition to the SAT resulted from the elimination of Achievement Test requirements by many colleges during the 1960s. By the 1970s, some of the administrations included only the SAT, as the ratio of SAT candidates to Achievement Test candidates changed from approximately three to one in 1956-57 to about five to one in 1977-78. Since 1975-76, Achievement Tests have been administered in the morning, at the same time as the SAT, on most test dates.

Expanded Offerings. By the time the first edition of this handbook was published in 1971, the College Board, then over 70 years old, had become a truly national organization. It had also broadened its perspective in an effort to respond to the greater variety of demands on the educational facilities of the country. In 1954, the Board had initiated the College Scholarship Service (CSS) to provide assistance in determining the need of students applying for financial aid and in administering scholarship programs. By the late 1970s, the CSS had surpassed the ATP in the number of individuals and institutions served. In addition to the SAT and Achievement Tests of its Admissions Testing Program, the Board also offered the Preliminary Scholastic Aptitude Test, the Advanced Placement Program, the College Placement Tests Program, the Comparative Guidance and Placement Program, and the College-Level Examination Program (CLEP).

In 1971, the National Merit Scholarship Corporation began using the Preliminary Scholastic Aptitude Test in its scholarship competitions. The test was renamed the Preliminary Scholastic Aptitude Test/National Merit Scholarship Qualifying Test. At about the same time, the College Board also developed a program of Spanish language admission tests for administration by its Puerto Rico office, and it offered, as a joint sponsor with ETS and later the Graduate Record Examinations Board, the Test of English as a Foreign Language (TOEFL), which measures the proficiency of foreign students in the English language. Finally, the Board had begun a program of seminars for admissions officers and another for guidance counselors and a validity studies computation service. As the 1960s came to an end, with opportunities for postsecondary education being more and more widely extended to youths who in the past would not have been college-bound, the Board, through its Commission on Tests, was reexamining its test offerings to see if they should be modified and extended to assess a wider range of talent.

The 1970s saw continued expansion in higher education. The Board moved to adapt to the many new problems it confronted by revising its governing structure and recognizing more ways in which institutions could hold membership. Within the ATP, the Student Descriptive Questionnaire (SDQ) was introduced (1971-72), as was the Summary Reporting Service (1972-73), a compilation of the information derived from the SDQ and the admissions tests.

Shortly thereafter, two new services were put into operation. The first, the College Locater Service, provided students with detailed information about colleges that met the students' criteria and an estimate of the likelihood of success if the students enrolled in specified colleges. The second, the Student Search Service, utilized test-taker files to help colleges identify specific kinds of students that they sought to attract. Each of these services indicated the Board's intention to implement the ''symmetrical'' set of services to students and institutions that the Commission on Tests had urged (College Board 1970). Although the College Locater Service was discontinued in 1973-74 for lack of sufficient interest, the Student Search Service has expanded each year through 1983.

Another major development throughout the seventies was the emergence of nontraditional education. Early College Board involvement in this area took the form of the Exxon-supported Commission on Nontraditional Study. An Office of New Degree Programs was jointly supported by the Board and ETS from 1971 through 1977. In the late 1970s, the Board launched another major initiative, Future Directions for a Learning Society. Each of these activities indicated both the importance of the new trends in higher education and the continued evolution of the nature of the Board itself. As the decade came to a close, the organization changed its name from the College Entrance Examination Board to simply the College Board. While the Admissions Testing Program remained the Board's largest enterprise overall, the Board's broad involvement in a variety of other areas indicated that during its more than 80-year history it had moved well beyond any single focus on entrance examinations.

SAT Score Decline. Nonetheless, it was the Admissions Testing Program that generated the most public attention during the 1970s as the mean SAT scores of test-taking juniors and seniors declined annually. The phenomenon, which actually began in 1963, continued throughout the seventies. A brief account is provided in Chapter IX of this handbook. The identification of the decline, and the release of information about it to the media and to the public, were facilitated by the introduction of Board-sponsored reports prepared by the Summary Reporting Service, notably, the annual publication of summary data in *National College-Bound Seniors* (College Board, 1983d).

The complex causes of the score decline were outlined in the report of the Advisory Panel on the SAT Score Decline, a blue-ribbon committee of educators and measurement specialists who met under the chairmanship of Willard Wirtz, and whose report *On Further Examination* (College Board 1977) delineated the major changes in American social life and in the schools that probably underlie the shift. The phenomenon thrust the Board and the SAT into unfamiliar and unwanted roles as evaluators of American secondary school curriculums and instruction. It led the Board to issue repeated warnings that the SAT is not intended as a measure of a school's educational accomplishments, and that one cannot evaluate the quality of a school's programs by the average SAT score of those students who choose to take the SAT. Nationwide, about one-third of all high school graduates take the SAT, but the percentage varies greatly from one school to another. Moreover, the verbal section of the SAT is so broadly constituted, and its item types typically so far removed from school-centered materials, that no precise curriculum counterpart exists for the test. The verbal section reflects learnings that are acquired in a variety of settings, and of these, the school system is merely one. To some extent, this is true of the mathematical section of the SAT also. While mathematics education is almost entirely centered in the schools, the mathematical section of the SAT consists predominantly of material commonly covered in the first nine grades. Only a few questions relate to material normally covered in first-year geometry.

The Coaching Issue. With the issuance of the Wirtz Panel's report and the abating of the pace of the SAT score decline in the late seventies, public attention to the phenomenon decreased. Admissions testing, however, was not out of the limelight. Coaching for ATP tests, an issue that emerged in the sixties, became a topic of lively debate in the seventies.

The role of ATP tests in admissions decisions gives them considerable—sometimes exaggerated—importance in the eyes of students. Not unnaturally, students seek a preparation strategy that will enhance their scores. Various forms of short-term intensive preparation or coaching for the SAT have been offered both by schools and by outside commercial groups, but their usefulness is disputed. Some of the issues and findings concerning coaching for the SAT are described in Chapter III.

Concern about the coaching issue has influenced the nature and development of the ATP. For example, the extensive explanations of item types and the sample questions in the ATP publications provided free to students are intended to help make all test takers equally "testwise." In the SAT, verbal test material that would require special knowledge or preparation is avoided, and for the mathematical portion, review of basic math concepts is recommended. Comments specific to the coaching issue are also included in the annually revised ATP publications.

For the Achievement Tests, which are directly related to curriculum and instruction, coaching is not an issue. Rather, the problem facing the committee of school and college teachers responsible for the content of each test is that of identifying the common core of subject matter included in most secondary school courses and those parts of the secondary school curriculum that are the necessary basis for college work.

Changing Test Populations. As the ATP grew in the sixties and seventies, it attracted not only a greater number of students, but an increasingly diverse group. In a society concerned about equity for its minority groups, equality of access to education became a national goal, and the proper role of admissions tests in the access of minorities became a major question for the College Board. As more and more minority students sought access to college,* the College Board tests began to change. Their fundamental psychometric properties remained the same, but increasingly their content was made to reflect the subcultural diversity of the larger society. Minority educators undertook increased involvement in the making of the tests; there was increasing sensitivity to and recognition of the varieties of backgrounds that test takers reflected.

As noted by Hanford (1976, p. 6), the Board's focus on minority problems was not limited to con-

cerns for its tests. He wrote, "It can be seen that the College Board's response to the basic social issues has taken essentially four forms, or more properly has taken place in four arenas—its forums, the demonstration projects in which it has participated, its testing programs, and its financial aid services." Within the testing programs, a number of responses are not centrally concerned with the technical aspects of the tests at all, as in Board policies for fee waivers, for minority student searches, and for the training of admissions personnel in the problems unique to identifying minority talent.

The shifting patterns in test populations were also reflected in the increasing proportion of female test takers. While the absolute number of males taking the test declined in recent years, the absolute number of females increased, so that in the late seventies females constituted approximately 51 percent of the group. At the same time, there was increasing variation in the age of college entrance; more older people who had deferred college now wished to continue their education. The ATP was increasingly called upon to serve not only a larger population, with a broader range for both test takers and colleges, but to facilitate decision making for a wider array of educational life patterns.

Testing Under Scrutiny. Increasing diversity in the population being tested for admission to colleges and universities coincided with a greater emphasis on the law as a medium for social change in America. It is not surprising, then, that the College Board has had to consider the implications for its work of major courtroom decisions such as the Supreme Court's ruling in *Bakke v. Board of Regents.*† As Fincher (1979) noted, the Bakke decision may be interpreted as a confrontation between individual rights and group rights, and as a ruling that individual rights may not be denied by group considerations. A diversification of admissions criteria is now public policy.

The College Board recognized the far-reaching effects of such legal precedents. It was becoming clear that efforts to maintain test fairness, while protecting the rights of both the test takers and the score-using institutions, would be a continuing challenge. The legal issues that influence the Board's attempt to meet this challenge and impact upon the structure

*The proportion of ethnic minority students among test takers rose from 11 percent in 1973 to almost 19 percent in 1983. Although all minority groups showed increased rates of participation, the largest was that for Oriental students, which doubled from 2 percent in 1973 to more than 4 percent in 1983. The number of Black students increased from 7 percent of all students in 1973 to more than 9 percent in 1980, but has declined slightly in each of the years since 1980.

†The celebrated *Bakke* case concerned a lawsuit by a medical school applicant who alleged that his constitutional rights were infringed when he was denied admission in spite of formal criteria, including test scores, that were superior to those of minority students admitted under a special program.

of the Admissions Testing Program include: 1) student rights to control the dissemination of the test scores* and 2) the need for proper procedures when testing organizations try to validate the authenticity of a test score against the evidence of impersonation, copying answers, or similar deviations.

In the late 1970s, critics of testing began calling for specific legislation to control the operations of testing organizations. The first of these laws, passed in June 1979 in New York State, required extensive and last-minute changes in the ATP for the 1979-80 testing year. The New York bill was introduced by Senator Kenneth P. LaValle and became effective January 1, 1980. Commonly referred to as the "disclosure" law, it required testing agencies to do the following (among other things):

1. Disclose all postsecondary admissions tests after each administration. (The Achievement Tests were specifically exempted.)
2. Provide any test taker, on request, with the test questions, correct answers, and a copy of his or her own answer sheet, so that both question content and scoring accuracy could be checked. (A reasonable fee could be charged for this service.)
3. File with the state's education commissioner copies of all studies related to the tests.
4. Provide students with information explaining what each test is designed to measure, its limitations, and how it is scored.

In order to comply, the ATP had to cancel some test administration dates in New York that had already been announced. However, for most of the test administrations, test disclosure services were made available to New York test takers, in conformance with the new law.

Difficulties with the new legislation led to several amendments in June 1980, only six months after its implementation. The major changes, which expanded the requirements to the Achievement Tests, included:

1. The exemption of low-volume tests from annual disclosure, but with the requirement that each of these tests be disclosed within three years of their administration in the state.
2. The requirement that opportunities for testing be made available to those who cannot test on Saturdays for religious reasons in the same ratio to regular administrations as before legislation, with at

least one non-Saturday administration intended for disclosure.

These amendments basically determined the ATP non-Saturday schedule for New York in 1980-81. Because the ratio of non-Saturday to Saturday ATP administrations before legislation had been one to one, there were four Sunday test dates, one for each of the Saturday dates. One of these, the legal minimum, was disclosed. By law each of the four Saturday tests was disclosed. In 1983, additional amendments were passed, altering the disclosure requirements for achievement tests. Depending on student volume, disclosure cycles of five and eight years were established.

In the spring of 1981, the College Board decided to offer the SAT disclosure services to all students who were tested on the test dates slated for disclosure. The new offering, named the SAT Question-and-Answer Service, allowed a student to order for a fee ($6.50 in 1982-83) a copy of the test questions, the correct answers, a copy of his or her answer sheet and raw scores, and instructions for scoring. More than one million students took the SAT in 1982-83 on the four Saturdays and one Sunday designated for disclosure. Of these, about 20,000—less than 2 percent—chose to use the service.

Throughout the 80-year history of the Board there have been various criticisms of admissions testing—and College Board tests, in particular. These criticisms have included the charge that the Board's tests are biased against minorities, that teachers inappropriately teach to the tests, or that the tests do not reflect well the potential of the educationally gifted. More recently, social critics have attacked the Board itself as inordinately and inappropriately secretive and powerful. This is, of course, a somewhat paradoxical charge to bring against a membership organization of over 2,500 colleges, universities, schools, school systems, and associations.

The latest criticism stresses the relationship of student and Board as that of consumer and agency. It is not surprising that the strong societal concern for equality of opportunity has brought testing as a system for educational differentiation under scrutiny. The courts, however, have recognized that valid and appropriate methods of educational assessments can make a valuable contribution to an institution's goals of an able and appropriate student body.

The attacks of the social critics, and the concern for the legal aspects of testing in selective admissions, do not obscure one fundamental finding: on the whole, the students themselves, who, as applicants, are the ones most affected by the testing, tend

---

*Presently, the best-known source of such rights is the Family Educational Rights and Privacy Act of 1974 (the "Buckley Amendment"), which enumerates seven major areas of privacy protection, including the need for written consent before a disclosure to third parties (American Association of Collegiate Registrars and Admissions Officers 1976).

to feel that the tests are both fair and appropriate. Such is the conclusion to be drawn from the results of a survey by Response Analysis Corporation (1978) on high school students' views of the SAT and college admissions. Such surveys show that students tend to feel that they will derive important benefits from the objectivity of the test scores; some of them feel that their high school record is not valid because of problems they have had in demonstrating their full capacity.

The ATP in the Early Eighties: Handling Today's Challenges

The College Board Admissions Testing Program today consists of the Student Descriptive Questionnaire (SDQ), the Scholastic Aptitude Test, the Test of Standard Written English (TSWE), and 14 Achievement Tests: English Composition, Literature, French, German, Hebrew, Latin, Spanish, American History and Social Studies, European History and World Cultures, Mathematics Level I, Mathematics Level II, Biology, Chemistry, and Physics.* All the tests at each administration are entirely multiple-choice, except the December English Composition Test (ECT), which includes a 20-minute essay. The SAT and the TSWE are given jointly in a three-hour testing session. The SAT yields a verbal score, a mathematical score, and two verbal subscores (reading and vocabulary). The TSWE score reflects basic writing skills. The Achievement Tests, each one hour long, are given in a single three-hour test session, during which a student may take any one, two, or three tests. Each Achievement Test yields a single score.

During the 1982-83 academic year, the SAT with TSWE was offered on six test dates—in November, December, January, March, May, and June (except in New York state where it was administered only in November, December, May, and June). In addition, the SAT was offered in October in six states (California, Florida, Georgia, Illinois, North Carolina, and Texas). The larger-volume Achievement Tests were offered on five test dates—in November, December, January, May, and June. The European History and World Cultures, German, Hebrew, and Latin Achievement Tests were offered only on the December and May test dates. Students could take either the SAT or the Achievement Tests (not both) on a given test date. The tests were given on Saturdays, with Sunday sessions provided to accommodate students who cannot test on Saturday for religious reasons.

*The description of the ATP ''today'' refers to 1982-83, the last full testing year prior to preparation of this handbook.

The College Board also makes available special editions of the tests for handicapped students, which are administered at a time and place convenient to students and test administrators. Students with diagnosed handicaps may request special testing arrangements, such as braille, large-type editions, or cassettes. It is also possible to arrange for extended time, for separate test rooms, or for individualized supervision or instructions in order to minimize the effects of a handicap on test scores. All reasonable assistance is permitted, such as the use of a magnifying glass, a typewriter, or an abacus. The test taker may have another person read the test aloud, convey the content manually by signs, or record the answers. Colleges are informed that the scores were obtained under nonstandard conditions intended to minimize any adverse effect of the handicap on test performance. Because the individual circumstances vary so widely, no score interpretive data is provided for these special cases.

By the 1982-83 academic year, the College Board membership had expanded to about 2,500 institutions, including colleges and universities, schools, and educational associations. Approximately 1,175 colleges and universities were members and many of these required or encouraged their applicants to take the SAT. Students directed their score reports to about 3,600 colleges and scholarship sponsors. Only about 200 (mostly selective colleges) required some or all of their applicants to submit Achievement Test scores; in 1982-83 about 18 percent of the students who participated in the Admissions Testing Program took Achievement Tests.

Over 1.5 million Scholastic Aptitude Tests were taken in 1982-83 at approximately 3,800 test centers, about 500 of which were located in 100 foreign countries on six continents. The number of students who take the tests on a given date varies considerably. The colleges typically set individual deadlines for filing for admission, and the students plan their own test taking accordingly. The following table shows the numbers of students tested at each administration in 1982-83:

	SAT	Achievement Tests
October (six states)	84,328	Not offered
November	408,128	27,696
December	195,903	91,703
January	183,752	46,650
March	177,280	Not offered
May	302,748	25,738
June	231,259	88,362
Total	1,583,398	280,149

These figures include students who may have taken the test more than once. In addition to the volumes shown above, approximately 17,000 students take tests each year through special programs, such as the one for the handicapped. Most students taking the SAT will already be familiar with a similar test through their participation in the Preliminary Scholastic Aptitude Test/National Merit Scholarship Qualifying Test, which is widely administered in the fall of the junior year of high school.

As the table shows, the most popular test dates are November for the SAT and December for the Achievement Tests. For some years, this most popular date has been pushed back from the late spring of the senior year to the fall of the senior year, as the process of application for college begins earlier and earlier. In addition, more and more students, particularly able students, choose to take the SAT in the spring of their junior year. Slightly less than 50 percent of the students taking the SAT in the fall of their senior year have taken the test in their junior year.

Because a student may repeat the tests a number of times and because a number of test forms (editions) are now disclosed each year, the number of active, secure forms must be sufficiently large to allow flexibility in the reuse of forms at Sunday and make-up administrations as well as those for handicapped students. To keep the pool of active forms large enough to meet these needs, about ten new forms of the SAT and at least one new form of most Achievement Tests are introduced into the program each year. In 1982-83, for example, nine new SAT forms were introduced.

The large size of the ATP administrations has some positive consequences; it makes possible more accurate estimates of the statistical measures of test difficulty and reliability. This, in turn, allows more accurate control of the differences among the various test editions. The usual sample size for an item analysis of the SAT rose from 370 in 1961 to approximately 2,000 in 1975. These larger numbers may in the future enable specialists to develop uses for even more sophisticated techniques, such as the application of item response theory (IRT)* to the pre-equating of tests.

Another benefit of size is the dramatic savings in the relative cost of testing each student, made possible by the greater numbers of test takers and the development of computer applications. The SAT fee in 1982-83, for example, was 57 percent of the fee in 1952-53 in terms of adjusted dollars. While the functions of the College Board expanded during this period, and the demands on its resources for research and development were greater than ever before, the interests of the students and their families retained a

primacy, as is reflected in these lowered relative costs. Had the fee kept up with inflation, it would have been $19.00 in 1982-83, instead of $10.50.

Administration of the Tests. Each ATP administration involves the following activities, handled by ETS with policy direction from the College Board: 1) providing information to students and to schools and colleges about the tests and their proper use; 2) bringing together the students and the tests at the proper time; 3) providing the students with a standardized testing environment; 4) scoring the tests accurately and reporting the results; and 5) detecting and dealing with irregularities in administration or breaches of the security of the tests, should any occur.

Students are informed about the program through a series of publications. The most basic is the *Student Bulletin,* which is updated annually and distributed to secondary schools before the beginning of the school year. The *Student Bulletin* contains information about the tests, the times and places that the tests are given, the Student Descriptive Questionnaire, and a form for registering for the tests. The Registration Form provides students with an opportunity to purchase *The College Handbook* and *Index of Majors,* published by the Board, at reduced prices. *The College Handbook* offers general facts about over 3,000 colleges and brief descriptions of their specific characteristics, such as admission and test requirements, cost of attendance, available financial aid programs, and, in some cases, information and statistics about the academic qualifications of enrolled students. The *Index of Majors* identifies the colleges that offer specific programs of study.

To assist the student in preparing for the tests, free booklets describing the SAT and the Achievement Tests are also available. *Taking the SAT* contains a complete sample SAT and TSWE and is distributed in bulk to all secondary schools so that everyone who registers for the SAT can get a preview of the test. Students who register for the Achievement Tests receive a booklet describing each Achievement Test and containing sample questions from all of them.

When completing the Registration Form from the Student Bulletin, the student indicates a choice of either the SAT or Achievement Tests. Students planning to take Achievement Tests, however, do not indicate which specific test or tests they will take until the day of the administration. The Registration Form also contains the answer spaces for the Student Descriptive Questionnaire. The SDQ contains questions about the student's background, academic record, extracurricular activities, plans for college study, and more. From lists in the *Student Bulletin,*

---

*See Chapter II for a discussion of item response theory.

the student selects the test center and finds the code numbers of the colleges to which the scores are to be sent; then he or she enters this information on the Registration Form and sends it to College Board ATP.

After receiving the completed Registration Form, the ATP will send the student an admission ticket to the test center. Test centers for each administration are usually established a year in advance at secondary schools and colleges. The effort to ensure that tests are administered properly begins with the appointment and instruction of the test center supervisors. The supervisor of a test center is usually a member of the administrative staff of the institution where it is located. About two weeks in advance of a test date, the supervisor receives the test books and answer sheets for the test administration. Approximately one week in advance, he or she receives a roster of the names of the students assigned to the center. A comparison of the tickets and the roster by the center supervisor provides a final check on the students registered for a particular center. Each supervisor receives the *Guide for Administering ETS Tests,* which describes the general requirements of test center management: for example, the type of facilities and staff needed, the proper handling of test materials, seating of test takers, timing, and maintaining test security (including the acceptable identity documents). In addition, the ATP *Supervisor's Manual* contains detailed rules for conducting the test sessions, verbatim directions to be read aloud to test takers, and forms for reporting on the administration, including any irregularities that may occur.

Nonstandard Administrations.

In its role as the operational arm of the College Board, ETS has an obligation to ensure that no student is permitted an unfair advantage over others and to issue scores that accurately reflect the abilities of the test takers. ETS staff members regularly review test center operations by observing test administrations. In addition, records are kept of student complaints, cases of confirmed cheating, and other reported administrative irregularities. Whenever testing conditions are found to be inadequate at a particular center, corrective action is taken; this may include changing the test center procedures, reducing the number of students assigned to a center, or, if necessary, moving the center to another location.

Because of these procedures, irregularities arise in only a very small percentage of the test administrations. In fact, less than one-tenth of one percent of the annual 1.5 million test takers ever receives a letter from ETS in connection with a possible irregularity.

When an irregularity is reported or ETS employees discover a possible irregularity while scoring the tests, ETS conducts an investigation. If the investigation indicates that the scores should be questioned, they are referred to the Board of Review, a panel of senior professionals. Currently, any single member of the three-person committee chosen from the Board of Review may clear the scores or may recommend further investigation before reaching a decision. If all three members decline to clear the scores, the student is notified and given these choices: 1) ETS can cancel the scores; 2) the student may take a retest to confirm the scores; 3) the student may submit explanatory information to the Board of Review to resolve the questions about the scores; 4) the student may ask ETS to send a summary of the file to any institution for an independent decision; or 5) the student may request arbitration by the American Arbitration Association. The score review procedures are carried out in strict confidence.

Score Reporting.

Within four to six weeks after an administration, the test scores are sent to the designated colleges, the students, and the high schools. The task of translating the response marks on test answer sheets into interpretable score reports is accomplished largely by scoring machines and computers. To ensure accuracy in this scoring and reporting operation, the data processing system contains a series of checks. The system is programmed to reject cases in which the scoring machine is unable to clearly "read" the student's marks on the answer sheet. These cases are scored by hand. Studies of scoring accuracy show that virtually 100 percent of the SAT and Achievement Test answer sheets are accurately scored when the student marks his or her answer sheet according to instructions. When problems do occur, usually due to student marking errors, they almost always cause no more than a 10-point difference on the standard score scale. All answer sheets are kept on file for 18 months should any question arise concerning the accuracy of a score. Students may order a photocopy of their answer sheet, the answer key, and scoring instructions if they care to check the accuracy of the scoring. A computer record of scores and background information (but not answers to individual questions) is maintained indefinitely in some form. Because many students elect to take the test more than once, the record is cumulative, containing all of a student's test scores and the latest responses to the Student Descriptive Questionnaire. The full content of this cumulative record is reported to the student and to the colleges and high school he or she designates.

The foregoing brief summary of the ATP as it was in 1982-83 indicates the complexity of program operations and the annual cycle of events that must occur in order to carry out a test administration properly. The history of the ATP that preceded this discussion also demonstrates the evolving nature of the program; the ATP of the future will undoubtedly differ greatly from that just described.

The Eighties and Beyond: Confronting the Future

The role of the computer in the emergence of the modern ATP has been noted. Larger numbers of test takers and institutions are given a greater number of services for relatively lower costs, and the basis for this is the greater power of the computer. Technology has altered the scoring and information-processing characteristics of the program, and it may be anticipated that it will alter the administration of the tests. Technology may also alter the *production* processes for the tests as well. The development of modern text-processing equipment, for example, has led to possible applications in the development of test forms. While computer-assisted test construction is not yet operational, the flexibility in layout and editing that is made possible by text processors is ideal for an edit-intensive activity such as test development. Increasingly, professional test developers may be able to draft material and revise it in cost-effective ways by relying upon new and more sophisticated equipment.

The success of computer-assisted test construction processes has been hampered, however, by the complexity of the decision processes involved in item selection. While many test development steps could be carried out as the kind of binary decision activity that the computer does best, human judgment is needed at critical moments, for no item classification system completely describes all the ways in which items may overlap. In light of this, more recent strategies involve systems that allow for greater interaction between test constructor and computer.

The emerging technology may also impact upon the measurement models for the ATP. Efforts to make tests for the diverse test populations of the eighties have led increasingly to consideration of models that abandon the traditional "one-test-for-all-students" approach and attempt to match the material to the students. This approach is called "adaptive testing," in which a student's performance on a test item or set of items determines the next item or set of items given. To date, no feasible means of introducing such flexible testing strategies into the ATP have been developed. In part, the implementation of such innovations must await the development of appropriate technology.

This chapter makes extensive use of material supplied by William H. Angoff and Henry S. Dyer for the first edition of this handbook.

Principal author: Thomas F. Donlon
Contributors or reviewers: William H. Angoff, Nancy W. Burton, John A. Centra, Linda M. Heacock, Richard J. Noeth, Barton M. Perlman, June Stern, and Peggy A. Thorne.

CHAPTER II

Psychometric Methods Used in the Admissions Testing Program

Introduction

The psychometric issues of the Admissions Testing Program are not fundamentally different from those encountered in the production and interpretation of any battery of tests having multiple forms. Selecting items, establishing score scales, equating different test forms, and determining the reliability and validity of tests are necessary activities for any testing program, and techniques for accomplishing these ends are described in the journals and texts that serve the measurement profession. The basic procedures, then, for establishing test characteristics are not unique to the ATP. However, the effort to maintain measurement consistency over time and to serve the users and purposes of the program in a context of strong public concern for the probity and fairness of the procedures complicates the operations and occasionally demands solutions that are somewhat out of the ordinary. This chapter offers a description of the basic psychometric procedures that are followed in the ATP for the establishment and maintenance of the score scales, for item analysis, and for test analysis.*

The ATP procedures are not immutable, and, in fact, have been changed over the years to reflect changing needs and concerns. For instance, SAT scores used to be reported on a scale that was defined anew each year. The institution of a "permanent" score scale for the SAT, referenced to the 1941 test-taking population, was a response to an external change: the introduction of additional test dates confronted the program with the need to equate the results of tests from two different administrations that were attended by two self-selected groups differing in ability. The procedures described in this chapter are components of a program that attempts to meet and exceed the professional criteria in the *Standards for Educational and Psychological Tests* (American Psychological Association 1974, revision in progress); they reflect technical standards established in keeping with the goal of offering a program that serves both individuals and institutions.

Scoring Methods

At the present time, all the multiple-choice tests in the Admissions Testing Program are scored by the formula (Number Right)−(Number Wrong)/(k-1), where k = the number of choices per item. (The number of choices varies somewhat from item type to item type, but is usually five.) In testing programs where the decision based on scores is not a critical one, differences in scores that result from differential tendencies to guess are more easily accepted. However, in the case of the Admissions Testing Program, the value of college acceptance is perceived to be important. The College Board must consider the effects of its test directions and scoring procedures, however small or rare these effects may be, when the test scores are used in making admissions decisions. Since 1953 the directions for taking the tests have discouraged strictly random guessing, and the SAT and Achievement Tests have been scored by formula. Prior to this date, test takers had been discouraged from guessing, but number right scoring had been used. The change to formula scoring in 1953 was based primarily on the concern that students who were more inclined to guess were likely to earn higher scores on a rights-scored test—given under directions that discouraged random guessing—and possibly gain an unfair advantage over students who were not inclined to guess. This argument was supported by the results of a study conducted by Swineford and Miller (1953), which was designed to investigate the effect of different guessing directions on actual guessing behavior. It led to the conclusion that, when test takers are discour-

---

*Portions of this chapter have been adapted from Angoff, William H. (ed.) *The College Board Admissions Testing Program.* Princeton, N.J.: College Entrance Examination Board, 1971.

aged from guessing, formula scoring is preferable to rights scoring.

A review by Diamond and Evans (1973) does not substantially diminish the force of this argument. Further, it pinpoints the role of the instructions. Although results are varied, studies such as that of Slakter (1969) suggest that subjects low in risk taking are penalized in multiple-choice test scores in many disciplines if they are discouraged from guessing by the test directions. However, others hold the view that encouraging students to guess at items about which they have little or no knowledge or do not reach when taking a test is educationally unsound and perhaps morally improper. The problem is difficult, for it is usually necessary to provide some encouragement to make *informed* guesses, and the role of instructions in moderating student behavior to produce the proper amount of guessing is clearly central to the problem. It is difficult to give the students directions that are completely structured and informative; yet Cureton (1966) has stated that unless students are explicitly instructed to mark every item, it is unethical *not* to use the correction for guessing.

Students differ greatly in their understanding of probability. Since they can be confused if the instructions are too detailed, the instructions must be carefully worded to balance clarity against excessive detail. The present instructions concerning guessing for the SAT, which are printed on the back cover of the test book, are as follows: "Students often ask whether they should guess when they are uncertain about the answer to a question. Your test scores will be based on the number of questions you answer correctly minus a fraction of the number you answer incorrectly. Therefore, it is improbable that random or haphazard guessing will change your scores significantly. If you have some knowledge of a question, you may be able to eliminate one or more of the answer choices as wrong. It is generally to your advantage to guess which of the remaining choices is correct. Remember, however, not to spend too much time on any one question."

The decision to adopt formula scoring brought with it the possibility of negative scores, which occur in a test with five-choice items when the number of wrongs is more than four times the number of rights. Negative scores are simply chance-level scores and, as such, are not unique to formula scoring. But since the possibility of random responding is more obvious for negative scores, a special study of their properties was made. Boldt (1968) found valid discrimination among students in the region of negative formula scores. Although in theory formula scoring allows discriminations as low as –21 on the verbal part of the SAT and as low as –17 on the mathematical part, virtually no students earn scores lower than –10. A brief review of research on the properties of low-level scores was reported in the first edition of this handbook (Angoff 1971). Studies by Cliff (1958), Levine and Lord (1958), Angoff (1964), Boldt (1968), and Hills and Gladney (1968) were considered. The conclusion was (p. 174): "It would appear then, on the basis of the combined evidence of the various studies summarized here, that chance-level scores do not behave much differently from above-chance-level scores, especially in the prediction of an adequate criterion."

Research by Angoff and Schrader (1981) studied the impact of test instructions concerning guessing or omitting on test taker behavior. Students were randomly assigned to either of two test-taking situations. Each situation was identical in test content, but in one case students were told that the material would be scored using the rights only method, and they were encouraged to guess. In the other case, students were told that the material would be formula scored, and they were given the standard, cautionary SAT advice regarding guessing. Students did make more responses under the rights only instruction, and earned a higher average rights only score when taking the test this way. However, when formula scoring was applied to the records generated under rights only instructions, the resulting formula score means and standard deviations were not significantly different from the comparable values secured under formula scored instructions.

Angoff and Schrader interpret this as supporting the "Invariance Hypothesis." Essentially, the Invariance Hypothesis states that any "additional" marks made under conditions of rights only instructions will yield a rights score increment no greater than *chance*. It suggests that test equating operations could continue to use the formula score even if students were instructed, correctly, that rights only scoring would be used to compute individual scores. Thus, the option for a return to rights only scoring probably could be exercised if it were ever judged to be necessary.

The SAT Score Scale

The SAT scores reported to test users and to the students are scaled scores. These scores have been computed in such a way as to be comparable across different forms of the test and across different groups of test takers. That is, a particular scaled score (for example, 470) represents the same level of ability on each form of the test. In contrast, a raw score (formula score) depends on the difficulty of the test as well as the student's ability.

The SAT scores are reported on a scale that ranges from 200 to 800. A score of 200 does not mean that the student did not answer at least one question correctly; it is simply the lowest score reported. Similarly, a score of 800 does not necessarily mean that the student answered all the questions correctly—although that has been the case for all recent forms of the SAT.

One of the most persistent misconceptions of the SAT score scale is that it is a standard score scale on which 500 represents the mean score of "all College Board test takers" in some recent year and 100 represents the standard deviation of their scores. Similar misconceptions are that 500 and 100 represent the mean and standard deviation of "all college freshmen" in some recent year or that 500 and 100 represent the mean and standard deviation of "all current secondary school seniors." The fact is that the numbers 500 and 100 simply refer to the mean and standard deviation of the group of 10,654 students who took the verbal portion of the SAT in April 1941. (The mathematical scale was linked to the verbal scale in April 1942 by setting the scaled score mean and standard deviation of the mathematical test equal to the mean and standard deviation of scaled scores on the verbal test at that administration.) Because the base group is of interest only from a historical point of view and has no normative significance or usefulness in interpreting College Board scores, the 500 score similarly has no special significance (except that it is midway between 200 and 800). The real significance of the SAT score scale is its continuity in the face of changing test forms and changing test-taking populations.

The process of scoring the SAT consists of the following steps:

1. As indicated earlier, the student's "raw score" is computed by counting the number of right answers and subtracting a fraction of the number of wrong answers.

2. The raw score is converted to a scaled score by applying a "raw-to-scale conversion" (See Table 2.1). This conversion is determined by a procedure called "equating," as explained later in this chapter.

3. The scaled score is rounded to the nearest multiple of 10 for reporting purposes. If the scaled score is below 200 it is reported as a score of 200; if it is above 800, it is reported as a score of 800. (For some scores, notably those for TSWE and for the reading and vocabulary subscores of SAT-verbal, the trailing zero is dropped and a two-digit score is reported.)

Equating the SAT

Several different forms of the SAT, constructed to be as similar in content and in difficulty as possible, are administered every year. However, it is not practically possible to make all forms of the SAT precisely equal in difficulty for test takers at every ability level. Therefore, it is necessary to use a statistical procedure called score equating to make scores on different forms of the SAT comparable. The use of score equating prevents the test takers who encounter a slightly more difficult form of the SAT from being penalized with lower scores. It permits comparisons among groups of test takers taking the SAT at different times. Score equating also makes it possible to measure changes in college applicants' verbal and mathematical skills over a period of years.

The procedures used for equating SAT scores are based on the linking of each form of the SAT to one or more previous forms. Each new form includes an "anchor test" that has been administered with a previous form. The anchor test is a miniature version of the SAT. Because it is taken by both the current group of test takers and the previous group, the anchor test provides a link between the current form and the previous form. This link makes it possible to convert raw scores on the new form to scaled scores in such a way that each scaled score represents approximately the same level of ability on the new form as on the previous form. For example, if the new form of the SAT is slightly easier than the previous form, a test taker may need one or two more correct answers on the new form than on the previous form to attain a score of 450. If the new form is slightly more difficult, a test taker may earn a score of 450 with one or two fewer correct answers.

The anchor tests used in equating the SAT are "external"; that is, the anchor test is not included in computing the students' raw scores. Each test booklet containing a new form of the SAT is printed in several different versions. Four of the six sections of each version are "operational SAT sections"; they contain the questions used to compute the students' raw scores. A fifth section contains the Test of Standard Written English (TSWE). Typically, these five sections are the same in all versions of the test. The remaining section—the "variable" section—is different in each version. It may contain a verbal anchor test, a mathematical anchor test, or a collection of SAT verbal, mathematical, or TSWE questions being "pretested" or administered for research purposes. (Pretesting helps identify and correct questions that are ambiguous, inappropriate, or flawed in some way. It also provides an estimate of the difficulty of each question. Every SAT question is pretested at least once in an unscored "variable" section before being included in a scored "operational" section, but it may be revised slightly before being used in the operational section.) The variable section makes it possible to include several different anchor tests in each new form of the SAT, with different students taking each anchor test. The different versions of the test form are "spiraled," that is, packaged in a repeating sequence. This system ensures that the groups of students taking each variable section will be closely representative of the population of all students taking the SAT at that administration. (See Chapter III for details on spiraling.)

A typical form of the SAT includes at least six different anchor tests, three verbal and three mathematical. Two of the three verbal anchor tests are "old" anchor tests, linking the current form with previous forms; the third is a "new" anchor test, to link the current form with future forms. A similar pattern is used for mathematical anchor tests. The "old" anchor tests make it possible to equate the new form to two (or more) previous forms. This practice provides at least two independent estimates of the raw-to-scale score conversion for the new form. Typically there are two estimates for verbal scores and two for mathematical scores. Usually the estimates agree closely, and they are averaged. However, if there is evidence that one of the estimates is more accurate than the other, that estimate may be given more weight in establishing the raw-to-scale score conversion for the new form. Figures 2.1 and 2.2 show the patterns of equating linkages among SAT forms over the years. These "genealogical" charts indicate the "parental" and "ancestral" linkages for each form from 1983 back to 1941. Each line in the diagram that connects two forms of the test indicates that the more recent form has been equated to the older form and through it to the basic reference scale. The chart shows that since 1954 there has been a practice of two separate equatings, carried out independently and averaged to produce the final, operational values. As more and more new forms are introduced each year, the complexity grows. The system provides for the "braiding" and interweaving of forms to avoid the development of separate "strains" and to ensure an internally consistent and homogeneous network.

The foregoing description reflects the procedures that are typically followed. During the 1970s, the equating design deviated from the standard. In some cases in the early 1970s, the new edition contained an internal anchor that was an external anchor to the old form. In some cases in the mid-1970s, the equating items were internal to both the new and old forms. During the 1977-78 testing year,

Figure 2.1

Genealogical Chart for SAT-Verbal Equating Forms

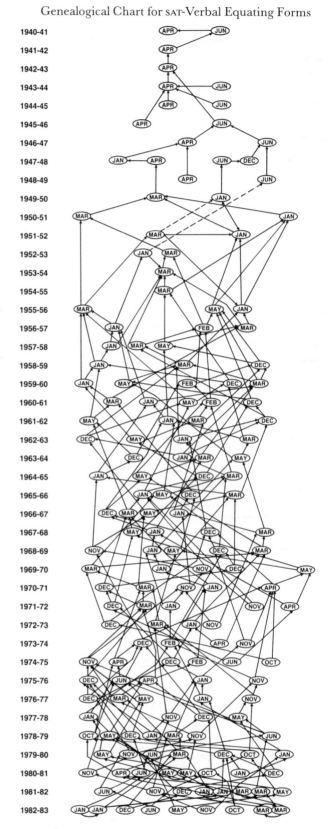

one of the external anchors used was common to an old form that was administered concurrently with

Figure 2.2

Genealogical Chart for SAT-Mathematical Equating Forms

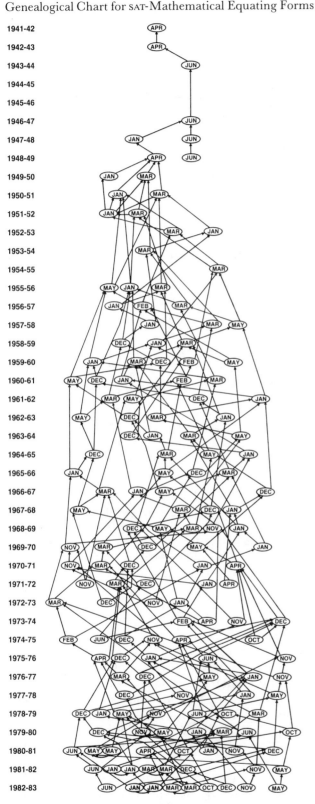

(1) fairness to the test takers taking different forms of the test and (2) preservation of the meaning of the reported scores. Ideally, it should be a matter of indifference to test takers at any ability level which form of the test they take; scaled scores on any two forms should indicate the same levels of ability. In practice, these goals can never be perfectly achieved, but they can be approximated very closely—more closely by some equating methods than others. Before 1982, SAT scores were typically equated by linear equating methods. These methods assume that the relationship between the raw scores representing the same ability level on the tests to be equated can be represented on a graph by a straight line. Linear equating methods consider scores on two different SAT forms to be comparable if they correspond to the same number of standard deviations above or below the mean of a reference group of test takers. Ideally, this reference group would be a group of test takers who take both of the two forms of the SAT. However, since each student typically takes only one form, the performance of such a reference group cannot be directly observed. It must be estimated from the test takers' scores on the anchor test and on one form or the other of the full SAT.*

The stability of the scale through successive linear equatings has been a continuing concern. A study by Stewart (1966) showed that the SAT-verbal score scale had drifted approximately 20 points from 1948 to 1953 (in the direction of higher scores for the same level of ability) but had remained stable from 1953 to 1963. Modu and Stern (1975) conducted a similar study on both the verbal and mathematical score scales, equating the December 1963 and December 1966 forms of the SAT to the December 1973 form. Their results indicate average scale drifts in an upward direction of about 14 points on the SAT-verbal section and about 17 points on the mathematical section. That is, a scaled score of 500 in 1963 equated to scores of 514 on verbal and 517 on mathematical in 1973. To verify this result, Modu and Stern conducted another study (1977) in which approximately 3,000 high school students each took two SAT-verbal sections, one from 1963 and one from 1973. (Half the students took the 1963 form first; the other half took the 1973 edition first.) The results indicated that a student taking the SAT in 1973 would have been likely to receive a slightly higher reported SAT-verbal score than a student of the same ability who had taken the SAT in 1963. Two pairs of SAT forms were compared; the average scale drift was 5 points for one pair of forms and 14 points for the other.

the new form. The standard design, however, is essentially as described above.

Score equating has two fundamental goals:

---

*Linear equating methods will be described in greater detail in the section on "Equating the Achievement Tests."

17

Since 1982, SAT scores have been equated by a method based on a mathematical model of the test-taking process called item response theory, or IRT (Lord 1980). (IRT is sometimes referred to as item characteristic curve theory or latent trait theory.) IRT equating methods are much more complicated than linear equating methods, but they make it possible to equate test scores more accurately. Unlike other equating methods, which involve only the test takers' total scores on the full test and on the anchor test, IRT methods make use of the additional information contained in the students' responses to the individual questions on the test.

The decision to change from linear to IRT methods was preceded by a series of research studies investigating the stability of the SAT score scale and comparing the accuracy of various equating methods. The first of these recent studies comparing various equating methods was undertaken by Marco, Petersen, and Stewart (1983). This study compared the accuracy of several linear and nonlinear equating methods over a wide range of conditions, varying the difficulty of the tests to be equated and the ability of the students tested. The most consistently accurate equating method was an IRT method.

The second comparative study of equating (Petersen, Cook, and Stocking 1983) compared the effects of several equating methods on the stability of the SAT-verbal and SAT-mathematical score scales. The IRT equating methods resulted in less scale drift in SAT-verbal and about the same scale drift in SAT-mathematical as conventional linear procedures.

The change in 1982 to IRT equating was made in conjunction with a change in the difficulty specifications for the verbal portion of the SAT: the number of extremely difficult questions on the verbal portion was reduced slightly. A change of this type could be expected to produce a curvilinear relationship between verbal scores on 1982 editions and verbal scores on previous forms. A continued application of linear equating methods would have resulted in some inaccuracies. The likelihood of such errors was reduced by the change to IRT equating.

A brief description of the new approach may assist some readers. IRT assumes that the probability that a test taker will answer a test question correctly* depends on one and only one characteristic of the test taker—his or her mastery of the particular competency or skill that the test measures. This characteristic is commonly referred to as the test taker's "ability" and is usually represented in mathemat-

ical formulas by the Greek letter theta (θ). Because of this assumption, IRT will logically be most appropriate when the test developer considers that each question on the test measures some aspect of the same general ability.

IRT assumes that the probability that a test taker of any given ability (θ) will answer a given question correctly can be represented by a particular kind of mathematical function, called an "item response function." Each test question (or "item") has its own item response function. The IRT model that is used to equate SAT scores assumes that all the item response functions can be expressed by the formula:

$$P = c + \frac{1-c}{1 + e^{-1.702a(\theta-b)}}$$

The letter P in this formula represents the probability that the test taker will answer the question correctly. The values of a, b, and c in the formula will differ from one test question to the next. These item parameters each describe a different aspect of the test question. Parameter c indicates the probability that a test taker of very low ability will answer the question correctly. Parameter b indicates the difficulty of the question, that is, the ability level for which the probability of success equals $c + .5(1-c)$. Parameter a indicates how sharply the question discriminates among students at different ability levels and is proportional to the slope of the curve at ability level b.

Equating the SAT involves two completely separate applications of the same procedure, one for the verbal score and one for the mathematical score. In equating the SAT, the item parameters a, b, and c for each test question are estimated from the responses of a reasonably representative sample of the eleventh and twelfth grade students taking that form of the test at that administration to the individual test questions. The item parameters for the verbal questions on the previous form, the new form, and the anchor test are all estimated together in a single computer run; likewise for the mathematical questions. Including the anchor test items in this process serves the important purpose of placing the item parameter estimates for the new form and the previous form on the same θ-scale. That is, the inclusion of the anchor test items provides the link that ensures that the numerical values of the item parameters will have the same meaning on the new form as on the previous form.

The estimates of the item parameters for equating a new SAT form are based on data from four samples of test takers: two samples from the group taking the current form (each taking a different anchor test) and one sample from the group taking each of two

---

*This probability can be interpreted as the proportion of test takers of equal ability who would answer the question correctly.

Figure 2.3

Matrix of Item Response Data for Equating a Typical Form of the SAT

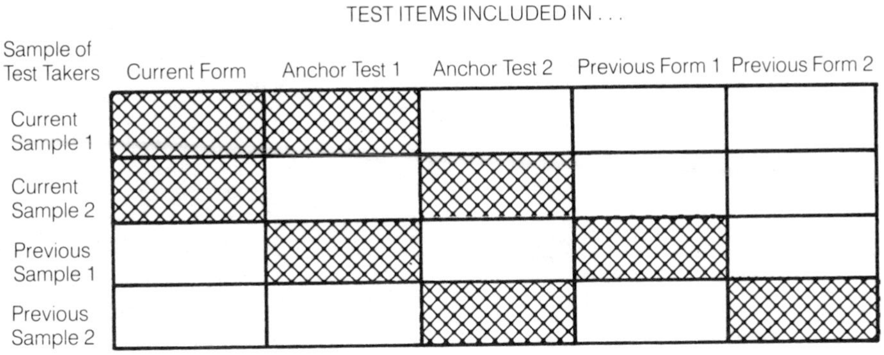

TEST ITEMS INCLUDED IN . . .

Sample of Test Takers	Current Form	Anchor Test 1	Anchor Test 2	Previous Form 1	Previous Form 2
Current Sample 1	▨	▨			
Current Sample 2	▨		▨		
Previous Sample 1		▨		▨	
Previous Sample 2			▨		▨

previous forms. Each of the four samples includes approximately 3,000 students. Figure 2.3 illustrates the data matrix for a typical equating of the SAT. The shaded areas represent the available data, in the form of students' responses to the test items.

Once the item parameters have been estimated for each question in a form of the SAT, it is possible to compute an expected raw score for any given value of θ (for a test taker with any given level of ability). When this computation has been made for two forms of the SAT, the two expected raw scores corresponding to a given value of θ can be considered equivalent and assigned the same scaled score. For example, suppose that a θ-value of 0.5 leads to an expected raw score of 42 on the previous form and 45 on the new form. If a raw score of 42 on the previous form corresponds to a scaled score of 480, then a raw score of 45 on the new form should also correspond to a scaled score of 480.

To determine the expected raw score corresponding to a given value of θ, the item parameters are used to compute P for each question on the test. The sum of these P values for all questions on the test is the expected number of right answers for a test taker of ability θ who attempts all the questions. The expected number of wrong answers is the sum of $(1-P)$ for all the questions. Applying the correction for guessing formula, if each question has k choices, the expected raw score for a test taker who answers all the questions is

$$\Sigma P - \frac{1}{k-1} \Sigma (1-P)$$

The procedure actually used to equate SAT scores (verbal or mathematical) is as follows:

1. Estimate the item parameters for each question on the old and new form of the test.
2. For each possible whole-number raw score on the *new* form, determine the corresponding value of

θ, by an iterative procedure, that is, a series of successively closer approximations. This calculation is also performed for raw scores that are halfway between whole-number values, (48.5, 49.5, etc.) for more accurate interpolation in Step 4.
3. For each of these values of θ, compute the corresponding expected raw score on the *previous* form of the test. (In general, these raw scores will not be whole numbers.)
4. Using interpolation, find the scaled score that corresponds to each of these raw scores on the previous form and assign that scaled score to the corresponding raw score on the new form.

Notice that the equating procedure does not involve the estimation of θ for each student taking the SAT. The procedure does estimate θ for a sample of these students, but these θ estimates are used only for estimating the item parameters. The item parameters are used to determine a raw-to-scale conversion, and this conversion is used to convert each test taker's raw score to a scaled score for reporting. The computer program that estimates the item parameters is called LOGIST (Wingersky 1983; Wingersky, Barton, and Lord 1982). LOGIST estimates the parameters iteratively by the maximum likelihood method, modified because of the missing responses from students who omit test questions.

Often the equating will produce raw-to-scale conversions such that the test will not "scale to 800"; that is, the maximum possible raw score will convert to a scaled score less than 795 (which, when rounded, will result in a reported score of less than 800). In this case the raw-to-scale conversion is adjusted at the upper end to ensure that at least one raw score converts to 800. The adjustment is chosen on the basis of two principles: (1) to affect the reported scores of as few students as possible and (2) to avoid sharp changes in the slope of the raw-to-scale conversion. The choice of the adjustment represents a compromise between these two conflicting principles; however, the choice is always made in such a way as to affect the reported scores of less than 5 percent of the test takers. Data on the ranges of scaled scores that were observed at selected raw score levels of the SAT are provided in Table 2.1.

Table 2.1

SAT-Verbal, SAT-Mathematical, and TSWE
Raw Scores Converted to Scaled Score Ranges

| | College Board Score Ranges | | |
Raw Score	SAT-Verbal (85 Questions)	SAT-Math (60 Questions)	TSWE (50 Questions)
85	800		
80	750-770		
75	700-730		
70	660-690		
65	610-650		
60	580-620	800	
55	540-580	740-760	
50	510-550	690-720	60+
45	480-510	640-670	57-60+
40	440-480	600-630	52-55
35	410-440	560-580	47-50
30	380-410	510-530	42-45
25	350-370	470-490	37-39
20	310-340	430-450	31-34
15	280-310	380-400	26-29
10	240-270	340-360	21-24
5	210-240	290-320	20
0	200-210	250-280	20

Note: The ranges for the College Board scores are based on all forms of the SAT and the TSWE given from November 1977 through June 1981.

Subscores of the SAT

Two subscores are reported on the verbal portion of the SAT. The reading comprehension subscore is based on the reading comprehension and sentence completion items; the vocabulary subscore is based on the antonym and analogy items. These subscores are reported on a 20-to-80 scale that corresponds to the 200-to-800 scale used for the total verbal score. For example, a score of 43 on the vocabulary subscore is intended to represent the level of general verbal ability that is indicated by an SAT-verbal score of 430. The raw-to-scale conversion for each of these subscores on a new form of the SAT is determined by scaling the subscore to the total verbal score. The numerical procedures are the same as those for equating the SAT to previous forms and make use of the same item parameter estimates:

1. Estimate the item parameters for the verbal questions. This step is done as part of the equating of the total verbal scores.

2. For each possible whole-number raw score on the subscore, determine the corresponding value of θ. Do the same for raw scores ending in .5.

3. For each of these values of θ, compute the expected raw score on the full (total) verbal portion.

4. Find the scaled score that corresponds to each of these raw total verbal scores. Divide these scaled scores by 10 and assign them to the corresponding raw subscores.

If the scaling procedure results in a maximum possible scaled score of 78 or 79, the SAT subscores are not forced to 80 in the way that the verbal and mathematical scores are forced to 800. However, if the scaling procedure results in a maximum possible scaled score less than 78, the scores are forced to 78. The procedure for choosing the adjustment is chosen to be consistent with that used for forcing the verbal scaled scores to 800.

Scaling and Equating the Test of Standard Written English (TSWE)

Scores on the TSWE are reported to the nearest whole number on a two-digit scale that corresponds to the first two digits of the 200-to-800 score scale used for the SAT. However, the TSWE score scale ranges only from 20 to 60. Scores of 60 or above are reported simply as 60+, because the TSWE is not designed to discriminate at the higher ability levels. The TSWE scale was originally linked to the SAT scale by setting the mean and standard deviation of TSWE scores at one-tenth of the mean and standard deviation of the SAT-verbal scores of the same group of test takers.

Each new TSWE form is equated, by linear methods, to several (5 to 15) previous TSWE forms. (Linear equating is described below in the section on "Equating the Achievement Tests.") SAT-verbal scaled scores are used as an external anchor, since each student taking the TSWE also takes the SAT. (Because the SAT scaled scores are equated, scaled scores on different forms of the SAT can be used interchangeably.) This procedure yields approximately 5 to 15 independent estimates of the raw-to-scale conversions for the new TSWE form—a separate estimate for each of the several previous TSWE forms to which the new form is equated. These results are examined for consistency, and any deviant results are excluded. The remaining estimates are averaged to produce the raw-to-scale conversion for the new TSWE form. Table 2.1 provides information on the ranges of scaled scores that were observed for selected raw score levels on a number of forms of the TSWE.

Table 2.2

Summary Statistics for English, Mathematics, Science, and Social Studies Achievement Tests
for Samples of Students Taking Both the SAT and Achievement Tests in 1979-80*

	Eng. Comp.	Lit.	Am. His. & Soc. Stu.	Eur. His. & World Cul.	Bio.	Chem.	Phys.	Math Level I	Math Level II
Number of Test Takers	5,279	7,373	5,471	2,849	6,386	5,392	6,164	5,156	5,874
MEAN									
SAT-Verbal	508	524	507	565	510	525	537	495	551
SAT-Mathematical	560	521	544	554	550	614	644	550	652
Achievement Test	517	526	502	542	524	565	588	534	651
STANDARD DEVIATION									
SAT-Verbal	107	113	107	109	106	104	109	103	107
SAT-Mathematical	109	105	107	106	107	99	93	100	89
Achievement Test	106	109	106	101	106	102	98	92	91
CORRELATION									
SAT-Verbal vs. Achievement Test	.80	.84	.75	.72	.72	.59	.57	.51	.47
SAT-Mathematical vs. Achievement Test	.59	.54	.52	.48	.67	.68	.69	.83	.81
SAT-Verbal vs. SAT-Mathematical	.61	.60	.55	.53	.63	.57	.55	.58	.54

*Based on data obtained in rescaling Achievement Tests. The sample sizes do not reflect the relative total volumes.

Scaling the Achievement Tests

The College Board offers 14 different Achievement Tests. The use of these tests in admissions is not limited to selection; a discussion of placement and other applications is provided in Chapter V, which reviews the Achievement Tests. If the scores are to be useful for selection purposes, comparing students who take tests in different subjects, the score scales should be as comparable as possible. For example, the level of achievement in American history indicated by a score of 560 on the American history test should be as similar as possible to the level of achievement in biology indicated by a score of 560 on the biology test. But what does it mean to say that one student's achievement in American history is comparable to another student's achievement in biology? The Admission Testing Program's answer to this question, which forms the basis for scaling the Achievement Tests, is as follows. Suppose student A's relative standing in a group of American history students is the same as student B's relative standing in a group of biology students. Now suppose the group of American history students is equal to the group of biology students in general academic ability. Then it is meaningful to say that student A's achievement in American history is comparable to student B's achievement in biology.

The groups of students who choose to take the different Achievement Tests, however, cannot be assumed to be equal in general academic ability. Their SAT scores often provide evidence that they are not. Tables 2.2 and 2.3 show the mean SAT-verbal and SAT-mathematical scores of samples of students taking the different Achievement Tests in 1979-80. Obviously, the differences are quite large in some cases and cannot be disregarded.

To adjust for these differences, the Achievement Test score scales are based on a hypothetical reference group for each test. These hypothetical reference groups are specified in terms of their SAT scores in order to make all the reference groups equal in verbal and mathematical ability. The reference group for each Achievement Test was originally specified as a group of the students taking that test, having a distribution of SAT scores with the following properties: (1) a mean of 500 and a standard deviation of 100 on SAT-verbal; (2) a mean of 500 and a standard deviation of 100 on SAT-mathematical; (3) a correlation of .40 (covariance of 4000) between SAT-verbal and SAT-mathematical scores.†

---

†When the Achievement Tests were originally scaled, the reference group was specified to have an SAT verbal-mathematical correlation of .40. Since then the empirically observed correlations have grown larger, and the formulas are now based on a reference group with a correlation of .60 between SAT-verbal and SAT-mathematical scores.

Table 2.3

Summary Statistics for Language Achievement Tests for Students
Taking Both the SAT and Achievement Tests in 1979-80*

	French	German	Hebrew	Latin	Russian†	Spanish
Number of Test Takers	5,616	3,054	518	1,137	298	5,536
MEAN						
SAT-Verbal	544	544	563	574	575	509
SAT-Mathematical	570	591	571	592	603	549
Achievement Test	540	519	581	528	526	498
STANDARD DEVIATION						
SAT-Verbal	104	104	110	105	114	104
SAT-Mathematical	100	99	106	100	111	105
Achievement Test	98	103	99	103	123	101
CORRELATION						
SAT-Verbal vs. Achievement Test	.54	.42	.47	.56	.18	.38
SAT-Mathematical vs. Achievement Test	.44	.31	.41	.50	.35	.32
Achievement Test vs. Semesters of Study	.37	.30	.33	.28	.20	.39
SAT-Verbal vs. Semesters of Study	.17	.11	.06	.15	.02	.20
SAT-Mathematical vs. Semesters of Study	.12	.04	.05	.10	.12	.14
SAT-Verbal vs. SAT-Mathematical	.57	.53	.67	.54	.57	.60

*Based on data obtained in rescaling Achievement Tests. The sample sizes do not reflect the relative total volumes.

†Russian is not currently offered in the ATP.

The score scale for each Achievement Test was defined so that the scaled scores would have a mean of 500 and a standard deviation of 100 for this hypothetical group. The equations that make up the scaling process for an Achievement Test can be specified in terms of SAT and Achievement Test scores.

Notation:

x = Raw scores on the Achievement Test to be scaled.

S = Scaled score on the Achievement Test

v, m = Scaled scores on SAT-verbal and SAT-mathematical sections.

M, s, s_{gh} = Observed statistics (mean and standard deviation) for group taking Form x. $s_{gh} = r_{gh}s_g s_h$.

μ, σ, σ_{gh} = Designated statistics for hypothetical subgroup. $\mu_v = \mu_m = 500$; $\sigma_v = \sigma_m = 100$;

$\sigma_{vm} = \rho_{vm}\sigma_v\sigma_m = 6{,}000$ (previous procedures used a value of 4,000)

$b_{gh.ij...}$ = Partial regression coefficient for predicting g from h, holding constant variables i, j, . . .

The data for scaling Achievement Test x are assembled by drawing all, or virtually all, of the population of students taking that test at its first administration, calculating the means, variances, and covariances among SAT-verbal, SAT-mathematical, and Achievement Test x, and entering the appropriate values in the equations below.

$$\hat{\mu}_x = M_x + b_{xv.m}(\mu_v - M_v) + b_{xm.v}(\mu_m - M_m) \quad [1]$$

$$\hat{\sigma}_x^2 = s_x^2 + b_{xv.m}^2(\sigma_v^2 - s_v^2) + b_{xm.v}^2(\sigma_m^2 - s_m^2) \quad [2]$$
$$+ 2b_{xv.m}b_{xm.v}(\sigma_{vm} - s_{vm}).$$

The equation relating raw scores on Achievement Test x to the standard score scale S is then derived by designating the mean and standard deviation of scaled scores on that test for the hypothetical subgroup as 500 and 100, respectively:

$$\frac{S - 500}{100} = \frac{x - \hat{\mu}_x}{\hat{\sigma}_x}$$

which yields the linear equation relating raw scores on Test x to the scale:

$$S = a_{sx}x + b_{sx},$$
where $a_{sx} = 100/\hat{\sigma}_x$ and $b_{sx} = 500 - a_{sx}\hat{\mu}_x.$ \quad [3]

Clearly, equation [3] applies only to the particular form of Test x for which these calculations were made. When a new form of Test x is produced and administered to a student group, that form must be equated to a previous form of the test in order to derive a new conversion equation appropriate for it.

The process just described applies to all the Achievement Tests in the College Board Admissions Testing Program except the language tests. In the late 1940s, as a result of a study by L. R Tucker (Angoff 1961) of differences in language Achievement Test scores associated with levels of language training, a third variable, semesters of language training, was added to the SAT-verbal and SAT-mathematical predictors in setting the scales for the tests in French, German, Latin, and Spanish. This variable was added in an effort to make the scales for the language tests reflect the differences in amount of language training that were characteristic of students who took the different language tests. The equations for estimating the mean and variance of raw scores on the language tests for the hypothetical subgroup correspond precisely to equations [1] and [2], except that a third predictor variable is added. Thus, if n is used to designate the number of semesters of training, equations [1] and [2] become respectively, equations [4] and [5]:

$$\hat{\mu}_x = M_x + b_{xv.mn}(\mu_v - M_v) + \quad\quad [4]$$
$$b_{xm.vn}(\mu_m - M_m) + b_{xn.vm}(\mu_n - M_n)$$

$$\hat{\sigma}_x^2 = s_x^2 + b_{xv.mn}^2 (\sigma_v^2 - s_v^2) +$$
$$b_{xm.vn}^2 (\sigma_m^2 - s_m^2) + b_{xn.vm}^2 (\sigma_n^2 - s_n^2) \quad [5]$$
$$+ 2b_{xv.mn}b_{xm.vn}(\sigma_{vm} - s_{vm})$$
$$+ 2b_{xv.mn}b_{xn.vm}(\sigma_{vn} - s_{vn})$$
$$+ 2b_{xm.vn}b_{xn.vm}(\sigma_{mn} - s_{mn}).$$

The values of μ_v, μ_m, σ_v, σ_m, and σ_{vm}, were respectively, 500, 500, 100, 100, and 4,000 (current procedures use a value of 6,000). The values of μ_n, σ_n, σ_{vn}, σ_{mn} were taken from the original data collected by Tucker in his study of language Achievement Test scores. The specified values of these statistics in the hypothetical group were set equal to their observed values in the combined group of students taking French, German, Latin, and Spanish.

In general, the system of scaling the Achievement Tests allows the scores on those tests to reflect the level and dispersion of SAT scores for students who typically choose to take them. Specifically, the system has the effect of raising the scale score values for a test that is typically taken by high-ability students (as measured by the SAT) and lowering the scale for a test that is typically taken by lower-ability students. In the case of the foreign language tests, for which the number of years of language study is added to the set of predictors, it also increases the scaled scores for a test in a language that is typically studied for an extended period of time in secondary school and lowers it for a test in a language that is typically studied for a short period of time. It broadens the scales for tests that are taken by heterogeneous groups of students (heterogeneous in terms of SAT scores and/or length of language study) and produces narrow scales for tests taken by homogeneous groups of students.

The reason for this system of scaling the Achievement Tests is to avoid some of the inequities that would result if, for example, each test were scaled by using all the students taking that test as a reference group. Such a system would yield the same proportion of high scores on all the Achievement Tests, even though some tests are taken by groups of students that are more able than the groups taking other tests. The Achievement Test scaling system awards a larger proportion of high scores on tests taken by groups that include a higher proportion of academically able students.

Although the Achievement Test scaling procedure attempts to make scores comparable across subject areas, the comparability is not perfect. The main problem is that scores on the different Achievement Tests do not correlate equally with the SAT. When an Achievement Test is scaled, the mean score of the students taking the test is assigned a scale value that depends on the correlation of the students' Achievement Test scores with their SAT scores. The higher the correlation of the Achievement Test scores with the SAT-verbal scores, the closer the scale value of the mean Achievement Test score will be to the students' mean SAT-verbal score, and similarly for the SAT-mathematical score. The lower the correlations between the Achievement Test score and the SAT scores, the closer the scale value of the mean Achievement Test score will be to 500. Because the mean SAT scores of students taking one or more Achievement Tests are above 500, the scaling procedure tends to assign somewhat higher scaled scores on tests that are more highly correlated with the SAT.

Equating the Achievement Tests

The scaling process is carried out when an Achievement Test is first introduced and periodically thereafter. Between rescalings the comparability of scores on different forms of the same Achievement Test is maintained by an equating of each new form to one or more previous forms of the test. For most of the

Achievement Tests, the link to each previous form is provided by common items, that is, questions included in both the new form and the previous form. These questions are selected to represent, insofar as possible, the full range of content and difficulty of the questions on the test. Since they are included in computing the student's raw score, they constitute an "internal" anchor test. One exception is the Literature Achievement Test, which does not use common items, but instead uses SAT scaled scores as an external anchor. Another exception is the English Composition Achievement Test, which uses a combination of internal anchor (common items) and external anchor (SAT scaled scores). The trial conversion is typically a weighted aveage of the results of the two approaches. Similarly, when more than one old form is used to provide internal anchor items, the results are combined or averaged to produce the final conversion.

The type of equating most commonly used to equate the Achievement Tests is linear equating. Linear methods are based on a definition of equating that considers scores on two tests as equal if they represent the same number of standard deviations above or below the mean of a reference group. For example, if a raw score of 43 on Test X and a raw score of 44 on Test Y are both 1.2 standard deviations above the mean of the reference group, then a 43 on Test X is assumed to represent the same level of ability as a 44 on Test Y. In most cases, however, there is no group of students taking both of the forms to be equated. Therefore, it is necessary to specify a reference group of test takers and estimate the mean and standard deviation of the reference group on each of the two tests. For the methods used to equate the Achievement Tests, the reference group consists of a combined sample of students from the groups taking each of the two forms of the test to be equated, approximately the same number from each group. The formulas most commonly used for linear equating of the Achievement Tests are as follows:

Variables:

x, y = Raw scores on test forms to be equated. Form x is new; Form y is the old form to which Form x is to be equated

u = Raw score on anchor test u, the test common to both Form x and Form y

S = Scaled score on the Achievement Test

M, s = Observed statistics (mean and standard deviation) for group taking Form x.

b_{gh} = Regression coefficient for predicting g from h.

Groups:

α = Group taking new Form x and anchor test u

β = Group taking old Form y and anchor test u

t = Combined group formed from Groups α and β

The equating relationship between raw scores on the new Form x and the old Form y is specified in terms of their means and standard deviations in Group t. Raw scores x and y are assumed to represent the same level of ability if

$$\frac{x - M_{x_t}}{s_{x_t}} = \frac{y - M_{y_t}}{s_{y_t}}$$

Since Group t does not actually take either Form x or Form y, the means M_{x_t} and M_{y_t} and the standard deviations s_{x_t} and s_{y_t} must be estimated. The estimation procedure most often used is based on the assumption that the regression of either form of the full test (x or y) on the anchor test (u) has the same slope, intercept, and residual variance in the total group (Group t) as in the group taking that form (Group α or Group β). For the new Form x in Groups t and α,

$$b_{xu_t} = b_{xu_\alpha}$$

$$M_{x_t} - b_{xu_t} M_{u_t} = M_{x_\alpha} - b_{xu_\alpha} M_{u_\alpha}$$

$$s_{x_t}^2 (1 - r_{xu_t}^2) = s_{x_\alpha}^2 (1 - r_{xu_\alpha}^2)$$

and similarly for the old Form y in Groups t and β. These assumptions yield the following estimates:

$$\hat{M}_{x_t} = M_{x_\alpha} + b_{xu_\alpha}(M_{u_t} - M_{u_\alpha});$$

$$\hat{M}_{y_t} = M_{y_\beta} + b_{yu_\beta}(M_{u_t} - M_{u_\beta});$$

$$\hat{s}_{x_t}^2 = s_{x_\alpha}^2 + b_{xu_\alpha}^2 (s_{u_t}^2 - s_{u_\alpha}^2);$$

$$\hat{s}_{y_t}^2 = s_{y_\beta}^2 + b_{yu_\beta}^2 (s_{u_t}^2 - s_{u_\beta}^2).$$

(Since all test takers in Group t take the equating section u, the mean M_{u_t} and standard deviation s_{u_t} can be computed.)

Substituting the estimated means and standard deviations into the equation that defines the equating relationship yields a formula for translating raw scores on the new Form x into equivalent raw scores on the old Form y:

$$\hat{y} = Ax + B$$

where $\quad A = \hat{s}_{y_t} / \hat{s}_{x_t}$

and $\quad B = \hat{M}_{y_t} - A\hat{M}_{x_t}$

Substituting into the existing equation relating Form y raw scores to the standard scale

$$S = a_{sy} y + b_{sy},$$

the equation relating Form x raw scores to the scale is obtained:

$$S = a_{sx} x + b_{sx}$$

where $\quad a_{sx} = a_{sy} A$ and

$$b_{sx} = a_{sy} B + b_{sy}.$$

The formulas presented above were originally derived by L. R Tucker (Angoff 1961) under assumptions appropriate to observed scores; they have been found to operate quite effectively when the groups taking the new and old forms (Groups α and β) do not differ sharply in ability, as indicated by their scores on the anchor test. In those instances, however, when the groups differ by a substantial amount, a different set of formulas, derived by R. S. Levine (1955) is used. Levine's formulas are based on the assumption that both full test forms (x and y) are randomly parallel to the set of equating items (u), that is, that the items may all be considered as having been drawn at random from the same item pool. For this reason the Levine formulas are used only when the groups taking the two forms differ substantially in ability.

A second type of equating method used to equate different forms of the same Achievement Test is equipercentile equating. Equipercentile equating methods are based on a definition of equating that considers scores on two tests as equal if they represent the same percentile rank in some reference group. The type of equipercentile equating most often used for the Achievement Tests is a two-stage procedure. Scores on the new form are equated to scores on the anchor test in a sample of the students taking the new form. The scores on the anchor test are then equated to scores on the previous form in a sample of the students who took the previous form. The resulting raw-to-scale score conversion may require "smoothing" to remove small-sample irregularities, particularly at the upper and lower ends of the score scale, where the number of test takers is not large.

The main advantage of equipercentile equating over linear equating is that it allows for a curvilinear raw-to-scale score conversion; that is, one that would appear as a curved line on a graph. Both linear and equipercentile equating are routinely performed in equating each Achievement Test. If the equipercentile equating does not clearly indicate a curvilinear relationship, the linear equating results are used. If the relationship does appear to be curvilinear, the equipercentile equating results are used in place of or to modify the linear results in parts of the score range. (Sometimes the equipercentile curve is approximated by a series of connected line segments.)

In some cases, the raw-to-scale conversions resulting from the scaling and equating are such that the maximum raw score would be assigned a reported scaled score less than 800. In most of these cases, the raw-to-scale conversion is adjusted to ensure that at least one raw score converts to a scaled score of 800, by means of an adjustment similar to that used for the SAT (as described earlier in this chapter). However, the Achievement Tests are required to scale to only 780.

In other cases, the scaling and equating result in raw-to-scale conversions such that a perfect score and other very high scores yield scaled score equivalents greater than 800. This situation occurs for the most difficult tests, such as Mathematics Level II, which are taken by groups of students of very high ability. In these cases, a student can miss several questions and still receive the maximum reported score of 800.

Rescaling the Achievement Tests

As the population of students taking the Achievement Tests changes over time, the statistical relationships between the SAT and the Achievement Tests tend to change (Wilks 1961). As a result, it is not possible to maintain strict form-to-form comparability of scores on the Achievement Tests and still maintain comparability of scores on different Achievement Tests. The Admissions Testing Program has dealt with this problem by periodically rescaling the Achievement Tests. The rescaling procedure is similar to the procedure by which the tests were originally scaled, except that the reference group now is specified to have a correlation of .60 between SAT-verbal and SAT-mathematical scores. Also, the reference group for the foreign language tests is specified to resemble the current combined group of students taking all those tests in terms of the statistics involving the number of years of language study. The usual practice for adjusting the score scale after a rescaling is to average the results of the rescaling with those of the equating. This practice is intended to prevent an abrupt shift in the score scale. Rescaling improves the effectiveness of the Achievement Tests for the purposes of selective admissions, but it diminishes their effectiveness for other purposes, such as in the accumulation of historical data and the placement of students in courses.

The Achievement Tests were rescaled every year from 1965 through 1972 and in 1974, 1976, 1978, 1979, and 1980. The results of each rescaling were applied to all forms administered after April of the year in which the rescaling was done. Frequently a new form of an Achievement Test will be equated to a previous form that was last administered before the most recent rescaling. In that case, the raw-to-scale conversion for the previous form is adjusted to reflect the results of the rescaling. The equating will then produce a raw-to-scale score conversion for the new form that reflects the results of the rescaling. Consequently, scores on the rescaled form (and on subsequent forms) will not be comparable to scores on previous forms of that test.

Table 2.4 provides information about the shift in the Achievement Test score scale that has resulted from some of the rescaling operations to date. It presents scaled scores for the 14 Achievement Tests on the current scale (established in 1980) corresponding to selected scaled scores on the 1972 and 1979 scales. For example, a scaled score of 250 on the 1972 English Composition Test corresponds to a score of 245 on the current scale. Similarly, a score of 250 on the 1979 English Composition Test corresponds to a score of 251 on the current scale. As indicated by the data in Table 2.4, for most tests rescaling has relatively small effects over a short period, as, for example, 1979 to 1980. Of the 39 differences implicit in the table for those years, 33 are 10 points or less. For longer time periods, for example, 10 years, the effects may be substantial. Achievement Test users who are interested in interpreting trends in these scores over time or in comparing scores reported several years apart should take into consideration the effects of rescaling.

Table 2.4

Scaled Scores on the Current Scale Corresponding to Scaled Scores on the 1972 and 1979 Scales for ATP Achievement Tests*

Achievement Test	1980 Scaled Scores Corresponding to 1972 Scaled Scores of			1980 Scaled Scores Corresponding to 1979 Scaled Scores of		
	250	500	750	250	500	750
English Composition	245	488	731	251	497	744
Literature	242	488	735	247	494	742
American History	270	506	743	266	508	751
European History	265	514	763	248	504	761
French	232	470	708	240	494	748
German	237	461	685	256	498	741
Hebrew	203	492	782	221	492	762
Latin	268	511	753	272	515	758
Spanish	227	458	688	257	507	757
Biology	244	474	704	254	498	743
Chemistry	237	478	720	254	500	745
Physics	254	494	734	253	503	752
Mathematics Level I and II	244	486	729	247	500	754

*The current scale was established in May 1980.

Scaling and Equating the PSAT/NMSQT

Each year two new forms of the PSAT/NMSQT are assembled from items originally written for the SAT. Most of these items are taken from two retired forms of the SAT, called the "parent" forms. The PSAT/NMSQT scores are scaled through the parent forms of the SAT, not through previous forms of the PSAT/NMSQT. However, because the SAT scores are equated, this scaling procedure results in equated scores for the PSAT/NMSQT. Each of the two PSAT/NMSQT forms has a number of items in common with each of the two parent SAT forms. These common items are used as anchor items in the scaling and equating of the PSAT/NMSQT. The anchor items contained in each form of the PSAT/NMSQT are "internal"; that is, they are used in computing the student's raw score. Figure 2.4 shows the pattern of linkages for a typical form of the PSAT/NMSQT.

Figure 2.4

Linkages Between New PSAT/NMSQT Forms and "Parent" SAT Forms

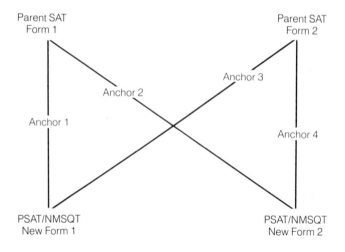

Since the PSAT/NMSQT scores are scaled through the SAT parent forms, the PSAT/NMSQT score scale corresponds to the SAT score scale. The final zero is dropped from PSAT/NMSQT scores, so that the score scale ranges from 20 to 80. For example, a PSAT/NMSQT score of 48 corresponds to an SAT score of 480. However, the PSAT/NMSQT is both shorter and easier than the SAT. Because the PSAT/NMSQT contains fewer difficult questions than the SAT, the relationship between raw scores on a PSAT/NMSQT form and on a parent SAT form tends to be curvilinear. This curvilinear relationship cannot be determined by linear scaling methods, but it can be determined by applying item response theory. Since October 1982, the correspondence between each new PSAT/NMSQT

Figure 2.5

Matrix of Item Response Data for Scaling a Typical Form of the PSAT/NMSQT

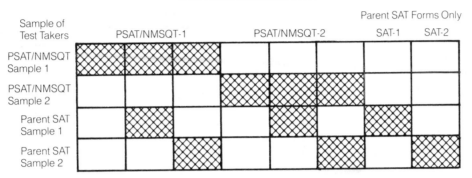

The IRT scaling procedure for the PSAT/NMSQT typically produces a raw-to-scale score conversion that does not reach to 80; that is, even a student who answered all the questions correctly would not receive a scaled score of 80. However, beginning in October 1982 the PSAT/NMSQT score conversions have included an adjustment at the upper end to force the scores to 80. This adjustment is made in the same manner as described earlier for SAT scores. Before October 1982, PSAT/NMSQT scores were not forced to 80, as is reflected in Table 2.5 for raw score of 65. However, the highest possible score was adjusted to be the same for both PSAT/NMSQT forms, in the interest of fairness to the students who answered all items correctly. Table 2.5 provides information on the ranges of scaled scores observed at selected raw score levels across a number of forms.

form and each of the parent SAT forms has been determined by IRT procedures like those used for equating the SAT. (Before October 1982, linear methods were used.) The item parameters for all the items in both new forms of the PSAT/NMSQT and both parent SAT forms are estimated in a single application of the computer program LOGIST. The estimates are based on item response data from a sample of students taking each new form of the PSAT/NMSQT and a sample of test takers from each of the two parent SAT forms. Figure 2.5 illustrates the data matrix for estimating the item parameters. The interlocking pattern of items assures that all item parameter estimates will be expressed on the same θ scale. Once the item parameters for the two new PSAT/NMSQT forms and the two parent SAT forms have been estimated, the raw-to-scale score conversion is determined in the same way as for a new form of the SAT.

Item Analysis

The processes of scaling and equating ensure a practical comparability among scores. Nonetheless, these processes cannot guarantee perfect results. An evaluation of the psychometric properties of the tests is typically carried out by the preparation of two special summaries: the item analysis and the test analysis. Item analysis is used at two points in the test development process. During the pretest stage, item analysis is used to assess the appropriateness of questions for use in a final test form. After the final form has been taken by students, item analysis is used to reveal the extent to which statistical specifications were met and to obtain a final check on the adequacy of the pretest analysis. The scope and content of item analysis is described on the following pages; test analysis is described in a later section.[*]

Table 2.5

PSAT/NMSQT Scaled Scores for Selected
Formula Raw Scores

Raw Score	PSAT-Verbal (65 questions)	PSAT-Mathematical (50 questions)
65	77-80	
60	70-73	
55	65-68	
50	59-63	77-80
45	55-59	69-73
40	50-54	63-68
35	46-50	58-61
30	42-45	53-56
25	38-41	48-51
20	34-37	43-46
15	30-33	39-41
10	25-28	34-36
5	20-24	29-31
0	20	24-27

NOTE: The ranges for the College Board scores are based on all regular administrations of the PSAT given from October 1975 through October 1983.

[*]Further information concerning item analysis is provided by Hecht and Swineford (1981); additional information on test analysis is furnished by Walker (1981).

A systematic program of pretesting and item analysis is used to control the statistical properties of the test forms. This pretest program includes steps intended to assess the difficulty and discriminating power of the items, to select items of appropriate statistical characteristics, and to detect sources of ambiguity and other reasons for failure to provide adequate discrimination.

Although the analysis of items yields a variety of information, the principal statistics are the indexes of item difficulty and item discrimination. The index of difficulty, "delta," ($\triangle$) is a function of the percent passing the item. It is the baseline normal deviate of the point above which lies the proportion of correct responses to the item. It is expressed in terms of a scale whose mean is 13 and whose standard deviation is 4.*

The use of delta is based upon some statistical advantages that such baseline measures offer over percentages. Equal differences in percentages do not reflect equal differences in item difficulty if the percentages themselves vary widely. For example, the difference in intrinsic difficulty reflected by percentages of 95 and 90 is probably greater than the difference in intrinsic difficulty reflected by 55 and 50, because there are so many fewer individuals at the extremes of the ability distribution. Throughout much of the middle range of difficulty, the relationship between the percent correct (p) and delta is fairly linear, but at the extremes small differences in percentages become greater differences in delta.

The scale for delta is inversely related to the scale for p. Thus the more difficult the item, the smaller is the value of p and the greater the value of delta. Typically, a delta of 13.0 is equivalent to 50 percent marking the correct answer, a delta of 9.0 is equivalent to 84 percent marking the correct answer, and a delta of 17.0 is equivalent to 16 percent marking the correct response.

Delta is corrected for the effects of dropout by the amount by which the mean of the "still working" group differs from 13.0. For example, if 20 percent of the group drop out, 80 percent are still working. If 40 percent of the "still working" group succeed on an item, the first estimate of delta is 14.0, the usual equivalent on the delta scale to a success rate of 40 percent. But, typically the average ability of the group still working is greater than 13.0 (for example, 13.3). Then the first estimate of raw delta is modified upward by 0.3, the observed increment in

the mean. The new estimate, 14.3, is the working estimate of item difficulty for this item.

Samples may differ in level of ability from the standard reference group that was originally used to scale the tests. Therefore, it is necessary to render the raw, or observed, deltas obtained from successive pretestings comparable to one another by an equating procedure. This procedure requires that the pretest material consisting of new items be administered together with a number of previously used items whose standard, or equated, deltas are known. For each item, an observed delta is calculated based on the pretest sample. When these new observed delta values for the previously used items are plotted against the equated delta values on graph paper, the resulting scatterplot typically falls in an elongated, narrow ellipse reflected in a high correlation coefficient, usually in the upper 90s. The line defined by this plot, calculated from the means and standard deviations of the observed and equated deltas, is used to convert the item difficulties for the pretest samples (observed deltas) to item difficulties as estimated for the reference population (equated deltas). Figure 2.6 gives an example of such a plot and the resulting line. Although the observed deltas

Figure 2.6

Sample Item Plot Used in Delta Equating

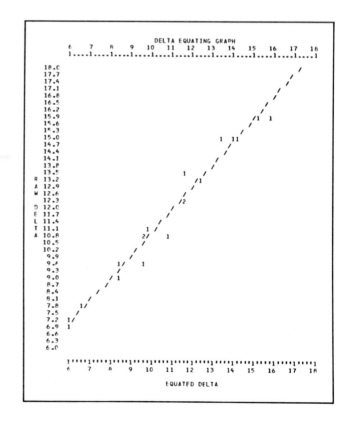

EQUATED DELTA

---

*The parameters 13 and 4 were chosen early in the history of the College Board's objective testing program to avoid negative scores or scores requiring two-decimal accuracy. This was a practical consideration because all computations were done manually.

lack comparability, because they are dependent on the abilities of the various groups to whom the items have been administered, the equated deltas are all defined in terms of the same standard reference group and are, therefore, directly comparable (Thurstone 1947).

A second statistic regularly calculated for every item is the biserial coefficient of correlation between the item and an appropriate criterion, usually the total score on the test. The biserial coefficient was chosen from a variety of other coefficients because of its theoretical independence from the difficulty of the item being evaluated. Other indexes—for instance, the point biserial or the phi coefficient—do not share this property. When the score on an item is correlated against the total score on the test and the item is included in the total score, the inclusion tends to increase or inflate the observed level of correlation. (In an SAT pretest, the item itself is not included in the criterion, which is the total score on the appropriate section of the SAT.) Because this effect is generally quite small and because it tends to affect all the items in a similar manner, no attempt is made to apply statistical corrections intended to deal with this difficulty.

The biserial correlations are used for three purposes: 1) to identify items that may be ambiguous or incorrectly keyed, 2) to assess the worth of items as discriminators, and 3) to provide a basis for checking on the degree of homogeneity among the items of the test. This last consideration has a bearing on the parallelism among test forms. Because a certain degree of heterogeneity is regarded as desirable, especially for the Achievement Tests, and is in part predetermined by the content specifications of the test, some items with relatively low biserials as well as items with relatively high biserials may be included in each new form. Consequently, the degree to which the means and standard deviations of the biserial correlations over forms agree becomes an important consideration in controlling the parallelism among the several forms.

The first step in conducting an item analysis is to draw a random sample of scored answer sheets. The scores from these answer sheets are then transformed by curvilinear methods into special criterion scaled scores with a normal distribution, a mean of 13.0, and a standard deviation of 4.0. The general distribution of the resulting criterion scores is described in Table 2.6.

In the item analysis, an "omit" response is distinguished from a "not reached" response. An "omit" is any blank response that is followed by at least one item to which there is a marked response. A "not reached" response is a blank response to any

Table 2.6

General Distribution of the Normalized Criterion Score

Criterion score	Relative Rank of the Answer Sheets
20 or above	highest 5%
18 or above	highest 10%
16 or above	highest 20%
14 or above	highest 40%
above 13	upper half
below 13	lower half
12 or below	lowest 40%
10 or below	lowest 20%
8 or below	lowest 10%
6 or below	lowest 5%

item after the last marked item. The frequency and criterion score mean for the omit response are shown as for any other response. This is not done for the not reached response. However, the percentage still working is reported, together with the mean criterion scaled score of the group still working.

The size of the sample selected for analysis depends on the number of test takers available. For both the SAT and the major Achievement Tests the sample is approximately 1,500 to 2,000 students for final forms, but varies. For SAT pretests, it ranges from 1,500 to 1,700; for small volume Achievement Test pretests, from 200 to 300. Pretesting for the Achievement Tests takes place outside of the regular administrations on the campuses of cooperating colleges (see Chapter V).

The data routinely produced in the item analysis are particularly useful in making revisions to items. These data include the number of people choosing each option of the item, the percentage passing the item, the number of people omitting the item, the number not reaching the item (presumably due to insufficient time), the mean total score on the test for those choosing each option (as well as for those omitting the items), and the number of people in each of five groups of equal size (as defined by the total score on the test) choosing each option. From these frequencies and means, it is possible to determine, for example, whether an incorrect option is sufficiently attractive to the less able test takers to be helpful, and whether it draws so many of the more able students that it may indicate the presence of an ambiguity. The analysis by score-level groups makes it possible to determine approximately where on the score continuum the item is making its maximum discrimination and, in an approximate way, whether the response pattern (curve) for each of the item options, including the correct option, is as it should be.

Table 2.7 on the next page presents a sample item analysis for an SAT item. The frequencies of response

Table 2.7

Example of Item Analysis Computer Report
(Item 19 of Scholastic Aptitude Test, May 1983)

ITEM NO: 19	TIS NO: 5061	TEST: VERB 1	FORM: FSA056IP	BASE N: 1505	DATE TABULATED: 6/20/83

	RESPONSE CODE	LOW N₁	N₂	N₃	N₄	HIGH N₅	
	OMIT	21	25	26	22	9	
EDUCATIONAL	A	82	48	21	17	4	ITEM ANALYSIS
TESTING	B	50	57	65	35	19	
SERVICE	C	51	57	75	75	43	
MM NR	D	29	62	80	108	199	
0 0	E	68	52	34	44	27	
0.0 0.0	TOTAL	301	301	301	301	301	* DENOTES CORRECT RESPONSE

FORM	BASE N	OMIT	A	B	C	D	E	M_{TOTAL}	$\triangle_E$ SCALE	$\triangle_E$	CRITERION
FSA056IP	1505	103	172	226	301	478*	225	13.0	BOARD	14.0	IS085

TEST CODE	ITEM NO.	M_O	M_A	M_B	M_C	M_D	M_E	P_{TOTAL}	P+	$\triangle_O$	r_{bis}
VERB 1	19	12.2	9.8	12.1	12.9	15.4	11.7	1.00	0.32	14.9	0.55

for each option for each of the five groups, and the N for each group, 301, are presented in the 5 × 7 matrix in the central portion of the item report. Thus, there are 82 persons choosing option A in the lowest scoring fifth, as opposed to 4 persons choosing option A in the highest fifth. For the keyed response, D, the lowest scoring group shows 29 responses; the highest scoring group, 199.

The information in the two-row strip below the 5 × 7 matrix can be read as follows, from left to right, and from top to bottom within a column:

Column	Upper/ Lower	Category Label	Content
1)	U	Form	Form designation (FSA056IP)
	L	Test Code	Type of material: section (Verb 1)
2)	U	Base N	Sample size (1,505)
	L	Item No.	Item number (i.e., sequential location in the test) (19)
3-8)	U	Omit, A, etc.	For example, Omit has 103 students with a mean of 12.2; option A has
	L	M_O M_A, etc.	172 students with a mean of 9.8, etc.
9)	U	M Total	Mean criterion score of group reaching item (13.0)
	L	P Total	Proportion of group reaching item (1.00)
10)	U	$\triangle_E$ Scale	Reference scale for equated delta (College Board)
	L	P +	Proportion succeeding on item (0.32)
11)	U	$\triangle_E$	Equated delta (14.0)
	L	$\triangle_O$	Observed delta (14.9)
12)	U	Criterion	Item analysis criterion code: the criterion contained the item (I), was composed of similar items (S), and there were 85 items (085). (IS085)
	L	r_{bis}	The biserial correlation (0.55)

In the case of this sample SAT item, 32 percent of the group reaching the item marked the correct response. The delta corresponding to 32 percent is 14.9. The estimated delta for the College Board standard reference group, the "equated" delta, is entered just above the "observed" delta computed from the data. It is 14.0, indicating that the item would have been different in difficulty, somewhat easier, for the standard reference group than for this sample. Each sample may be expected to differ from other samples; the description of difficulty in terms of a standard reference group enables these differences among samples to be reduced.

The index of discrimination, the biserial coefficient of correlation (r_{bis}) of the item with the total score, is entered at the extreme right. It is 0.55. There is a space above the biserial correlation for identifying the criterion, which was the total formula score on the test, based on all items including the item being correlated.

As shown, the item analysis provides the test developer with considerable information about students' responses to the items. This particular analysis strongly suggests that the specific item is suitable for the test. It is neither too hard nor too easy, all options are functioning properly, and there is no evidence of ambiguity. The item discriminates sharply between high-scoring and low-scoring students.

"External" Criteria in Item Analysis

The use of the total score on a test as the criterion for item analysis has sometimes been criticized on the grounds that the use of such a criterion could gradually lead to measuring progressively narrower aspects of an area. Ideally, it is argued, each question should make an independent contribution to the measurement of the total. Therefore, the best item is one that has a low correlation with other questions in the test but measures some important aspect of the criterion performance.

From time to time, criteria other than the total scores on a test may be used. However, in the construction of College Board Achievement Tests, the item analysis procedure supplements, rather than substitutes for, the judgment that the item is appropriate and useful. Generally, the test writer asks: "Is the biserial correlation for this item high enough to reduce the possibility that it is ambiguous or irrelevant?" This is quite a different question from: "Of all the items that have been written, which have the highest biserial correlations?" Item analysis is used as a guide to help identify defective items, not to determine which items will be selected for a test.

Carl Brigham, who, with Cecil Brolyer, was responsible for devising the basic item analysis procedures applied to College Board tests, recognized that the item-test correlation is a useful index of the item's discriminating power, but he wondered about possible inconsistencies between item-test results and item-criterion results. He had constructed the verbal aptitude test for the purpose of predicting performance in liberal arts colleges, particularly in English classes. Therefore, he carried out an item analysis in which he correlated the antonym items in Form C of the SAT with grades obtained in English courses six months after the administration of the test. The results were compared with those obtained from the analysis against the total score on the test. His conclusions (Brigham 1932, p. 367) read: "More important than the range of biserial r's, however, is the fact that these items derive their validity from exactly the same traps or from the same characteristic item pattern which indicated their validity when the total score in the scholastic aptitude test was used as a criterion. Changing the criterion did not alter the pattern of the item charts materially."

If one is attempting, by a purely empirical procedure, to construct a test that will predict performance of a complex and not very well understood criterion, a process of item analysis based on correlations with an external and independent measure of that criterion may be the only justifiable approach. But when one is evaluating test items that have been judged appropriate, in terms of their content, for inclusion in a test designed to assess achievement in an academic field, the total score on a representative sample of such questions is likely to be a highly satisfactory criterion. It is assumed, of course, that systematic studies will be made of the relationship of the total score criterion to whatever other criterion measures may be available. Usually, the information obtained from studies that correlate test scores and performance is more definitive than that obtained by correlating items with performance criteria. This is particularly true when, as in college admissions, there are as many criteria as there are colleges and schools within the colleges.

This conclusion is strongly supported by data from a study that compared various methods of item selection for the Law School Admission Test (Olsen and Schrader 1953). The test in its original form consisted of numerous different subtests, each created on the basis of rational judgment and then refined through item analysis procedures with the total score on the subtest as the criterion. The total testing time was approximately six hours, and it was decided to attempt to shorten the test by selecting from the total pool of questions those most predictive of performance in law schools. In this situation, the external criterion for item analysis did not prove to be superior to the internal criterion for this purpose.

Test Analysis

After the first formal administration of each newly developed test form, a sample of answer sheets (usually 1,500 to 2,000) is drawn for item and test analysis purposes, and a report of a detailed test analysis is made. Reliabilities and standard errors of measurement of the separately timed parts of the test are calculated, as well as intercorrelations among the parts and the total score. Assessments of speededness are made. Distributions of the total formula scores are also presented (not only for this special sample, being subjected to analysis, but for all students taking that form). In addition, the distributions, means, and standard deviations are given for the number of items answered correctly, the number answered incorrectly, the number omitted, and the number not reached. As an additional check on speededness, a bivariate plot is made of score versus number of items marked, and the ratio of the variance of items not reached to score variance is reported. Finally, distributions, means, and standard deviations are reported for item difficulties and biserial correlations for each separately timed section of the test. These findings are presented together with an introductory text to each test analysis, which is then used as a guide for the development of future forms of the test.

Examples of the test analysis data for the November 1982 SAT form are presented in Tables 2.8, 2.9, 2.10, 2.11, and 2.12 (see pages 32-34). Table 2.8 contains the distribution of scores for the group of 381,570 test takers. At the bottom of the table, summary statistics (means and standard deviations) are given. In Table 2.8, the mean raw score on the 85-item verbal section of the test was 36.79; for the 60-item mathematical section of the test, it was 26.02. In each case, the mean is reasonably close to the midpoint of the total possible score range. The possible score range on the verbal section is from -21 to +85, or 107 points, and the midpoint of this range is 32. The possible score range for the mathematical section is from -17 to 60, or 78 points, and the midpoint of this range is 21.5. Further, there are approximately three standard deviation units between the mean and the maximum obtainable raw score. For the verbal section, there are 2.96 standard deviation units, and for the mathematical section, 2.67. There are no obvious floor or ceiling effects.

Table 2.8

Example of Score Distributions and Conversion Data Reported in Test Analyses (Scholastic Aptitude Test, November 1982)

VERBAL - 85 ITEMS				MATHEMATICAL - 60 ITEMS			
RAW SCORE X	STANDARD SCORE S	FREQ	% RANK OF LOWER LIMIT OF INTERVAL	RAW SCORE X	STANDARD SCORE S	FREQ	% RANK OF LOWER LIMIT OF INTERVAL
85	800	40	100.0	60	800	213	99.9
80- 84	730-780	1242	99.7	57- 59	760-780	1290	99.6
75- 79	680-720	3789	98.7	54- 56	730-750	3646	98.7
70- 74	640-670	6750	96.9	51- 53	700-720	8194	95.2
65- 69	610-630	10264	94.2	48- 50	670-690	12486	91.9
60- 64	580-600	14716	90.4	45- 47	640-660	15524	87.9
55- 59	550-570	20236	85.1	42- 44	620-640	20700	82.4
50- 54	520-540	26446	78.1	39- 41	590-610	25826	75.7
45- 49	490-510	33462	69.4	36- 38	560-580	28169	68.3
40- 44	460-480	39956	58.9	33- 35	530-550	31458	60.0
35- 39	420-450	44871	47.1	30- 32	510-530	33339	51.3
30- 34	390-420	46311	35.0	27- 29	480-500	31581	43.0
25- 29	360-390	42951	23.7	24- 26	450-470	31399	34.8
20- 24	320-350	35365	14.5	21- 23	420-440	28956	27.2
15- 19	290-320	25493	7.8	18- 20	400-420	25741	20.5
10- 14	250-280	16053	3.1	15- 17	370-390	23663	14.3
5- 9	210-240	8739	1.3	12- 14	350-360	19659	9.1
0- 4	200	3837	0.3	9- 11	320-340	14702	5.3
- 5-- 1	200	947	0.0	6- 8	300-310	11195	2.5
-10-- 6	200	99	0.0	3- 5	250-260	5585	0.9
-15--11	200	3	0.0	- 3-- 1	220-240	2393	0.2
				- 6-- 4	200-210	766	0.0
		381570		- 9-- 7	200	106	0.0
				-12--10	200	5	0.0
				-15--13	200	0	0.0
				-18--16	200	1	0.0
						381570	

| M_x = 36.79 Mdn_x = 35.67 σ_x = 16.27 Max_x = 85 Min_x = -15 M_s = 432.78 Mdn_s = 426.71 σ_s = 104.82 Max_s = 800 Min_s = 200 α_3 = 0.258 | CONVERSION DATA — Raw scores were placed on Board standard scale via IRT true-score equating to Forms 3CSA1 and 3DSA05. Equating tests gy and gq, in common with each old form respectively, were used in calibration. See page a.3 for raw-to-scaled conversion table. | M_x = 26.02 Mdn_x = 26.04 σ_x = 12.75 Max_x = 60 Min_x = -17 M_s = 472.15 Mdn_s = 470.44 σ_s = 114.73 Max_s = 800 Min_s = 200 α_3 = 0.064 | CONVERSION DATA — Raw scores were placed on Board standard scale via IRT true-score equating to Forms 3CSA1 and 3DSA05. Equating tests gz and gr, in common with each old form respectively, were used in calibration. See page A.4 for raw-to-scaled conversion table. |

Although the possible score range is sufficiently great, much of that range is theoretically possible through random responding, a factor that complicates the evaluation of test difficulty. The nonchance ranges for the SAT-verbal and SAT-mathematical sections (i.e., the range of scores significantly greater at the .01 level [one-tailed test] than the expected chance score) are, respectively (and approximately), 7 to 85 and 6 to 60. Most scores fall within this range, and they are positively skewed. The sections tend to be quite difficult for the average student, who will only succeed on about 50 to 55 percent of the questions in either section, even with a certain amount of "guessing." This difficulty and the resulting proportion of answers that cannot be distinguished from chance levels are the probable consequence of the effort to provide adequate measurement in the upper score levels. The lower average ability for students in recent years has exacerbated the problem of the difficulty of the test; the average attainment has decreased but the requirement for an accurate assessment at the top has remained.

The remainder of the test analysis is based on the special sample of 1,610 cases. Data on reliability and test speededness are presented in Table 2.9.

Table 2.9

Example of Data on Reliability and Speededness of Sections Reported in Test Analyses (Scholastic Aptitude Test, November 1982)

```
SCORING FORMULAE AND RELIABILITY COEFFICIENTS FOR SECTIONS

                                    -- RELIABILITIES --   --OBSERVED SCORE DATA--
                        SCORING                SEM    SEM                  OBTAINED
   TEST SECTION         FORMULA     REL.       RAW  SCALED^d  MEAM   S.D.  RANGE

   I. VERBAL 1          R-.2500W   0.868^a    3.27           19.42   9.00  -2 -  45
  II. VERBAL 2          R-.2500W   0.859^a    3.14           17.69   8.35  -5 -  40
  READING SUBSCORE      R-.2500W   0.868^a    3.15    4.2    17.23   8.69  -5 -  40
  VOCABULARY SUBSCORE   R-.2500W   0.868^a    3.24    4.2    19.90   8.91  -6 -  45
  I+II. TOTAL VERBAL    R-.2500W   0.926^b    4.53   29.3    36.98  16.70  -6 -  84
                                   0.921^c    4.70   30.4

  IV. MATH 1            R-.2500W   0.800^a    2.47           11.03   5.52  -4 -  25
   V. MATH 2            R-KW^e     0.862^a    2.94           15.17   7.90  -8 -  35
  IV+V. TOTAL MATH      R-KW^e     0.911^b    3.84   34.5    26.07  12.86  -5 -  59
                                   0.910^c    3.86   34.7
```

^{d} DRESSEL ADAPTATION OF KUDER-RICHARDSON FORMULA 20.

^{b} SEE EQUATION 2 IN TEXT.

^{c} SEE EQUATION 3 IN TEXT.

^{d} SEE TEXT, PAGE 8.

^{e} K EQUALS .250 FOR 5-CHOICE ITEMS AND .333 FOR 4-CHOICE ITEMS.

```
                        SPEEDEDNESS OF SECTIONS

                        PCT COMPLETING   VARIANCE    # ITEMS    TOTAL
   TEST SECTION         100%     75%     INDEX OF    REACHED    # OF
                                         SPEED.^f    BY 80%     ITEMS

   I. VERBAL 1          51.1    95.7      0.18         41        45
  II. VERBAL 2          74.6    99.9      0.06         38        40

  IV. MATH 1            62.1    99.4      0.05         24        25
   V. MATH 2            58.0    98.7      0.07         34        35
```

^{f} VARIANCE INDEX OF SPEEDEDNESS IS THE RATIO OF THE VARIANCE OF THE NUMBER OF ITEMS NOT REACHED AND THE VARIANCE OF SCORES.

Brief discussions of these aspects of the test evaluations are presented later in this chapter. Table 2.10 shows a detailed section analysis, in this case, the first 45-item verbal section of the November 1982 SAT. It provides the analyst with the frequency distributions for four specific types of responses to the test: right answers, wrong answers, omitted responses, and those items not reached. Furthermore, the bivariate plot enables the analyst to estimate the

Table 2.10

Example of Detailed Data on Speededness Reported in Test Analyses (Scholastic Aptitude Test, November 1982)

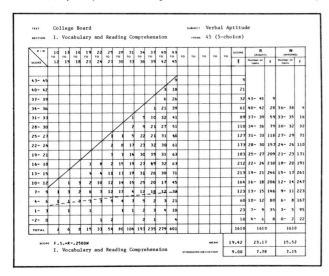

extent to which work rate alone determines the distribution of scores for the group that fails to complete the test.

The item analysis procedures were explained earlier. As Table 2.11 shows, a summary of item analysis data is included in the test analysis and the distribution of deltas is compared with the specifications. A summary of the item analysis for several recent forms is provided, as shown in Table 2.12 (page 34), to further help the test development staff evaluate their work.

Table 2.11

Example of Item Analysis Summary Data Reported in Test Analyses (Scholastic Aptitude Test, November 1982)

Test   College Board

Subject   Aptitude   Form   3ESA08

Frequency Distributions, Means, and Standard Deviations of Observed (Obs.), Equated (Equ.) and Specified (Spec.) Deltas

| Delta | Mathematical | | | | |
| | Obs. | | | | |
	IV	V	IV+V	Equ.	Spec.
19.0 up					
18.0-18.9					3
17.0-17.9	2	2	4	7	4
16.0-16.9	2	4	6	4	4
15.0-15.9	3	3	6	5	4
14.0-14.9	0	3	3	3	4
13.0-13.9	4	4	8	8	4
12.0-12.9	2	1	3	2	4
11.0-11.9	5	3	8	8	8
10.0-10.9	2	8	10	9	8
9.0- 9.9	3	4	7	4	8
8.0- 8.9	1	2	3	6	5
7.0- 7.9	1	0	1	2	1
6.0- 6.9		0	0	1	2
5.9 down		1	1	1	1
Total ...	25	35	60	60	60
Mean	12.6	12.5	12.5	12.3	12.2
σ	2.8	2.9	2.8	3.3	3.3

Equated Δ = a(Observed Δ) + b

     a = 1.1502

     b = -2.0824

Δ (index of item difficulty) = $13-4z$, where z is the normal deviate corresponding to proportion correct.

Table 2.12

Example of Multi-Form Item Analysis Summary Data Reported in Test Analyses
(Scholastic Aptitude Test, November 1982)

Form	3ESA03	3ESA04	3ESA05	3ESA06	3ESA07	3ESA08
Administration	March 1982	March 1982	May 1982	June 1982	Oct. 1982	Nov. 1982
Total-Group N	148,578	35,872	290,137	214,659	79,606	381,570
Sample N	1,915	2,015	1,490	1,670	1,510	1,610
Total-Group Statistics						
Formula-Score Information						
Mean	23.98	23.68	25.30	23.94	25.26	26.02
S.D.	13.45	13.44	12.67	13.49	12.80	12.75
Possible Range	-17-60	-17-60	-16-59	-17-60	-17-60	-17-60
Obtained Range	-12-60	-10-60	-12-59	-14-60	-10-60	-17-60
Median	23.31	23.12	25.32	23.41	25.40	26.04
Skewness	.24	.18	.04	.19	.05	.06
Scaled-Score Information						
Mean	456	458	486	479	480	472
S.D.	116	115	114	118	117	115
Possible Range[a]	120-800	200-800	120-800	110-800	110-800	110-800
Obtained Range[a]	160-800	200-800	150-800	130-800	170-800	110-800
Median	444	451	483	474	474	470
Sample Statistics						
Formula-Score Information						
Mean	24.63	24.54	26.16	24.93	26.29	26.07
S.D.	13.60	13.72	12.83	13.65	12.58	12.86
Obtained Range	-9-60	-7-60	-7-59	-5-60	-6-60	-5-59
Median	24.04	24.22	26.64	24.38	26.87	26.42
Skewness	.18	.10	-.08	.14	-.00	-.04
Scaled-Score Information						
Mean	462	466	494	488	489	473
S.D.	117	117	116	119	115	116
Obtained Range[a]	190-800	210-800	200-800	210-800	210-800	210-780
Median	450	462	496	484	489	474
Item Statistics						
Number of Items	60	60	59	60	60	60
Mean Proportion Correct	.52	.51	.54	.52	.54	.53
Mean Observed Delta	12.8	12.8	12.5	12.7	12.5	12.5
S.D. Observed Delta	2.7	2.6	2.8	2.8	2.9	2.8
Mean Equated Delta	12.1	12.3	12.2	12.4	12.2	12.3
S.D. Equated Delta	3.2	3.2	3.3	3.2	3.3	3.3
Mean R-Biserial	.57	.56	.55	.57	.55	.55
S.D. R-Biserial	.11	.12	.11	.12	.09	.11
No. R-Biserial <.20	0	0	0	0	0	0
Test Statistics						
Reliability	.919	.920	.912	.921	.910	.911
Raw Std. Error of Meas.	3.87	3.88	3.80	3.85	3.78	3.84
Scaled Std. Error of Meas.	33.4	33.2	34.3	33.6	34.6	34.5
Special Score Data						
Mean Rights	31.02	30.84	31.96	31.32	32.13	32.07
Mean Wrongs	23.09	22.77	20.74	23.11	21.25	21.73
Mean Omits	4.91	4.54	4.73	4.33	4.68	4.36
% in Chance-Score Range						
Section IV	19	21	16	20	17	17
Section V	20-23	22-25	15-19	20-23	13-17	15-19
Speededness (Section IV)						
% Completing Section	85.6	56.8	73.1	76.2	52.3	62.1
% Completing 75%	99.1	96.7	98.5	99.2	97.9	99.4
# Items Reached by 80%	25	23	24	24	22	24
# Items in Section	25	25	25	25	25	25
Mean Not Reached	.40	1.27	.72	.64	1.29	.72
S.D. Not Reached	1.27	2.04	1.60	1.43	1.90	1.29
NR Variance/Score Variance	.05	.13	.09	.06	.12	.05
Speededness (Section V)						
% Completing Section	77.5	76.6	76.3	75.5	82.1	58.0
% Completing 75%	99.5	99.5	99.6	99.6	99.1	98.7
# Items Reached by 80%	34	34	34	34	35	34
# Items in Section	35	35	35	35	35	35
Mean Not Reached	.58	.59	.86	.61	.66	1.12
S.D. Not Reached	1.68	1.48	1.89	1.53	1.87	2.06
NR Variance/Score Variance	.04	.03	.06	.04	.06	.07

[a]If scores are not truncated at 200 and 800, with the exception of Form 3ESA04, for which converted scores below 200 were not derived

This discussion only partially characterizes a test analysis. Walker (1981) has prepared a more complete statement on the procedures, criteria, and decisions that underlie the analysis. The test analysis is primarily a working document, intended for the staff members and external committees. It serves as a means of quality control and as a guide for the development of successive forms. Collectively, such analyses constitute a historical record of certain aspects of a test. The contents of the analyses may be summarized in connection with certain types of research studies, of which Swineford's systematic studies (1956, 1974) of item-test properties are perhaps the best example.

The following sections discuss the procedures used in test analyses to assess test reliability, test speededness, and the parallelism of forms. Validity is not routinely evaluated in a test analysis, nor are such important matters as item and test bias considered. Instead, such topics tend to be the subject of special separate reports. The test analysis is not intended to describe all the psychometric properties of the test; it is limited to the concerns of test developers and committees as they seek to develop forms that meet the specifications.

Reliability Information

The reliability of scores from each form of the test in the ATP is estimated as a part of the test analysis that follows its first formal administration. The estimates for the verbal and mathematical sections in the sample data in Table 2.9 are found at the top of the table. The primary approach to this estimation follows Kuder-Richardson 20 (1937), an internal-consistency estimation. The specific formulas are an adaptation presented by Dressel (1940), extending KR-20 to formula scores. This adaptation is equivalent to coefficient alpha when items have the same number of alternatives. The reliability of composite scores, derived from combining separately timed sections, is estimated by summarizing the error variance for each section, as follows:

$$1 - \frac{\Sigma \sigma_e^2}{\sigma_x^2},$$

where the σ_e^2 are the error variances of the sections and σ_x^2 is the variance of total scores.

The appropriateness of the Kuder-Richardson estimates depends upon several considerations and assumptions, of which unspeededness and unidimensionality are primary. Additional estimates are used, based on formulas developed by Angoff (1953) and later by Feldt (1975) using scores from separately timed sections. These coefficients are superior to a Kuder-Richardson approach when subtests are speeded. In general, there is a very high level of correspondence between the Angoff-Feldt estimates and Kuder-Richardson estimates.

The reliability coefficients that are reported in a given test analysis are accompanied by corresponding estimates of the standard error of measurement. These standard errors are often a more useful index of the consistency of the results than are the reliability coefficients, because the standard errors are less sensitive to the character of the sample used. In the course of an academic year, it is likely that the group tested at a given administration will show a distribution that is somewhat different from the distributions shown by groups at other administrations. The reliability coefficients, however, are sensitive to these distributional characteristics, and so the task of interpreting a specific reliability coefficient and conceptualizing the general reliability of the measurements is somewhat complicated.

The test analysis reliability data are based on internal consistency methods and influenced by a number of factors (for example, test speededness) that might tend to increase the reliability estimate. Further, new forms are introduced at different administrations, and because the variability of the groups attending these administrations is not constant, reliability estimates based on standard groups are often better appraisals of performance. Reliability, however, is always a statement about scores derived from tests in the context of certain groups. Within the ATP, no single number is established as *the* reliability of the test. Instead, evaluations must take into account the various available estimates and their relevance for different kinds of appraisals.

However, for those who use ATP results, the reliability coefficients and standard errors of measurement associated with any particular form are meaningful only as components of a larger evaluation. Because the specific test form that a student may take is essentially unpredictable, the important question is whether the general level of reliability is sufficiently high and reasonably uniform. The test user must be confident about the scores from *any* of a number of unspecified forms with a general confidence in them all. Thus, form-to-form comparability must be considered in evaluating reliability.

In some cases, particularly for the SAT, data derived from alternate forms are available. Such correlations are reported in Chapter III (page 54) for six typical patterns of test taking: March/April, May, or June of the junior year and November or December of the senior year. The correlations average approximately .88 for the verbal and mathematical sections, about .03 lower than the internal consistency estimates, and constitute a lower boundary for the reliability of the SAT.

Assessing Speededness

It has long been the policy within the Admissions Testing Program to regard a test as essentially unspeeded if at least 80 percent of the group reach the last item and if everyone reaches at least 75 percent of the items. These are arbitrary criteria and are not rigidly applied. They are useful from a practical standpoint, because the 80 percent who finish are likely to include all the able students; if additional time were allowed, the other 20 percent would be unlikely to change their relative position substantially. When the not reached variance is judged to be large compared to the score variance, (for example, a ratio of .25) the test is considered speeded. It is important to understand, however, that the application of these criteria does not determine whether the test is speeded or not. The full evaluation of speededness involves the kind of data available in Table 2.10: the bivariate distribution of scores and attempts, the distribution of omits, of not reached items, and of rights and wrongs separately. The combination of these factors into the evaluation of speed is primarily a matter of judgment.

Parallelism of Forms

Estimates of reliability generally assume that the successive forms of any particular test are parallel in respect both to content and difficulty (Lord 1964). To the extent that these assumptions are not met, the "actual" standard error of measurement for a score (the standard error irrespective of which test form was taken) will be slightly larger than the standard error reported for a score on a given form. The assumption of parallelism does not hold exactly from form to form, and the degree to which it does hold varies from test to test within the ATP.

The effort to achieve parallelism among the forms requires well-defined test specifications and the de-velopment of test forms that adhere to the specifications. Such specifications may often include these elements: 1) the distribution of item difficulties, 2) the average of item-test correlations, and 3) the distribution of item content. Indexes of item difficulty and of item-test correlation yield some information about parallelism in successive forms of a test, but these statistics provide only indirect information about the parallelism of item content. The content aspect of the specifications is necessarily less rigorous because: 1) it depends upon verbally defined categories of topics and processes, and these leave room for interpretation on the part of the item writers; and 2) with the accumulation of new data on the changing nature of the test-taking population, the secondary school curriculums, and the intellectual demands of the colleges, there is a continuous need to change the content of the tests. In short, strict parallelism in test content, even if it were attainable, would tend over time to bring about a reduction of validity if it were adhered to blindly. This problem is met by a conscious compromise in the content specifications: changes in content are introduced slowly and continually so that the active forms in use over any five-year period are approximately interchangeable as far as content is concerned. The rate of change in the content of the SAT is, of course, less rapid than that of most Achievement Tests.

When possible, the test analysis summarizes data pertinent to the control of form-to-form statistical parallelism, as indicated in Tables 2.11 and 2.12. The spread of the deltas and the average biserial correlation are the most powerful factors for controlling such test score properties as reliability and standard deviation. Such data need to be interpreted in the light of known characteristics of the groups tested at various administrations.

This chapter makes extensive use of material supplied by William H. Angoff and William E. Coffman for the first edition of this handbook.

Principal authors: Thomas F. Donlon and Samuel A. Livingston

Contributors or reviewers: William H. Angoff, Nancy W. Burton, Gary L. Marco, Christopher C. Modu, Nancy S. Petersen, June Stern, and Nancy K. Wright.

CHAPTER **III**

The Scholastic Aptitude Test

Introduction

The Scholastic Aptitude Test (SAT) is a measure of developed verbal and mathematical abilities. It was introduced in 1926, and throughout most of its long history, it has provided a separate score for each of these two areas. Because of the large numbers of students who have taken it, over more than 50 years, the SAT is the best known test in college admissions. As such, it has been much studied and much discussed. In recent years, as the result of the decline in the average score from year to year, the test has been the subject of increased scrutiny and public attention.

The Purpose of the SAT

The SAT is not intended to be used as the sole criterion for admission to college; rather, it is designed to supplement the high school record and other information in assessing a student's competence for college work. See "Guidelines on the Uses of College Board Test Scores and Related Data" in the *ATP Guide for High Schools and Colleges* (College Board 1982a). The usefulness of such a supplementary measure, of course, stems partly from the unique objective information it provides about the student and partly from its ability to confirm or to question other assessment sources. When test scores are inconsistent with the high school record, or subjective information, they provide a signal that should lead to the search for more data about a student.

This supplemental nature of the SAT is worth some emphasis, for it is often forgotten. The SAT was originally intended to provide some redress for possible errors and inconsistencies in secondary school records and in the results of the essay examinations of the 1920s and 1930s, which were tailored to highly specific curriculums. By stressing the direct measurement of basic developed abilities, the test allowed a more balanced assessment of the student who had limited exposure to these specific curriculums. Further, it could help to identify the under-

achiever. Similarly, it served to identify the occasional case where achievements in subject-matter areas were gained through unusual expenditures of effort, or where the secondary school record was more a reflection of a pleasing personality than of substantive accomplishment.

In practice, the SAT-verbal and the SAT-mathematical scores are often made part of a formal regression equation that includes information from the high school record, the results of other tests, and other predictors as well. Alternately, test scores may be used to resolve conflicts in admission deliberations. In all these applications, the model urged for the SAT is that it not be used by itself.

In a large number of regression equations, the SAT has clearly and repeatedly demonstrated that it makes a unique contribution to the prediction of college success. (See Chapter VIII for extensive information on this subject.) The SAT showed this ability to contribute something of its own from the very beginning. The "Second Annual Report of the Commission on Scholastic Aptitude Test," prepared by Carl Brigham and published in *A Study of Error* (Brigham 1932, p. 346), contains the following statements: "The fact that the Scholastic Aptitude Test does contribute something to the prediction of college grades . . . justifies its inclusion as a member of a team, and the findings to date indicate that it is a useful supplementary measure. Its inclusion helps the prediction of college grades."

Given its essentially supplementary nature, the SAT is not ordinarily evaluated through the simple correlation with college grade point average. Much greater interest attaches to its *incremental* effectiveness, that is, to the degree to which it can improve the prediction of college grades when combined with high school academic records or perhaps Achievement Test scores. One value of the SAT, therefore, is the extent to which it can add something unique to the correlation exhibited by the other measures.

Because the high school record is largely a reflection of locally controlled curriculums and grading practices (which themselves are dependent on the nature of the student body and on the objectives of the school), there are variations from school to school in the meaning of grades. This fact inevitably works to the advantage of some college applicants and to the disadvantage of others. The SAT, on the other hand, represents a standardized independent measure of a defined set of mental tasks with the results expressed on a common scale for all students. Thus, it operates as a kind of "leveling agent," cutting across differences in local customs and conditions and affording the admissions officer a concise piece of information common to the records of all applicants. Especially in the case of students coming from schools with which the admissions officer is unfamiliar, the SAT can provide information that would otherwise be unavailable or, at best, difficult to obtain.

The Definitions of Aptitude

The field of measurement does not offer any single universally accepted definition of an aptitude test. In general, an aptitude test is thought of as a means for measuring potential for a particular kind of behavior. SAT scores are intended to predict future academic performance, and they do, as the validity evidence demonstrates.

The SAT measures aspects of developed ability, rather than innate characteristics. Indeed, in common with other tests, it cannot possibly be designed to measure innate qualities. Instead, it makes use of the kind of basic verbal and mathematical skills that develop over the years, both in and out of school. The content of the test does not reflect specific curriculums, although it is designed to be consistent with school-based learning. In measuring aptitude, previous experience or training on the part of the individual is assumed to be reasonably constant for all individuals comprising the population considered. Given this assumption, differences in developed abilities may plausibly be used to infer differences in future academic success, in accordance with the principle that those who have demonstrated the stronger attainment in the past are likely to demonstrate the stronger performance in the future.

The distinction between an achievement test and an aptitude test cannot be precisely drawn. (See discussion in Chapter VII.) Even though the information tested in the SAT is relatively curriculum free, students must have had experience with the skills being tested. An *aptitude* test points toward future performance; an *achievement* test may be used in this way, but assesses past attainment. Developed ability, however, *is* an achievement, and aptitude test scores can and do change. Thus, aptitude scores

provide a basis for a prediction at a given time, not forever. If low aptitude scores are the result of educational deficits, these deficits may be overcome.

Differences in background and in interests will influence the amount and kinds of information acquired by the students, and test content is carefully balanced to avoid as much as possible inequities in selection for any subgroup of test takers. For example, although students who take the SAT vary in the number of years of mathematics studied in high school, the mathematical sections of the test require as background one year of algebra and exposure to a limited number of topics in geometry. A few of the mathematical questions will probably be more readily solved by a student who is equipped with skills learned in advanced mathematics courses, but it is possible for a student equipped only with basic arithmetic, algebraic, and geometric skills to solve all of the problems.

There is no intrinsic reason why the SAT could not include measures of other domains in addition to the verbal and mathematical. There has, in fact, been considerable research to identify other domains that might be relevant to the prediction of college success, and such research into new measurement methods is a continuing concern. However, over the more than 50 years of the SAT's existence, no other measures considered by the College Board have demonstrated such a broadly useful relationship to the criterion of college achievement as have the verbal and mathematical tests. (See Chapter VIII.)

The SAT provides effective discrimination over most of the range of academic ability of college-bound students. The test is aimed not only at contributing to the decisions of institutions that have high-scoring students but also at describing levels of ability among average or lower-scoring students. The requirement that the SAT be useful for a variety of types of colleges and students strongly determines its content, for in order for the test to be efficient it must contain questions that involve content suitable for measuring the abilities of the majority of students who take it. It would not make sense to widen the scope of its content at the expense of requiring most students to be tested on material that has little relevance to their preparation or to their particular college objective. Although no statistical index of such relevance controls the inclusion of content material or measures, the test is not likely to be altered in order to reflect special conditions that may exist in a small number of colleges. Instead, it is intended to describe what is useful for most colleges and to be adapted to a given institution by varying the relative weights given to the SAT-verbal and SAT-mathematical scores. These weights are generally based upon statistical studies done by individual colleges and may take into account the scores on one or more of the Achievement Tests or other predictors that are already available from the high school record. (See Chapter VIII.)

Over the years, the test has evolved somewhat in the way it measures verbal and mathematical abilities. Table 3.1 shows the variation in the composition of the test since its beginning. By the fifth year after its introduction (1930), the period of experimentation was over, and a verbal test consisting of antonyms, paragraph reading, and double definition was offered. Paragraph reading was basically the ''ancestor'' of the present day reading comprehension test, and double definitions the precursor of the sentence completion items. With the reintroduction of an analogy item format in 1936, the present pattern was essentially established. Modifications in item format were introduced in later years in each general area, and sentence completions were not used from 1942-45, but the general framework has remained the same.

The rationale for selecting the item types is not narrowly psychometric. The values of several item formats, each somewhat distinctive but all yielding relatively high intercorrelations, include freedom from coaching, a more varied and interesting test, wider content sampling, and efficient time per item averages. The four principal verbal item types emerged from a larger set of possibilities that Brigham and his committee considered from 1924-1930, including, as Table 3.1 indicates, tests of artificial language and logical inference. These early comparisons, however, proved decisive; while all of the measures had some plausibility, the four item types comprising the verbal test seemed most useful.

General mathematics items have been found in the mathematical sections since the earliest days of the SAT; however, the mathematical sections have not been given as continuously as the verbal sections. As Table 3.1 shows, it was not until 1941 that the mathematical sections won a permanent place, having been ''suspended'' during 1928-29 and from 1936-40.

The earliest form of the mathematical sections had a special mathematical item type called number

Table 3.1

Item Types Used in the SAT-Verbal and SAT-Mathematical Sections, 1926-1983

Item Type	1926-27	1928	1929	1930-35	1936-40	1941	1942	1943-45	1946-51	1952-58	1959-74	1975-83
Verbal												
Antonyms												
Six-choice	•	•	•	•	•	•	•	•	•			
Five-choice										•	•	•
Word relations				•								
Analogies												
Select fourth term	•	•										
Select two terms			•		•	•	•					
Select second pair								•	•	•	•	•
Paragraph reading	•	•	•	•	•	•	•	•				
Easy paragraphs		•										
Reading comprehension									•	•	•	•
Double definition		•	•	•	•	•						
Sentence completion									•	•	•	•
Definitions	•											
Classification	•	•										
Artificial language	•											
Logical inference	•											
Synonyms (two-choice)		•	•									
Mathematical												
Fill-in problems				•								
Six-choice problems						•						
Five-choice problems								•	•	•	•	•
Arithmetic word problem	•											
Data sufficiency											•	
Number series completion	•											
Quantitative comparison												•

series. However, it was almost immediately discontinued, and it was not until 1959 that a variation in mathematical item format was introduced. This was the data sufficiency item, which consisted of a question followed by two statements. The five possible responses made assertions about the sufficiency of the statements to provide an answer to the question. This item type had attractive features because it stressed insight and diminished the need to compute an answer. Data sufficiency items were answered more swiftly, on the average, than general mathematical items. However, they were somewhat complex and were also somewhat susceptible to coaching (Pike and Evans 1972).

In 1974, data sufficiency items were replaced by quantitative comparisons. The new items resemble data sufficiency items in that they have precoded meanings for the answers, can be answered more rapidly, and maximize the opportunity for the student to apply insight and avoid calculation. They differ in that they are somewhat less complex and easier to understand, have a reduced reading load, and show less minority bias. While apparently somewhat coachable, their advantages outweigh their disadvantages (Schrader 1973).

In contrast to the primarily "literary" focus of its content during the twenties, thirties, and forties, the verbal test has been eclectic since the fifties. It has drawn from the social, political, and scientific areas as well as from literary, artistic, and philosophical topics. In mathematical material, the test did not reflect the new curriculums of the sixties and early seventies. The skills and abilities tested were consistent with the move in curriculum toward an emphasis on understanding, but the special notation and symbolism that characterized the modern mathematics movement were avoided because many schools continued to offer traditional mathematics. As the country moved toward the metric system in the early seventies, the SAT began to contain a few problems in metric units. However, because the United States has been slow to convert to the metric system, the test in the early 1980s contains both metric and nonmetric questions as well as a few measurement questions in which neither metric nor nonmetric units are used. At the present time, no questions involve conversions between systems, and few demand within-system conversions, such as the conversion of centimeters to meters. Additional changes have been made to reduce the complexity of directions and to reduce the correlation between verbal and mathematical scores. These goals have been accomplished in part by eliminating complex item types, such as the early artificial language items and the data sufficiency mathematics items.

A significant constraint upon the test is the requirement of form-to-form comparability, which limits the rapidity with which changes can be made. The college admissions officer must be able to compare large numbers of SAT scores based on different forms of the test, taken at different times of the year, and often taken in different academic years. In order to remove the variations from one form to another in the meaning of a given raw score, scores on all forms of the test are equated and converted to the 200-to-800 standard score scale for ATP tests. Since no equating process can cope with major differences in the factorial structure of the test forms, the task of changing the SAT is one of a controlled introduction of new test content.

Organization of the Test

The total testing time of three hours is divided into six equal segments of 30 minutes each. Of these, two are verbal, two are mathematical, one is the Test of Standard Written English (described in Chapter IV), and one is reserved for the equating, pretesting, and research sections described below.

The verbal sections contain a total of 85 questions involving four types of questions:

> Antonyms—25 questions
> Analogies—20 questions
> Sentence Completions—15 questions
> Reading Comprehension—25 questions

Since 1974, students have received a vocabulary subscore based on the antonyms and analogies, and a reading subscore based on sentence completion and reading comprehension questions. Each operational verbal section contains all four types of questions.

The mathematical sections of the SAT consist of a total of 60 items and include only two formally distinct item types: regular mathematics items, which have five choices and require no special directions, and quantitative comparison items, which have four choices, require special directions, and call for a determination of the relative size of two expressions or quantities.

Within each section, blocks of items of a similar type are arranged in approximate order of increasing difficulty. The average difficulty of each item type is approximately equal; that is, the difficult items are not all antonyms nor the easy items all sentence completions. Rather, there is an effort to achieve the same level and range of difficulty for each item type, a goal which is, of course, only approximated in practice. Usually, the arithmetic reasoning questions are somewhat easier than those involving algebraic or geometric content. The difficulty arrangement of the test may be indicated by the following idealized diagram of a verbal section:

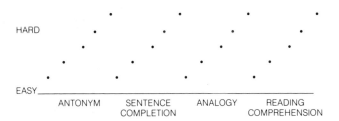

Items in any block are generally presented in order of difficulty. The exceptions to this rule are the reading comprehension questions, which are usually presented in the order that was used for the pretesting (the administration for item tryout); the order at pretest is based on the logic and organization of the passage. Figure 3.1 shows the actual pattern of item difficulty sequences for the shorter verbal section in a recent form of the SAT.

The test is corrected for guessing, with a fraction of the wrong answers subtracted from the correct responses: $R-\frac{1}{4}W$ for five-choice items; $R-\frac{1}{3}W$ for four-choice items; generally, $R-\frac{1}{K}W$ (R = right

answers, W = wrong answers, and K is the number of wrong choices available). A discussion of this scoring method is provided in Chapter II.

Instructions. Students are encouraged to become thoroughly familiar with the directions before they take the test, and the booklet *Taking the SAT* (College Board 1983f), which includes a full-length test, makes this possible. On the day of the test, the instructions, which are printed on the back cover of each test book, are read aloud to all students by the proctor before the test begins (see Figure 3.2). Within the test book, there are statements at the beginning of each of the six sections as to the number of items in that section and the total time allowed for working on it, and examples are provided for each item type, where practical. The versions of these instructions used in 1982-83 are presented in Figures 3.3 and 3.4. The examples are provided to suggest to the student the mental process involved in each of the various item types and to stress that this process is fundamentally one of judgment—of finding the *best* answer, rather than the only answer. To some extent, also, the directions and examples are aimed at ensuring an understanding of the multiple-choice format.

Variable Section. One section in each test book is "variable," so called because its contents vary from

Figure 3.1

Item Difficulty Sequences for a Typical SAT-Verbal Section
(Based on a Form of the SAT Introduced in March 1983)

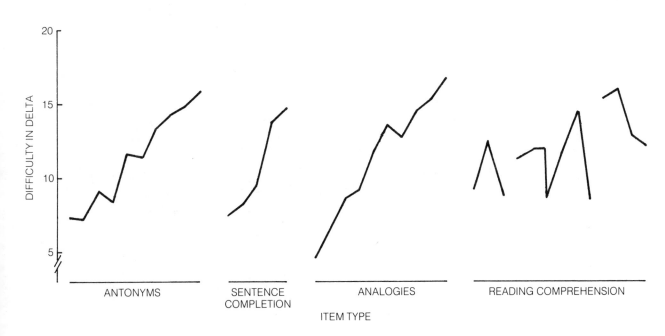

Figure 3.2

Instructions Printed on the Outside Back Cover of the SAT Test Book

YOUR NAME (PRINT) _____

　　　　　　　　　　　　　　LAST　　　　　　　　　　FIRST　　　　　　　　　　MI

TEST CENTER _____

　　　　　　　NUMBER　　　　　　　NAME OF TEST CENTER　　　　　　ROOM NUMBER

IMPORTANT: The following codes are unique to your testbook. Copy them on your answer sheet exactly as shown.

2. TEST FORM

Copy this in box 2 → 204025
on your answer sheet.

3. FORM CODE

Copy this code in box 3
on your answer sheet. Then
blacken the corresponding
ovals exactly as shown.

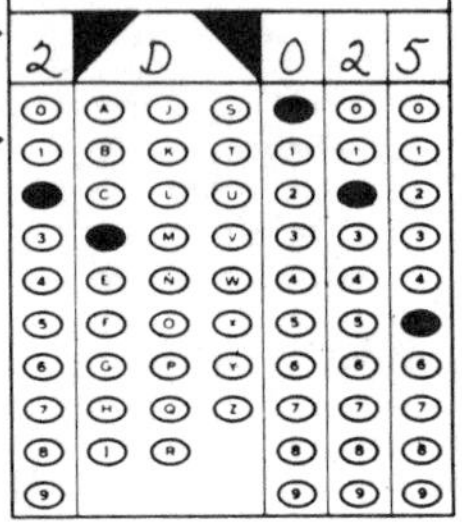

SCHOLASTIC
APTITUDE TEST

and Test of Standard Written English

You will have three hours to work on the questions in this test book, which is divided into six 30-minute sections. The supervisor will tell you when to begin and end each section. If you finish before time is called, you may check your work on that section, but you are not to work on any other section.

Do not worry if you are unable to finish a section or if there are some questions you cannot answer. Do not waste time puzzling over a question that seems too difficult for you. You should work as rapidly as you can without sacrificing accuracy.

Students often ask whether they should guess when they are uncertain about the answer to a question. Your test scores will be based on the number of questions you answer correctly minus a fraction of the number you answer incorrectly. Therefore, it is improbable that random or haphazard guessing will change your scores significantly. If you have some knowledge of a question, you may be able to eliminate one or more of the answer choices as wrong. It is generally to your advantage to guess which of the remaining choices is correct. Remember, however, not to spend too much time on any one question.

Mark all your answers on the separate answer sheet. Mark only one answer for each question. Since the answer sheet will be machine scored, be sure that each mark is dark and that it completely fills the answer space. In each section of the answer sheet, there are spaces to answer 50 questions. When there are fewer than 50 questions in a section of your test, mark only the spaces that correspond to the question numbers. Do not make stray marks on the answer sheet. If you erase, do so completely, because an incomplete erasure may be scored as an intended response.

You may use the test book for scratchwork, but you will not receive credit for information written there.

(The passages for this test have been adapted from published material. The ideas contained in them do not necessarily represent the opinions of the College Board or Educational Testing Service.)

DO NOT OPEN THIS BOOK UNTIL
THE SUPERVISOR TELLS YOU TO DO SO.

ANTONYMS

For each question in this section, choose the best answer and blacken the corresponding space on the answer sheet.

Each question below consists of a word in capital letters, followed by five lettered words or phrases. Choose the word or phrase that is most nearly <u>opposite</u> in meaning to the word in capital letters. Since some of the questions require you to distinguish fine shades of meaning, consider all the choices before deciding which is best.

Example:

GOOD: (A) sour   (B) bad   (C) red
(D) hot   (E) ugly   Ⓐ ● Ⓒ Ⓓ Ⓔ

ANALOGIES

Each question below consists of a related pair of words or phrases, followed by five lettered pairs of words or phrases. Select the lettered pair that <u>best</u> expresses a relationship similar to that expressed in the original pair.

Example:

YAWN : BOREDOM ::   (A) dream : sleep
(B) anger : madness   (C) smile : amusement
   (D) face : expression   (E) impatience : rebellion
        Ⓐ Ⓑ ● Ⓓ Ⓔ

SENTENCE COMPLETIONS

Each sentence below has one or two blanks, each blank indicating that something has been omitted. Beneath the sentence are five lettered words or sets of words. Choose the word or set of words that <u>best</u> fits the meaning of the sentence as a whole.

Example:

Although its publicity has been ----, the film itself is intelligent, well-acted, handsomely produced, and altogether ----.

(A) tasteless. .respectable   (B) extensive. .moderate
  (C) sophisticated. .amateur   (D) risqué. .crude
    (E) perfect. .spectacular   ● Ⓑ Ⓒ Ⓓ Ⓔ

READING COMPREHENSION

Each passage below is followed by questions based on its content. Answer all questions following a passage on the basis of what is <u>stated</u> or <u>implied</u> in that passage.

REGULAR MATHEMATICS

In this section solve each problem, using any available space on the page for scratchwork. Then indicate the <u>one</u> correct answer in the appropriate space on the answer sheet.

The following information is for your reference in solving some of the problems.

Circle of radius r: Area = πr^2; Circumference = $2\pi r$
   The number of degrees of arc in a circle is 360.
The measure in degrees of a straight angle is 180.

Definitions of symbols:
   < is less than $\leqq$ is less than or equal to
   > is greater than $\geqq$ is greater than or equal to
   $\perp$ is perpendicular to $\parallel$ is parallel to

Triangle: The sum of the measures in degrees of the angles of a triangle is 180.
If $\angle$CDA is a right angle, then

(1) area of $\triangle ABC = \dfrac{AB \times CD}{2}$

(2) $AC^2 = AD^2 + DC^2$

Note: Figures which accompany problems in this test are intended to provide information useful in solving the problems. They are drawn as accurately as possible EXCEPT when it is stated in a specific problem that its figure is not drawn to scale. All figures lie in a plane unless otherwise indicated. All numbers used are real numbers.

QUANTITATIVE COMPARISONS

<u>Questions 8-27</u> each consist of two quantities, one in Column A and one in Column B. You are to compare the two quantities and on the answer sheet blacken space

   A if the quantity in Column A is greater;
   B if the quantity in Column B is greater;
   C if the two quantities are equal;
   D if the relationship cannot be determined from the information given.

Notes: 1. In certain questions, information concerning one or both of the quantities to be compared is centered above the two columns.
       2. A symbol that appears in both columns represents the same thing in Column A as it does in Column B.
       3. Letters such as x, n, and k stand for real numbers.

	EXAMPLES		
	Column A	Column B	Answers
E1.	2×6	$2 + 6$	● Ⓑ Ⓒ Ⓓ
E2.	$180 - x$	y	Ⓐ Ⓑ ● Ⓓ
E3.	$p - q$	$q - p$	Ⓐ Ⓑ Ⓒ ●

book to book for the same form. In addition, its order within five other sections will change from form to form. Although questions in this section do not contribute to the student's score, they do serve three broad purposes.

First, they are used to gather the information necessary to equate the tests. Second, they are used to try out items for future use in the test, and third, they may be used for research purposes. In a typical administration, six variants are dedicated to the equating function. The number of variants allocated for pretesting varies according to the need for replacement items, and in recent years has averaged about 100 per year. Each new form requires 210 items from the pools (85 verbal operational, 40 verbal equating, 60 mathematical operational, and 25 mathematical equating). The current level of pretesting, which generates about 300 new items at an administration, is the required maintenance level, particularly since item writers cannot predict the difficulty of the items with precision. Although in the past items could be reused, recently enacted test disclosure legislation, and the introduction of the SAT Question-and-Answer Service, which enables students to obtain their test, preclude most item reuse.

To ensure that the student's effort on these items is equal to his or her effort on the operational items—a condition that is clearly necessary to guarantee reliable results—the variable items are made, insofar as possible, indistinguishable from the operational items. As mentioned, the position of the section is moved from administration to administration in order to make it difficult for the test taker to identify the variable section.

While some use is made of older forms for special Sunday administrations and sometimes two or three SATs are used concurrently, in general there is a single new SAT for most major national administrations that is taken by all students. Accordingly, although the variable section items differ for a given test taker and his or her neighbors in the testing room, for most administrations the five sections on which the students' scores are based are the same for all students in the testing room—and, indeed, are probably the same for almost all students taking the SAT on that particular date anywhere in the world.

The test books are arranged for distribution in a manner called "spiraling." Assuming 10 variant sets of items, the stacks of test books are arranged in sequence so that books 1 to 10 consist of variants 1 to 10, books 11 to 20 repeat variants 1 to 10, and so forth. The result is that any sizable block of test books selected for shipment to a center will contain the 10 variants in almost equal proportions.

The intent of spiraling is to effect systematic, or spaced, samples, one such sample for each group of students taking a different variant section. Because the supervisors are instructed to hand out the test books in the order in which they are received, the students who work on a given variant are a representative sample of the total group tested at an administration. Random samples drawn from the total group may be expected to retain this property.

The powerful simplicity and usefulness of the variable section, which was first introduced by Brigham, must be stressed. This notion of a section containing material not used in computing the student's scores has made possible the pretesting of SAT questions under virtually ideal conditions. In addition, it has provided a way for the introduction of experimental material for preliminary trial. If the quality of the test is due to any one factor, it is probably due to this constant infusion of new items having statistical properties that can be ascertained with relative precision.

The use of the variable section is sometimes criticized as a misuse of the students' time; it is felt that the students are required to spend an extra half-hour for purposes (pretesting, equating, experimental development) that are of no immediate benefit to them. These students, however, are the direct beneficiaries of the system through the time contributed in this way by other students tested earlier. The control of test characteristics and the equating of the tests do work directly to the benefit of all test takers. Seen in this way, the extra half-hour is by no means inappropriate.

Test Assembly

From 1926 to 1941, the SAT was essentially the creation of Carl Brigham, Associate Secretary for the College Board, who, with Cecil R. Brolyer, put the SAT on a firm psychometric footing. Since 1948 the actual assembly of the test has been the responsibility of Educational Testing Service. The work at ETS is reviewed both by the College Board staff and by an external advisory committee. Since 1977, this committee has been called the Scholastic Aptitude Test Committee. It consists of prominent educators from a variety of backgrounds, who oversee the general development of the test. Table 3.2 (see following page) lists the names and periods of service for members to date.

The techniques for the assembly of the SAT, which are described below, have grown increasingly formal and prescriptive over the years. In the late 1950s, the ETS staff, under the guidance of the College Board's Committee of Examiners in Aptitude

Table 3.2

Members of the Scholastic Aptitude Test Committee 1977 to Fall 1983 with Terms of Service*

Name	Institution	Term of Service
Mary Ellen Ames	Wellesley College (MA)	1977-1980
Anne Anastasi	Fordham University (NY)	1977-1980
Henry F. Bedford	Phillips Exeter Academy (NH)	1977-1981
Joan Bollenbacher	Cincinnati Public Schools (OH)	1977-1979**
James R. Buch	University of Oregon (OR)	1982-
Nancy S. Cole	University of Pittsburgh (PA)	1980-1983
William Controvillas	Farmington High School (CT)	1982-
Barbara W. Davis	Charlotte-Mecklenburg Schools (NC)	1977-1981
William A.G. Fisher	Taylor Allerdice High School (PA)	1977-1979
Margaret Fleming	Cleveland Public Schools (OH)	1981-
Lynn H. Fox	Johns Hopkins University (MD)	1982-
Joella Gipson	Wayne State University (MI)	1983-
Gustavo González	University of California—Santa Barbara (CA)	1977-1979
Jeanette B. Hersey	Connecticut College (CT)	1980-1983
Jeremy Kilpatrick	University of Georgia (GA)	1977-1982†
Walter H. MacGinitie	Teachers College, Columbia University (NY)	1977-1980
Willie M. May	Wendell Phillips High School (IL)	1979- ‡
Alberta E. Meyer	Trinity University (TX)	1983-
Robert S. Moore	South Carolina Department of Education (SC)	1981-
Allen Parducci	University of California—Los Angeles (CA)	1980-1983
Paul Pressly	Savannah Country Day School (GA)	1983-
Alonzo F. Rodriguez	Metropolitan State College (CO)	1979-1982
Emory A. Sigler, Jr.	Highland Park High School (TX)	1979-1982
Nathaniel Teich	University of Oregon (OR)	1977-1981
Hammet Worthington-Smith	Albright College (PA)	1981-

*The present Scholastic Aptitude Test Committee is not the first such overview committee with responsibilities for this test. Several predecessor groups served during earlier periods.
**Chairperson 1977-79
†Chairperson 1979-82
‡Chairperson 1982

Testing, developed detailed specifications for the content of the test and for the statistical characteristics of the items. These specifications, with occasional adjustments, remain the basis for the present development techniques. Control charts, content and statistical specifications, and many reviews govern the process. It is a more rigorous system than in the earlier years, and some of the items considered appropriate for the early tests would be unacceptable by today's standards. The need for greater control is evident: more people are now involved in the assembly of the test, and more forms are assembled within a given year. Further, today's system of form-to-form equating makes heavy demands on the parallelism of successive forms, heavier than in Brigham's day, when each year's form was independently scaled to a mean of 500 and standard deviation of 100. In addition, staffing changes, while not excessive, are more frequent now than in Brigham's time (Brigham's own tenure lasted about 18 years), so that the direct responsibility for the test may pass through successive hands in a relatively short time. Finally, concerns for content bias, particularly for minorities, have led to extensive formal test sensitivity review processes. For these reasons, the specifi-

cations for the assembly process need to be detailed, demanding, and explicitly stated.

The SAT is assembled to meet both content and statistical specifications. Items are classified not only by subject matter, item type, and difficulty, but by other dimensions as well. (See Table 3.3.) These additional dimensions are controlled in an effort to create test forms that are highly similar in content and difficulty.

Test specifications sometimes embody process dimensions as well as content dimensions, differentiating the items in terms of the solution processes they seem to demand. In the mathematical sections, some aspects of these solution processes are made an explicit component of the specifications, and the test is controlled for the proportions of items judged to demand routine versus nonroutine solutions. In the verbal sections, there are no obvious process differentiations within the specifications. However, it is clear that the several verbal item types themselves demand somewhat different mental operations, with antonyms and analogies requiring more associational reasoning steps, while sentence completion and reading comprehension demand an ability to infer meaning and logical relationship from context.

Table 3.3

Classification Scheme for SAT-Verbal Items

Item Type	Classification Dimensions	Number of Questions
Sentence Completions	Content	
	Aesthetics/philosophy	4
	World of practical affairs	4
	Science	4
	Human relationships	3
	Structure	
	One missing word	5*
	Two missing words	10*
Antonyms	Content	
	Aesthetics/philosophy	6
	World of practice affairs	6
	Science	7
	Human relationships	6
	Generality of required distinction	
	General distinctions	14*
	Fine distinctions	11*
	Structure	
	Single word	15*
	Phrases	10*
	Part of speech used	
	Verb	7†
	Noun	7†
	Adjective	11†
Analogies	Content	
	Aesthetics/philosophy	5
	World of practical affairs	5
	Science	5
	Human relationships	5
	Abstraction of terms	
	Concrete	6*
	Abstract	6*
	Mixed	8*
	Independence of stem and options	
	Independent	13*
	Overlapping	7*
Reading Comprehension	Content	
	Narrative	4‡
	Biological science	4‡
	Argumentative	4‡
	Humanities	4‡
	Social sciences	4‡
	Physical science	4‡
	(One of the foregoing passages must have a minority orientation.)	
	Functional skill tested	
	Understanding main idea	5
	Understanding supporting idea	5
	Understanding intended inference	9
	Applying external information	2
	Evaluation of author's logic	2
	Evaluation/appreciation of style	2

*A deviation of ± 2 is permitted.
†A deviation of ± 3 is permitted.
‡Modest deviations of two to three items are permitted in these categories; for reading comprehension, three passages will have five questions, the remainder two to four.

Because the proportions of the various verbal item types are fixed, their process dimensions are likewise fixed. These additional dimensions are controlled in an effort to create test forms that are highly similar in content and difficulty.

Assembly of the SAT-Verbal Sections

Content Specifications. The principal dimensions of the content specifications for the verbal sections are summarized in Table 3.3. The sentence completion, antonym, and analogy items are discrete, that is, they are complete in themselves, rather than associated with a passage as are the reading comprehension questions. The discrete items fall into four content categories: 1) aesthetic and philosophical areas, 2) the world of practical affairs, 3) science, and 4) human relationships.

The foregoing classification scheme represents an ideal. Actually, with complex stimuli such as the analogies or the sentence completion items, it is frequently quite difficult to assign a question clearly to one or another of the four categories, nor can the categories be ideally named. Inevitably, they suggest a correspondence with subject categories that does not exist. Thus, the aesthetic/philosophical category for antonym stems includes not only such obvious items as EXQUISITENESS and INIQUITOUS, but also more general words, such as LATENT and LUCID. Science antonyms might embrace ERUPT as well as COAGULATE. In view of this necessary latitude in classification, some unreliability in the actual assignments is not surprising. Nevertheless, the items are placed in the categories to the best of the test assembler's judgment.

In the reading comprehension questions, the narrative passage is fiction and the argumentative passage is typically propaganda or polemical material. All the passages are examples of writing in the various areas that might appeal to a college student who is not a specialist in the area. It is intended that all passages be limited to topics that are not normally covered in the scope of secondary school curriculums. The sources are chosen so as to make it unlikely that any student has read the particular selections in advance, since those who were familiar with the source might perform deceptively well.

The other classification dimensions (besides content) are different for the various item types. Three of these dimensions concern the purely formal characteristics of the test items and are intended more as guides to item writers than as intrinsically desirable characteristics of the test, although it may be argued that they relieve the test of repetitiveness. These three are the "number of blanks" dimension in the sentence completion item type, the "number of words in options" dimensions in the antonym item type, and the "part of speech" dimension, also in antonyms.

Three other dimensions, however, are felt to govern more important characteristics of the items and to facilitate the measurement of ability by means of an assortment of complex tasks: 1) the "general definition vs. fine distinction" dimensions in the antonyms, 2) the "concrete vs. abstract" and "independent vs. overlapping" dimension in the analogies, and 3) the six categories that classify the functional skill tested in the reading comprehension questions. These three dimensions may be explained as follows:

1. A "general definition" item requires only a general knowledge of the word in the stem, for only one genuinely possible contender is presented among the options. In a "fine distinction" item there is more similarity among the options and the item may require considerable reflection.

2. Among the analogies, a concrete relationship would be HOUSE : ROOF, an abstract one ELECTORATE : DEMOCRACY, while a mixed analogy might contain a relationship such as SHERIFF : JUSTICE. An analogy is said to be independent if the relationship in the stem would not normally directly suggest the relationship in the answer, but it is said to overlap if the stem suggests the key. Thus, FIRE : ASHES : : EVENT : MEMORIES demonstrates independence, while FAMINE : FOOD and DROUGHT : WATER overlap.

3. The six categories for assigning items according to the reading skill tested are

   a. the comprehension of the main idea as explicitly stated,

   b. the comprehension of a supporting idea as explicitly stated,

   c. the completion of an intended inference,

   d. the application of some principle stated in the passage to a hypothetical case,

   e. the evaluation of the logic of the language in the passage,

   f. the perception of the style and tone of the passage.

The first two categories are basic comprehension questions. The next three categories stress logical reasoning, and the sixth category calls for a sensitivity to various aspects of language. There are some natural correlations among these categories and the content of the passages with which they are associated. Thus, questions about style and tone tend to be asked of narrative passages, and there are only rare instances in which a style and tone question is appropriate for a science passage.

The frequencies with which the SAT-verbal items fall into the various categories are specified, and there is a genuine effort to meet these specifications. Satisfaction of the specifications results in parallelism of content among the test forms and the assurance that the performances of students taking the different forms will be based on essentially the same content dimensions.

Statistical Specifications. The test assembler must construct a test that meets not only the specifications for the content and other classification dimensions, but certain statistical criteria as well, including those for item difficulty and biserial correlation. All specifications on item difficulty are developed in terms of delta, which, as described in Chapter II, is a normal curve deviate corresponding to the percentage passing, with an arbitrarily defined mean of 13 and standard deviation of 4 and an effective range from 5 to 19. The index of item discrimination is the biserial correlation between the item and the total score on the operational test.

Specifications for the verbal and mathematical sections call for a particular mean and standard deviation for the difficulty index and a specified average level for the biserial correlations. Further, each individual item must show a satisfactory correlation with the total score, usually a minimum biserial correlation of 0.2. Most biserial correlations fall well above this minimum in the 0.3 to 0.7 range. To ensure the desired mean and dispersion of difficulties, a detailed distribution of deltas is specified. Table 3.4a presents the current specifications for the verbal sections of the SAT and some data on the actual assembly of a particular form. As indicated, the currently specified distribution of deltas yields a mean delta of 11.4 and a standard deviation of deltas of 3.0, and the mean r-biserial for the total test must be between .41 and .45. The delta distribution is stated in terms of equated deltas, using as a reference group a sample of students who took the SAT in early years. For this reference group, the mean equated delta of 11.4 would have been somewhat easy. The bimodal distribution of deltas and the constraints on the r-biserial are necessary in order to ensure that scaled scores up to 800 are more likely on every test form. This new distribution is a recent development; for years prior to 1974, the test was more nearly of middle difficulty, and the distribution of deltas was essentially bell-shaped. In 1974, the test was shortened by five items in order to allow time to administer the Test of Standard Written English to

Table 3.4a

Statistical Specifications and Data at Assembly of the Verbal Sections of the SAT

Item Difficulty Equated Delta	Specified Item Difficulty Frequency	Actual Frequencies at Assembly, Form Administered June 1983	Actual Frequencies at Administration, Form Administered June 1983
17	—	1	1
16	2	2	1
15	6	6	6
14	14	13	13
13	10	10	10
12	8	8	10
11	7	7	6
10	7	7	7
9	10	10	11
8	8	8	10
7	6	6	4
6	4	4	4
5	3	3	2

the students taking the SAT, and a new delta distribution was established at that time. It was revised in 1981 to the values presented in Table 3.4a. The total verbal score is based on two separately timed sections of 40 and 45 questions each of which must be highly similar in psychometric characteristics to each other and to the overall specifications.

In addition, students are given a reading subscore based on the combination of the reading comprehension items and the sentence completion items, and a vocabulary subscore based on the combination of analogies and antonyms. In order to ensure that the reading and vocabulary subscores cover the entire score range, it is necessary that the specifications for the set of reading items and for the set of vocabulary items parallel the specifications for the total test as much as possible.

Table 3.4b shows the mean difficulty, the standard deviation of the difficulties, and the mean biserial correlation actually achieved in the assembly of the verbal section of one form of the test. The close similarity between the specified and actual values reflects the strong effort to meet the specifications. The results presented here are typical. Table 3.4b also shows the principal statistical characteristics for the item sets comprising the various logical subdivisions of the test: its separately timed sections, the sets of items on which subscores are based, and the item types. The data indicate that the mean item difficulties are quite similar from subtest to subtest.

Assembly of the SAT-Mathematical Sections

Content Specifications. The assembly of the mathematical sections parallels in broad logic that of the verbal sections. As stated earlier, there are only two formally recognized item types in the mathematical sections: regular mathematics and quantitative comparisons. Each of these is classified as to the content and setting. In addition, general mathematics items are classified as to solution process. Solution process is less applicable within the format of quantitative comparison items, which require a judgment of magnitudes, rather than a complete solution. There are four content categories, applicable to both item types: arithmetic reasoning, algebra, geometry, and miscellaneous.

The arithmetic category includes the four basic operations of addition, subtraction, multiplication, and division; properties of odd and even integers; and percentages and averages. The algebra category includes linear equations, simple quadratic equations, factoring, and exponents; it does not include

Table 3.4b

Internal Balance of Assembled Sections for SAT-Verbal (June 1983)

Test or Subtest	Number of Items	Statistical Characteristics		
		M eq$_\triangle$	SD eq$_\triangle$	M$_{bis}$
Total Test				
Specified Assembly	85	11.4	3.0	.41-.45
Actual Assembly	85	11.4	3.0	.45
Separately Timed Sections				
Verbal Section I, Actual Assembly	40	11.4	3.0	.45
Verbal Section II, Actual Assembly	45	11.4	3.1	.45
Subscores				
Reading Subscore Items	40	11.5	2.6	.47
Vocabulary Subscore Items	45	11.3	3.4	.43

the quadratic formula, fractional or negative exponents, or logarithms. The geometry category includes the properties associated with parallel lines and measurement-related concepts such as area, perimeter, volume, the Pythagorean theorem, and angle measure in degrees. Knowledge of special triangles such as isosceles, equilateral, and 30-60-90 is also assumed. However, only topics that should have been encountered informally and independent of any formal study of deductive Euclidean geometry are included in the SAT. An item that involves both geometry and either arithmetic or algebra is usually classified as geometry. The basic geometric formulas required are printed in the descriptive booklet and are included for reference in the test book. Unusual notation is used only when it is explicitly defined for a particular question. Language and symbols used throughout the test are neutral with respect to curriculums.

The miscellaneous category includes problems dealing primarily with logical analysis and newly defined symbols or operations. The ability to grasp quickly and work with a new definition in the test is consistent with the demands of much college work. The subject-matter prerequisites for the mathematical sections of the SAT include arithmetic, a year of algebra, and geometric concepts that are typically taught in the elementary and junior high school years.

The setting for a mathematical question may be concrete or abstract. A setting is concrete if it relates to the real world. For example, questions dealing with money or automobile rates are classified as concrete; those concerned with parallel or perpendicular lines would be classified as abstract.

In addition to indicating the mathematical content tested by each question (for example, arithmetic, algebra), the specifications also indicate the ability or thought process necessary to solve the question. Every question is classified according to the following broad categories adapted from Benjamin Bloom's (1956) taxonomy of educational objectives for the cognitive domain:

0 Recall factual knowledge
1 Perform mathematical manipulations
2 Solve routine problems
3 Demonstrate comprehension of mathematical ideas and concepts
4 Solve nonroutine problems requiring insight or ingenuity
5 Apply "higher" mental process to mathematics

There are no rigid specifications for the number of questions in each category. The typical test emphasizes categories 2, 3, and 4 with a few questions in each of the other categories.

The insightful reasoning item is an interesting process item. This item type was introduced into the test as a result of a validity study by French (1964). An insightful reasoning item often goes beyond the limits of the normal nonstraightforward process item in that it requires an unusually insightful technique. An example of an insightful reasoning item follows:

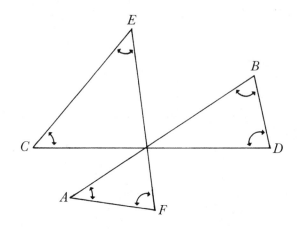

9. In the triangles above, if *AB, CD,* and *EF* are line segments, what is the sum of the measures of the marked angles?
   (A) 180   (B) 360   (C) 540   (D) 720
   (E) It cannot be determined from the information given.

Seeing that the correct answer to the question is (B) requires an ability to perceive the problem in a nonroutine manner. The solution involves recognizing that the sum of the three unmarked angles in the triangles is 180. Since the total number of degrees in all three triangles is 540, the sum of the measures of the six marked angles is 540–180 = 360.

Statistical Specifications. Table 3.5a presents the distribution of specified item difficulties for SAT-mathematical sections and data on the extent to which these were followed in an actual assembly. Table 3.5b presents similar information about the summary specifications: the observed mean difficulty for the mathematical items is 12.2, which is the midpoint for the specified range; the observed mean biserial, .47, is the value specified. The distribution for the mathematical sections, like that for the verbal sections, reflects a wide spread of deltas; the standard deviation of the deltas is 3.3.

Table 3.5a

Statistical Specifications and Data at Assembly
of the Mathematical Sections of the SAT

Item Difficulty Equated Delta	Specified Item Difficulty Frequency	Actual Frequencies at Assembly, Form Administered June 1983	Actual Frequencies at Administration, Form Administered June 1983
19			1
18	3	3	
17	4	3	4
16	4	5	6
15	4	4	3
14	4	4	3
13	4	4	5
12	4	4	6
11	8	8	10
10	8	8	6
9	8	8	6
8	5	5	4
7	1	1	3
6	2	2	1
5	1	1	2

Table 3.5b

Internal Balance of Assembled Sections for
SAT-Mathemetical (June 1983)

Test or Subtest	N	Characteristics M eq$_\triangle$	SD eq$_\triangle$	M_{bis}
Total Test				
Specified Assembly	60	12.17-12.27	3.1-3.3	.47
Actual Assembly	60	12.2	3.3	.47
Separately Timed Sections				
Mathematics Section I	25	12.3	3.2	.48
Mathematics Section II	35	12.2	3.3	.46

General Comments on Test Assembly

The practice of using detailed statistical specifications to assemble the SAT does not mean that these specifications are not reexamined for their appropriateness from time to time, and, if necessary, revised. Table 3.6 shows varying statistical specifications for both the SAT-verbal and SAT-mathematical since approximately 1960. As the table indicates, a number of different sets of specifications have been used, both for the verbal sections and for the mathematical sections. The changes in the test have reflected such new factors as a need to reduce the time requirements, to introduce new item types, and to conform the test to the pool of available items. As the means and standard deviations indicate, however, the test is changed only gradually over time.

Although the need for parallelism provides the major basis for a system of controls, it alone cannot justify the specific numbers of items in each content category. Why, for example, in the verbal sections of the SAT is it important to have one reading passage from each of six major areas? Why not some other configuration? In order to avoid favoring one type of student over another, the materials are controlled so as to provide a variety of content situations. The specific frequencies, of course, are derived by judgment; there is no formula by which one can assert that a test in which the 20 analogy items are divided into subgroups of 5-5-5-5 among the four broad content categories is the most equitable. The existing set of specified frequencies is not un-

Table 3.6

Changes in SAT Statistical Specifications over Time

Difficulty (in terms of delta)	Verbal Pre-1966	1966-1974	1974-1981	1981-Present	Mathematical Pre-1966	1966-1974	1974-Present
≥ 18	0	0	0	0	0	3	3
17	1	2	2	0	1	4	4
16	4	4	4	2	3	4	4
15	4	8	10	6	4	4	4
14	13	10	10	14	10	5	4
13	8	10	6	10	7	5	4
12	9	10	6	8	5	5	4
11	9	10	6	7	5	8	8
10	14	10	8	7	7	8	8
9	10	8	8	10	10	7	8
8	6	7	10	8	4	4	5
7	7	6	8	6	3	2	1
6	3	3	4	4	1	1	2
5	2	2	3	3	0	0	1
N	90	90	85	85	60	60	60
Mean Delta	11.4	11.7	11.4	11.4	12.0	12.5	12.2-12.3
SD Delta	2.8	2.9	3.3	3.0	2.7	3.1	3.1-3.3
Mean Biserial r	.42	.42	.43	.41-.45	.46	.47	.47

reasonable, however, and some empirical evidence shows that it contributes to a better balance for the scores between the sexes. Thus, a number of studies of sex differences in performance (Coffman 1961, Donlon 1973, Strassberg-Rosenberg and Donlon 1975) report data that support the notion that the categories designated ''world of practical affairs'' and ''science'' are typically easier for males, whereas the categories designated ''aesthetics/philosophy'' and ''human relationships'' are easier for females. Just as the frequencies are specified by judgment rather than by an explicit rationale, so the very nature of the categories themselves cannot be defended as the only rational approach to controlling the desired content properties of the test. Nonetheless, the definition of major content categories and the establishing of balanced frequencies across them seem to accomplish their purpose. Further evidence on this point has been provided by the item fairness studies described in Chapter X. Finally, the introduction of explicit, minority-related reading passages seems to provide some partial balancing of the comparative difficulty of the test for minority groups.

The Pretest Program

In the early days of the ATP, only one form of the SAT was required each year. A conversion from raw to scaled scores was effected for that form by arbitrarily setting its mean scaled score and standard deviation of the scaled scores at 500 and 100, respectively. Since 1941, each form has been equated to predecessor forms. In the 1982-83 academic year, nine new forms were assembled for use. These forms must be closely parallel to permit the application of equating techniques. As described above, the specifications for the SAT have been established in great detail, and they are followed in the assembly as scrupulously as the pool of available items allows. It is only through an extensive pretesting program that the items taken from the pool through the assembly of new final forms and equating items can be replaced. Table 3.7 presents data on the number of items pretested for both verbal and mathematical sections during 1978-79. This table shows the distribution of difficulties that the items exhibit and the number of satisfactory items that were achieved within each difficulty level and for the total pretest program. The data in Table 3.7 are displayed in Figure 3.5.

The salient characteristics of this table are the general tendency for the pretest efforts to yield markedly fewer verbal and mathematical items at the extremes of difficulty, both hard and easy, and for the proportion of items with satisfactory biserial correlations to be associated with the level of difficulty. The difficult (high delta) items face an even greater hazard in that when an item has high diffi-

Table 3.7

Distribution of Equated Deltas for SAT-Verbal and
SAT-Mathematical Items at Time of Pretest: 1978-79

Equated Deltas	Verbal Items			Mathematical Items		
	Frequency of:			Frequency of:		
	All Items	Satisfactory Items*	Proportion of Satisfactory Items at This Level	All Items	Satisfactory Item*	Proportion of Satisfactory Items at This Level
19+				13	3	.23
18	1	0	.00	21	9	.43
17	10	0	.00	44	16	.36
16	24	6	.25	73	33	.45
15	46	20	.43	82	51	.62
14	86	42	.49	97	60	.62
13	103	77	.75	96	63	.66
12	107	83	.78	77	60	.78
11	118	104	.88	87	75	.86
10	128	115	.90	67	56	.84
9	106	97	.92	26	22	.85
8	82	75	.91	17	15	.88
7	53	50	.94	9	4	.44
6	49	45	.92	10	9	.90
5	20	17	.85	7	7	1.00
Total	933	731	.78	726	483	.67

*An item is considered satisfactory if it has a biserial of .30 or greater.

Figure 3.5

Proportion of Satisfactory Items at Varying Levels of Equated Delta for
SAT-Verbal and SAT-Mathematical Pretests of 1978-79

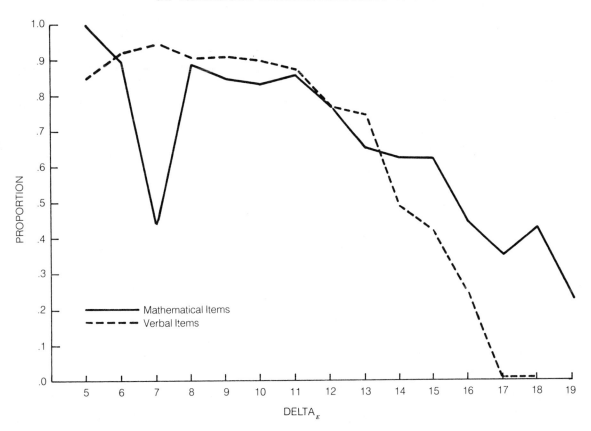

culty, it frequently fails to yield a satisfactory bi-serial correlation. In statistical theory, no relation-ship between difficulty level and biserial correlation is anticipated, for the coefficient, unlike the point bi-serial, is not inherently limited by item difficulty, but retains the full range of possible values from –1.00 to +1.00 regardless of item difficulty. How-ever, it is not easy to write difficult items that are ap-propriate for the whole SAT population and free of subtle ambiguities, and many items are discarded because of their failure to discriminate appropriately. The effects of "chance success" may also help to ex-plain this phenomenon. Items of equated delta 15 or greater are usually answered correctly by relatively small proportions of the total group—some below the 20 percent chance level for five-choice items. The mean ability level of the correct response may be dramatically lowered by the chance success of the less able group. On easy items, however, the pro-portion of students succeeding by guessing is so small that they do not lower the mean ability of the passing group to any extent.

The inability of the item writers to produce suffi-cient numbers of items at the extreme levels of diffi-culty is a perennial problem in test construction. This limited ability to forecast item difficulty or bi-serial leads inevitably to a higher volume of pretest-ing than would be necessary if the staff could make more accurate predictions.

The data in Table 3.7 may be related to the total volume of items that were required for the SAT in the 1978-79 academic year: 775 verbal and 595 mathe-matical items. This means that somewhat fewer items were being pretested in that year for each ver-bal form than was required. After the rejection of items with unsatisfactory biserials, the pretest pro-gram still supplies the bulk of the items that are used, but some older material, available from the pool, must be drawn upon. In addition, there is some reliance on questions from older, inactive forms. This reliance is limited by guidelines that restrict the total proportion of the newly assembled test that can derive from previously administered forms and constrain the overlap between a new test and any given prior form. With the introduction of public disclosure of several tests each year, very few individual items on an SAT form are likely to be reused.

Table 3.8

Internal-Consistency Reliability Estimates and Scaled Score Standard Errors of Measurement for Nine SAT Forms—October 1982 to June 1983

Form: Date of First Administration	Verbal Sections		Mathematical Sections	
	Reliability*	Scaled Score Standard Error of Measurement	Reliability*	Scaled Score Standard Error of Measurement
October 1982	.92	30.0	.91	34.6
November 1982	.93	29.3	.91	34.5
December 1982	.91	30.4	.91	32.7
January 1983†	.92	30.7	.92	32.1
January 1983†	.92	29.5	.91	33.4
March 1983†	.91	31.6	.92	34.3
March 1983†	.93	30.9	.92	34.0
May 1983	.92	29.2	.92	34.2
June 1983	.91	30.3	.91	35.2

*These reliability estimates are based on Dressel's (1940) modification of the Kuder-Richardson formula (20) (1937), adapting it to formula scoring.
†More than one form of the SAT was introduced at these administrations.

Table 3.9

Test-Retest Correlations for SAT Scores*

	VERBAL SECTIONS					
Year	March/April November	May- November	June/July- November	March/April December	May- December	June/July December
1971	.89		.87	.89		.88
1972	.89		.88	.89		.88
1973	.89		.88	.88		.88
1974	.88		.88	.87		.88
1975	.88		.87	.87		.67
1976	.88		.88	.87		.88
1977	.88	.88	.88	.88	.88	.88
1978	.88	.88	.87	.87	.88	.88
1979	.89	.88	.87	.87	.88	.86
1980	.89	.88	.88	.87	.87	.87
1981	.88	.88	.88	.88	.87	.88
1982	.89	.88	.88	.89	.88	.88

	MATHEMATICAL SECTIONS					
Year	March/April November	May- November	June/July- November	March/April December	May- December	June/July December
1971	.88		.86	.88		.87
1972	.88		.87	.89		.88
1973	.88		.87	.88		.89
1974	.87		.87	.87		.88
1975	.89		.87	.88		.88
1976	.89		.88	.90		.90
1977	.88	.89	.88	.88	.89	.88
1978	.88	.88	.88	.88	.88	.88
1979	.88	.88	.88	.88	.88	.88
1980	.88	.87	.86	.87	.87	.87
1981	.87	.88	.88	.87	.88	.88
1982	.88	.87	.88	.89	.88	.88

*These correlations are based on students who take the SAT in the spring of their junior year in secondary school and repeat the test in the winter of their senior year. See Table 3.17 for sample sizes and standard deviations of the 1977 to 1982 groups.

Parallelism and Reliability of the SAT

The reason for the conformity to test specifications during assembly is the need to produce reliable tests with a high degree of parallelism. Table 3.8 gives some evidence of the extent to which the processes succeed: the internal consistency reliability of both the verbal and mathematical sections is consistently greater than .90. Although there is some variation from administration to administration that would reflect population differences as well as slight differences between forms, the overall picture is one of considerable similarity among forms.

This single-form appraisal of reliability may be supplemented by the kind of interform reliability estimate provided in Table 3.9. Here, the results for students who elect to take the test in the spring of their junior year and again in the autumn of their senior year are correlated. These correlations are lower than true parallel form reliability estimates because of the long interval between testings. The interform estimates are also slightly lower than the single-form values, but they indicate a high degree of similarity among forms.

Correlation Between the SAT-Verbal and SAT-Mathematical Scores

The usefulness of the two separately reported scores for the SAT has been established by the numerous demonstrations of the various weights they receive in prediction equations. This capacity for an independent contribution, of course, is strongly influenced by the extent of the correlation between them. If this correlation becomes too high, the resulting redundancy in measurement diminishes the likelihood of independent contributions of the scores. Table 3.10 shows the recent experience with these correlations for nine test forms. The values have an average of .67 and a range of .08, which again indicates the stability of the assembly processes for these tests. A comparable table, presented in the earlier edition of this handbook, shows that the 12 forms from the years 1966 to 1969 also had an average value of .67 (Angoff 1971, p. 31). The introduction of quantitative comparisons into the SAT-mathematical sections in 1974, then, did not markedly affect this correlation although this item type is somewhat less verbal than the data sufficiency item type that it replaced.

The correlation between verbal and mathematical parts rose over the period of 1945 to 1965 from .54 to about .67, stabilizing at this upper level. Table 3.11 shows the average values for selected periods during the span from 1950 to 1983. In the early

Table 3.10

Correlation Between SAT-Verbal and SAT-Mathematical Scores for Nine Forms—October 1982 to June 1983

Form: Date of First Administration	Correlation of Verbal and Mathematical Scores
October 1982	.64
November 1982	.66
December 1982	.68
January 1983*	.67
January 1983*	.69
March 1983*	.65
March 1983*	.72
May 1983	.68
June 1983	.64
	Average .67

*More than one form of the SAT was introduced at these administrations.

1940s, the comparable figures were .40 to .45. No single explanation can be advanced for the increased values. Possibly it was due to increasing variability in the population taking the test, as more and more students sought admission to college. Such increased values, however, could also have been caused by changes in the item content of the tests.

Although studies have been made of the extent to which individual items in the verbal sections of the SAT correlate with the mathematical total score, and vice versa, no method for controlling the correlation through test content has been introduced. Thus, the stability of the last 12 to 15 years is not the result of direct monitoring actions by the test developers, but of some leveling in the underlying processes that produced the rise.

This increasing correlation has had implications for the models that are used for scaling the Achievement Tests, because, as described in Chapter II, the correlation between the verbal and mathematical

Table 3.11

Trend in the Correlation Between SAT-Verbal and SAT-Mathematical Scores

Time Period	Number of New Test Forms	Average Correlation
1950-1953	6	.54
1953-1956	6	.56
1956-1959	9	.62
1959-1962	14	.64
1962-1965	12	.66
1965-1969	16	.67
1969-1972	15	.68
1972-1975	14	.67
1975-1978	14	.66
1978-1981	22	.67
1981-1983	17	.67

sections is a parameter of these models. Initially set at .40 in the forties, reflecting the then current conditions, this parameter was increased to .60 during the 1970s to more accurately reflect the trends shown in Table 3.11. The apparent stability of the present level of correlation between the two test scores supports the appropriateness of this decision.

Validity

The long history of the SAT has produced a wealth of validity coefficients, many of which are summarized in Chapter VIII. Because there is no routine formal validity study for each new form of the SAT, colleges that use the SAT undertake validity studies of their own. These studies are based on their own criteria of college success and are usually conducted with the aid of the College Board Validity Study Service. The results of these studies are supplemented by special research investigations, carried out on behalf of the College Board, which contrast new item types with those appearing in operational forms of the SAT. In these studies it is apparent that the SAT is substantially correlated with college grade point average at a variety of institutions. Undergraduate populations at these institutions have a wide range of ability levels.

The primary validity for the SAT is criterion-related validity, in this case, the ability to predict freshman year college grades. However, the evaluations of validity must be extended to consider both content and construct validity. Chapter VII is devoted to these aspects of validity for the SAT.

Speededness

Over the years, the SAT has evolved as a power measure, with increasing amounts of time per item for both the verbal and mathematical sections. As in any timed test, however, speed is inevitably a determinant of performance to some extent, and the factor analyses of both the verbal and mathematical sections reveal factors associated with the last items in the test that seem attributable to speed. Such factors have typically accounted for no more than 5 to 10 percent of the variance.

Some data on speed are provided in Table 3.12, which shows the percentage of students completing each of the four operational sections of the test on a number of forms. This measure of completion depends somewhat on the properties of the last item. Because this item is usually a very difficult question and is not marked by many students even though they may consider it, the "percentage completing 100 percent of the test" drops off considerably. This factor, coupled with variation in the average level of the students from administration to administration, must be considered in the evaluation of the differences from form to form. Another index is the number of items comprising 75 percent of the test. In general, almost all students are given enough time on the SAT to enable them to consider this percentage of the items.

Time-per-item is also a factor. For the verbal sections of the test, the section with the greater time-per-item is completed by a larger proportion of the students in eight of nine comparisons in Table 3.12. For the mathematical sections, the section with

Table 3.12

Percentage of Students Completing 75 Percent and 100 Percent of the SAT for Nine Selected Forms—October 1982 to June 1983

Form:	Verbal Sections				Mathematical Sections			
	45-Item Section*		40-Item Section*		25-Item Section*		35-Item Section*	
Date of First Administration	75%	100%	75%	100%	75%	100%	75%	100%
October 1982	96	58	100	77	98	52	99	82
November 1982	96	51	100	75	99	62	99	58
December 1982	96	62	99	64	98	64	99	61
January 1983†	99	56	99	57	99	65	99	60
January 1983†	99	87	99	64	99	84	99	66
March 1983†	99	55	99	74	99	80	99	70
March 1983†	98	63	99	72	99	80	100	77
May 1983	97	59	99	81	100	75	100	53
June 1983	97	59	100	71	99	74	100	81

*Each section is allotted 30 minutes of testing time.
†More than one SAT form was introduced at these administrations.

Table 3.13

Mean and Standard Deviation of the Number of Items Not Reached for
Nine SAT Forms—October 1982 to June 1983

Form:	Verbal Sections				Mathematical Sections			
	45-Item Section*		40-Item Section*		25-Item Section*		35-Item Section*	
Date of First Administration	M	S.D.	M	S.D.	M	S.D.	M	S.D.
October 1982	2.20	3.66	0.85	2.00	1.29	1.90	0.66	1.87
November 1982	2.13	3.79	0.95	1.96	0.72	1.29	1.12	2.06
December 1982	2.05	3.79	1.14	2.25	0.95	1.69	1.02	2.09
January 1983†	1.35	2.35	1.73	2.71	0.64	1.32	0.86	1.72
January 1983†	0.73	2.39	1.62	2.73	0.46	1.30	1.08	2.12
March 1983†	1.18	2.53	1.04	2.32	0.55	1.33	0.69	1.69
March 1983†	1.54	2.90	1.20	2.41	0.61	1.56	0.66	1.71
May 1983	1.59	3.11	0.75	2.08	0.50	1.02	0.99	1.75
June 1983	1.85	3.32	1.01	2.04	0.48	1.12	0.58	1.54

*Each section is allotted 30 minutes of testing time.
†More than one form of the SAT was introduced at these administrations.

more time-per-item is completed by more students seven times in the nine comparisons.

Table 3.13 offers yet another approach to the assessment of test speededness. Those items that are left blank at the end of a test are classed as not reached. Table 3.13 shows the mean and standard deviation of items not reached for the various forms and sections. On the average, students fail to reach only one or two items, although there is quite a bit of variation in this markedly skewed distribution. While Table 3.12 shows that approximately 51 percent of the students in November 1982 completed the 45-item verbal section, the data in 3.13 indicate that the average test taker at this administration reached about 43 of the total of 45 items. The regularity of these results and the relatively small magnitudes involved demonstrate that the speed factor is in relatively good control.

Table 3.14 shows the ratio of the not reached variance to the total score variance. Swineford (1974) has suggested that as long as this ratio is less than .25, the test may be considered unspeeded. The typical value for an SAT section is well within this guideline. Only 3 of the 36 entries are greater than .15, all for the 45-item verbal section.

In evaluating the role of speed in completion of the SAT, it should be recognized that there is a tension between the program requirements for relatively unspeeded tests and the contraints of a practical administration. When time limits are set too generously, more students will finish, but many students will have too much time at the end. Even

Table 3.14

Ratio of the Variance of the Not Reached Scores to the Total Scores for
Nine SAT Forms—October 1982 to June 1983

Form:	Verbal Sections		Mathematical Sections	
	45-Item Section NR Variance/ Total Variance	40-Item Section NR Variance/ Total Variance	25-Item Section NR Variance/ Total Variance	35-Item Section NR Variance/ Total Variance
Date of First Administration				
October 1982	.17	.07	.12	.06
November 1982	.18	.06	.05	.07
December 1982	.18	.10	.09	.06
January 1983*	.07	.13	.05	.04
January 1983*	.07	.11	.05	.07
March 1983*	.09	.09	.05	.04
March 1983*	.09	.08	.08	.04
May 1983	.11	.07	.03	.05
June 1983	.15	.07	.04	.04

*More than one form of the SAT was introduced at these administrations.

under optimum conditions, the idleness of some students could have a troubling effect on other students who have not yet finished. Further, proctors may complain that their work is, consequently, more difficult.

Effects of Preparation on Test Performance

Because SAT scores can contribute to important decisions, there has been a continual concern about the students' preparation for the test. The adequacy and fairness of the test preparation are two major areas of concern. For this reason, individuals have questioned the practice of "coaching" for the SAT, in fear that students who have been coached will have an advantage over those who haven't. But the concern for preparation is truly a broader topic than just "coaching." It covers the general adequacy of all students' preparation and the question of the specific resources for preparation that the College Board can appropriately make available.

Positions on Coaching. The College Board (1965a, p. 4) has offered the following definition: "The word coaching . . . refers to a variety of methods used in attempting to increase in a relatively short time students' mastery of the particular skills, concepts and reasoning abilities tested by the SAT." The problems of definition were clear, however; while "coaching" clearly refers to test preparation, the exact form of the preparation is not specified.

Over the years the College Board has supported a variety of investigations of coaching for the SAT. Messick and Jungeblut (1981) classified these and other studies according to the presence or absence of a control group, and prepared the summaries presented in Tables 3.15 and 3.16 (see pages 60 and 61). The studies are a diverse collection, varying greatly in the adequacy of their experimental design, in the quality of their instructional treatment, and in the motivation of their participants. Nonetheless, they are an important aggregate because they provide the basis for the general conclusion that elaborate interventions may often be inordinate investments of a student's time, money, or effort.

This general conclusion is reached because of the inconsistency with which statistical significance occurs, even under seemingly optimum conditions, and by the rarity of any strikingly positive outcomes even when statistical significance is achieved. The trustees of the College Board (1968, p. 8), in an early comment on the studies through 1962, stated, "The evidence collected leads us to conclude that in-

tensive drill for the SAT, either on its verbal or its mathematical part, is at best likely to yield insignificant increases in scores." More recently, the Board restated this fundamental position, in the message to students presented in Figure 3.6. This message is reprinted from *Taking the SAT* (College Board 1981).

A critical component of the Board's stand is a judgment as to the practical value associated with a slight gain in an individual's score. Most individuals would not object to an extra 15 points added to their scores. However, 15-point increases could occur simply upon retesting, and few admissions officers are likely to make distinctions on the basis of such slight differences. The costs in time and money associated with efforts to produce the gain, when coupled with a fundamental uncertainty as to whether it can be achieved, seem inordinate.

Another critical component of the Board's conclusion is the judgment that the studies upon which it is based constitute a reasonable sample of the effective intervention strategies. Although the studies do reflect a wide variety of efforts, there is some reluctance to believe that this sample of effective strategies is sufficient. For example, none of these studies specifically focused on testwiseness, although a study by Pike and Evans (1972), described in Chapter X, devoted some attention to it.

While the studies generally support the Board's position, there are no simple answers to these complex questions. As a consequence, the Board continues to actively review the area of special preparation. The study by Alderman and Powers (1979), for example, focused on the effects of special preparation offered by secondary schools on SAT-verbal scores. In summarizing the results of eight schools, the researchers reported (p. 20), "It would seem that programs devised and implemented by secondary schools for the explicit purpose of improving student scores on a verbal aptitude test such as the SAT exert little influence on actual test performance." In the light of such findings, the Board's position seems appropriate; expensive outlays of time and money in preparation for these tests may not be justified.

Test Familiarization Materials: *Taking the SAT.* The College Board supplies each test taker with a variety of information concerning the nature and purpose of the test. Over the years the form of these preparation materials has varied. At one time, there was a genuine concern that multiple-choice testing might not be well understood, and students were required to present completed workbooks that had been mailed to their homes in order to gain entry to the test.

Figure 3.6

Six Points About Special Preparation for the SAT (Reprinted from *Taking the SAT*, 1981)

A Message to Students

The question is frequently asked: What can I do about raising my SAT scores or about making them better than they would be otherwise? The answer is: Quickly and immediately probably not much; over longer periods it depends upon how much time, effort, and concentration goes into the preparation.

The Scholastic Aptitude Test measures the extent to which your reasoning ability and skills with words and mathematical concepts have been developed up to the time you take the test. These are abilities that are related to academic success in college and that grow over a lifetime through learning experiences such as those in the family, in school, with your friends and associates, and in reading and independent study. The best preparation for the SAT is to have had varied opportunities of this kind and to have made the most of them.

The skills and abilities the SAT tests tend to grow relatively slowly and at different rates for different people. Whether you have more or less of these abilities does not say anything about your worth as an individual. Many other individual qualities not measured by the SAT, such as motivation, creativity, and artistic skills, have much to do with your sense of satisfaction and your success in life.

If you or your parents have been thinking about special preparation for the SAT outside your regular classroom activities, these six points are worth remembering:

1. The SAT measures developed verbal and mathematical reasoning abilities that are involved in successful academic work in college; it is not a test of some inborn and unchanging capacity.

2. Scores on the SAT are subject to improvement as educational experience, both in and out of school, causes these verbal and mathematical abilities to develop.

3. Development of these abilities is related to the time and effort spent; short-term drill and cramming are likely to have little effect; longer-term preparation that develops skills and abilities can have greater effect.

4. While drill and practice on sample test questions generally result in little effect on test scores, preparation of this kind can familiarize you with different question types and may help to reduce anxiety about what to expect. You can help yourself to become familiar with the test by using the explanations and full sample test in this booklet.

5. Whether longer preparation, apart from that available to you within your regular high school courses, is worth the time, effort, and money is a decision you and your parents must make for yourselves; results seem to vary considerably from program to program, and for each person within any one program. Studies of special preparation programs carried on in many high schools show various results averaging about 10 points for the verbal section and 15 points for the mathematical over and above the average increases that would otherwise be expected from intellectual growth and practice. In other programs results have ranged from virtually no improvement in scores to average gains as high as 25-30 points for particular groups of students or particular programs. Recent studies of commercial coaching have shown a similar range of results. You should satisfy yourself that the results of a special program or course are likely to make a difference in relation to your college admissions plans.

6. Generally, the soundest preparation for the SAT is to study widely with emphasis on academic courses and extensive outside reading. SAT score increases of 20-30 points correspond to about three additional questions answered correctly. Such a result might be obtained by independent study in addition to regular academic course work.

Table 3.15

Average Difference Between Experimental and Control Groups in Studies of SAT Interventions
(Adapted from Messick and Jungeblut 1981)

| Study/Design | Sample Characteristics | | | Characteristics of the Special Preparation | SAT-Verbal Difference[a] | Significance Level[b] | Exp./Control N | SAT-Math Difference[a] | Significance Level[b] | Exp./Control N |
	School	Level	Sex							
Dyer (1953)/control, different school	Private	High school seniors	M	12 30-60-minute sessions for Verbal; 5 60-90 minute sessions for Math	4.6	<.05	225/193	12.9	<.01	225/193
French (1955)/control, different school	Public	High school seniors	M & F	10 Verbal and 10 Math coaching sessions using ETS item materials	18.3	<.01	161/158	6.2	<.01	161/158
French (1955)/control, different school	Public	High school seniors	M & F	4½ hours of vocabulary coaching, 10 sessions of Math coaching using ETS item materials	5.0	<.05	110/158	18.0	<.01	161/110
Dear (1958)/control, same and different schools	Public & Private	High school seniors	M & F	Approximately 6 weekly 2-hour, 2-person coaching sessions, plus 1 hour of home-work each week	-2.5	ns	60/526	21.5	<.01	60/526
Dear (1958)/control, same and different schools	Public & Private	High school seniors	M & F	Approximately 12 weekly 2-hour, 2-person coaching sessions plus 1 hour of home-work each week	[c]	[c]		23.6	<.01	71/116
Frankel (1960)/control, same school statistically matched	Public	High school seniors	M & F	10 3-hour, 25-person coaching sessions	8.4	ns	45/45	9.4	ns	45/45
Whitla (1962)/control, statistically matched	Public & Private	High school seniors	M & F	Proprietary coaching school, 5 2-hour sessions plus homework in Verbal and Math	11.0	ns	52/52	-5.3	ns	50/50
Roberts & Oppenheim (1966)/randomized	Public	High school juniors	M & F	7½ hours of programmed instruction in test taking and in Verbal and Math content	14.4[d]	<.05	154/111	8.1[d]	ns	188/122
Evans & Pike (1973)/randomized	Public	High school juniors	M & F	Test-taking skills and math content, 7 3-hour sessions, 21 hours of homework	No coaching for SAT-Verbal			16.5	<.05	288/129
Alderman & Powers (1980)/randomized	Public & Private	High school juniors	M & F	Varied strategies, at eight schools, emphasizing reading and analogies; 5-45 hours	8.4	.05	239/320	No coaching for SAT-Math		
FTC (1979; see also Stroud, 1980)/control, test-score files	Public & private	High school juniors and seniors	M & F	School A: 40 hours commercial coaching; School B: 24 hours commercial coaching	31.7[e] / 5.2[e]	<.01 / ns	393/1729 / 163/1720	24.9[e] / 7.5[e]	<.01 / ns	393/1729 / 163/1729
Average weighted by size of experimental sample.					14.3[f]			15.1[f]		

Note: SAT = Scholastic Aptitude Test; M = male; F = female; ETS = Educational Testing Service; ns = nonsignificant.

[a] The coaching effects are intercept differences between regression lines for experimental and controlled groups or (for Frankel, 1960; Whitla, 1962; Roberts & Oppenheim, 1966; and Pike & Evans, 1972) average score increases of experimental over control groups, both weighted in the case of multiple experimental or control groups by their respective sample sizes.

[b] As shown for coaching effects reported in original text.

[c] Not calculated; variances and regression slopes differed significantly for experimental and control groups.

[d] This study employed the Preliminary Scholastic Aptitude Test as both pre- and posttest; the averages shown have been converted to the SAT score scale ranging from 200 to 800 points.

[e] Weighted mean score effects pooling juniors and seniors across test administration years from Stroud's reanalysis of Federal Trade Commission (FTC) data.

[f] If Rock's (1980) estimates for FTC School A of 16.9 for SAT-Verbal and 30.6 for SAT-Math (N = 192) are substituted for Stroud's (1980) estimates, the weighted averages become 9.7 for Verbal and 14.5 for Math.

Table 3.16

Adjusted Average Score Gains in Studies of SAT Instructional Interventions Having No Control Groups
(Adapted from Messick and Jungeblut 1981)

Study	Sample Characteristics School	Level	Sex	Characteristics of the Special Preparation	SAT-Verbal Adjusted Average Score Increase[a]	N	SAT-Math Adjusted Average Score Increase[a]	N
Pallone (1961)	Private	High school seniors and graduates	M	90-minute daily instruction and practice in developmental reading skills over 6 weeks	81	20+		
Pallone (1961)	Private	High school seniors and graduates	M	50-minute daily instruction and practice in developmental reading skills, with stress on logical inference and analogic analysis over 6 months	68 (43)[b]	80–		
Marron (1965)	Private	High school seniors and graduates	M	Full-time daily sessions aimed at verbal and mathematical content and test-taking skills over 6 months	Group 1 54 Group 2 33 Group 3 24 Group 4 12 } 35	83 600 5 26	Group 1' 59 Group 2' 59 Group 3' 46	232 405 78
Coffman & Parry (1967)[c]	Public	College freshmen	M & F	6-hours weekly of instruction in accelerated reading over 8 weeks	4[d]	19		
Average weighted by size of experimental sample					38 (36)[b]		54	

Note: SAT = Scholastic Aptitude Test; M = male; F = female.

a To estimate instructional or program effects, average score increases in the Pallone (1961) and Marron (1965) studies were adjusted by the average of four adjustments, those suggested by (a) the authors of the original articles—Pallone suggested 35 points on SAT-Verbal as normal expectation of gains during the final year of secondary school (15 points for the 5-month interval between tests in the short-term program), and Marron suggested 24 and 26 points, respectively, for SAT-Verbal and SAT-Mathematical as typical gains for high school seniors over 6 months; (b) Slack and Porter (1980)—average gains in national administrations of junior-to-senior year retesters having the same initial average score levels as Pallone's and Marron's groups; and (c) Pike (1978)—average gains of control students in superior schools from other studies of proprietary programs; as well as, (d) average gains of control students in other studies who have average initial score levels roughly comparable to those of Pallone's and Marron's groups.

b Due to discrepancies in Pallone's tables, there is some uncertainty as to whether the average adjusted score effect in his long-term program should be 68 points or 43 points (see Messick and Jungeblut, p. 195)

c The 15-week program in Coffman and Parry was not included because the 29-point mean decrease in scores was considered atypical and possibly indicative of motivational and test administration programs.

d The two 8-week programs in Coffman and Parry were combined, but adjustments were made only by the Slack and Porter procedure, which attenuated by only a few points an already tenuous effect. None of the suggested comparison groups of SAT takers appeared to provide even remotely reasonable yardsticks for gauging score gains of students already enrolled in a college not requiring the SAT.

Today, this means of preparation would be unnecessary. Still, concern for the level of student preparation remains. *Taking the SAT*, introduced in 1978, contains a complete test form and answer key, together with extensive comment and advice about the test-taking experience. This booklet was evaluated by Alderman and Powers (1979). They found that students who received it did no better on the test, in terms of the average score, than students who had not received it. In spite of the absence of specific score gains, however, the reaction of the students was overwhelmingly positive. About 95 percent of the group found the booklet useful, and most of its contents were found to be appropriate and helpful by sizable subgroups of the students. Therefore, *Taking the SAT* makes the total test-taking experience more comfortable. Familiarization can lead to important psychological benefits even when the score is not increased, but this benefit can be easily secured without purchasing coaching materials. The Board's publications about the SAT are comprehensive and widely available, enabling students to secure full and adequate preparation at no cost.

With the introduction of test disclosure, the College Board has adopted the practice of making available copies of the disclosed tests, which may also be used by those who wish to spend more time reviewing actual SATs. These copies are generally available in multiform editions, of which the most recent is *10 SATs* (College Board 1983g), containing, as its name suggests, ten forms of the test, or about 20 hours of test-taking experience. It is also possible for students to evaluate their actual performance on the SAT by using the SAT Question-and-Answer Service. This service was initially instituted in response to state legislation mandating disclosure, but has, since 1981-82, been available to *all* test takers for at least one major national administration. Upon request, and for a fee, the student may receive 1) a copy of the questions from the two verbal and two mathematical sections that are the basis of the SAT scores, 2) a copy of his or her answer sheet, 3) a list of correct answers, 4) the raw scores used to calculate the reported scores, and 5) a table to convert the raw scores to College Board scaled scores.

Scores from Repeated Testing

A sizable proportion of the students take the SAT more than once. The most frequent pattern of repetition involves a first testing in the spring of the junior year and a second testing in the fall of the senior year. The fact that these students have two scores, based on testings separated by several months, introduces the problems of score changes, for student growth, practice effects, and the inherent error of measurement make it unlikely that precisely the same score will be achieved by the same student the second time. How is the resulting information to be used?

Score change is of significant interest both to students and admissions officers. For the student, it involves questions concerning the best timing or the best patterning of the test taking. If the first score seems fairly high, should the test be taken again given the risk of obtaining a lower score? For the admissions officers, it raises questions concerning the best way to combine or use the multiple-score information in order to secure the most accurate estimate of future success. Should the most recent score be used? Should they be averaged?

Three factors—growth, practice, and error—contribute to score change. Errors of measurement do not produce change in any consistent direction. There are a number of error-increasing factors in the test-retest situation: random variation associated with the use of two independent forms, random variation associated with equating, and random variation associated with the changes in student performance over time. In most cases, growth and practice produce a score increment over the five-to-eight-month period between the testings. This increment is not large; it averages about 12 points each for the verbal and mathematical scores over the seven-month period from April to November. These averages are based on the data presented in Tables 3.17 and 3.18 (pages 63 and 64), which show the average gains for verbal and mathematical scores for different patterns of testing in each of six years. In spite of these factors, however, the high level of correlation between junior year and senior year performance reported in Table 3.9, approximately .88, is observed.

In a substantial number of cases, the decision of students to repeat the test in an effort to raise their scores does not produce the desired result. Tables 3.17 and 3.18 show that the percentage of repeating students who receive *lower* scores on their second testing is around 35 to 40 percent. This finding can appear disconcerting to students, to their parents, and to school personnel, whose expectations of gain are often very high. Confronted with the evidence of a loss in an individual score, or of a sizable proportion of losses in a roster of scores, the student or counselor often wonders if something is wrong with the test. Such an interpretation is seldom reached when the personal expectations are confirmed, and higher scores achieved. Yet, many of these gains are essentially as much the product of chance factors as

Table 3.17

Six-Year Summary of Change in SAT-Verbal Scores from March/April, May, or June of the Junior Year to November or December of the Senior Year

	March/April to November						March/April to December					
	1977	1978	1979	1980	1981	1982	1977	1978	1979	1980	1981	1982
N (in thousands)	77	58	55	51	63	47	19	15	16	17	15	11
Senior Scores												
Mean	452	451	452	448	451	453	436	428	428	435	433	430
Standard Deviation	99	98	100	99	100	97	98	98	96	97	95	98
Junior Scores												
Mean	435	437	440	438	444	445	413	417	417	412	419	421
Standard Deviation	97	94	100	97	96	98	96	93	97	93	96	98
Senior Minus Junior Scores												
Mean	16.9	14.3	12.0	9.3	7.6	8.5	23.0	10.7	11.3	22.9	14.2	8.5
Standard Deviation	47.5	46.5	47.2	46.5	48.2	45.8	47.7	47.0	49.0	47.7	47.7	46.9
Percent Showing Decrease	32	34	36	38	40	38	28	37	37	28	34	39

	May to November						May to December					
	1977	1978	1979	1980	1981	1982	1977	1978	1979	1980	1981	1982
N (in thousands)	75	81	82	77	77	115	21	23	24	29	24	25
Senior Scores												
Mean	457	452	450	448	450	453	441	430	424	432	429	428
Standard Deviation	100	97	99	98	99	97	100	98	95	97	94	97
Junior Scores												
Mean	438	442	437	432	436	444	417	422	411	405	409	419
Standard Deviation	98	95	97	95	96	93	99	94	96	92	93	93
Senior Minus Junior Scores												
Mean	19.3	10.7	12.6	15.4	13.8	9.8	24.2	8.2	12.5	27.2	20.1	9.1
Standard Deviation	48.1	46.8	47.7	47.7	47.0	45.8	49.2	47.1	47.5	49.0	47.4	47.2
Percent Showing Decrease	30	37	35	33	35	37	28	39	35	25	30	38

	June to November						June to December					
	1977	1978	1979	1980	1981	1982	1977	1978	1979	1980	1981	1982
N (in thousands)	42	42	45	41	46	64	16	18	19	22	20	22
Senior Scores												
Mean	446	444	442	439	439	437	428	418	418	422	420	416
Standard Deviation	98	98	98	97	97	94	98	97	95	97	93	95
Junior Scores												
Mean	434	428	436	435	431	424	409	404	411	406	405	404
Standard Deviation	96	99	98	96	96	91	96	97	95	94	95	94
Senior Minus Junior Scores												
Mean	12.1	16.2	6.1	3.5	8.7	12.6	18.8	14.2	6.6	16.4	15.8	12.2
Standard Deviation	48.1	46.6	49.3	48.2	46.8	45.8	47.8	47.7	50.3	48.7	47.1	46.6
Percent Showing Decrease	36	32	41	43	39	35	31	34	41	33	33	35

Table 3.18

Six-Year Summary of Change in sat-Mathematical Scores from March/April, May, or June of the Junior Year to November or December of the Senior Year

| | March/April to November | | | | | | March/April to December | | | | | |
	1977	1978	1979	1980	1981	1982	1977	1978	1979	1980	1981	1982
N (in thousands)	77	58	55	51	63	47	19	15	16	17	15	11
Senior Scores												
Mean	497	490	500	493	492	496	480	477	480	482	484	483
Standard Deviation	106	106	107	106	106	107	109	107	108	107	110	109
Junior Scores												
Mean	481	482	478	478	486	484	463	463	458	457	466	465
Standard Deviation	102	107	103	103	102	103	102	109	104	101	105	106
Senior Minus Junior Scores												
Mean	15.8	8.5	21.5	15.7	5.5	12.4	17.8	14.0	22.2	25.4	18.4	17.9
Standard Deviation	50.9	52.5	50.9	51.5	52.8	52.2	51.3	52.7	51.3	53.3	55.1	51.6
Percent Showing Decrease	34	40	30	34	42	37	32	36	29	28	33	33

| | May to November | | | | | | May to December | | | | | |
	1977	1978	1979	1980	1981	1982	1977	1978	1979	1980	1981	1982
N (in thousands)	75	81	82	77	77	115	21	23	24	29	24	25
Senior Scores												
Mean	500	492	498	493	492	499	485	481	477	480	482	481
Standard Deviation	106	106	105	106	106	107	111	108	108	108	110	109
Junior Scores												
Mean	485	484	483	488	487	495	468	467	462	461	463	472
Standard Deviation	104	105	104	103	105	103	107	107	105	105	105	106
Senior Minus Junior Scores												
Mean	15.2	8.7	15.4	4.8	4.4	3.4	17.4	13.3	15.5	18.9	19.0	8.6
Standard Deviation	49.7	51.5	51.8	52.3	52.0	52.9	50.3	51.5	52.3	53.6	53.5	52.5
Percent Showing Decrease	34	40	34	43	43	44	32	36	35	32	32	40

| | June to November | | | | | | June to December | | | | | |
	1977	1978	1979	1980	1981	1982	1977	1978	1979	1980	1981	1982
N (in thousands)	42	42	45	41	46	64	16	18	19	22	20	22
Senior Scores												
Mean	491	485	491	485	484	482	474	469	471	472	474	471
Standard Deviation	106	105	106	104	104	104	109	106	108	107	108	106
Junior Scores												
Mean	481	484	476	474	479	479	460	465	456	450	457	461
Standard Deviation	105	104	104	101	104	105	108	106	105	103	106	110
Senior Minus Junior Scores												
Mean	10.2	0.5	15.3	11.7	4.8	3.6	13.7	3.5	15.5	22.1	17.3	9.5
Standard Deviation	51.2	52.1	51.3	53.7	52.0	52.3	52.3	52.3	52.0	54.5	53.3	52.3
Percent Showing Decrease	38	46	34	38	43	44	36	43	34	31	33	39

are the declines in scores. About 1 student in 20 will show a score increase of 100 points or more; about 1 student in 50 will show a decrease of 100 points or more. Thus, there is a good chance of a score increase upon a retesting some months later; the average of such gains upon retesting will be quite small and there is a substantial probability of a decline upon retesting.

A complicating factor in these discussions, of course, is the relationship between the initial score and the score change. In general, because low initial scores are likely to reflect negative errors of measurement, and high initial scores are likely to reflect positive ones, there is a greater likelihood for a gain through retesting when the initial score is lower. Figure 3.7 reflects this pattern, describing the average expected retest gain as a function of the initial score. Although the line describing SAT changes is only an approximation, it indicates that low scoring students, in the range surrounding 300, may anticipate average gains of around 40 points; the better students with initial scores of 700 will show average losses of about 10 points. These data are based on experience with the PSAT/NMSQT and the SAT for both the verbal and mathematical sections. Of course, minor differences between the verbal and mathematical tests in these characteristics exist, but these distinctions are not so great as to diminish the general utility of a single line, as shown in Figure 3.7.

The variation in average anticipated gain for given initial scores can pose some complicated problems in personal decision making for the students. Students who have high scores may be less likely to win a gain upon retest. The fundamental fact re-

mains, of course, that for both low scoring and high scoring students, errors of measurement only rarely produce a change so great as to be important in the decision process. For most purposes, students need only take the test a single time, and need not wonder about which administration to attend. The means in Tables 3.17 and 3.18, when compared with the means for all students, indicate that the group of students who do elect to repeat the test are, on the average, more able than those who do not. This indicates that the typical student repeating the test is not motivated to repeat by scores as low as those in the 300-400 range. It is probably true that most decisions to repeat the test are motivated by assumptions that the experience of the first testing will confer a meaningful advantage in the second performance, and that the submission of two scores guards against a negative error in a single one. This second benefit is, of course, a real possibility, because the average of two scores will be somewhat more stable than any one. However, to view the second testing as insurance for better performance is not without obvious risks.

Because many students do take the SAT more than once, the admissions officers often need to deal with two or more sets of scores. The best way to use such data is often a matter of concern. Although it is possible to combine such multiple-score information by statistical methods that take into account the effects of changes over time, these complex methods of analysis do not conform to the intuitive expectations of admissions officers. In 1982-83, the admissions officer was simply given the following information, in the publication *ATP Guide for High Schools and Colleges* (College Board 1982a, p. 18):

Most admissions officers consider all the scores in a student's report. However, some admissions officers prefer to give students credit for their best performances and use the highest scores. The student who takes the SAT two or three times will probably receive at least one score higher than the score of the equally capable student who takes it only once. When admissions officers use only the highest scores, the student who can afford to take the test only once might be at a disadvantage compared with the student who has taken the test more than once.

Some admissions officers prefer to use a student's most recent SAT scores. This choice may be less subject to error of measurement than using the student's highest scores. The most recent scores may better reflect a student's current ability.

Other admissions officers calculate an average of all the student's SAT-verbal scores and an average of all the SAT-mathematical scores. This method may be the most equitable of the three, if scores span a short period.

Figure 3.7

Average Expected Retest Change as a Function of Initial Score (Based on 1983 *ATP Guide for High Schools and Colleges*)

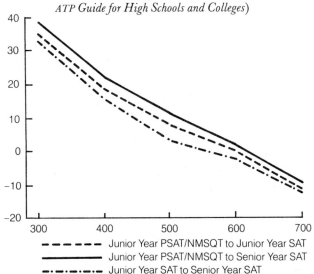

- - - - - Junior Year PSAT/NMSQT to Junior Year SAT
———— Junior Year PSAT/NMSQT to Senior Year SAT
-·-·-·- Junior Year SAT to Senior Year SAT

The advice in the guide is essentially nondirective and suggests that the average of the results is probably the superior method of evaluation in the absence of other information. In most cases, the two scores are within 25 points of each other; therefore, the errors introduced through the selection of less appropriate methods for combining multiple scores are not great.

The 800 Score

Because 800 is the highest score that is reported on the College Board scale, it has acquired a mystique of its own. In fact, the concept of perfect test performance has come to be popularly, albeit incorrectly, attached to an 800 score. Actually, an upper limit of 800 is arbitrarily imposed on all scaled scores in the College Board's ATP. This is done mainly to control for the inevitable variation in difficulty from form to form of the test, and, consequently, the variation in the maximum scores earned by highly able students who are taking different test forms. The 800 limit operates in such a way that if, for example, the maximum raw score of 60 on the SAT-mathematical sections is established by linear equating to be 812 on the scale, the reported score is nonetheless 800. The same, but opposite, restriction is imposed at the lower end of the scale by the 200 scores, which are the lowest reported. For most forms of the test, an SAT-mathematical score of zero is not as low as 200. Because valid differentiation is possible among formula scores lower than zero (Boldt 1968), the use of these scores makes it possible to extend the scale to the desired limit.

Difficulties arise, however, when the test form is slightly easier than ideal and the maximum raw score converts by ordinary equating to something less than 800. In such cases, no student, however capable, could achieve the score of 800 without the special adjustments that are carried out. Conversely, when the test turns out to be more difficult than the specifications called for, the maximum raw score converts to a scaled score too far above 800, and the 800-score limit causes the loss of many differentiable raw score units near the end of the test. Neither of these problems is fully solvable by equating. It is best to avoid them as much as possible through uniform control in the test development process. Accordingly, the statistical specifications for the SAT reflect careful attention to this problem.

The procedures for scaling and equating the tests are described in Chapter II. As indicated, IRT methods have replaced linear methods in recent years.

The Preliminary Scholastic Aptitude Test/National Merit Scholarship Qualifying Test

The PSAT/NMSQT is a slightly shorter, somewhat easier version of the Scholastic Aptitude Test. It is not part of the Admissions Testing Program, but its tests are parallel in content to the SAT and constructed from the questions that were used on previous, undisclosed forms of the SAT. One of the purposes of the PSAT/NMSQT is to assist students and counselors in their guidance decisions related to postsecondary education. Further, it is a useful experience for students who plan to take the SAT itself as part of the college admissions process. Cosponsored by the College Board and the National Merit Scholarship Corporation, the test is used by the latter in preliminary selection of candidates for consideration for scholarship awards.

To enhance the usefulness of the PSAT/NMSQT test-taking experience, the PSAT/NMSQT reports the test outcome on a Report of Student Answers, which provides the correct answers and the student's responses to the questions, as well as the student's raw scores, scaled scores, and percentile ranks. This information is presented to the student with a copy of the test book. This packet of information is broadly similar to the optional SAT Question-and-Answer service, described earlier, but is provided automatically to all students. In addition, schools and school systems may order a Summary of Answers, which summarizes their students' responses to each question on the test and also provides national data.

Because of its similar format and content, the PSAT/NMSQT is an excellent predictor of performance on the SAT. Test scores are reported in two digits, rather than the three digits of the SAT, but because the third SAT digit is uniformly zero, there is no basic difference in the scales. Because the SAT and PSAT/NMSQT populations are somewhat different in ability, the observed mean scores differ somewhat, with those taking SAT having the higher means.

The statistical procedures for placing the PSAT/NMSQT on the SAT scale are described in Chapter II. Each PSAT/NMSQT form is linked to designated "parent" SAT forms and there is careful adherence to content specifications that closely parallel those of the SAT; statistically, the PSAT/NMSQT is somewhat easier, with mean deltas of 11.0 for the verbal items and 12.0 for the mathematical items. (These compare with values of 11.4 for SAT-verbal items and 12.2 for SAT-mathematical items.) The test contains 65 verbal items (versus 85 on the SAT) and 50 mathematical items (in contrast to 60 on the SAT). These items are organized into two 50-minute sections, rather than into the modular 30-minute sections that are used for the SAT. There is no variable section; a form of the TSWE is not included.

The PSAT/NMSQT is administered in October of each year. It is currently taken by approximately 1.3 million students. Most of these students are in their junior year of high school; however, an increasing number of sophomores are choosing to take the test. For the convenience of the schools, there are two new forms each year (one administered on Tuesday and one on Saturday). Each school, however, must select one of the two test dates. Schools may arrange for individual students whose schedules do not permit testing at their own school to take the test at a nearby school that is giving the test on the other test date.

Principal author: Thomas F. Donlon, with the cooperation of James S. Braswell

Contributors or reviewers: William H. Angoff, Nancy W. Burton, Pamela I. Cruise, W. Edward Curley, Gary L. Marco, Geraldine I. May, Nancy S. Petersen, June Stern, and Nancy K. Wright.

CHAPTER IV

The Test of Standard Written English (TSWE)

Introduction

The assessment of writing skills has been a continuing concern of the College Board, which over the years has used a variety of methods to assess students' skills in writing English. The early practice of assessing writing skills by means of an essay test eventually gave way to a reliance on multiple-choice questions, with occasional use of essay and other free-response questions. Palmer (1960, p. 8) wrote in his review of the College Board English Composition Achievement Test that "Mankind . . . someday will undoubtedly achieve the perfect English composition test . . . . In 60 years of trying . . . the College Board . . . has not . . . ." The development of the all-multiple-choice English Composition Achievement Test; the inclusion of free-response interlinear exercises and, later, of a 20-minute essay in forms of that test; the use of the all-essay General Composition Test from 1954 to 1956; and the administration of the Writing Sample from 1960 to 1968 are all milestones in the history of the Board's efforts to provide colleges with useful appraisals of their applicants' writing skills.

In the early 1970s, American educators and the general public sensed a "writing crisis" developing among students. A renewed interest in measuring the basic writing skills of the entering college student began to emerge. Because effective instruction must be geared to the needs of the pupils, colleges need to know whether their applicants have acquired the kinds of writing skills that college courses require, or whether the colleges must teach those skills to their students. The English Composition Achievement Test and the SAT-verbal sections had relevance to the identification of language skills, but an instrument was needed that was specifically designed to identify students who might have difficulty in handling college writing assignments. After much discussion and development, some of which is described below, the TSWE was introduced experimentally as part of the College Board's Admissions Testing Program in fall 1974; it became a permanent part of the program in 1977.

Purpose of the TSWE

The TSWE is designed to assess a student's ability to deal with the conventions of standard written English, the language most often used in college reading and writing assignments. Because the TSWE is targeted for students who are relatively deficient in standard English expression, it is much less difficult than the SAT or the English Composition Achievement Test. Although it is printed in the same test book as the SAT and administered at the same time, it is basically an achievement test rather than an aptitude test. The TSWE is intended primarily to assist those who must place students in freshman writing courses of varying content and difficulty.

The test assesses the students' use of the conventions of standard written English by measuring their skill in dealing with a variety of writing problems, and it provides only a global writing skills score. Accordingly, no single writing problem is tested more than a few times in any one form of the test; therefore, the TSWE is inappropriate for diagnosis of particular writing difficulties. Recognized as an indirect measure of writing ability, the TSWE is designed to be highly correlated with more direct measures, such as essays. Furthermore, the test is a more reliable measure than single scored essays alone; it has been estimated that to obtain a reliability equal to or higher than the reliability for the TSWE, an essay test of writing skills would have to require each student to write three different essays, and each essay would have to be scored by two independent readers (Breland 1977c).

Preliminary Development of the Test

The value of teaching standard written English has been the subject of much discussion within the teaching profession. Some teachers believe that forcing students to write "correctly" is nothing more than forcing them to use White, middle-class dialect, a dialect that is no better or worse than any other dialect. Other aspects of writing, they believe, are far more important: the communication of ideas and feelings, for example. They argue that these ideas and feelings can be stultified if the writer must express them in what are, to him or her, essentially foreign structures and idioms.

Proponents of correctness, on the other hand, point out that what is called standard English is the general vehicle for communication in the United States—the language of those who hand out jobs, award contracts, admit people to universities, and distribute grades. Not to teach this standard language to those who speak or write in a nonstandard dialect is, according to this argument, to deny them significant opportunities for advancement in this society. In the fall of 1973, as part of general test development activity, questionnaires were sent to English departments at 196 four-year colleges and 111 two-year colleges in the United States. The survey was an attempt to find out about English instruction in these schools and about the kinds of tests that English faculty members would consider most useful. Awareness of the controversy in the field of English prompted many of the questions in the survey. The responses, as reported by Alloway and Conlan (1974), indicated that a test like the as-yet-undeveloped TSWE would have widespread applicability. Despite the controversy, standard written English was still being taught and required at many of the two- and four-year colleges in the United States.

The survey asked the English departments to indicate which aspects of composition they tend to reward in grading students' writing. The 124 departments responding to the question indicated their preferences as follows (p. 77):

	Percentage
Logical organization	86
Unity	81
Quality of thought	78
Correctness of expression	69
Awareness of situation and audience	65
Sophistication of sentence structure	65
Originality of expression	63
Economy	58
Sophistication of vocabulary	54

When asked to identify the specific kinds of information they would like tests to provide about incoming students, the English faculty indicated interest in securing the following information about students:

	Percentage
Knowledge of standard written English	81
Ability to write expository material	79
Ability to write critical essays	65

	Percentage
Vocabulary	61
Ability to deal with verb forms, sentence structure, etc.	60
Ability to analyze literature	57
Knowledge of mechanics	57

The survey thus confirmed that there was widespread attention to standard written English, regardless of any controversy as to its proper role.

Review of Pertinent Journal Articles. In addition to the questionnaire survey, a review of the relevant professional journals was undertaken. For the most part, the articles indicated that although the teaching of mechanics and grammatical structure was considered worthwhile, the teaching of such matters should not be given priority in the English classroom. There was concern that undue emphasis on correct mechanics might suggest to students that form is more important than substance and might wrongly indicate that voicing emptiness correctly is better than saying something important in a less-than-perfect composition.

This concern is perhaps epitomized in the following quotation from Nelson (1974, p. 45): ''We tend to teach writing as if there were something intrinsically worthwhile about the product, about the composition itself, rather than the process of writing—the process of sorting and discovering and creating. Thus, when we teach composition as some kind of end in itself, we reduce ourselves to dealing with commas and semicolons and paragraphs rather than with death and sex. . . . Now I am not saying that such things as commas, semicolons and paragraphing are not important; but I am saying that they are not our students' primary concern, and they should not be our primary concern.''

Thus, while the authors of professional journal articles did advocate training students in what might be considered the more mechanical aspects of writing, they viewed the teaching of those aspects of writing as subordinate to the teaching of other, less easily defined aspects: the creation of the composition, the transference of ideas and feelings to paper.

Survey of Relevant Instructional Content. A second survey (Breland, Conlan, and Rogosa 1976), conducted after the introduction of the TSWE, also proved useful for assessing the test's content. College English teachers were asked to indicate the importance they attached to possible areas of instruction in regular freshman English courses. No mention of the TSWE was made in the brief 40-item questionnaire itself or in the accompanying letter.

Table 4.1

Rank Ordering of Regular Freshman English
Course Topics in Terms of Importance as
Perceived by English Faculty Members
(Based on Breland, Conlan, and Rogosa 1976)

Rank	Mean Score	TSWE Problem*	Questionnaire Number and Instructional Topic
1	3.93		6. Writing a unified essay
2	3.93		15. Using supporting detail
3	3.88		17. Arranging argument logically
4	3.87	X	3. Making verbs agree with subjects
5	3.86		10. Writing expository prose
6	3.77		39. Distinguishing fact from opinion
7	3.75	X	33. Using words precisely
8	3.74	X	23. Making pronouns agree with antecedents
9	3.73	X	26. Subordinating and coordinating ideas in sentence
10	3.72	X	19. Avoiding run-on sentences
11	3.72	X	29. Using acceptable verb forms
12	3.70	X	30. Recognizing flaws in logic
13	3.68		4. Engaging the reader's interest
14	3.68	X	18. Avoiding sentence fragments
15	3.64	X	34. Writing concisely
16	3.63		14. Using a topic sentence
17	3.62	X	24. Avoiding vague reference of pronoun
18	3.60	X	30. Maintaining tense sequence
19	3.57	X	25. Using acceptable pronoun case
20	3.54		1. Using transition words properly
21	3.51	X	8. Avoiding dangling modifiers
22	3.49		36. Using all punctuation acceptably
23	3.46	X	28. Maintaining parallel structure
24	3.45	X	2. Using idiom properly
25	3.43		32. Suiting language to audience
26	3.41		27. Using sentence variety
27	3.41		35. Using comma acceptably
28	3.38		31. Establishing point-of-view (voice)
29	3.35		37. Using capitalization acceptably
30	3.27	X	7. Avoiding the double negative
31	3.27	X	9. Comparing modifiers acceptably
32	3.15		40. Expressing the writer's own feelings
33	3.14		21. Improving vocabulary
34	3.14		11. Writing from an outline
35	3.01		16. Using summary statement in the conclusion
36	2.87		5. Using figurative language
37	2.71		22. Syllabifying properly
38	2.18		11. Writing dialogue
39	1.88		12. Writing fiction
40	1.58		20. Reading graphs and charts

*An X indicates that this instructional topic is covered in the TSWE.

All 50 states were represented in the sample, with the relative size of the population of a state determining the number of mailings to that state. Of the 200 questionnaires sent, 116 were returned. All the questionnaire recipients were professors in College Board member colleges; however, English teachers in colleges that had participated in the earlier survey were not included.

Of the 40 writing problems listed in the questionnaire, 17 were problems actually covered in the TSWE. These included the almost mechanical, such as subject-verb agreement; matters of clarity of statement, such as clear reference of pronoun; and matters of logic, such as proper subordination and coordination. The problems ranged from those that are totally dependent on a knowledge of standard written English to those that are almost free of such dependence.

Table 4.1 shows the importance professors of English assigned to the topics covered by the TSWE and to the other topics. An index of the importance of each of these topics was achieved by computing a weighted average of the rating (Very Important = 4, Of Some Importance = 3, Not Important = 2, and Irrelevant = 1). The highest values shown in Table 4.1 were obtained by questionnaire items 6 (writing a unified essay) and 15 (Using supporting detail). Although neither of these topics is tested directly in the TSWE, each of the problems included in the TSWE received a rating indicating that respondents considered it to be of some importance.

Description of the Test

TSWE scores are reported on a scale that ranges from 20 to 60+; the score of 20 is equivalent to the score of 200 on the 200-to-800 SAT scale. However, because the TSWE is not designed to make discriminations among more able students, the test is much easier than the SAT, and TSWE scores seldom scale much above 60 (equivalent to 600). Some of the students who receive scores of 60+ would probably have scored higher if the test had been longer or if it had been more difficult. Such assessment is beyond the scope of the test, however, and other measures, such as the English Composition Test, can be used to discriminate among students at these higher ability levels.

With a large domain to be tested in a 30-minute, multiple-choice format, the item types used in the TSWE must be able to test a variety of problems. They must have efficient and relatively simple formats and produce scores that correlate highly with the scores derived from actual writing samples. The two types of items chosen for the TSWE, usage and sentence correction, meet these criteria.

Requiring the test takers to recognize writing that does not follow the conventions of standard written English, the first item type consists of a sentence with four words or phrases underlined and lettered, as shown in Figure 4.1. Students are asked to choose the one underlined word or phrase that must be changed in order to make the sentence acceptable in standard written English. If students think that the sentence is acceptable as written (as some sentences are), they can choose the fifth option, "No error." This item type can be used effectively to test such basic conventions of standard written English as the use of appropriate tense sequences, the agreement of pronoun with its antecedent, and the use of appropriate idiom and diction.

The sentence correction item type requires students not only to identify unacceptable phrasing in a sentence, but also to choose the best way of rephrasing that sentence (See Figure 4.2). For this item type, part of a sentence or the entire sentence is underlined. Five ways of rewriting the underlined part are listed below the sentence. Choice (A) is always the same as the underlined part; that is, if the student considers the sentence correct as it is, he or she marks (A). On the other hand, if the student believes the sentence should be changed, he or she chooses the answer that will produce the correct and

most effective sentence. That sentence will be clear, precise, and correct; it will be neither awkward nor ambiguous. Because the student can be asked about many elements of a sentence, and even the entire sentence, in items of this type, such items can be used to present not only easily corrected errors, but also other faults in the logic or structure of a given sentence that might require considerable change.

The test contains 35 usage items and 15 sentence correction items. The choice of these two item types restricts to a certain extent the problems that can appear in the test. Thus, in the TSWE, the organization of ideas into paragraphs is not tested, nor is the use of supporting detail. Punctuation is tested only insofar as it affects the construction of sentences. The test assesses only the ability to deal with writing problems related to expository prose; it does not assess ability to create imaginative writing such as fiction or poetry. At its simplest level, the test deals with such basic matters as identifying sentence fragments. At a more sophisticated level, the items ask students to recognize when the logic of a particular comparison is flawed. None of the items test knowledge of spelling, capitalization, or the formal terminology of grammar.

In spite of the limitations imposed by the two item types used, the two types do permit testing of a wide variety of problems in a format that is easily understood. The content of the sentences used covers a

Figure 4.1

Example of Usage Item and Instructions for the Test of Standard Written English (1982-83)

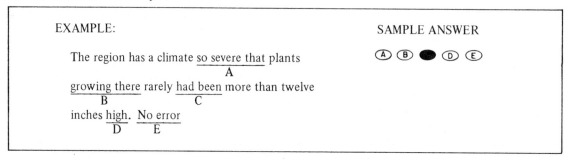

Directions: The following sentences contain problems in grammar, usage, diction (choice of words), and idiom.

        Some sentences are correct.
        No sentence contains more than one error.

You will find that the error, if there is one, is underlined and lettered. Assume that elements of the sentence that are not underlined are correct and cannot be changed. In choosing answers, follow the requirements of standard written English.

If there is an error, select the one underlined part that must be changed to make the sentence correct and blacken the corresponding space on your answer sheet.

If there is no error, blacken answer space Ⓔ .

EXAMPLE: SAMPLE ANSWER

The region has a climate so severe that plants
                         A

growing there rarely had been more than twelve
    B   C

inches high. No error
     D   E

Ⓐ Ⓑ ● Ⓓ Ⓔ

Figure 4.2

Example of Sentence Correction Item and Instructions for the Test of Standard Written English (1982-83)

Directions: In each of the following sentences, some part or all of the sentence is underlined. Below each sentence you will find five ways of phrasing the underlined part. Select the answer that produces the most effective sentence, one that is clear and exact, without awkwardness or ambiguity, and blacken the corresponding space on your answer sheet. In choosing answers, follow the requirements of standard written English. Choose the answer that best expresses the meaning of the original sentence.

Answer (A) is always the same as the underlined part. Choose answer (A) if you think the original sentence needs no revision.

EXAMPLE: SAMPLE ANSWER

Laura Ingalls Wilder published her first book   Ⓐ ● Ⓒ Ⓓ Ⓔ
and she was sixty-five years old then.

(A) and she was sixty-five years old then
(B) when she was sixty-five years old
(C) at age sixty-five years old
(D) upon reaching sixty-five years
(E) at the time when she was sixty-five

---

range of subject matter and reflects a plurality of interests, including those of minorities and women. The sentences are presented in varied structures to provide a diverse sample of language use and to sustain students' interest. To ensure that the context in which the problem is being tested does not hinder the students' ability to identify or correct the problem, abstruse vocabulary and content are avoided, as are extremely complicated sentence structures.*

Use of the TSWE in College English Placement

The use of survey information to guide the early development of the test ensured that the test would be relevant in content and format to English instruction in the colleges. An empirical validation of the new test, however, was also required, and the College Board commissioned studies of these aspects of the test. As information about the scores accumulated, research carried out by users or potential users was also reported. The following sections describe some of these developments.

*The development of the test is reviewed for the College Board by the TSWE Committee. Members of the committee for 1982-83 were: Ronald B. Newman, University of Miami, Coral Gables, Florida, *Chairperson;* Carlota Cárdenas de Dwyer, University of Texas, Austin, Texas; Michael C. Flanigan, University of Oklahoma, Norman, Oklahoma; Maurice A. Lee, Bard College, Annandale-on-Hudson, New York; Marjorie G. Roemer, Brookline High School, Brookline, Massachusetts.

Studies Sponsored by the College Board. With the development of trial TSWE forms, attention shifted to studies of the relationships between TSWE scores and decision making about students and courses. The study by Breland (1977c), for example, was an attempt to examine the performance of the new test before it became a permanent part of the Admissions Testing Program.

In general, students should experience gains, through instruction, in those abilities that are measured by a placement test. Placement theory considers it improper to base a student's placement upon aptitude, intelligence, or other measures of long-term developed abilities, for it is usually impossible to relate instruction to any score deficiency. The Breland study, in seeking to examine the relevance of the TSWE for placement, also sought to examine the relevance of instruction to changes in scores.

Because college placement decisions are complex, the study was conducted intensively with only four colleges. For the study, the definition of an instructional outcome was broad, including: 1) performance on TSWE posttests administered toward the end of the courses; 2) performance on special essay posttests, also administered toward the end of the courses; and 3) students' satisfaction with their English courses and their placement within them. Preliminary data included information on performance on the TSWE and performance on a special essay pretest administered at the beginning of the first freshman English course. In addition, background data on the students, including information from the Student Descriptive Questionnaire and SAT scores, were obtained from the College Board files.

The colleges offered nine different courses, which were classified (in terms of their content and relation to other courses in the instructional sequence) as Exemption, Group Pacing, Remediation, Vertical Sectioning, Compensatory Programming, and Assignment after a model suggested by Willingham (1974). The study generated a large amount of correlational data on the relationships between the TSWE and other variables. Particular importance was attached to such questions as:

1) How do TSWE scores correlate with scores on actual essay tests?
2) How do scores on one form of the TSWE correlate with scores on another form of the TSWE administered at some other time and place?
3) How well do TSWE scores predict outcomes of English courses, such as course grades or end-of-course essay-writing ability? Alternately, how do preliminary TSWE scores predict end-of-course scores on the TSWE?
4) How well do TSWE scores predict the outcome of English courses in comparison with predictions based on SAT-verbal scores or precourse essays?

Three TSWE scores were available for the students in the Breland study: one generated from participation in the ATP, one obtained at the end of a one-semester course ending in the fall, and one generated at the end of a two-semester course ending in the spring. Similarly, three essay scores were available: one prior to, one at the beginning, and one toward the completion of a one-semester or two-semester course. Table 4.2 shows the resulting correlations between the TSWE scores and the essay scores.

Table 4.2

Correlation of TSWE Scores and Essay Scores
(Adapted from Breland 1977c)

	TSWE Posttest (Fall)	TSWE Posttest (Spring)	Essay Pretest (Fall)	Essay Posttest (Fall)	Essay Posttest (Spring)
TSWE Pretest (ATP)	.83	.84	.63	.58	.58
TSWE Posttest (Fall)		.84	.63	.56	.62
TSWE Posttest (Spring)			.57	.52	.58
Essay Pretest (Fall)				.52	.51
Essay Posttest (Fall)					.50

As these data show, the three separate administrations of the TSWE yielded high intercorrelations. A value of .83 or .84 is a reasonable test-retest reliability estimate, particularly when, as in this case, intervening instruction serves, by its differential effects,

to diminish or attenuate the correlations. The intercorrelations among the essays are, of course, reduced by similar factors. But the absolute level of the intercorrelations among the essays is considerably below that of the TSWE forms; for the essays, values of .50-.52 are observed. Nine intercorrelations between the multiple-choice TSWE and the various essays have a median value of .58. These data indicate that the typical TSWE form is more highly related to an essay score than is another essay score. Therefore, it seems fair to conclude that the TSWE, in spite of its indirect approach to the assessment of writing skills, has a demonstrated relationship to writing. There is a substantial relationship, .76, between a composite score based upon three TSWE administrations, or 90 minutes of indirect appraisal of writing ability, and a composite score based on three essays, or 60 minutes of essay writing. This correlation tends to establish that TSWE scores are validly consistent with essay scores.

Another major question about TSWE scores is their relationship to grades. It is plausible to anticipate that students who enter courses with higher levels of attainment in writing skills, as evidenced by higher TSWE scores, will tend to retain their superior positions. Because of the differential effects of instruction on tests and grades, however, there should be reduced correlation between grades and TSWE scores. Table 4.3 offers some relevant data derived from the Breland study.

Table 4.3

Correlations Between TSWE Scores, SAT-Verbal Scores, Essay Scores, and Grades
(Adapted from Breland 1977c)

	English Grade	
	Fall	Spring
TSWE Pretest (ATP)	.27	.33
TSWE Posttest (Fall)	.28	.36
TSWE Posttest (Spring)	.25	.28
Essay Pretest (Fall)	.28	.26
Essay Posttest (Fall)	.23	.27
Essay Posttest (Spring)	.25	.23
SAT-Verbal Score	.25	.28

The table shows modest levels of test-grade relationships for the TSWE. The six correlations, based on three TSWE administrations at three different times and on two course grades, average about .30. The six correlations between essay scores and course grades, based on essays written at times roughly comparable to the administration dates of the TSWE, average about .25. The SAT scores show correlations of .25 (fall grades) and .28 (spring grades). While these relationships are not strong, they are not unusual for grades in individual English courses, which are presumably influenced by factors other than writing skill (class attendance, promptness in submitting papers, etc.). The TSWE-grade correlation compares favorably with the levels of prediction afforded by the SAT and essay scores, and confirms that TSWE appraisals are reasonably consistent with the evaluations made by instructors at the end of a course.

External Assessments. Among the limited but growing number of studies conducted by users of the TSWE is a report by Bailey (1977) on the usefulness of the TSWE for placement into English 1 courses at a California state university. The following data are the results for 145 students who completed the course and were awarded a grade:

Grade in Course	N	TSWE Mean	TSWE S.D.
A	43	45.0	9.3
B	64	43.0	9.2
C	27	37.0	9.3
D	6	42.0	4.5
F	5	32.0	3.9

After considering the evident but moderate relationship between TSWE scores and grades in English 1, Bailey concluded (p. 73), "The College Board statement that students having high scores on the TSWE probably do not need remedial help in writing may be an accurate one." The converse assumption, it was pointed out, need not hold (p. 73): ". . . some students who do not score well on the TSWE do very well in English 1." The final conclusion was a guarded one (p. 73): ". . . the TSWE, although effective as a gross screening device, may not be completely suitable for student placement in English courses."

A study by Hackman and Johnson (1977) reported an application of the TSWE at Yale. The authors asked (p. 82), "How do precollege measures, including . . . the new experimental placement test (Test of Standard Written English) relate to Yale freshmen essay ratings and to grades in English courses?" The Yale sample was markedly skewed: 38.3 percent got the highest possible score, 60+; 13.9 percent got 59. But, Hackman and Johnson noted (p. 91), "The original purpose of the TSWE and the extreme skewing of Yale's TSWE scores make it surprising that fairly strong relationships are still found for the Yale freshmen between TSWE and the essay ratings and freshmen English grades."

The TSWE correlated best with mechanics of writing, at both the subsentence and sentence level (.57 each). The frequency distributions indicated that students scoring below 56 on the TSWE were consistently rated below average on the six essay categories. "However," the authors note (p. 93), "a maximum TSWE score of 60+ is no guarantee of high essay ratings." Comparing their results to the results of previously reported Board research (Breland, Conlan, and Rogosa 1976), the authors found their correlations with mechanics (p. 92) "almost identical to the correlation of .52 found by ETS," in spite of the fact that (p. 93) "the Yale freshman's average TSWE scores are considerably higher than those at any of the 12 diverse colleges in the ETS preliminary study. Even the lowest 19 percent of Yale scores would fall in the top 50 percent of the 12 ETS study schools." However, many low-scoring Yale students studied English as a foreign language. The report also noted that (p. 93) "TSWE appears to correlate slightly better than the SAT-verbal score or the English Composition Test with grades in English courses."

Osterlund and Cheney (1978) studied the correlation between the TSWE and a criterion derived from composite holistic essay reading. Specifically noting Bailey's concern for the role that nonstandardized English grades played in producing moderate relationships between test scores and grades, Osterlund and Cheney were able to define a small sample of 42 students who took the TSWE at the beginning of a course and whose members wrote two short, holistically scored essays at its conclusion. The TSWE correlated .42 with end-of-course grades, but .61 with scores on the essays. The authors concluded (p. 173), "Whether the .61 correlation between the TSWE and the composite (essay scores) is practical is a matter of judgment. It is certainly more practical than the .32 obtained by Bailey." Osterlund and Cheney added (p. 173), "The composite essay score is preferable to grades as the criterion of choice for testing the empirical validity of the TSWE."

Michael and Shaffer (1979) studied more than 500 freshmen at California State University at Northridge, comparing the California State University and College-English Placement Test (CSUC-EPT) and the SAT with TSWE to see whether the latter might supplant the CSUC-EPT. Comparisons were made with respect to four criterion measures: 1) grades in a written expression course; 2) grade point average for fall; 3) grade point average for spring, and 4) grade point average for the full year. The authors concluded (p. 131), "The TSWE requiring 30 minutes of test-taking time is very nearly as valid as the CSUC-EPT, which involves 2 hours and 45 minutes of working time, in the prediction of success in the general English composition course." Both the TSWE and CSUC-EPT test (p. 131) "predicted English course grades better than either SAT-V alone or a brief essay test. From the standpoint of cost effectiveness, serious consideration should be given to the replacement of the CSUC-EPT with the TSWE.''

In general, then, the results of external researchers confirm the work of Breland, Conlan, and Rogosa (1976): the TSWE is a valid predictor. It is related to appraisals of writing ability based on actual writing and apparently fulfills its designers' expectations that it would be most sensitive to the lower levels of ability. It is essentially a screening test, useful in broad-scale planning, rather than a diagnostic test to be used in instruction.

Data on Test Fairness

Breland (1977a) reviews the experience of 18 colleges in using the TSWE to evaluate the writing ability of minority students and to place them in appropriate courses. The study was intended to assess the extent of any differences in the usefulness of the test for both sexes and for minority students.

Because of the small number of students in each particular racial-ethnic/sex category at a given institution, the data from the colleges were pooled by year; the 14 colleges in the 1974-75 study were considered as one group and the 4 colleges in the 1975-76 study as another. These two groups were further subdivided into majority and minority groups, separately by sex. Minorities included those students who described themselves as American Indian; as Black, Afro-American, or Negro; as Mexican American or Chicano; as Puerto Rican; or as Oriental or Asian American. Majority students were those who described themselves as White or Caucasian.

There were 888 minority students among the 6,708 students at the 14 colleges in 1974-75; for 667 of the minority students, all the information needed for Table 4.4 was available. Table 4.4 presents information on the relationship between score level and grades for majority and minority applicants.

As indicated by the right-hand column in the table, some of the percentages in a category are based on very small numbers. For instance, only 28 individuals constitute the group of majority test takers scoring 60+ on TSWE and receiving the modal grade of A; only 2 individuals constitute the similarly defined minority group. There is obviously considerable sampling variation in such numbers. In general, the differences in proportions within a score level are smaller than the differences in the group as a whole.

The degree of consistency between test and course grades reflected in Table 4.4 may be assessed by phi

Table 4.4

Proportions of TSWE Score-Level Groups in English Course-Grade Category for Varying Score-Level Groups, Majority vs. Minority* (Adapted from Breland 1977a)

TSWE Score-Level Category		A	B	C	D	F	N
60+	Majority	.53	.40	.08	.00	.00	53
	Minority	.50	.50	.00	.00	.00	4
50-59	Majority	.26	.48	.22	.02	.02	619
	Minority	.13	.49	.33	.02	.03	61
40-49	Majority	.18	.40	.35	.05	.05	773
	Minority	.08	.43	.39	.02	.08	171
30-39	Majority	.08	.31	.43	.10	.07	516
	Minority	.05	.28	.52	.05	.10	240
20-29	Majority	.06	.25	.48	.14	.07	121
	Minority	.02	.16	.40	.04	.37	191
Total	Majority	.17	.39	.33	.06	.05	2,082
	Minority	.06	.31	.43	.04	.06	667

*Modal categories within a score level are underlined.

coefficients in order to provide a more systematic analysis of the relationship. For this purpose, the score of 40 was arbitrarily selected as the differentiating score for the test, while the grade of B was chosen as the differentiating level for the grades. As Table 4.5 shows, there was some difference in the strength of relationship determined when the groups were divided in these ways.

Table 4.5

Strength of Relationship (Phi Coefficients) Between TSWE and Grades for Four Subgroups: Males, Females, Majority Students, and Minority Students (Adapted from Breland 1977a)

	Males (1,541) A or B C, D, or F			Females (1,859) A or B C, D, or F	
TSWE ≥ 40	510	434	TSWE ≥ 40	855	442
TSWE < 40	174	423	TSWE < 40	193	369
	phi = .24			phi = .29	

	Majority (2,082) A or B C, D, or F			Minority (667) A or B C, D, or F	
TSWE ≥ 40	929	516	TSWE ≥ 40	129	107
TSWE < 40	240	397	TSWE < 40	114	317
	phi = .25			phi = .28	

On the basis of these phi coefficients, the relationships between TSWE scores and freshman English grades are slightly stronger for women and for minorities than they are for males and the majority (White) group. A slightly higher level of predictability for females is not an unusual finding in correlational research concerning course grades of this type. The finding for the minority sample is somewhat reassuring: the test is at least as well correlated with grades for this group as it is for the majority group.

The arbitrary levels selected for the computation of phi coefficients may occasionally produce quite different impacts on the values observed. To explore this facet of the data, Breland presented additional two-way contingency tables, using the cutting score of 35, rather than 40. The resulting recalculated phi coefficients were:

Males .17	Females .27
Majority .17	Minorities .27

As these phi coefficients show, while the validities declined slightly in all samples, the relationships between the sexes and between the ethnic groups remained. All the coefficients reported here have high statistical significance, indicating a modest, but real, relationship between TSWE scores and course grades in all samples.

In another phase of this study, Breland considered the intercorrelations among 14 variables, using the pooled data from the 14 colleges. Certain of these correlations seem exceptionally pertinent to an evaluation of the merits of the appropriateness of the TSWE for minorities. The correlation between TSWE scores and end-of-semester fall grades in English composition was reported for each of the four samples and for each of two additional subgroups. These subgroups were differentiated according to their placement by the college in either the short sequence, usually considered to demand a higher level of preparation, or the long sequence, which usually involved more courses and a slower pace designed for students who need more work to reach the college's acceptable level of competence. The following table shows the correlations with grades and essays for the TSWE and the pretest essay written by students prior to entering the course.

TSWE Correlations with First-Semester Grades

	Males	Females	Majority	Minority
Short Sequence	.39	.36	.34	.43
Long Sequence	.30	.42	.30	.33

Essay Pretest Correlations with
First-Semester Grades

	Males	Females	Majority	Minority
Short Sequence	—	.17	.30	.17
Long Sequence	.33	.21	.21	.25

With the exception of long-sequence males, for all groups the TSWE pretest score was a better predictor of grades than was the score derived from the writing of an essay. This finding is consistent with the principal findings in much previous research using other multiple-choice measures (Angoff 1971). Unless extraordinary measures are undertaken to enhance the reliability of the score based upon essay writing, as in Godshalk, Swineford, and Coffman (1966), multiple-choice measures of language skills tend to be better predictors of grades, even when grades are based heavily, as they typically are, on essay test performance. Thus, the TSWE is a better predictor of grades for minorities than is the essay pretest score.

The Breland analysis for the four colleges in the second academic year, 1975-76, did not differentiate between the long-sequence and the short-sequence subgroups. The reported correlations between grades and precourse essay scores and precourse TSWE scores for the four groups were as follows:

Correlations with Grades

	Males	Females	Majority	Minority
TSWE Score	.27	.25	.25	.20
Essay Score	.28	.27	.27	.15

As these data show, there was little difference between the predictors in three of the four samples, but for the minority group the TSWE score was slightly more predictive than a score based upon actual writing. Again, the evidence sustains the view that the TSWE is not seriously biased against minorities. Minority grades in this analysis were more difficult to predict.

Breland and Griswold (1981) extended the evaluation of the fairness of the TSWE to different sexes and ethnic groups. The basic information available reflected eight test scores: TSWE, SAT-verbal, SAT-mathematical, and five scores based on the CSUC English Placement Test, a two-hour and forty-five minute English language skills assessment: (1) EPT-Reading, (2) EPT-Sentence Construction, (3) EPT-Logic and Organization, (4) EPT-Essay, and (5) EPT-Total. A correlational analysis demonstrated the close relationship among SAT-verbal, SAT-mathematical, TSWE, and the EPT scores. The groups studied and the number of students in them were as follows: men (4,766), women (5,908), Asian American (606), Black (583), Hispanic (445), and White (5,236). There was some overlap among groups; overall, 10,674 different students were included.

The White student sample consistently yielded lower correlations for all comparisons than did the other groups. This was attributed to attenuated variances. Most importantly for the present discussion, the TSWE correlated with EPT-Essay (an actual writing sample) as well as any other measure for any of the groups. In the regression analysis, TSWE tended to *overpredict* minority performance in essay writing, as did the other measures; and as has been repeatedly demonstrated in such studies, women's essay writing scores, on the other hand, were underpredicted.

A "score interval" analysis considered these relationships within stratified ranges of the test scores. In general, these descriptive comparisons were similar for all groups, and were in agreement with similar previous studies.

College Validity Studies

The predictive validity of tests in the Admissions Testing Program is reviewed in Chapter VIII. However, because this validity is so relevant to an evaluation of TSWE, the following distribution of validities derived from studies reported by the Validity Study Service (VSS) is presented here.

Percent of Colleges with Validity Correlations Higher Than Designated Level	Level of Validity (Correlation Between TSWE and Freshman English Grade)
10	.53
25	.44
50	.38
75	.25
90	.22
Mean Validity	.37
Standard Deviation Validity	.16

As this table shows, the TSWE is reasonably predictive of freshman English grades. This is the case in spite of the fact that the test is designed to produce skewed distributions of a sort that result in lower correlations for groups with average or greater-than-average writing skills, and in spite of the fact that the content of the test (by intention) reflects only a part of what is being evaluated in course work.

The nature of the courses and the students in the samples is, of course, relevant to any evaluation of these results. This descriptive information, however, is not available through the statistical summaries of the Validity Study Service. The observed TSWE correlations, however, may be evaluated by comparison with the typical correlation between freshman English grades and the SAT-verbal sections. For 72 colleges, many also represented in the TSWE table above, the average validity for the SAT-verbal sections against freshman English grades was .36. Thus, the TSWE was able to predict English grades about as well as the SAT itself.

In spite of the similarity in the level of correlations

attained, the TSWE and the SAT-verbal sections tap somewhat different aspects of the criterion, for their combined prediction is greater than that of either one alone. This is demonstrated by the average multiple correlation for the TSWE and the SAT-verbal sections with grades at 47 institutions included in the VSS studies. The average correlation for these studies of both predictors, .44, is significantly greater than the levels of approximately .35 that were attained with a single predictor.

Specifications for the Test

Each form of the Test of Standard Written English is carefully constructed to conform to detailed specifications concerning both content features and statistical properties. Table 4.6 provides basic information on content aspects, showing that the percentage distribution of the items across a number of error-type categories is carefully specified. The meaning of a category is carefully defined for the item writers, and there are specified subcategories to assist the writers in preparing a diverse collection of appropriate material. The separate functions of the two item types, usage and sentence correction, are suggested by the differences in the categories used to

Table 4.6

Content Specifications for the Test of Standard Written English

Usage Items (Total = 35 Items)	
Error-Type Category	Percentage of Test Section
Subject-Verb Agreement	11
Tense	9
Verb Form	6
Connectives	6
Sentence Logic	6
Modifiers	6
Pronouns	17
Diction	6
Idiom	14

Approximately 20 percent of the usage items will have no error.

Sentence Correction Items (Total = 15 Items)	
Error-Type Category	Percentage of Test Section
Parallelism	20
Sentence Fragment	14
Comma Splice	13
Improper Subordination	14
Improper Coordination	13
Dangling Modifier	13
Miscellaneous	13

govern their properties. In general, with eight functioning error-type categories for the usage items and seven for the sentence correction items, the items are spread quite evenly across a wide number of writing problems. In addition to this spread, the topic content of the sentences used is also carefully distributed. The content categories (the topics referred to in the sentence) are spread across six major areas, with additional widespread dispersion within a major category such as arts and social science. Examples of such content categories are:

Arts	Music, Dance, Crafts, Painting, Architecture, Literature, Film, Theater, etc.
Social Science	Psychology, Sociology, Economics, History (Western and Non-western), Anthropology, Language, etc.
Science	Biology, Ecology, Physics, Chemistry, Astronomy, Medicine, Technology, Computer Science, Agriculture, etc.
Public Life	Business, Politics, Law, Communications, Professional Athletics, Transportation, etc.
Student-Relevant	Curriculum, Career Planning, Classroom and Extracurricular Activities, etc.
Everyday Activities	Family, Hobbies, Travel, etc.

The statistical specifications for the TSWE are presented in Table 4.7. The most difficult items are in the $\triangle$12.0-12.9 range, on which approximately 40 to 50 percent of the group will succeed; all other items are easier than these. The average delta for the test is 9.37, which is intended to produce a test with a marked negative skew, facilitating comparisons at the lower end of the score range. The relatively high average biserial requirement ensures a reasonable level of reliability for the test and guards against the introduction of items that center on some idiosyncratic element of the content domain.

Description of TSWE Characteristics

Like every other College Board test, each form of the TSWE is evaluated by means of an item and test analysis after its administration. The results of these analyses are carefully reviewed to ensure that the new form meets the statistical specifications for the TSWE. The results of such analyses may be cumulated for a number of forms to show the consistency with which the test development process yields intrinsically equivalent forms, minimizing the burden that must be borne by the equating.

Tables 4.8 and 4.9 demonstrate the extent to which raw scores on alternate forms of the TSWE yield closely equivalent scaled scores. The typical range of scaled score equivalents between one test form and another is about two to three points. As this indicates, the level of adjustment demanded of the equating process is not great; the detailed test specifications are reliably conformed to, and their effect on constraining form-to-form variation is evident. The methods used for scaling the TSWE are described in this handbook in Chapter II on psychometric methods.

Table 4.7

Statistical Specifications for the Test of
Standard Written English

Difficulty Category (in Terms of $\triangle$)	Usage Items (N = 35)	Sentence Correction (N = 15)	Total Test (N = 50)
12.0-12.9	2	1	3
11.0-11.9	5	2	7
10.0-10.9	7	3	10
9.0- 9.9	7	3	10
8.0- 8.9	8	2	10
7.0- 7.9	3	2	5
6.0- 6.9	2	1	3
5.0- 5.9	1	1	2
	Mean $\triangle$		9.37
	Mean r-biserial		.45 $\pm$ .02

Order of the item types:
  1–25 Usage (include $\triangle$ 12 items here)
26–40 Sentence Correction
41–50 Usage

Table 4.8

Scaled Score Ranges for Selected Raw Scores on the
Test of Standard Written English*

Raw Score (50 Questions)	Scaled Score
50	60+
45	57-60+
40	52-55
35	47-50
30	42-45
25	37-39
20	32-34
15	27-29
10	22-24
5	20
0	20

*Based on all forms of the TSWE given from October 1980 through November 1982.

Table 4.9

Means and Standard Deviations of Raw and Scaled Scores and the
Measures of Skewness for the Eight Forms of the TSWE
Administered Between November 1981 and June 1983

Date of First Administration of TSWE Form	N	Raw Scores M	Raw Scores S.D.	Scaled Scores M	Scaled Scores S.D.	Skewness
Nov. 1981	334,394	29.98	10.62	42.93	10.53	−0.40
Jan. 1982	118,891	25.40	10.67	39.92	10.80	−0.09
March 1982	184,450	28.11	10.70	41.94	10.89	−0.19
June 1982	214,659	29.23	10.07	42.64	10.41	−0.30
Nov. 1982	381,570	30.67	11.05	43.14	10.45	−0.43
March 1983	169,430	27.44	10.88	41.98	10.99	−0.23
May 1983	285,570	30.01	10.49	43.88	10.44	−0.37
June 1983	219,003	29.28	10.24	42.46	10.51	−0.28

Table 4.9 shows the means and standard deviations of both the raw scores and the scaled scores for each of eight recent forms, together with the estimates of skewness. The raw score means and standard deviations show highly consistent values, indicating that the test forms are highly similar in terms of their difficulty and dispersions. Some of the variation in the raw-score data is in part explained by the variation in ability level of the test-taking groups. For example, the ability levels of the January and March groups described in the table are typically somewhat lower than those for other administrations; as a result, so are the corresponding raw-score means. The table presents the pattern of a tightly controlled test-development process that produces a uniform set of tests, with highly equivalent properties. As the estimates of negative skewness indicate, the median lies above the mean, and the test differentiates better in the lower score ranges than in the upper. This is consistent with the intentions of the test specifications.

Table 4.10 presents information on the speededness of the test forms. Virtually all students complete 75 percent or more of the test. A somewhat smaller number of students at each administration, typically about 85 percent of the group, complete the entire test. The range of the percentages of students completing the test is from 82 to 90 percent.

The mean number of items that have not been reached varies little, ranging from 0.69 to 1.27, indicating that most students have sufficient time to complete all, or almost all, of the questions. This equivalence among forms is further supported by the data on the number of items omitted, which is typically quite small. Thus, students are reaching the last items without skipping over any significant number of earlier ones.

The standard deviations of the number of items not reached are quite small, indicating little speed-edness. One index of the contribution of speed to the total information provided by the test is the ratio of the variance of the number of items not reached to the score variance. If the ratio is relatively large, variance due to speed may be a primary factor contributing to overall score variance. If the ratio is relatively small, the test developer may safely disregard speed as a factor in solving variance. In general, values for this index greater than .25 are arbitrarily considered speeded. The score for the TSWE is corrected for guessing, so that the score variance is somewhat greater than it would be if it were based on rights only scores. As the data in Table 4.10 show, the levels of the index for TSWE forms nevertheless are typically well under the critical .25 level. For TSWE forms, the variance in the number of questions that were not reached is about 8 percent of the score variance.

The data in Table 4.10 project an overall picture of the appropriateness of the time limits for the test. The time allowance for the average question is 36 seconds; this would seem to be ample for the average student to read the brief sentences and respond, because the typical sentence used as a question in the test is 15 to 20 words long; a sentence of 25 words would be unusually long. Sentences of this length can be read easily by a college-level reader in about 10 seconds, at a reading rate of only 150 words per minute. This would leave over a third of a minute for reflection and response. Because the majority of the test requires students to deal only with clear errors in writing, errors easily recognized by most college students, the time allowed for the task seems ample.

In the years following the introduction of the TSWE, the committee of English teachers responsible for the appropriateness of the Test of Standard Written English has specifically focused on the time limits of the test for minorities and carefully studied the

Table 4.10

Values of Speededness Indicators for the Eight Forms of the TSWE
Administered Between November 1981 and June 1983

Date of First Administration of TSWE Form	Percentages Completing 75% of the Test	Percentages Completing 100% of the Test	Number Not Reached M	Number Not Reached S.D.	Ratio of the Variance of the Number Not Reached to the Variance of Scores
Nov. 1981	98.3	85.8	0.88	2.91	.08
Jan. 1982	97.4	82.1	1.27	3.45	.10
March 1982	97.7	84.5	1.17	3.34	.10
June 1982	98.4	83.5	1.03	3.03	.09
Nov. 1982	97.7	84.4	1.04	3.15	.08
March 1983	98.1	88.1	0.83	2.91	.07
May 1983	98.7	87.4	0.79	2.69	.07
June 1983	99.0	90.1	0.69	2.49	.06

time limits and content of the test in light of the statistical information available. Consequently, certain restrictions have been placed on the content of items and the overall balance of the test. Items are to be excluded if they exhibit characteristics that seem to lead to unusual time demands, specifically items using relatively sophisticated syntax or items with heavy conceptual load or esoteric content. In each case, the unusual time required by the item is peripheral to its central measurement goal. In addition, the overall balance of each test form in terms of sentence length was reviewed in order to avoid lengthy items requiring a greater proportion of the test taker's time than is usually demanded.

Correlations with SAT-Verbal Scores

The TSWE, when first introduced, was expected to correlate very highly with the SAT-verbal sections. The English Composition Test, the existing Achievement Test related to writing ability, had already demonstrated a high level of relationship to the verbal aptitude measure, and the new test, made up of items similar to those in the English Composition Test (though less difficult), would reasonably be expected to continue this pattern.

Adding a new measure to the ATP requires some justification. The major problems involve a) a possible redundancy and overlap among measures and b) the extent to which correlation may be used to infer a criterion. Clearly, the use of measures with demonstrated true-score equivalence would be discouraged as a waste of time. However, the fact that the SAT-verbal score is highly predictive of writing ability does not mean that it should be substituted for scores on the TSWE and the English Composition Test, which contain items that are more logically and directly related to measuring this ability. The

TSWE also provides finer differentiation at the lower score levels, where the placement decisions to which it contributes are focused. The SAT correlates with the TSWE, but it is not equivalent; the SAT is a more broad-gauge admissions test that stresses different skills than the TSWE and measures higher ability levels as well.

The data in Table 4.11 show the correlations between TSWE scores and each of four other scores derived from the SAT: total verbal score, mathematical score, vocabulary subscore, and reading subscore. The patterns of these correlations demonstrate that the TSWE is highly correlated with the other verbal information. Given the reliabilities of the various tests, one can expect true-score intercorrelations in the .90s. However, as mentioned above, correlations of this magnitude would not indicate a perfect equivalence for the measures. The distinction between the knowledge and skills tapped by the TSWE and those measured by the SAT is apparent in the

Table 4.11

Correlations Between TSWE Scores and the Various SAT
Scores: Verbal, Mathematical, Vocabulary, and Reading
(November 1981 to June 1983)

Date of First Administration of TSWE Form	Verbal	Mathematical	Vocabulary	Reading
Nov. 1981	.80	.64	.76	.75
Jan. 1982	.80	.65	.77	.77
March 1982	.78	.67	.74	.74
June 1982	.76	.60	.72	.72
Nov. 1982	.78	.64	.75	.74
March 1983	.77	.65	.73	.72
May 1983	.78	.64	.74	.75
June 1983	.77	.59	.71	.75
Average	.78	.64	.74	.74

item content of the tests. Thus, the measurements are consistent, rather than equivalent.

With respect to its correlation with the mathematical sections of the SAT, the TSWE shows a level of relatedness that is slightly less than that of the verbal sections. A rise in the correlation between the verbal and mathematical components of the SAT was observed over a 15-year span from about 1950 to 1965, after which the correlation stabilized at its present level, approximately in the upper .60s. The causes of this coming together of verbal and mathematical attainments are not well understood. They have been attributed to changes in the populations going to college and the nature of instruction. For whatever reason, the correlation demonstrated by the TSWE is about what would be anticipated.

The reliability of the test and the raw score and scaled score standard errors of measurement are presented in Table 4.12. As these figures show, the test is highly reliable despite its modest length. The items systematically tap a homogeneous vein, and the resultant inter-item correlations yield a high internal-consistency reliability. The standard error for scores in the upper ranges is probably somewhat greater than the standard error for scores in the critical range, because the skewed distribution shifts the region of greatest average error to the upper levels, where fewer critical decisions need to be made.

The estimates of internal-consistency reliability for the total test are typically in the upper .80s. Parallel-form reliability will ordinarily not be this great. However, as Table 4.13 indicates, the median test-retest correlation is about .82. This median value is based on intervals that vary in length, but that average about six months. Intervals of this length would, of course, tend to lower the reliability estimate. On the other hand, the test-retest correlations are not based on random samples of students,

as are the internal-consistency estimates, but on samples of those students who elect to take the test in the spring of their junior year and again in the winter of their senior year. While this is a large and varied group, the distortions that are possible though self-selection cannot be assessed.

Table 4.13

Test-Retest Correlation for TSWE Scores*

Year	March/ Apr.- Nov.	March/ Apr.- Dec.	May- Nov.	May- Dec.	June- Nov.	June- Dec.
1977	.82	.81	.82	.82	.82	.82
1978	.81	.82	.82	.83	.80	.80
1979	.83	.82	.84	.83	.84	.83
1980	.82	.82	.83	.83	.83	.83
1981	.81	.80	.83	.81	.83	.82
1982	.82	.82	.83	.82	.82	.82

*These correlations are based on samples described in Table 4.14.

Tables 4.12 and 4.13 demonstrate that the TSWE is so constructed that it consistently secures an appropriate level of reliability. The basic applications for the test are not in highly crucial selection decisions, but in guidance and placement. For these applications, less precision is required than is needed for selection, usually a reliability of approximately .80 rather than .90 or greater. The various reliability estimates for TSWE indicate that suitable levels are achieved for this test.

Information on Score Change

Table 4.14 presents the test-retest data to show the mean and the standard deviation of the score changes. As might be expected, there is an incre-

Table 4.12

Internal Consistency Reliability Estimates and Standard Errors of Measurement, Raw and Scaled, for the Eight Forms of the TSWE Administered Between November 1981 and June 1983

Date of First Administration of TSWE Form	Reliability*	Standard Error of Measurement Raw	Scaled	Sample Mean Raw	Scaled	Sample Standard Deviation Raw	Scaled
Nov. 1981	.885	3.59	3.7	30.18	43.1	10.59	10.9
Jan. 1982	.881	3.77	3.9	26.24	40.7	10.94	11.5
March 1982	.885	3.67	3.8	28.23	42.1	10.80	11.3
June 1982	.865	3.64	3.9	29.64	43.1	9.92	10.6
Nov. 1982	.904	3.55	3.5	30.69	43.2	11.43	11.2
March 1983	.887	3.69	3.8	28.02	42.5	10.95	11.4
May 1983	.882	3.59	3.7	29.81	43.8	10.47	10.8
June 1983	.868	3.65	3.8	29.31	42.5	10.04	10.5

*These reliability estimates are based on Dressel's adaptation (1940) of Kuder-Richardson (20) (1937).

Table 4.14

Six-Year Summary of Change in TSWE Scores for March/April, May, or June
of the Junior Year to November or December of the Senior Year

	March/April to November						March/April to December					
	1977	1978	1979	1980	1981	1982	1977	1978	1979	1980	1981	1982
N (In Thousands)	77	58	55	51	63	47	19	15	16	17	15	11
Senior Scores												
Mean	45.6	45.3	45.5	45.0	45.1	45.6	44.1	43.5	43.8	43.6	43.6	43.9
Standard Deviation	9.4	9.6	9.8	9.6	9.6	9.5	9.8	10.0	10.0	9.9	9.7	10.2
Junior Scores												
Mean	43.9	38.5	44.8	44.4	44.6	44.5	41.5	41.7	42.5	41.6	42.1	42.2
Standard Deviation	9.9	9.9	9.8	9.7	9.7	9.8	10.1	10.3	10.1	9.9	10.0	10.2
Senior Minus Junior Scores												
Mean	1.7	1.3	0.7	0.6	0.5	1.1	2.6	1.9	1.2	2.0	1.4	1.6
Standard Deviation	5.9	6.1	5.7	5.7	6.0	5.7	6.2	6.2	6.1	6.0	6.2	6.2
Percent Showing Decrease	35	38	40	42	43	39	30	34	38	33	38	36

	May to November						May to December					
	1977	1978	1979	1980	1981	1982	1977	1978	1979	1980	1981	1982
N (In Thousands)	75	81	82	77	77	115	21	23	24	29	24	25
Senior Scores												
Mean	46.1	45.4	45.6	45.3	45.1	45.5	45.0	43.9	43.5	43.7	43.0	43.4
Standard Deviation	9.3	9.6	9.8	9.5	9.6	9.5	9.9	10.0	10.1	9.9	9.7	10.2
Junior Scores												
Mean	44.9	44.7	44.2	43.9	43.8	44.4	42.6	42.5	41.5	40.9	40.9	42.0
Standard Deviation	9.8	9.5	9.8	9.7	9.8	9.3	10.2	9.9	10.1	10.0	10.0	9.8
Senior Minus Junior Scores												
Mean	1.3	0.7	1.4	1.4	1.3	1.0	2.3	1.4	2.0	2.8	2.1	1.4
Standard Deviation	5.6	5.7	5.5	5.6	5.7	5.5	6.0	5.9	5.9	5.9	6.1	6.0
Percent Showing Decrease	38	41	35	36	37	38	31	36	33	27	33	35

	June to November						June to December					
	1977	1978	1979	1980	1981	1982	1977	1978	1979	1980	1981	1982
N (In Thousands)	42	42	45	41	46	64	16	18	19	22	20	22
Senior Scores												
Mean	45.0	44.5	44.8	44.4	44.1	44.0	43.5	42.7	43.0	42.6	42.2	42.3
Standard Deviation	9.3	9.7	9.9	9.5	9.7	9.6	10.0	10.0	10.1	10.1	9.8	10.2
Junior Scores												
Mean	44.3	43.9	44.1	44.1	43.4	42.9	41.9	41.5	41.6	40.9	40.8	40.9
Standard Deviation	9.4	9.7	10.0	9.8	9.6	9.8	10.1	10.0	10.2	10.2	10.0	10.1
Senior Minus Junior Scores												
Mean	0.7	0.6	0.6	0.3	0.7	1.1	1.6	1.2	1.4	1.7	1.5	1.4
Standard Deviation	5.7	6.1	5.6	5.7	5.7	5.8	5.9	6.3	5.9	5.9	6.0	6.1
Percent Showing Decrease	40	42	41	44	40	39	35	38	37	34	36	37

ment in average score when testing is repeated at intervals of six or seven months. This mean increment varies somewhat from one test-retest pattern to another. The range in Table 4.14 is from 0.3 scaled score points from June to November 1980, to 2.8 scaled score points from May to December 1980. The mean of the 16 means of changes reported in Table 4.14 is 1.4 scaled score points. This result is reasonably consistent with what is known of mean score changes on the SAT scales and indicates on the average a gain of about .25 scaled score points per month on the TSWE scale.

The general pattern of gain, however, is by no means the same for everyone. On the average, over a third of those repeating the test show score decreases, as Table 4.14 indicates. This finding is consistent with any test of about this reliability for which the average upward shift over time is approximately 40 percent of the standard error of measurement. The sources of these gains cannot be established precisely, but it seems reasonable to attribute them to continued exposure both to schooling and to language.

Content-Construct Validity

The origins of the content specifications for the TSWE are indicated in Table 4.1, which details a number of subdimensions for the test (verb agreement, precision in word use, pronoun-antecedent agreement, etc.). Table 4.6 provides the current working values. The content validity of this collective set of specifications is indicated in the discussion that accompanies Table 4.1: the mean scores for the various instructional topics are the means of the ratings of the topics in terms of ''importance as perceived by English faculty members.'' The uniformly high average rating for the various elements sampled by the TSWE is evidence of the appropriateness of its content. While some elements that the faculty members consider important are not measured, the TSWE content consists entirely of elements judged to be important.

The construct validity of the test is perhaps best demonstrated by the fact that when writing is evaluated by professional English faculty members, they tend to include a dimension that is consistent with the aspect of writing measured by the TSWE. Thus, in the study by Hackman and Johnson (1977) the categories for evaluation included ''subsentence level'' mechanics (spelling and punctuation), the use of idiom and of vocabulary, as well as the use of sentences with proper grammar, control of meaning and syntax, and structure. Hackman and Johnson, in turn, justify their rating categories by referring to a study by Diederich, French, and Carlton (1961), which found that ''usage'' and ''sentence structure'' constitute important elements of rating that are emphasized by one major subgroup of English specialists.

Principal author: Thomas F. Donlon.
Contributors or reviewers: J. Evans Alloway, Hunter M. Breland, Roberta H. Camp, Gertrude C. Conlan, Robert J. Jones, Geraldine I. May, June Stern, and Nancy K. Wright.

CHAPTER V

The Achievement Tests

Introduction

The College Board Achievement Tests are specifically intended to measure attainment in subject-matter areas. In this, they contrast with the Scholastic Aptitude Test, which is designed to identify those individuals who, regardless of the subjects they might have studied in secondary school, possess the general academic skills necessary for successful college work. Historically, the Achievement Tests predate the SAT by over a quarter of a century. They were the basis for the initial organization of the College Board in 1900, long before the development of aptitude testing. In the years following their introduction, they have served a variety of purposes: the principal three are outlined in the following pages.

In recent years, the College Board has offered 14 different Achievement Tests, in five broad subject-matter areas, as follows:

English
English Composition
Literature

Foreign Languages
French
German
Hebrew
Latin
Spanish

History and Social Studies
American History and Social Studies
European History and World Cultures

Mathematics
Mathematics Level I
Mathematics Level II

Sciences
Biology
Chemistry
Physics

The discussion that follows describes the purposes of the Achievement Tests, the history of their evolution, and the manner of their development. Because the same types of tests are offered year after year—history, English, the sciences, mathematics, and foreign languages—the Achievement Tests appear to be unchanging. This seeming stability, however, belies continuing changes and adaptations. Achievement testing, by its very nature, is geared to education; as education changes, so does the testing of its outcomes.

Since the founding of the College Board at the beginning of the twentieth century, there has been a major shift from essay tests to multiple-choice tests, a shift that has had powerful implications for the entire field of achievement testing. A steady evolution in the approach to achievement testing has occurred in recent years. One may not be able to point to dramatic changes, but the area is far from static. William Coffman reviewed achievement test development for the first edition of this handbook (1971). The current chapter extends the description of the Achievement Tests to cover the events of the past decade. It was a decade marked by a decline in the number of students taking the Achievement Tests, but also by substantial and continued vigor in the evolution of each of the tests.

Purposes of College Board Achievement Tests

The Achievement Tests are typically required as part of the college application process for one or more of the following reasons: 1) to determine whether an applicant for admission is adequately prepared in a particular subject, 2) to assist in placing new students into appropriate college courses, and 3) to combine with other variables in the prediction of college performance. These different purposes overlap in the kinds of tests required and in the ways in which the information derived from the tests is used. There is, of course, a great deal of variation in the way that individual Achievement Tests are used on individual campuses, but some generalizations can be made.

Determining Adequate Preparation. Many colleges and universities expect students entering their courses to have a particular level of competence, and they wish to select only students who can meet this prerequisite. For example, an engineering college may begin the study of mathematics with a course in calculus and analytical geometry. In such a setting, it is assumed that the entering students have already developed an understanding of algebra, trigonometry, and elementary functions along with the mathematical skills that will permit them to master the concepts in the course. Some evidence of this understanding is provided by passing grades in appropriate secondary school courses, but the requirements for this passing grade vary from school to school. The Mathematics Achievement Tests, by providing a common sample of problems for all the students, can furnish evidence of the extent to which the applicants from different schools—and with different types of exposure to the subject matter—have reached a common level of achievement. In the same way, the English Composition Test can be used to indicate that acceptable levels of skill in the basic elements of composition have already been achieved in secondary school.

The use of tests to verify the adequacy of preparation may be particularly important in certain colleges where there is no provision for devoting time during the freshman year to the development of such skills. The use of tests in this way is similar to but subtly different from the use of tests alone or in combination as predictors of success. When used to indicate competence, an Achievement Test is used essentially in a criterion-referenced fashion. The critical criterion level is that level of competency that is judged necessary for an entering student to succeed in the course. This use of a particular test as a kind of specific insurance against failure in a key subject gives a critical importance to the use of a test. College faculty members, recognizing that the ability to write clear and correct English is critical for success in college, frequently require the English Composition Test as a means of assessing whether entering students have developed that ability.

Related to this use of the Achievement Tests is the use of test results to indicate that a student has the level of competence in a particular subject that is required by the institution for graduation. Such applications are usually made with respect to a general educational goal and lead to the waiver of a requirement rather than the granting of college credits. For example, students may be allowed to meet a foreign language graduation requirement by achieving a suitable score on one of the foreign language Achievement Tests.

Assisting in Placement. Colleges, recognizing individual differences among their students, offer a variety of courses and place students in these courses on the basis of the level of achievement demonstrated at the time of admission. The College Board Achievement Tests, because they can be administered prior to admission to college, provide a convenient way of developing schedules and assigning students to appropriate classes so that they can begin course work promptly.

The use of Achievement Test scores for placement requires a college to determine a score level appropriate for the placement decision. This determination can be made by a number of methods, differing in their formality. One method, for example, would be for a college to establish an appropriate score level for entry into its third-semester French course by administering the French Achievement Test to students completing the *second*-semester course. The average score achieved by the students in this second-semester course who received a grade of C is then required of entering students wishing to register for the third-semester course.

Improving Prediction. The Achievement Tests can be used, with the SAT and the high school record, to predict academic performance. Some colleges require particular Achievement Tests, most commonly English Composition and Mathematics, judged to be relevant to the requirements of their curriculum. The scores on these required tests may be used to estimate the likelihood of the applicant's success in completing the required course(s) in the particular subject.

Other institutions permit applicants to choose any combination of Achievement Tests. Typically, the average of the several scores is used as a single index, on the assumption that the subjects selected will usually reflect the areas in which a student feels best prepared. The average of the scores provides a measure of the student's performance in areas where motivation and interest are high. Because students frequently select college courses for these same reasons, the average of the Achievement Test scores has proven to be a useful variable in predicting overall college performance.

Based on validity studies conducted for Achievement Test takers who entered college in 1964 through 1981, the average of the Achievement Tests taken correlates .37 with freshman grade point average. For many institutions this average usually makes only a modest addition to the predictive information derived from the combination of the SAT scores and the high school record. The median multiple R between freshman grade point average and the combination of SAT scores and high school grades for this group is .52; with the addition of the Achievement Tests, the multiple R is .55. (See Chapter VIII for more validity data.)

Certain highly selective colleges receive a large number of applicants scoring in the upper ranges of the SAT score scale. Consequently, they find the greater variability in the Achievement Test scores useful in distinguishing among such very able applicants. Any user of Achievement Test scores should be aware that a student's performance on these tests is more dependent on the specific curriculum and learning opportunities of the secondary school attended than is performance on a more general measure of potential such as the SAT.

Historical Background of the Achievement Tests

The College Board Achievement Tests result from a series of adaptations in a program that has been in continuous existence since the first tests were administered in 1901. Although a general overview of the history of the College Board is included in Chapter I, it will be helpful to review here the history pertaining specifically to the Achievement Tests. The College Board was established for the purpose of bringing together schools and colleges with a common concern for establishing sound and uniform practices in the transition from school to college. One of the first actions of the Board was to establish a common set of admission tests to replace the many different sets of tests required by individual colleges.

Originally, the "College Boards," as the tests came to be called, consisted of a series of essay questions for each of the commonly taught college preparatory courses. At that time the tests were seen as providing evidence that students had mastered course content at an acceptable level. Typically, the tests were given at the end of the school year in which courses were taken, and it was assumed that passing grades indicated that necessary credits had been attained. The series of tests, which in some instances extended over the course of a week, were administered in June and graded in July and August; the results were reported to colleges before the opening of the fall session in time for them to notify their applicants of their acceptance or rejection.

Responsibility for constructing the tests was placed with committees of examiners appointed by the College Board, one committee for each test. Originally, "the definition of the requirement in each area was taken from the recommendations of national committees: for example, the requirements

in Latin were based on the recommendations of the American Philological Association; those in French met the demands of the Committee of Twelve of the Modern Language Association; and the requirements in history followed closely the outline submitted by the Committee of Seven of the American Historical Association'' (Fuess 1950, p. 41). To supplement the work of these committees, the Board appointed special commissions to consider developments in secondary school curriculums and their implications for the tests.

It was recognized, however, that major responsibility for the quality of the tests must rest with the examiners. The success of the Board's program depended, finally, not on the statements of national committees about what the tests should be, but rather on the extent to which these qualified committee members were able to produce tests that were recognized by the institutional membership of the Board and the academic community at large as relevant, fair, and effective. Therefore, every effort was made to induce leading educators to accept appointment as examiners and to provide sound subject-matter support. The list of examiners over the years is a testimony to the success of those efforts.

The process has always required, and received, statistical studies and other technical support. Among the early studies were those conducted before 1920 indicating that tests were not strictly equivalent from year to year and that a student's test score might depend to a considerable extent on the year in which the test was taken and on the person who happened to read the paper and assign the grade, rather than simply on the quality of the student's answers. In response to these findings, systematic efforts were made to improve the reliability of the reading and to reduce the variability in test difficulty from year to year. In 1937, to provide tests for scholarship purposes, the College Board contracted with the Cooperative Test Service of the American Council on Education in New York to provide a series of one-hour, multiple-choice achievement tests that could be administered along with the SAT on a single day in April and scored in time to make scholarship awards in May. In the following years, responsibility for constructing the multiple-choice scholarship tests was gradually shifted from the Cooperative Test Service to the College Board committees of examiners, who also prepared the June essay tests.

With the onset of World War II, colleges began operating on a full-year schedule, admitting students to a summer quarter directly from high school. Because of this change and because there were fewer teachers available to read the essay tests, the multiple-choice Achievement Tests were substituted temporarily for the June essay tests. Within a short time, it became clear that the multiple-choice tests were giving admissions officers the information necessary for making their decisions much earlier than had been possible with the essay test program. As a result, the essay tests were not reinstated after the war, and the multiple-choice Achievement Tests were used for admissions and placement as well as the awarding of scholarships.

At the end of World War II, the Admissions Testing Program consisted of a morning session, in which the Scholastic Aptitude Test (Verbal) and a Mathematical Attainment Test were administered, and an afternoon session in which 10 Achievement Tests—English Composition, Social Studies, French, German, Latin, Spanish, Chemistry, Physics, Biology, and Comprehensive Mathematics—and a Spatial Relations aptitude test were administered. The student chose one, two, or three of the one-hour tests according to the requirements of the colleges to which he or she was applying and according to his or her own abilities and training.

Each Achievement Test consisted of questions selected from files or written by the committee of examiners appointed by the College Board. Responsibility for coordination and technical work on the tests rested with the College Board technical staff, who were located in Princeton with the group of specialists in charge of the SAT. All policy decisions and the final approval of each Achievement Test question remained with the respective committee. The technical staff in Princeton formed part of the staff of Educational Testing Service when that organization was founded in 1947; ETS formally began operations on January 1, 1948.

The formation of ETS did not change fundamentally the relationship between the technical staff and the committees of examiners. Examiners continued to have responsibility for the content specifications for the tests and for approving the questions to be included in each new test; the technical staff continued to provide coordinating and editorial services and to prepare and interpret statistical analyses indicating how well each test had met expectations.

The Achievement Tests in Mathematics. In 1947 the Mathematics Attainment Test, a three-level examination from which each candidate elected one level, was eliminated. In its place, the program offered a single mathematical aptitude test, as one part of the morning SAT program, and two one-hour Achievement Tests—an Intermediate Test for students with two and one-half or three years of mathematics and an Advanced Test for students taking a fourth year of mathematics.

The revolution in mathematics education that began during the 1950s led to changes in the Mathematics Achievement Tests in the 1960s. The Committee of Examiners in Mathematics contributed to this revolution by requesting that the College Board set up a special commission to study the mathematics curriculum of the secondary schools and make recommendations for the future. The two-volume *Report of the Commission on Mathematics* (College Board 1959a) included outlines of recommended subject matter for grades 9 through 12, suggestions for the training of elementary and secondary school teachers, and proposed changes in college mathematics. In the appendixes to the report, the commission provided information, instruction, and materials for teachers. Some of the appendixes introduced new ideas and facts; others presented new methods for approaching old topics.

The report received widespread attention among mathematics educators. By 1963, so many changes in educational practices had taken place in the secondary schools that it became necessary to change the pattern of the tests again. The Level I (Standard) Mathematics Achievement Test, appropriate for students following the typical secondary school program, and the Level II (Intensive) Mathematics Achievement Test, appropriate for students in more advanced programs, were offered instead of the Intermediate and Advanced Tests.

The two Achievement Tests have continued to change gradually to reflect changes in the secondary school curriculum. Currently, the Level I test is the principal mathematics Achievement Test for use in college admissions. It is a broad survey test covering content typical of three years of college preparatory mathematics: algebra, plane and coordinate geometry, and an introduction to elementary functions. The Level II test is intended for students with three and one-half years or more of mathematics or those who have had three years of an accelerated or enriched mathematics curriculum. A greater proportion of this test is devoted to trigonometry, elementary functions, and advanced precalculus topics. Due to enriched mathematics curriculums and special programs, such as the Board's Advanced Placement Program in Calculus, more students are now prepared to take the Mathematics Achievement Tests prior to their senior year in high school.

The availability of inexpensive electronic calculators affected the elementary and secondary mathematics curriculum of the late 1970s and raised some concern about the continued relevance of certain topics included in the Mathematics Achievement Tests. (The use of calculators is not permitted at

Achievement Test administrations.) A study was conducted by Braswell and Herman (1980) to assess the impact of the use of hand-held calculators on the performance of students on multiple-choice questions, such as those used in the mathematical sections of the SAT and the Level I Mathematics Achievement Test. The results of the study did not show an appreciable difference between the performance of those students who were permitted to use calculators and those who were not. However, the mathematics committee will continue to monitor the impact of electronic calculators on the mathematics curriculum and student performance so that the tests will reflect current practices. This concern over the impact of calculators on instruction is shared by the committees in chemistry and physics, as well.

The Achievement Tests in Science. For a brief period from 1959 to 1963, a special examination in physics was offered for students who had studied a new secondary school course prepared by the Physical Science Study Committee (PSSC). However, a study using data collected from 1963 to 1967 demonstrated that it was possible for the committee of examiners to develop a test appropriate both for the traditional and the PSSC courses. Subsequently, the Project Physics curriculum was introduced in many secondary schools making it imperative for the test to be appropriate for students following any one of these major curriculums. During the 1960s and 1970s, the use of English units of measurement gradually declined in the physics curriculum; beginning in 1975, new forms of the Physics Achievement Test have used metric units exclusively. Forms constructed since 1978 have used the International System to represent these units.

As in physics, the biology and chemistry committees have been challenged to develop tests appropriate to both the traditional course of study and the curriculum funded by the National Science Foundation. The advent of the three versions of the Biological Sciences Curriculum Study (BSCS) program in biology and the CHEM-Study programs in chemistry, with their emphasis on the inquiry approach, led the committees to give greater emphasis in the tests to the experimental bases for major principles and concepts and to interpreting and drawing conclusions from laboratory data. Environmental concerns have received greater attention on recent forms of the tests, especially in biology, where 15 percent of the questions now relate to ecology.

The Achievement Tests in History and Social Studies. In 1963 the Social Studies Test was replaced by two separate tests, one in American History and Social Studies and another in European History and World Cultures. Each of these tests has continued to evolve to meet the changing nature of social science education in American secondary schools. The American History and Social Studies Achievement Test committee advocated the inclusion of a brief essay in the test; such an essay was administered once in 1971. The subsequent research showed that while the essay contributed to the total score variance of the test, the additional information was minimal in comparison to the pool of information about the student available from other sources. Consequently, the essay was discontinued.

The committee for the American History and Social Studies Test has attempted to recognize the increased use of the "inquiry" or "discovery" approach in the teaching of history by including items in the test that emphasize the understanding of data or evidence, an appraisal of its relevance and reliability, and its usefulness in evaluating hypotheses. Ideally, such items test both inquiry skills and a knowledge of history. The committee has also sought to expand the emphasis on social science concepts, particularly those that are encountered in the study of history.

The European History and World Cultures Achievement Test committee has gone through a parallel experience in trying to recognize the inquiry approach. A more noticeable change has been a de-emphasis on European history following the discovery that a majority of the students have taken world civilization courses.

The Achievement Tests in English. The history of the English Composition Test since World War II is the search for a balance between the use of direct measures of writing, with their inherent problems of achieving reliable scoring, and the use of indirect measures that can be scored reliably and economically. Early forms of the test consisted of a single essay written on an assigned topic. When it proved impossible to read such a test with an acceptable degree of reliability, modifications were tried in subsequent forms. However, a form of the test made up of three 20-minute essays and one made up of four 15-minute essays proved as difficult to score reliably as the single essay; therefore, efforts were made to develop ways of assessing writing that could be scored more reliably. Between 1945 and 1960 numerous multiple-choice and free-response types of questions were developed. These new item types produced scores of acceptable reliability, and most were demonstrated to have acceptable degrees of relationship to grades in English composition courses. Of particular interest was the "interlinear exercise," a free-response exercise that required students to edit (between widely spaced printed lines of text) an expository passage in which certain types of errors were intentionally embedded. The rationale for this exercise was that it placed students in a situation similar to the one they would be in when trying to edit first drafts of their own writing. Although the interlinear exercise could be scored with a high degree of reliability, it proved quite difficult for the average student.

During the 1950s the typical English Composition Test consisted of three completely multiple-choice sections or two multiple-choice sections and one interlinear section. Meanwhile, in response to the urging of those who felt that such indirect approaches to the measurement of writing ability were unacceptable, the College Board continued its efforts to develop acceptable essay tests. An experimental General Composition Test was administered for three years beginning in 1954, but proved no more satisfactory than the essay tests of the 1940s. By 1960, an hour-long Writing Sample on an assigned topic, copies of which were transmitted directly to the designated colleges for them to score and use at will, was competing with the English Composition Test for the students' time. The Writing Sample continued in the program until 1968 when it was discontinued because few colleges were using it.

In 1966 a study by Godshalk, Swineford, and Coffman demonstrated that an English Composition Test made up of a single short essay, read holistically and independently by three different readers, and two multiple-choice sections would produce scores that were both reliable and valid. The criterion for validity was a complex sample of actual writing. At the same time, the study produced evidence that the one-hour examination consisting of only multiple-choice items or combined multiple-choice and interlinear sections also provided reliable and valid information about the students who took the English Composition Test.

From 1963 until 1971, at least one administration a year offered a form of the English Composition Test that included a 20-minute essay. Supported by the validity data of Godshalk, et al., other forms used only multiple-choice items. In 1971, the College Board, in an effort to control costs, eliminated the essay component because of the expense involved in having each essay scored by three different readers. During the ensuing years, English teachers, working through committees of the College Board, pressed for the reinstatement of the essay component. As the writing crisis became a major concern in American education, the College Board responded by introducing the 20-minute essay once

again in December 1977, in order to signal the importance of writing in the secondary curriculum. The enormous expense of achieving reliable scoring continues to limit the inclusion of the essay component to one administration annually. Test forms that are entirely in a multiple-choice format are used at all other administrations.

Choosing essay topics for the December administrations of the English Composition Test is a difficult task because all students at one administration must write on a single topic. The topic must be one that is accessible to all students, regardless of their race, sex, or socioeconomic, educational, or regional background. In addition, it must be a topic that they can react to and begin writing about almost immediately.

Each year, a number of potential topics are pretested for use in future administrations. The essay pretests are administered to samples of college students enrolled in composition courses. The faculty committee responsible for the English Composition Test, assisted by a number of other experienced teachers, read the pretest essays and identify those topics to which students can respond readily and in a variety of ways and that allow different students to argue for different points of view.

The essays written for the English Composition Test are scored holistically; that is, they are read for the total impression they make on the reader. This total impression is created by every aspect of the essay; spelling, punctuation, organization, choice of words, and the host of other characteristics of writing are all considered. Readers are instructed to read the essays quickly and to score immediately while their impression of the total essay remains fresh. Further, the reader who scores holistically is encouraged to look at what students have done well rather than at what they have failed to do. The scorer does not mark a paper for errors.

Each essay is scored on a scale from 1 to 4, by each of two readers. (Actually, it is 0-4, since 0 is available to describe an unratable, off-topic essay). If these two readers disagree by 2 or more points, the essay receives a third reading, and the most discrepant score of the three is dropped. This system was introduced in 1978 after an initial year of evaluation based on a system that called for three ratings of all essays. The essay score is the sum of the two reading scores used. Reader reliability is determined by applying the Spearman-Brown formula to the observed correlation between the two reading scores that are used. The process of scoring the essay has been described in detail by Conlan (1978) and by Kirrie (1979).

The reliability of the English Composition Test with Essay is not reported as a specific value, but is estimated to be within a range, typically from .85-.90. To obtain this range, the score reliability for the total test is computed twice, once using a lower bound estimate of the *essay* reading reliability and once using an upper bound estimate of this reliability. The lower bound estimate of essay score reliability is based on an empirically determined value for essay grading reliability (.45) derived from the multiessay, multireader experiment reported by Godshalk, Swineford, and Coffman (1966). The upper bound is based on the reader reliability derived as described above, using data from the actual test administration. Typically, the upper bound estimates for essay reading reliability are .70-.71.

In 1959 the College Board appointed a Commission on English. The report of the commission, *Freedom and Discipline in English* (College Board 1965b), analyzed the conditions and practices of English teaching in America's secondary schools; made specific recommendations for the improvement of English instruction in the areas of teacher preparation, teaching conditions, curriculum, language, literature, and composition; and advised English teachers, curriculum planners, and supervisors on the basic approaches and methods necessary to accomplish the best possible teaching.

A report of such wide scope inevitably had an influence on the testing program of the Board, if only indirectly through its influence on teaching practices. At the May 1968 administration of the Achievement Tests, a test in literature was offered for the first time since 1941. This test, now administered regularly, does not assume that students have read particular works; rather, it assesses their ability to analyze a given literary text closely. The passages in the test are drawn from a variety of historical periods and literary genres.

The Achievement Tests in Foreign Languages. There has been great ferment in recent years in the areas of modern foreign languages, and that ferment has been reflected in the College Board Achievement Tests. In 1957, recognizing the need to examine listening skills as well as reading skills in modern foreign languages, the Board authorized a supplementary program that permitted schools to offer their students 30-minute listening comprehension tests in French, German, and Spanish. Tests of listening comprehension in Russian and in Italian and a reading test in Italian were subsequently offered in the Supplementary Achievement Test Program.

From 1971 to 1973, the Achievement Tests in French, German, Italian, Russian, and Spanish included both reading and listening components. Financial concerns led the College Board to revert to reading-only examinations in 1974 and to discontinue Italian entirely. The Russian reading examination continued in the program until May 1982.

The 1970s have seen an increase in the number of Hispanic students in Spanish classes and in the Spanish Achievement Test population. The Spanish committee of examiners has responded to the growing awareness of the differences of language and culture among the Hispanic groups in the United States by including reading comprehension passages drawn from the experience of the several Hispanic groups and by avoiding areas of the language that are in flux or that have variation in acceptable usage among the groups.

In 1979, a substantially revised Latin Achievement Test was introduced in response to concerns expressed by Latin teachers. These teachers felt that the older forms neither reflected contemporary Latin curriculums nor were appropriate for second-year students. The old version involved only questions based on unedited Latin passages. In the new version, the Latin passages have been edited, and discrete questions (questions that are not attached to any passage) have been added. The discrete questions require the student to translate from Latin to English; to determine the Latin original of an English derivative; to identify the correct grammatical form of a Latin word; to choose a Latin word, phrase, or clause that is closest in meaning to another; and to complete Latin sentences.

Publication of Achievement Tests

In 1983, in an effort to make more information about the Achievement Tests available to teachers, students, and others interested in the subject areas, the Board published a book containing a recent form of each test: *The College Board Achievement Tests: 14 Tests in 13 Subjects* (1983b). This publication, sold through both the ATP and commercial bookstores, includes not only the tests, but the test specifications, a discussion of the types of items used, an explanation of a number of sample items, and information about student performance on each item in the published test. All students registering to take the Achievement Tests continue to receive the free publication, *About the Achievement Tests* (1983a), that contains a description of each test and sample questions.

Development of the Achievement Tests

The preparation of a form of the Achievement Tests begins long before the actual administration, typically two years earlier. More than one new form of each test is usually being developed simultaneously. The pattern, therefore, is one of overlapping cycles, so that material being pretested for future years will be considered by an Achievement Test committee at the same meeting that the final draft of another test form is being reviewed prior to administration. Further, the results of the analyses of past forms are not only evaluations of those forms but the foundation for changes in future forms.

The processes, therefore, do not have a simple sequence of steps; there are interactions among the various activities and a need to keep the entire process sensitive to and articulated with the instructional programs in the schools. Accordingly, while the outline provided here is the principal logical sequence, it is considerably more complex than can be suggested. The development of tests in particular subject-matter fields may involve variants of the general steps described below; every test, however, must be developed in accord with procedural guidelines that have been established to assure compliance with the *ETS Standards for Quality and Fairness* (Educational Testing Service 1983), a basic statement of policies and principles governing the conduct of Educational Testing Service's activities.

The Committee System. Central to the development of the College Board Achievement Tests is the committee system. This system is based on the assumption that a representative committee of competent school and college teachers can oversee the construction of a single test (or in the case of mathematics, two tests) that will be appropriate for assessing the achievement of students who have been taught courses based on different textbooks with different emphases. These committees are the basic authority for the many subject-matter decisions in the test construction process. They bring to this task a fundamental knowledge of the curriculums, textbooks, and instructional methods in their fields, and, what is most important, a knowledge of the abilities and skills that are critical and how these might be demonstrated by the students. Committee members, who are appointed by and responsible to the College Board, work closely with members of the test development staff of Educational Testing Service in planning, developing, and approving new forms of the Achievement Tests.

The College Board in its charge to new committee members has defined the responsibilities of the Achievement Test committees as follows:

1. to specify the content, ability, and other dimensions to be used in developing the examination or examinations within the committee's purview.

2. to review all items proposed for use, to attest to their subject-matter relevance and accuracy, and to remove anything extrinsic to the characteristics, skills, or knowledge to be measured.

3. to review and approve each form of the examination before its initial administration, certifying its adherence to the specifications established for it.

4. to review all examination-related materials designed for those using or affected by the examination(s), to determine that such material fairly and accurately represents the forms of the examination currently administered.

5. to participate on occasion in efforts to inform other teachers about the examination(s);

6. to recommend research, validity studies, curriculum surveys, or other information-gathering activities aimed at improving the quality and usefulness of the examination(s).

Central among these responsibilities are the definition of a test that is appropriate to the national population that takes it and the critical review to ensure that the actual test matches this definition.

Because of the importance of these responsibilities, great care is given to the selection and appointment of each committee member. The first requirement for each committee member is that he or she be expert in the subject matter and experienced in teaching it at the secondary school or undergraduate level. Nominations for possible committee appointment are solicited from appropriate professional organizations and from members of the College Board regional staff who are in close contact with teaching institutions. Other potential committee members may be identified among participants in professional meetings or from teachers who have been involved in other College Board activities.

In addition to strong subject-matter competence, committee members must be well informed on recent trends in curriculum and preferred instructional strategies. Committee members must be skilled in working in small groups and willing to argue their judgments and perceptions with their colleagues on the committee while striving to produce a well-constructed test.

A second set of criteria for selecting committee members involves the goal of representativeness. The programs of the College Board are national in scope and there is a need to represent the variety of viewpoints that exist in American education. Diversity among committee members is critical to the appropriateness of the test for students from widely varying schools and curriculums and to the fairness of the test for students from different social and racial backgrounds. To provide balance within a committee, a variety of characteristics are considered.

Members with different specialities within the subject area, including experience with different curriculums, are included. Committee members are drawn from institutions with different characteristics; both secondary and collegiate institutions from the public and private sectors should be included. The size of the committee member's institution, its geographical location, and its membership in the College Board are also factors considered in assembling a representative committee.

Because of the commitment of the College Board and Educational Testing Service to equal opportunity for all people, high priority has been given during the last decade to the inclusion of women and racial minorities on the committees. This has been important both to the goal of representativeness of the committees and to aid in the broader social goal of breaking the stereotypes associated with particular subject fields, as for example, physics as a male domain.

Because only five or six members serve on any one committee, these expectations with respect to diversity are not realized in the composition of each committee every year. However, within each committee over time and across the several Achievement Test committees each year, the varied perspectives are well represented. The choice of each committee member represents a combination of the considerations described above. Thus, for example, the committee in chemistry might include a chairman who teaches in a major public university in the Southeast. His large freshman chemistry courses provide contact with a heterogeneous student body; he is also the author of a widely used exercise book in general chemistry. A second member might teach in a highly selective liberal arts college in the Midwest and be very active in the Division of Chemical Education of the American Chemical Society. A third member might be a high school teacher in the Southwest where she is very active in the regional activities of the College Board. A young, black chemist from a major urban public university in the Northwest might be the fourth member. As an active researcher, she might bring particular experience in teaching chemistry to students who enter the university with inadequate preparation. The fifth member might be the chairman of the science department of a public high school in the Northeast. Active in the National Science Teachers Association, he has served on the advisory board for its journal and has adapted curricular materials for use in secondary schools in West Africa. Such a committee, while not guaranteeing that all points of view are represented, does bring diverse training and experience to the development of a nationally useful examination. Some

indication of the diversity of the composition of the various committees is suggested by Figure 5.1, which is reproduced from the ATP booklet, *About the Achievement Tests* (1983a). The broad sampling of men and women, universities, colleges, high schools, and geographical regions is evident.

Changes in the membership of the committee occur annually with the rotation of one or two experienced members and the appointment of new members. Continuity of membership is needed to provide stability in the nature of the test and to ensure having experienced members throughout the development cycle. At the same time, however, there is a need to provide a steady infusion of new ideas and perspectives. Members typically serve three or four years. The chairman, chosen from among experienced committee members, may serve an additional two or three years in that role.

Each test committee has responsibility for a specific subject-matter test within the Admissions Testing Program. Some problems within a broad discipline area, such as mathematics or foreign language, are shared by the committees working on related tests within the field. There are certain common features of foreign language testing, for example, that make it necessary to coordinate the approach to language examinations. Consequently, the College Board has established Academic Advisory Committees in those broad areas in which more than one of the College Board programs offer a test: the Arts, English, Foreign Languages, History, Mathematical Sciences, and Science. These Advisory Committees advise the College Board on the interrelationship among its several tests in the subject and on the appropriateness of these tests to the curriculums and course patterns commonly found in secondary schools, colleges, and universities. In addition, these Advisory Committees provide a liaison between the College Board and members of their discipline. The Advisory Committees provide an additional mechanism for ensuring that the Achievement Tests are firmly set in the context of contemporary teaching practice in the field.

The ETS Test Development Specialist. Working closely with the committee and assuming responsibility for coordinating the work between meetings of the committee are the test development specialists of Educational Testing Service. The test development staff members are themselves subject-matter specialists holding advanced degrees in the appropriate areas. Typically, they have been teachers of the subject prior to joining the staff at ETS.

The specialist serves numerous functions for the College Board and the committee. Essentially, he or

Figure 5.1

College Board Achievement Test Development Committees, 1982-83

American History and Social Studies

Clayborne Carson, Stanford University, *Chairperson;* Estelle Feinstein, University of Connecticut – Stamford Campus; Jonathan Harris, Paul D. Schreiber High School, Port Washington, New York; Peyton McCrary, University of South Alabama; Fay D. Metcalf, Boulder High School, Boulder, Colorado

Biology

Anna R. Brummett, Oberlin College, *Chairperson;* Kendall Corbin, University of Minnesota; Stuart W. Hughes, Central High School, Philadelphia, Pennsylvania; Rena T. Jones, Spelman College; John W. Kimball, Tufts University; Joann M. Meyer, Dulles High School, Stafford, Texas; Cherry Sprague, Princeton High School, Princeton, New Jersey

Chemistry

Martin N. Ackermann, Oberlin College, *Chairperson;* Richard L. Humphrey, Harvard School, North Hollywood, California; Nancy H. Kolodny, Wellesley College; Edward K. Mellon, Florida State University; Michael A. Saltman, Bronxville School System, Bronxville, New York

English Composition

Roger K. Applebee, University of Illinois at Urbana-Champaign, *Chairperson;* Scott Baird, Trinity University; Ann L. Keenan, Braintree Public Schools, Braintree, Massachusetts; Ralph F. Voss, University of Alabama; Jacqueline W. White, Berkeley High School, Berkeley, California

European History and World Cultures

Paul W. Knoll, University of Southern California, *Chairperson;* Earl Clemens, The Fieldston School, Bronx, New York; E. Daniel Eckberg, Lindbergh High School, Hopkins, Minnesota; Jayne B. Williamson, Northeastern University

French

Jean Leblon, Vanderbilt University, *Chairperson;* Lucien R. Bosivert, Hamden High School, Hamden, Connecticut; Claire L. Gaudiani, University of Pennsylvania; André Maman, Princeton University; Frankie W. McCullough, West Side High School, Gary, Indiana

German

Kathy A. Harms, Northwestern University, *Chair-person;* Hans-Dieter Brueckner, Pomona College; D. Victoria Ellis, Princeton High School, Princeton, New Jersey; James R. McIntyre, Colby College; Alan L. Stiegemeier, Quincy Public Schools, Quincy, Illinois

Hebrew

Joshua Bakst, Ramaz Upper School, New York, New York; Edna Grad, Northwestern University; Paula Jacobs, Hebrew College; Samuel Schneider, Yeshiva University

Latin

Edwin S. Ramage, Indiana University, *Chairperson;* Rita M. Fleischer, Graduate Center, City University of New York; Glenn M. Knudsvig, The University of Michigan; Wade C. Stephens, The Lawrenceville School, Lawrenceville, New Jersey; Lura A. Wallace, Gardena High School, Gardena, California

Literature

Charles H. Long, Yale University, *Chairperson;* Thomas R. Arp, Southern Methodist University; Ann L. Hayes, Carnegie-Mellon University; Sandra Carter Jackson, Oakland Public Schools, Oakland, California; Richard D. S. Rickard, University School, Hunting Valley, Ohio

Mathematics

George W. Best, Phillips Academy, Andover, Massachusetts, *Chairperson;* Floyd L. Downs, Hillsdale High School, San Mateo, California; Richard M. Koch, University of Oregon; Jane Cronin Scanlon, Rutgers University; R. O. Wells Jr., Rice University

Physics

Gerald F. Wheeler, Montana State University, *Chairperson;* James C. Davenport, Virginia State University; William S. Dougall, Lakeside School, Seattle, Washington; Arnold Strassenburg, State University of New York at Stony Brook; Lora W. Wilhite, Carlinville High School, Carlinville, Illinois

Spanish

Carlos A. Solé, University of Texas at Austin, *Chairperson;* Mary C. Colín, Evanston Township High School, Evanston, Illinois; Alfred Ellis, Hillcrest High School, Jamaica, New York; Carmen Salazar Parr, Los Angeles Valley College; Roberto A. Véguez, Middlebury College

she is responsible for providing the committee with access to the resources and services of ETS. In addition to the test specialist's own knowledge of educational practice and assessment strategies in the subject field, these resources include other staff with expertise in measurement, printing, distributing, arranging pretest administrations of all new items, and preparing detailed statistical analyses of the pretests and the final tests.

The test development specialist assigned to the test also serves the committee as the nexus in a complex series of communications that must occur between meetings. At the regular meetings of each Achievement Test committee, time is reserved for those activities that benefit most from general discussion, that is, revising the specifications to reflect changing curricular trends, reviewing and approving the final form of a test, and reviewing pretests. The test development staff facilitates and coordinates other committee activities between meetings, such as reviewing and critiquing new items or reviewing publications pertaining to the test.

The committee and the test development staff have complementary roles. The committee, as the group appointed by the College Board, is responsible for the subject-matter accuracy and relevance of the test and for ensuring its appropriateness to the broad scope of American secondary school curriculums in that subject. The test development staff facilitate the work of the committee and are responsible for organizing the ETS resources to produce a test with the desired content validity as well as the best possible measurement characteristics obtainable within the broad constraints set by the nature of the Admissions Testing Program.

Planning the Achievement Tests. There are three general program constraints upon an Achievement Test committee: the test's time limit, the rate at which test specifications may change, and the budgetary implications of the testing process.

Each test is one hour in length, permitting a student to take three tests in a half-day administration. A student wishing to take more than three tests must register for and attend more than one administration. Having a common time allowance for the test also facilitates the test administration; students in the same room may work on different tests at the same time.

Test specifications change, but only gradually. Forms administered within a few months of each other must be very similar and yield comparable scaled scores. This is necessary because students who take the tests at adjacent administrations are likely to be compared with each other by a college during the admissions decision process. A score on the Chemistry Achievement Test taken in December should mean the same thing as a score earned on a different form given the following May. Such comparability is desirable even for administrations that are somewhat more than a year apart. Whenever scores derived from different forms of Achievement Tests in the same subject-matter discipline are likely to be compared, the various forms must be highly similar.

This constraint is counterbalanced, however, by the committee's responsibility for keeping the test closely related to the curriculums of the schools. As curriculums change, the content of the test must reflect these changes. Accordingly, while tests in successive years follow very much the same specifications, marked changes may be observed between two forms developed some years apart.

If a committee feels the need to change a test at a faster pace, a number of groups will be consulted, including the College Board and ETS staff, the standing committees that advise the Board, and, on some issues, the voting representatives of member schools and colleges. The cost of implementing a proposed modification is an important factor, and these costs must be carefully reviewed by Board staff. An example of one such costly change was the reintroduction of the 20-minute essay in the English Composition Test. The implementation of test changes with major budgetary implications are not within the discretion of the subject-matter committee. Rather, changes tend to originate with committees but must be processed through the College Board's policy-making structure.

Content and Ability Specifications. Within these general program constraints, however, important questions remain: what is to be tested and how it should be tested. The committees' decisions regarding these questions are expressed in the form of content and ability specifications for the test. The specifications are the blueprint for the test. They guide the development of a sound and useful test and are the outcome of extensive information gathering, deliberation, compromise, and decision. Specifications provide the framework within which the test development process can operate, and as such, they are the logical starting point in the work. Most Achievement Test committees, in practice, update already existing specifications; they rarely create them anew.

Content and ability specifications may be conceptualized as a grid, with content categories along one dimension and ability categories along the other. The first step is to establish the appropriate categories for each dimension and the defining characteristics for each. The second step is to decide the relative emphasis to be given each content or ability category.

The decision of which item type(s) to use is related to the decisions about the content and abilities to be measured. Although the tests are all multiple-choice (with the exception of some editions of the English Composition Test), there are important variations within this format, and decisions about the item type(s) to use may have important consequences for the test. For example, questions that are not complete within themselves, but depend upon a separate stimulus—such as a reading passage, a graph, or picture—may take more time, and fewer of them can be used within the time allowed. Alternatively, a format that has a limited set of common responses may provide a way of increasing the number of questions. Other decisions about item type are related to the cognitive skills or content that the committee believes to be tapped by a particular kind of exercise; for example, one item type might lend itself to testing control of grammatical structures and another might be more appropriate for measuring logical relationships. Or, as in the English Composition Test, there may be variations in the kinds of items that measure language usage: one type may require the identification of faulty diction; another may require the choice of a more efficient structural element. Because different item types vary with regard to the time a student needs to respond, the choice of item type determines the number of questions that can be asked within the one-hour limit.

Although the content and ability specifications are conceptualized as a grid, in practice most committees assign frequencies separately to the two dimensions. In effect, the frequencies reflect the relative importance that the committee attaches to each category. This is based on the committee's understanding of current curricular emphases in the wide generality of American secondary schools. Every few years the committee's perceptions may be supplemented by a survey of secondary school teachers of the subject and/or a detailed analysis of the most commonly used textbooks in the field. These latter activities would, typically, be done on the committee's behalf by the ETS test development specialist assigned to the test.

A committee always has a set of specifications in effect at any given time. A typical example is the 1983 outline for the Chemistry Achievement Test presented in Figure 5.2. The specifications are for a test of 85 items distributed over 12 content categories and 3 skills categories. Content specifications for each of the tests are presented in *The College Board Achievement Tests: 14 Tests in 13 Subjects* (1983b).

Statistical Specifications. The specifications for a test include more than a plan for sampling content and abilities or choosing item types. In addition, there are statistical specifications that ensure that the test will be appropriate in difficulty for measuring the knowledge and skills of the students who take the test. The quality of information derived from a test is a function of its statistical properties. If all the students who take a test receive the same score, there is no differentiation among them, and, hence, no information of use to an admissions or placement officer. There is a need to consider the score distribution carefully and to plan a test that will yield useful information across the full range of reported scores.

A member of the statistical analysis staff at ETS works with the test development staff member and the test committee to develop statistical specifications that must be met if the test is to be appropriate to the test-taking group. Table 5.1 presents the sta-

Figure 5.2

ATP Chemistry Achievement Test Content Specifications

Topics Covered	Approximate Percentage of Test
Atomic Theory and Structure, including periodic relationships	14
Chemical Bonding and Molecular Structure	10
States of Matter and Kinetic Molecular Theory	9
Solutions, including concentration units, solubility and colligative properties	6
Acids and Bases	9
Oxidation-reduction and Electrochemistry	8
Stoichiometry	10
Reaction Rates	2
Equilibrium	5
Thermodynamics, including energy changes in chemical reactions, randomness, and criteria for spontaneity	4
Descriptive Chemistry: physical and chemical properties of elements and their more familiar compounds, including simple examples from organic chemistry; periodic properties	16
Laboratory: equipment, procedures, observations, safety, calculations, and interpretation of results	7
	100

NOTE: Every edition contains approximately five questions on equation balancing and/or predicting products of chemical reactions. These are distributed among the various content categories.

Skills Specifications	Approximate Percentage of Test
Level I: Essentially Recall—remembering information and understanding facts	30
Level II: Essentially Application—applying knowledge to unfamiliar and/or practical situations; solving mathematical problems	55
Level III: Essentially Interpretation—inferring and deducing from available data and integrating information to form conclusions	15

tistical specifications current in 1982-83. Thus, in assembling the test, the committee and test development staff must choose items whose statistical characteristics will, in aggregate, provide a test with the desired statistical characteristics. Information about the statistical characteristics of each Achievement Test item is obtained through a special pretest administration of all new items. The results of the pretesting are summarized in an analysis of each item that is used by the test development staff and the committee in assembling a test that has both the desired content coverage and the desired statistical characteristics. A detailed description of item analysis is presented in Chapter II.

A constraint on the assembly of any test is the need to provide for the score equating procedures.

Table 5.1

Statistical Specifications for Each Achievement Test in 1982-83

Test	Number of Items	Mean Equated Δ*	Standard Deviation Δ	Mean r_{bis}	Number of Options
English Composition	90	12.0	2.4	.45	5
Literature	60	12.3	2.0	.45	5
French	85-90	11.7	3.1	.50	4
German	80-90	11.7	2.9	.54	4
Hebrew	90	12.5	3.0	.54	5
Latin	70-75	11.2	2.8	.46	4
Spanish	85-90	11.5	2.8	.48	4
American History and Social Studies	95-100	11.5	2.2	.44	5
European History and World Cultures	95-100	12.0	2.0	.47	5
Mathematics Level I	50	13.2	3.0	.50	5
Mathematics Level II	50	15.2	2.2	.48	5
Biology	95-100	13.0	2.2	.40	5
Chemistry	85-90	13.0	2.0	.46	5
Physics	75	14.0	2.2	.48	5

*Delta is the index of item difficulty. See Chapter II for further information.

These procedures, also described in Chapter II, make it possible to determine scaled score equivalents for the raw scores of any form of a test. The equating process adjusts for the minor differences among several forms of each test. In order to carry out score equating for the Achievement Tests, each test committee must include a set of questions carefully selected from a previous form.

Item Generation. Because the specifications impose a number of restrictions on the tests, the pool of items from which a test is assembled must be somewhat larger than the test itself. It is useful to have a pool of usable items that is at least one and one-half times the number of items in a given form. Because pretesting eliminates weak or ambiguous items, it is usually necessary to pretest at least twice as many test questions as will be needed in a given final form.

Although there is variation among the subjects, the typical pattern is for committee members to write some draft questions and the ETS subject-matter specialist to contribute others. In addition, other teachers in the field may serve as outside item writers. The committee members and the outside writers receive instruction from the ETS test development specialist in proven techniques of writing high quality items. Item writing assignments are made in view of the test specifications and with consideration of each person's area of expertise within the subject field. In order to avoid student confusion, certain editorial and stylistic constraints are imposed on the items, and it is the responsibility of the ETS test de-

velopment specialist to ensure that the items conform to these standards.

Even though pretesting reveals much about individual questions, the main approach to ensuring item quality is the test specialist and committee review process. Typically, the new items are reproduced and distributed by mail for committee members to review. The judgments and suggestions for revisions may be discussed at a committee meeting or collected by mail. The committee may discard an item as inappropriate for the test or return it to the writer or ETS staff for revision. The committee then approves the item in either its original or revised form for inclusion in a pretest.

Pretesting. Pretesting is a means of checking the quality of individual items and determining the statistical characteristics of the item. To obtain useful information, the items must be administered to a sample of students representative of the target population of the testing program. In the case of the Achievement Tests, pretests are administered in introductory college courses where the students are expected to have subject-matter preparation equivalent to that assumed in the test specifications. The pretesting depends on the cooperation of college teachers and students; on occasion, the sample of students participating in the pretesting is not as representative of the target population as is desirable. If the deviation is particularly pronounced, an additional pretest sample may have to be obtained.

Following the pretest administration, the answer

sheets are scanned and item analyses prepared. The resulting indexes are used by the test specialist to choose a set of items for the final form that will meet the statistical specifications.

Pretesting provides other information to the test specialist and the committee. The pattern of responses may indicate that the wording of the item is ambiguous, or that the best prepared students chose an option that was intended to be a distracter or foil. This information helps the test specialist decide whether to revise the item or discard it.

Assembly of New Forms. The establishment of specifications, the process of item writing and review, and the pretesting and subsequent item analysis create a pool of material that can be used to prepare a new form of the test. To save time at the meeting of the committee, the initial selection of a set of items that meets the specifications is made by the test development specialist, who sends this draft test to the committee members before the meeting. In reviewing this draft test, the committee members continue to examine the merits of the individual questions, even though they are the product of considerable review and have survived the rigors of pretesting. They also focus on the test as a whole; the test must have a coherence and internal consistency that furthers its fundamental purpose of providing a broad-gauge assessment in the field, and it must avoid redundancy or overlap. Sometimes, for example, one of two questions must be excluded from a given form because, while each is independently appropriate, one provides information that will assist in answering the other. Such interconnections may be subtle, and only when the entire draft test is assembled will they be revealed.

After a thorough discussion at the committee meeting, including the possible substitution of other pretested items for some of those chosen by the ETS test specialist, the committee approves the test. The committee's approval indicates that it meets the specifications set for it, that each item is appropriate and unambiguous, and that the test as a whole is a suitable measure of secondary school achievement in the subject.

The committee's approval must be given eight or nine months before the initial administration of that form of the test to permit adequate time for the complex production process. The length and complexity of the production process are the result of a series of quality assurance checks ensuring that the draft test approved by the committee is accurately transformed into a printed test book. Another subject-matter specialist of the ETS test development staff will review the test in great detail, looking for ambi-

guities that may have eluded committee review and pretesting, suggesting ways of clarifying the intent of particular items, independently ''keying'' the test and then checking his or her choice of answers against those recorded for the draft test. This provides a further check on the clarity of each item and protection against clerical errors in noting the keyed response or in failing to change the key when an item has been revised.

Each test is also reviewed by one of a number of specially trained ETS staff members to be sure that the test does not contain inappropriate or offensive material about women or members of minority groups, and to be sure that those tests referring to people contain a balance of references to men and women and to minority as well as majority persons.

Each test is edited by one of several test editors whose task is to ensure that the test follows the accepted ETS style. A member of the test development staff then ''takes'' the test and checks his or her answers against the established key to be sure that the key did not change as a result of any revisions during the several review and production steps. The primary responsibility for this postcommittee work is vested in the test development specialist, who works closely and continuously with test development colleagues, test editors, and the production staff. A proof of the test is then sent to the committee for one final review before it is printed. Any committee revisions that are incorporated into the test are then checked, as is the final key.

The final step in the process, from the standpoint of the committee, is the beginning of the next cycle when they receive feedback, occasionally in the form of letters from test center supervisors or students, but most often from the test analysis by ETS statisticians. This is the final evaluation of how well the test met established standards: its score distribution, its overall difficulty, the shape of its score distribution, its reliability, the evidence that most students could complete it within the allotted time, and so forth. This evaluation helps the committee determine whether modifications are needed in their plans for subsequent forms of the test. Table 5.2 presents statistics for a typical form of each of the Achievement Tests. A comparison of the values presented in this table, obtained when each test form was first administered, with the specified values (Table 5.1) for the mean and standard deviation of delta and the mean r_{bis} indicates a reasonably high degree of success in achieving the desired statistical characteristics for the several Achievement Tests. Those small variations from the statistical specifications that do occur are a result of giving priority to meeting the content specifications in situations where the pool of avail-

Table 5.2

Selected Test and Item Statistics for the Achievement Tests

Test	Analysis Sample N	Mean Equated Δ*	Standard Deviation Equated Δ	Mean r_bis	Reliability Coefficient	Scaled Standard Error of Measurement	Percentage Completing Test
English Composition (June 1982)	2,055	12.4	2.4	.45	.916	29.0	74.3
Literature (December 1982)	2,845	12.2	2.2	.48	.888	34.5	86.7
French (December 1982)	555†	11.8	3.1	.44	.900	31.3	79.5
German (May 1983)	315†	11.8	2.3	.62	.949	24.6	82.2
Hebrew (December 1982)	130	12.4	3.1	.57	.945	23.8	64.6
Latin (December 1982)	415‡	11.2	2.4	.52	.918	27.8	77.6
Spanish (May 1983)	415†	11.7	2.9	.58	.948	22.8	65.3
American History and Social Studies (December 1982)	2,470	11.7	2.1	.41	.899	31.5	69.1
European History and World Cultures (May 1983)	745	12.1	3.1	.44	.916	32.5	70.9
Mathematics I (May 1983)	2,290	13.8	3.1	.53	.884	33.6	64.8
Mathematics II (December 1982)	2,075	15.1	2.0	.49	.861	31.9	55.6
Biology (June 1983)	2,125	13.4	2.1	.44	.919	29.8	72.8
Chemistry (December 1982)	2,520	13.6	2.1	.45	.909	30.7	40.6
Physics (May 1983)	1,065	14.2	2.1	.50	.919	26.7	80.5

* Delta is the index of item difficulty. See Chapter II for further information.

† Sample does not include French, German, or Spanish students with less than two years of training, nor those test takers who failed to respond to the questionnaire or whose knowledge of the language did not come primarily from courses taken in grades 9 through 12.

‡ Sample does not include Latin students with only one year of training, nor those language students who failed to respond to the background questionnaire or who indicated they had learned the language outside of school.

able items does not permit the test assembler to meet both the content and the statistical specifications in every detail.

The last three columns of Table 5.2 present additional information about the psychometric properties of each test. The reliability coefficient is the Dressel adaptation of Kuder-Richardson (20). The standard error of measurement is reported in terms of the 200-to-800 score scale used in the Admissions Testing Program. As one index of speededness, the percentage of students completing each test is reported in the last column. The figures suggest that some of these forms were slightly speeded for the group of students who took them in the designated administration.

Table 5.3 (page 100) gives further information about the samples of students used in generating the test statistics in Table 5.2. The mean and standard deviation of the raw score distribution for each analysis sample is shown along with the mean and standard deviation of the distribution of scores converted to the ATP 200-to-800 score scale. Each correct answer counts one point toward the raw score. Omitted questions do not count toward the score. For each wrong answer, a fraction of a point is subtracted to adjust for random guessing. For five-choice questions, one-fourth of a point is subtracted for each wrong response; for four-choice questions, one-third of a point is subtracted.

Beyond the type of information provided by the test statistics, each committee is very interested in the number of students who have taken their test in the last year, how well those students performed on the test, and the academic calibre (as measured by

Table 5.3

Summary Statistics for Achievement Tests Analysis Samples

	Analysis Sample N	Number of Items	Raw Score		Scaled Score	
			Mean	Standard Deviation	Mean	Standard Deviation
English Composition (June 1982)	2,055	90	43.39	17.06	529	100
Literature (December 1982)	2,845	60	29.87	12.36	523	103
French (December 1982)	555†	85	32.84	15.59	513	98
German (May 1983)	315†	80	42.39	19.99	535	109
Hebrew (December 1982)	130	90	42.88	19.12	607	101
Latin (December 1982)	415‡	73	33.26	16.42	537	97
Spanish (May 1983)	415†	88	39.27	21.74	520	101
American History and Social Studies (December 1982)	2,470	95	39.38	16.20	503	99
European History and World Cultures (May 1983)	745	100	43.13	17.94	545	112
Mathematics I (May 1983)	2,290	50	23.00	9.73	547	99
Mathematics II (December 1982)	2,075	50	25.36	9.13	645	85
Biology (June 1983)	2,125	95	53.36	17.90	583	105
Chemistry (December 1982)	2,520	90	36.14	16.31	550	102
Physics (May 1983)	1,065	75	37.49	15.60	596	93

† Sample does not include French, German, or Spanish students with less than two years of training, nor those test takers who failed to respond to the questionnaire or whose knowledge of the language did not come primarily from courses taken in grades 9 through 12.

‡ Sample does not include Latin students with only one year of training, nor those language students who failed to respond to the background questionnaire or who indicated they had learned the language outside of school.

the SAT), of the students taking the test. Information of this sort, reprinted from *National College-Bound Seniors, 1983* (College Board 1983d, pp. 13-14) is presented in Table 5.4 for students who were secondary school seniors in 1983.

Test Dates and the Instructional Calendar. Test committees also have spent much time exploring the implications of variable test dates for the Achievement Tests in biology, physics, chemistry, European history, and American history. These subjects are usually taught for only one year, and typical November, December, or January test takers will either have completed their course in the subject in a previous year or find themselves in the middle of the course at the time of the test. In recent years, a deci-

sion has been made to construct each test in a one-year subject as if the test were to be taken near the end of the year of study. Colleges are urged to consider the number of years of study in the subject and the level of courses taken, and students are encouraged to register for tests in one-year subjects near the end of their period of study or shortly after they have completed the course. The result has been an increasing popularity of May and June dates for tests in the one-year subjects.

Student Views of the Achievement Tests

Student reactions to testing vary considerably. Most students, however, do not react negatively at all. In

Table 5.4

Achievement Test Scores for ATP College-Bound Seniors 1983
(Adapted from *National College-Bound Seniors, 1983*)

Score	ENGLISH COMPOSITION Number	%	LITERATURE Number	%	MATHEMATICS LEVEL I Number	%
750-800	1,136	1	86	1	2,243	2
700-749	6,597	4	619	4	6,330	4
650-699	13,312	8	1,562	9	13,188	9
600-649	21,664	12	2,450	14	21,112	15
550-599	29,425	17	2,749	16	27,838	20
500-549	31,312	18	2,758	16	26,352	19
450-499	29,142	16	2,567	15	22,490	16
400-449	22,758	13	1,959	12	14,861	10
350-399	14,647	8	1,377	8	6,042	4
300-349	5,559	3	677	4	1,591	1
250-299	1,490	1	160	1	253	0
200-249	317	0	13	0	6	0
Number	177,359		16,977		142,306	
Mean	518		523		543	
Std. Dev.	102		105		96	
SAT-V Avg.	512		524		500	
SAT-M Avg.	566		528		556	

Score	MATHEMATICS LEVEL II Number	%	BIOLOGY Number	%	CHEMISTRY Number	%
750-800	6,372	16	516	1	1,338	4
700-749	7,271	19	2,548	6	2,722	8
650-699	8,403	21	4,683	11	4,249	12
600-649	8,228	21	6,622	16	5,818	16
550-599	5,116	13	7,201	17	6,479	18
500-549	1,793	5	7,274	17	6,403	18
450-499	919	2	5,856	14	4,809	13
400-449	595	2	4,203	10	2,726	8
350-399	274	1	2,292	5	1,005	3
300-349	97	0	1,010	2	171	0
250-299	20	0	304	1	8	0
200-249	5	0	35	0	0	0
Number	39,093		42,544		35,728	
Mean	655		544		569	
Std. Dev.	90		104		98	
SAT-V Avg.	550		523		536	
SAT-M Avg.	649		570		624	

Score	PHYSICS Number	%	AMERICAN HISTORY Number	%	EUROPEAN HISTORY Number	%
750-800	1,188	7	659	2	84	3
700-749	1,672	10	1,535	4	146	6
650-699	2,460	15	2,961	7	261	10
600-649	2,785	17	4,612	11	381	15
550-599	2,933	18	6,555	15	439	17
500-549	2,675	16	7,854	18	451	17
450-499	1,845	11	7,767	18	450	17
400-449	777	5	6,544	15	266	10
350-399	166	1	3,632	8	115	4
300-349	6	0	1,224	3	26	1
250-299	0	0	212	0	5	0
200-249	0	0	17	0	0	0
Number	16,507		43,572		2,624	
Mean	595		516		549	
Std. Dev.	98		102		102	
SAT-V Avg.	536		513		563	
SAT-M Avg.	647		550		557	

Table 5.4 (continued)

Achievement Test Scores for ATP College-Bound Seniors 1983
(Adapted from *National College-Bound Seniors, 1983*)

Score	FRENCH Number	%	GERMAN Number	%	HEBREW Number	%
750-800	1,024	4	250	8	75	18
700-749	1,401	6	245	8	68	16
650-699	2,238	10	327	11	59	14
600-649	2,769	12	405	13	76	18
550-599	3,614	16	499	16	46	11
500-549	3,887	17	530	17	29	7
450-499	3,684	16	358	12	39	9
400-449	2,764	12	277	9	18	4
350-399	1,212	5	138	4	10	2
300-349	260	1	59	2	4	1
250-299	10	0	7	0	2	0
200-249	0	0	0	0	0	0
Number	22,863		3,095		426	
Mean	548		567		627	
Std. Dev.	108		115		119	
SAT-V Avg.	541		542		551	
SAT-M Avg.	571		586		588	

Score	LATIN Number	%	SPANISH Number	%
750-800	86	4	1,389	5
700-749	160	7	1,961	8
650-699	260	11	1,882	7
600-649	319	13	2,488	10
550-599	340	14	2,905	11
500-549	410	17	3,803	15
450-499	411	17	4,169	16
400-449	300	12	3,738	15
350-399	123	5	2,286	9
300-349	2	0	713	3
250-299	0	0	49	0
200-249	0	0	0	0
Number	2,411		25,383	
Mean	550		533	
Std. Dev.	104		120	
SAT-V Avg.	562		498	
SAT-M Avg.	591		542	

a 1975 survey conducted for the College Board by Response Analysis Corporation, students affirmed the value of admissions testing, from their point of view, for its objectivity. Although student use of the Achievement Tests has declined in recent years, as fewer colleges required the Achievement Tests, many students find the tests useful in demonstrating their competencies. There is no single best method of appraisal for all students. The Achievement Tests and the SAT are important elements in a testing system that serves to supplement and validate the appraisals implicit in the high school record.

In summary, the Achievement Tests of the Admissions Testing Program continue a tradition that was the basis for the initial creation of the College Board. Although taken in somewhat smaller num-

bers in recent years, the tests continue to play a vital role in admissions and placement decisions in a variety of contexts. The fundamental process by which they are produced is the committee process. The committees, working within the policy-making structure of the Board and assisted by the subject-matter and measurement specialists at ETS, consistently produce tests that appear to be highly appropriate for their purposes of evaluating subject-matter competence, course placement, and prediction of academic performance.

Principal author: Ernest W. Kimmel
Contributors or reviewers: William H. Angoff, Linda L. Cook, Thomas F. Donlon, and June Stern.

CHAPTER VI

The Student Descriptive Questionnaire, the Summary Reporting Service, and the Student Search Service

Introduction

The College Board introduced the Student Descriptive Questionnaire (SDQ) into the Admissions Testing Program in the fall of 1971. A response to a number of changes in the emerging patterns of college admissions, the SDQ was directly influenced by the advisory reports of the Commission on Tests, a panel convened in 1967 to "undertake a thorough and critical review of the Board's testing function in American education and to consider possibilities for fundamental changes in the present tests and their use in schools, colleges, and universities" (College Board, 1970, p. 1). The SDQ is a questionnaire that offers students an opportunity to describe themselves in a number of ways, including their academic performance, extracurricular activities in high school, socioeconomic background, plans for college study, and specific needs for assistance during the transition to college. This information goes beyond the test score information with which the Board's programs have historically been concerned. The introduction of this noncognitive instrument showed a willingness on the part of the Board to offer services that were relevant to a larger proportion of the admissions process than tests alone. Further, it signaled a maturity for the admissions process itself, a recognition of the vital role it plays in institutional life, and the emergence of some new and more sophisticated models for making admissions decisions.

How the SDQ Developed

The SDQ was formulated after consideration of a wide variety of possible instruments. Two major considerations limited the kinds of information that might be collected. The first was the need to maintain the students' privacy. The Board could not develop a dossier of highly personal information on the students, however useful some items might be. The

second concerned the limitations of many self-assessment instruments in terms of their construct and other validities. Although a number of interesting methodologies have been suggested for the assessment of noncognitive characteristics, some of the approaches have marked limitations. The Board chose not to implement any approaches that lacked a research base. In view of these considerations, the SDQ avoids highly personal data or attempts to reflect personal psychological characteristics. It is limited to a pragmatic core of basic information about a student's past experiences, current status, and future needs. Further, it draws upon the student's *direct* expression of self-perceptions with respect to his or her characteristics, plans, aspirations, and grades. In contrast, some approaches to noncognitive assessment rely upon less direct questionnaires, from which there is an *inference* concerning interest.

The SDQ reflects a number of assumptions concerning the role of this kind of measurement in the ATP. Some of the principal assumptions follow.

1. The biographical information should cover a wide variety of areas, limited to a few specific questions in each, rather than focusing extensive questioning on one or two areas.
2. Biographical data can inform the processes of counseling and guidance as well as those of selection and admissions. Information about the student's personal, social, and academic background provides the counselor or guidance officer with a superior basis for insight.
3. Biographical summaries can be useful to students in their formulation of plans for self-development. The content of the questionnaire covers many important considerations for those planning further education, and completion of the questionnaire can help students to perfect their understanding of these considerations.
4. Biographical data is the basis for a two-way flow of information between students and colleges. A questionnaire enables a student to describe him-

self or herself to a college. By summarizing the questionnaires of its students and applicants, the college can describe itself to the student. This two-way communication is the central goal of the recommendation of the Commission on Tests.

5. Biographical data can assist the student's transition from high school to college. For example, biographical data enable colleges to reach and communicate with defined subgroups of potential applicants, such as minority students, as in the Student Search Service (sss). Further, such data make it easier to assess and plan for the aggregate needs of students on campus.

While the SDQ was intended to serve a number of administrative admission functions, it was also intended to contribute to a prediction of college grades. The value of self-reported data for admissions purposes has sometimes been challenged, for several reasons. The prevailing criticism is that the student, through misguided self-interest or a biased self-perception, is likely to supply distorted information. This criticism is particularly directed toward self-reporting of grades. The potential problems were carefully evaluated before the introduction of the SDQ, and a brief review by Baird (1976) summarized the evidence supporting the validity of self-reporting. The technical concerns reviewed by Baird may be expressed as questions about the use of biographical data:

1. Are self-reported grades useful predictors of college success? How are they influenced by self-concept in general? How well does general biographical information contribute to prediction?
2. How well do biographical self-report data contribute to an understanding of major decisions such as: deciding to go to college, selecting a college, selecting a college residence, participating in campus-related activities, and remaining in college?
3. How well do biographical data assist in the understanding of students' educational backgrounds and needs, particularly students in the lower socioeconomic levels or minority students?
4. How well do biographical data assist in the understanding of student choice of major field or of vocational decision making?

The most general answer to each of these questions, as outlined by Baird, is that self-reported biographical data make useful contributions to all these areas. His report concludes that "there is considerable evidence that self-reported grades can be as useful as school-reported grades as predictors of college grades," (p. 10) and that "measures of accomplishment could be used for the early identification of students with the potential for high-level accomplishment" (p. 34).

Several strategies exist to reduce inaccurate grade reporting:

1) Efforts can be made to reduce ambiguities in the systems that are used to collect the self-reports (Maxey and Ormsby 1971; Armstrong and Jensen 1974).
2) Announcing that the students' actual grades may be verified and using a system spot check could decrease the rate of distortion.
3) Steps could be taken to find a pattern of variables that would lead to the identification of students who are likely to exaggerate their grades (Kirk and Sereda 1969).

This pattern of variables would be roughly analogous to the "lie" scales on personality and interest tests. The colleges could then check the grades of students who scored high on such a scale. To date, this remains a research possibility, rather than an established technique.

The usefulness of SDQ self-reported data has been confirmed by studies that compare the characteristics of SDQ self-reports with data from other sources. The Validity Study Service reports the following comparative data on validity in the prediction of freshman year grade point average.

Predictor	Mean Correlation
High School Rank	
Reported by Student	.43
Reported by High School	.49
High School Grade Point Average	
Reported by Student	.44
Reported by High School	.48

As these data show, the rank-in-class and grade point average reported by the high school are somewhat more predictive of college freshman grade point average than is the student-generated report. There is little evidence of a widespread effort by students to mislead admissions authorities by a wholesale "inflation" of the record; however, there is some difference between self-reported grades and school-reported grades. Although no serious distortion is likely in estimating group statistics from self-reports, there can be serious distortion for individuals in a few cases.

Certain self-descriptive information, such as sex, may add to predictions at a statistically significant level, but may violate the principles of equity underlying the admissions process. For example, there is ample evidence that the grades of women are more predictable and tend to be higher than those of men with equivalent scores (see Chapter VII and Abelson 1952, Jacobs 1959, Munday 1967, Seashore 1962). This may be attributed to differences in courses taken, but it underscores potential problems. Should a college deliberately admit more women because they can be expected to earn higher grades? Should it ignore the difference and put everyone into one regression equation, thereby overpredicting for men and underpredicting for women? Would this represent favoritism toward men and bias against women?

The position taken in the development of the SDQ was that most group-identification variables should not be used as part of the admissions decision except in rare marginal cases. Much biographical information is concerned with factors over which the individual has no control and which cannot change—sex, race, social background, etc. Even though these factors add predictive power, it does not seem reasonable to consider such things, since they are essentially accidental phenomena. Even fairly innocuous information can be used in objectionable ways. In this context, it is essential to secure an *informed* cooperation on the part of the student; each student who completes a questionnaire should be told the reasons he or she is being asked for the information and given the option of omitting any question thought to be objectionable.

What the SDQ Contains

The 1982-83 edition of the SDQ contained 63 questions. Of these about 70 percent were also asked, in the present format or in a closely related manner, in the first form of the SDQ, introduced in 1971-72. As the overlap indicates, the SDQ has defined a stable domain of interest, and the questions have required few changes in language.

The 1982-83 questionnaire is reprinted in its entirety at the end of this chapter. While the content of each SDQ question is clearly of interest, the structure and organization of the entire instrument is perhaps more meaningful, particularly in the light of its multiple purposes. The content of the survey is focused on common sense, practical, and factual information. Question 29, for example, simply asks, "When you enroll, do you expect to attend college during the (A) day (B) evening?" This kind of information is useful in administering student admission processes, alerting the school to likely class sizes, etc. It is not self-descriptive in the sense that could characterize, for example, questions concerning vocational

planning. In general, few of the questions asked on the SDQ are in any sense deeply probing, and there is little material that is potentially embarrassing, if revealed, under ordinarily foreseeable circumstances.

The dimensions of the SDQ can be indicated by categorizing its questions into clusters. Question 1 asks the student about his or her interest in participating in the Student Search Service. The remaining questions fall into six clusters:

	Area of Interest	Questions Relating to Area
I.	General personal characteristics	31, 32, 37, 38
II.	Previous academic attainment	2-18, 23, 25, 33-36
III.	Activities in high school	19-22, 45
IV.	Self-evaluation	47-60
V.	Family situation	39-43
VI.	Plans	24, 26-30, 44, 46, 61-63

The general content of each of these broad areas is conveyed by the following recasting of the questions into brief statements. The parentheses following each question contain the number of the question.

I. *General personal characteristics:*
Are you a U.S. citizen? (31) A veteran? (32) What ethnic group do you belong to? (37) Is English your best language? (38)

II. *Previous academic attainment:*
Are you in a public high school? (2) An academic program? (3) How large is your graduating class? (4) What is your standing in it? (5) How many years will you have studied English, mathematics, foreign languages, etc.? (6-11) What is the latest grade you received in these areas? (12-17) Have you taken advanced courses? (18) Have you won academic honors? (23) When is your graduation? (25) Have you previously attended college? (33) Are you still enrolled? (34) What grade point average have you achieved? (35) At what level do you expect to enter the new college? (36)

III. *Activities while in high school:*
How many hours did you work at a job? (19) How much did you participate in community/church groups? (20) How much in athletics? (21) How much in clubs/organizations? (22) How many of the eight listed activities did you take part in? (45)

IV. *Self-evaluation:*
How do you compare yourself with others in 14 abilities, such as acting, artistic talent, athletics, etc.? (47-60)

V. *Family situation:*

How far did your father get in school? (39) Your mother? (40) How many dependents do your parents have? (41) Are other dependents going to be in college when you enter? (42) What was your parents' approximate pre-tax income last year? (43)

VI. *Plans:*

What is the highest level of education you plan to pursue? (24) When do you expect to enter college? (26) Do you plan to seek financial aid? (27) Will you go full time? (28) Will you attend day sessions? (29) Where would you like to live? (30) Will you need special services like counseling, tutoring, job finding? (44) In what extracurricular activities do you plan to take part? (46) What field is your first choice as a major? (61) Your second choice? (62) What field do you think you will pursue after college? (63)

This content analysis is intended to display the direct factual nature of the instrument. As it demonstrates, the six areas cover numerous dimensions of the person and are broadly relevant to a number of decisions.

The Summary Reporting Service

SDQ data can serve numerous functions. One such functional analysis follows. As the analysis suggests, individual questions may serve multiple functions, both within a given area (college, school, student) and across areas. The Roman numerals in parentheses refer to the six areas of interest cited above (general personal characteristics, previous academic attainment, etc.).

1. Functions for colleges (or groups of colleges)
   • Admissions (I, II, III)
   • Recruitment (I, V, VI)
   • Academic programs and placement (II, VI)
   • Financial aid (V)
   • Student services (VI)
   • Overall planning, administration, and research (I-VI)

2. Functions for high schools (or groups of high schools)
   • Formulating academic programs (II, III, IV, VI)
   • Counseling, including college choice (IV, V, VI)
   • Providing extracurricular activities (III)

3. Functions for students
   • Initiating self-discovery/self-counseling (IV, VI)
   • Conveying personal information to colleges (III, IV)

4. Functions for governmental bodies
   • Evaluating financial assistance programs (V, VI)
   • Monitoring trends in student populations (I, II, V)

5. Functions for the general public
   • Understanding the college-bound process (II, III, V, VI)
   • Monitoring trends in student populations (I, II, V)
   • Monitoring trends in college-bound students' attainments (II, III, IV)

From its inception the SDQ had a potential for describing college-bound groups and individuals in ways that would be useful to the five broad audiences described above—the colleges, high schools, students, governmental bodies, and general public. Each of these audiences approaches the information that the SDQ provides from a somewhat different perspective.

Services to Colleges and Groups of Colleges. The information generated by the students who participate in the Admissions Testing Program is provided to the colleges in the Summary Reporting Service (SRS). The SRS is a series of statistical profiles of high school seniors at various points in the admissions process and into their freshman year in college.

The fundamental aim of the Summary Reports is to provide data that colleges can use in planning. Accordingly, the students who take part in the admissions process are analyzed and placed into a number of subgroups, as indicated in Figure 6.1. The reports are generated in three rounds:

Round 1: All colleges and scholarship sponsors designated as recipients of ATP score reports from at least 100 current high school seniors by March of their senior year automatically receive a Round 1 ATP Summary Report. Although it is not certain that these students will make application to these colleges or scholarship programs, this report is a profile of these students as prospective applicants.

Round 2: By informing the College Board that they wish to receive summary reports on their applicants, accepted applicants, and/or enrolling freshmen (and by indicating the admissions status of their prospective applicants), colleges may receive reports on these groups of students. These reports describe the

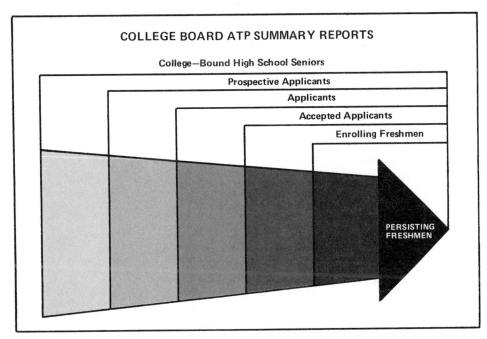

COLLEGE BOARD ATP SUMMARY REPORTS

College—Bound High School Seniors

Prospective Applicants

Applicants

Accepted Applicants

Enrolling Freshmen

PERSISTING
FRESHMEN

group in total and can be divided into as many as six subgroups (for example, out-of-state applicants, financial aid recipients, or engineering majors.)

Round 3: By supplying information on which enrolled freshmen persist to the end of the academic year, colleges may receive a profile of their persisting freshmen, their dropouts, or both (either of which can also be divided into as many as six subgroups). Further, by supplying criterion information, colleges may receive the results of a validity study based on data for their students, through the Validity Study Service (described in Chapter VIII).

The series of reports described above is also available to groups of colleges who elect to join together to pool information. A single college or group of colleges may receive a large number of summary descriptions of groups of its potential applicants, applicants, and students. These, in conjunction with ATP data that profile state, regional or national groups, provide a wide array of information to be used in institutional decision processes.

Because nearly 90 percent of all ATP students answer at least one SDQ question, a college requiring the Board's tests will observe that a substantial proportion of its applicants are described in the summaries. This proportion may be expanded through options permitting a college to supply additional information about non-ATP candidates for incorporation into the summary, or to ask the College Board

to include information about ATP candidates who have ultimately approached the college, although their college choices at the time of testing did not indicate an intent to apply.

The summary reports are considered confidential information and are sent only to the given college or to the designated coordinator for a group of colleges. The results of specific colleges or groups may be incorporated into summaries describing larger groups of institutions (such as all four-year private colleges), but the specific institutional designations are eliminated in these summaries.

Four basic comparisons may be derived from the data in the summary reports: (a) institutions or groups of institutions in different years, (b) a given institution or group with other institutions or groups, (c) institutions or groups at different stages in the admissions process, and (d) subgroups of special interest (minorities, out-of-state students, etc.). To facilitate these comparisons, the ATP compiles a report on all current high school seniors who have registered with the ATP at any time during their high school years. These national data can be supplemented by six regional reports and other reports describing the responses of students from each of the states and the District of Columbia. When considered in conjunction with summaries for selected reference groups, such as four-year public colleges or four-year private colleges, the total information base that a college can use is impressive.

The *College Guide to the ATP Summary Reports* (College Board 1983c), an annual publication, describes the system of reports and provides suggestions on using the results in areas such as admissions and placement. In addition, a variety of consultative services are available through the ATP and the Board's Regional Offices.

The summary reports do not incorporate all the information in the SDQ. For example, the data on participation in non-school activities such as community and church groups are no longer a regular component of the analysis, because a user survey indicated that these particular data were seldom useful. However, a college can still pursue an interest in such areas on its own. A computer tape providing all the information on all the prospective applicants to that college is made available at the end of the academic year. Using this tape, a given institution can consider its applicants, acceptances, admitted students, and persisting freshmen with respect to characteristics not included in the summary reports. The colleges may also use the Student Search Service, described on page 115, which attempts to match individual students to colleges that seek students having certain characteristics.

Summaries for High Schools and Groups of High Schools. Each high school from which an aggregate total of 100 or more seniors participated in the ATP during their high school career receives a complete summary report of ATP responses at the conclusion of an academic year. A high school that had 50 to 99 seniors participating during that time is sent an abbreviated version. In addition to their own ATP Summary Report, high schools are sent a copy of the *National College-Bound Seniors* (1983d) and the related state and regional summary.

The principal functions of these data at the secondary level are not so directly decision-oriented as the functions of the data in college admissions. However, the data are peripherally related to an evaluation of the college preparation programs within an individual school and community. The data provide the raw material for useful reports to school boards, parent groups, faculty committees, department chairmen, college admissions offices, local newspapers, and the students themselves. A sample of a report to community audiences is incorporated in the *School Guide to the ATP Summary Reports* (College Board 1983e) to encourage this kind of dissemination.

The SDQ summary of self-evaluations, family situation, and future plans offers the secondary school a concise framework within which to launch counseling discussions. The information in these areas

for all students completing the SDQ gives an indication of the effectiveness of the school's guidance activity in relation to student planning. The SDQ also provides high schools with a useful summary of the extracurricular activities reported by their students.

Other Uses of the SDQ

Use by Students. Although the SDQ is a self-report instrument, the student, in theory, can acquire some useful insights into himself or herself in relation to going to college by considering the implications of the questions. For the student, however, an important value of the SDQ lies in its capacity to make information available to interested colleges through the Student Search Service. The communications received from colleges via the Student Search Service may significantly expand the possibilities open to the student.

The booklet, *Your Score Report* (College Board 1983h, p. 7), which explains how colleges use ATP data, including SDQ results, contains the following comment: "Different colleges value different qualities in applicants: One college may be looking for leadership potential, while another may place more weight on various extracurricular activities. . . . Some will admit students with particular qualities they want, even if the students' grades and scores indicate they will have to make an extra effort.'' It should be noted, however, that while such a broad assessment of student characteristics is often ascribed to college admissions practices, a relevant study (Willingham 1982) does not confirm that the specific qualities mentioned are used as frequently in the admissions process as has been thought.

Use by Governmental Bodies. The Chief State School Officers annually receive analyses of the ATP performance of students enrolled in schools in their states; these analyses are valuable in state planning processes. Trends in individual decision making may be recognized more quickly in the context of a summary report, and SDQ information is useful in the more practical aspects of educational planning.

Because ATP summaries are based on self-selected groups, they cannot have the generalizability of random samples. However, as substantial aggregates of information, the summaries may be watched for year-to-year shifts in the type of broad questions that are the responsibility of governmental agencies. An awareness of changes in the patterns of high school courses taken, for example, as reflected in responses to SDQ questions, can be valuable to those charged with monitoring education.

Table 6.1

Percentage of Male and Female SDQ Respondents Indicating
Major Field First Choice in Business and Commerce and
Health and Medical Professions, 1975-1983

	1975	1976	1977	1978	1979	1980	1981	1982	1983
				Business and Commerce					
Males	13.5	14.0	15.4	17.2	18.2	18.5	17.6	17.5	17.0
Females	9.6	11.3	13.2	15.6	17.3	18.8	19.4	19.8	19.8
				Health and Medical					
Males	N/A	11.6	11.0	10.1	9.7	9.2	9.0	8.5	8.6
Females	N/A	23.7	23.5	22.1	20.7	19.5	19.3	19.3	20.1

Use by the Public. The uses of SRS data by secondary schools and governmental bodies include efforts by these agencies to provide information to the public. The College Board encourages this use of the information. Citizens need to be informed about the nature of those who enroll in college. The value of SDQ data for this function comes, in part, from its ability to show changes from year to year that reveal or clarify fundamental changes in the pursuit of and access to higher education. A good recent example is the increasing number of female students electing to major in business or commerce. Table 6.1 shows the trends for males and females from 1975 to 1983 in the percentage of SDQ respondents who indicate that their first choice for a major field is in one of two broad areas: business and commerce or health and medical professions.

As the table shows, in 1983 female students were electing the business and commerce option at a rate approximately twice that for females in 1975. In fact, although male interest in this area had also expanded, in 1980 and after, a slightly higher percentage of females than males indicated the intention to major in business. The experience in this area contrasts with that in the health and medical professions, which shows continued sex differences in the overall rate of expressed interest, but a similar pattern of gradual decline from 1976 to 1982.

Such information is broadly applicable for citizen involvement in educational planning and financing. Although SDQ data describe self-selected groups, and generalizations from these groups must be conservatively projected, the sheer size of the overlap between the group of SDQ respondents and the total of students entering college directly from high school gives considerable validity to the SDQ results.

Evaluations of the SDQ and the SRS

The introduction of the SDQ was based upon research and field trials of its feasibility. The first versions were recognized as tentative, and the underlying philosophy for the instrument is that it will be modified over time as the understanding of its properties is improved. To facilitate this understanding and to guide the changes, there has been an effort to obtain reviews of the SDQ from school and college measurement professionals. These approaches to improvement have been supplemented by occasional formal studies of reactions to the SDQ by the primary users for whom it is intended. Since its introduction, there have been five principal surveys of SDQ users: two surveys of students, two of college officials, and one of high school counselors.

How Students Evaluate the SDQ. Two surveys of students were conducted in the mid-1970s by an external organization (Response Analysis Corporation 1978). The first survey involved 430 students. The students were asked to indicate whether they thought each particular SDQ item would be hard to answer and whether it contained information that would be important to a college. At the end of the survey, the students were asked to provide "any other comments you would like to make about the Student Descriptive Questionnaire. . . ."

Overall, the items that students felt were *least* important were: the numbers of hours the student had worked during high school (only 44 percent considered it to be important), the extent of participation in community and church groups (53 percent), participation in athletics (43 percent), ethnic/racial background (25 percent). There was further doubt about some of the self-rating items, numbers 47-60.

Similar results were obtained in the second study, which surveyed 748 students concerning their views of the SDQ before they had taken the SAT. The students were asked whether they felt that it was "all right" that colleges should or should not receive the information requested in each item. Fifty-five percent thought that colleges should not get ethnicity data, 44 percent thought this way about church or community activities, and 32 percent thought this way about the number of hours worked during high school. These students were also asked whether it was all right for the College Board to collect information about the students' families, if the information was used only for research purposes. Sixty-two percent thought that the Board should not collect information about parents' educational achievement; 48 percent thought this way about their estimate of their parents' income; and 35 percent thought this way about the number of financial dependents their parents had. (Individual students could act on such judgments, of course, for if a student disapproves of a question, he or she is under no obligation to respond to it.)

Students were also encouraged to provide their overall opinions of the SDQ. Although it is difficult to assess the general comments, many students questioned the accuracy or significance of the self-rating items; some did not understand the item on class rank.

Although the results of the two studies agree, they are complicated by the fact that students with different characteristics responded differently. For example, about half the minority students saw the ethnicity question as important, compared to only 23 percent of the majority students. Similarly, although 60 percent of the White students objected to the ethnicity question, only 41 percent of the Hispanic students and 30 percent of the Black students objected. The general pattern was that if a student was directly involved in an area, his or her responses were likely to be different from others who were not so involved. This pattern was widespread: 78 percent of the students who earned varsity letters felt that information about athletic participation was important, in contrast to 32 percent of the students who did not participate in athletics. Similar results were obtained for the question on the number of hours worked during high school.

Researchers found that 50 percent of the students whose families had incomes of $20,000 or more a year objected to the collection of family income data, but that only 32 percent of students whose families had incomes of less than $10,000 a year objected. Although a majority objected to providing information about the parents' educational achievement, the percentage of those objecting was higher among students with better educated parents.

These results suggest that students who see some possible personal benefit in a question will regard it more positively than students who do not see such benefits. This complicates the use of student opinion in efforts to revise or evaluate the instrument. Some SDQ information probably should be requested, even if some students regard it as unimportant or objec-

tionable, if there is a counterbalancing group of students who would benefit from it. Further, there is a continuing need to explain clearly the reasons for collecting the information and to try to point out the ways each item would or could help students. Students tend to focus on individual uses of the data rather than on summary ones. It cannot be emphasized too strongly, however, that the student retains autonomy in the decision to provide *any* information in the SDQ. The instructions clearly state: "You are encouraged to answer all questions, although you may omit the answer to a specific question, if you wish."

Students do not leave out information capriciously. In 1982-83, for example, there were approximately 908,000 students supplying some SDQ information out of about 1,013,000 college-bound seniors taking the SAT before April 1983. Of these respondents, virtually all provided such basic information as "What type of high school did you attend?" (99 percent) or "Are you a U.S. citizen?" (98 percent). Most questions were answered by 850,000-890,000 test takers, or about 96 percent. Even the question on ethnic identity was answered by 96 percent of the respondents. The notable exception was question 43 on parental income (86 percent). In general, failure to respond is limited to very few individuals, and in many cases it may simply reflect uncertainty.

Opinions of College Officials. The College Board has conducted two surveys of the opinions of college and university officials. The first, in 1975, asked 91 institutions about their needs and their views of possible College Board services. The second survey, in 1977, was based on the responses of 229 admissions officers. Although the first was more a general "marketing" survey, several of its findings bear on the SDQ. One general finding was that smaller colleges found the SDQ information more useful than did larger colleges. Another general finding was that the most desired information tended to be data that would bear directly on the daily work of the admissions office and data that might identify any need for special treatment of students. For example, more than half of the colleges wanted the following information: (a) student's telephone number, (b) information on handicaps, (c) citizenship, (d) previous college attended, (e) participation in accelerated high school programs, and (f) state of residence.

In addition, at least half of some groups of colleges wanted information about the following: (a) veteran's status (59 percent of the public colleges), (b) years since high school graduation (62 percent of small colleges), (c) intention to enroll full time or part time (52 percent of small colleges), and (d) special athletic information (52 percent of small colleges).

The colleges indicated that they would like more information that could be used in the guidance of students about their educational, vocational, and career choices and other interests. More generally, the colleges indicated that their most pressing needs were to obtain help in making enrollment projections and to improve recruitment.

The second survey showed that several items in the current SDQ were not considered "important" by a majority of the 229 admissions officers. These included the following items.

Number(s) on SDQ		Percentage Describing Item as "Important"
21	Participation in athletics	41
39	Father's educational achievement	27
40	Mother's educational achievement	27
47-60	Self-ratings of abilities	28-48

In addition, the admissions officers were asked if there were any questions they would like to see deleted or added, and if there were items that were commonly misinterpreted or answered inaccurately by students. In response to these questions, the admissions officers indicated that they thought that the self-rating and the income items were of questionable validity. Some thought that the class rank, grade items, and the questions on the need for help or counseling were misinterpreted. The most common information they wanted collected in the SDQ was the students' choice of college and the reasons students might give concerning that choice.

The admissions officers also answered questions on how they used SDQ information. The most useful functions were recruiting, evaluating, and the Student Search Service (all more important among private colleges), and compiling institutional statistics (more important among public colleges). The following table shows the information considered particularly useful for recruiting and evaluating, two of the principal functions of the SDQ data.

Number(s) on SDQ	Item	Percentage Rating Item as "Useful" for Recruiting	Percentage Rating Item as "Useful" for Evaluating
61	Intended Field of Study	60	—
5	Class Rank	54	46
5, 12-17	High School Performance Based on Rank or Average	51	44
24	Educational Objective	48	—
12-17	Latest High School Grades	46	48
37	Ethnic Group	42	—
38	English Best Language	—	41
18	Honors Courses	—	41

Items whose propriety students question (for example, ethnicity) or whose accuracy admissions officers challenge (for example, class rank) are, in fact, considered useful in both of these functions.

In another aspect of the survey, the admissions officers provided evaluations of the SDQ information in terms of its contribution to seven main goals of college administration. The results are shown in Table 6.2.

As the table indicates, admissions officers at public and private colleges differ on the value of the SDQ for these purposes. In general, however, both groups show similar variation across areas, with the value of SDQ information being least for curriculum planning or placement and greatest for recruitment

Table 6.2

Overall Value of SDQ Information by Purpose for Public and Private Colleges

Purpose	Percentage Rating "Very Useful"		Percentage Rating "Somewhat Useful"		Percentage Rating "Not Useful"	
	Public	Private	Public	Private	Public	Private
Student Search	33	52	43	32	24	16
Recruiting	44	52	47	44	9	4
Evaluating Curriculum	36	42	52	47	12	10
Planning	10	15	48	42	42	43
Counseling Students	30	31	43	45	26	24
Compiling Institutional Statistics	44	38	45	46	11	16
Placement	22	19	46	49	31	32

and institutional evaluation. These data attest to a wide variety of uses for SDQ data in admissions work, and to a general satisfaction with the instrument on the part of admissions officers.

Surveys of High School Counselors. High school counselors have a very different perspective on the uses of the SDQ; they are concerned with advising students, many of whom they know quite well, or about whom they have a large amount of information. Because they already know their students, much of the information in the SDQ is redundant for them. Accordingly, two-thirds or more considered some SDQ information to be of little use for counseling students. These include:

Number(s) on SDQ	Item	Percentage of Counselors Rating Item "Not Useful"
37	Ethnic Group	91
18	Honors Courses	75
20	Community or Church Groups	73
21	Athletics	73
38	English Best Language	71
5	Class Rank and Size	72-73
12-17	Grades	72
22	School Organizations	69
45-46	Extracurricular Activities	68
19	Number of Hours Worked During High School	66

The items that were most useful for counseling included the intended major in college, the educational objective, and self-ratings of skills.

In contrast, high school counselors classified certain items they had described as unimportant for individual counseling as important for colleges. For example, 66 percent thought that information about scholastic honors and awards was not useful for counseling purposes, but 87 percent thought that this information was important for colleges. Perhaps the most striking results in this study are these: When presented with 19 types of SDQ information, a majority of the counselors considered only five useful for counseling, but a majority of counselors thought that every one of the 19 was important for colleges. More generally, counselors felt that the SDQ was most helpful in providing information for college admissions and for the Student Search Service.

The counselors were asked to indicate which SDQ questions were commonly misinterpreted by students, which questions should be deleted, and whether there were questions that should be added. Many said that questions about latest grades (Items 12-17) and class rank (Item 5) were misinterpreted. The questions about family incomes and self-ratings were also thought to be misinterpreted, especially among counselors who worked with minority and Spanish-speaking students. The questions that were thought to be misinterpreted were frequently recommended for deletion. Counselors' views about questions to be added were not strong, but two needs were identified—more information about how students planned to finance their college education and more information about students' interests.

Information Yielded by the SDQ

Some of the information provided in Chapter IX on the descriptive statistics of the ATP test-taker population is developed through the use of the SDQ. The distributions of ethnic background and parental income reported in that chapter are developed from the SDQ, as are the number of years of study in selected subject-matter areas. Additional selected distributions are included in this review of the SDQ in order to characterize the output it generates. For example, Table 6.3 shows the distribution of reported extracurricular activities in secondary school for males and females over the ten annual cohorts 1974-1983. The numbers of students providing self-descriptions via the SDQ represent a majority of the students using the ATP. Thus, the numbers of males and females in Table 6.3 represent over 80 percent of the groups, and, in the last two years, nearly 90 percent of the groups. The table reflects participation in a wide variety of activities and shows considerable similarity in the percentages reporting from year to year. There are some differences between the sexes. Although athletics, in some form, is the most frequently reported activity, the percentage of males reporting this activity is about 20 percent greater than that for females. On the other hand, the pattern of involvement in social or community clubs is reversed, with females showing about 15 percent greater involvement in these activities than males. The category concerning activities that center on music (band, orchestra, chorus) was broadened in 1977 to a more general "Artistic" category, with art and dance added. This increased the level of response in these categories by approximately 10 percent for females and 5 percent for males. Thus, the pattern of a relatively heavier involvement for females continued. Females also show somewhat greater overall involvement in student government, social clubs, departmental (subject-matter area) clubs, and religious organizations.

The patterns in Table 6.3, which reports extracurricular participation in high school, may be compared with the patterns in Table 6.4 (page 114),

Table 6.3

Percentage of Extracurricular Activities in High School as Reported by
sDQ Responses for Ten Annual Cohorts, 1974-1983

Year	1974	1975	1976	1977	1978	1979	1980	1981	1982	1983
MALE										
Athletics, Intramural and Community	78	80	81	81	81	81	80	80	80	81
Ethnic Organizations	7	6	6	6	6	5	5	5	6	6
Journalism, Debating, Dramatics	24	25	26	26	25	24	24	24	24	24
Music, Band, Orchestra, Chorus*	27	26	27	31	33	33	33	33	32	32
Departmental or Professional Clubs	31	11	12	11	10	10	10	10	11	11
Religious Organizations	31	30	32	31	30	29	29	29	30	30
Social or Community Clubs	40	38	32	37	36	35	35	34	35	36
Student Government	25	23	23	22	21	20	20	19	19	19
Number Responding to at Least One Activity	384,361	391,153	372,468	386,283	421,451	427,691	426,081	425,877	422,599	408,620
FEMALE										
Athletics, Intramural and Community	54	56	58	57	58	58	59	59	60	60
Ethnic Organizations	10	8	8	8	8	7	8	7	8	8
Journalism, Debating, Dramatics	35	35	37	35	34	34	33	33	33	33
Music, Band, Orchestra, Chorus*	41	41	42	49	53	53	52	52	52	52
Departmental or Professional Clubs	22	21	20	18	16	15	15	15	15	15
Religious Organizations	42	41	41	39	38	37	37	37	37	38
Social or Community Clubs	55	54	54	51	50	49	49	48	49	50
Student Government	30	29	29	28	27	27	27	27	27	27
Number Responding to at Least One Activity	407,664	416,571	403,701	425,210	466,850	479,241	480,263	480,826	475,875	459,249
TOTAL										
Athletics, Intramural and Community	66	68	69	68	69	69	69	69	70	70
Ethnic Organizations	9	9	7	7	7	6	6	7	7	7
Journalism, Debating, Dramatics	30	30	32	31	30	29	29	29	28	28
Music, Band, Orchestra, Chorus*	34	34	34	41	43	44	43	43	43	42
Departmental or Professional Clubs	17	16	16	14	13	13	13	13	13	13
Religious Organizations	37	36	37	35	34	34	33	33	34	34
Social or Community Clubs	48	46	47	44	43	42	42	42	42	43
Student Government	28	26	26	25	24	24	24	23	23	24
Number Responding to at Least One Activity	792,025	807,724	776,169	811,493	888,301	906,932	906,344	906,703	898,474	867,869

*Item changed to "Artistic," including "Art and Dance" in 1977.

which reports plans for extracurricular activity in college. For both sexes, about 13 percent fewer students plan a participation in athletics. Both sexes plan a reduced participation in religious organizations, about 10 percent fewer students. There are indications of increased interest in preprofessional, or departmental, clubs and in social clubs, but in general there is indication of a somewhat reduced level of activity in college than in high school, probably in consideration of the unknown challenge of college academic work.

The data in Tables 6.3 and 6.4 are based upon the entire national college-bound senior population as this is reflected in the tests of the Admissions Testing Program. The Summary Reporting Service of the ATP offers similar tables for states and for individual schools and colleges.

The data for students applying for admission to a

Table 6.4

Percentage of Planned Extracurricular Activities in College as Reported by
SDQ Responses for Ten Annual Cohorts, 1974-1983

Year	1974	1975	1976	1977	1978	1979	1980	1981	1982	1983
MALE										
Athletics, Intramural and Community	67	68	67	67	68	68	68	66	68	68
Ethnic Organizations	10	7	7	6	5	5	5	5	5	5
Journalism, Debating, Dramatics	25	22	24	22	21	21	21	21	21	21
Music, Band, Orchestra, Chorus*	19	18	19	24	26	26	26	26	26	25
Departmental or Professional Clubs	22	18	20	18	17	17	18	18	19	19
Religious Organizations	24	20	21	20	20	19	20	20	20	21
Social or Community Clubs	43	39	40	38	37	37	36	36	37	39
Student Government	26	20	21	19	19	18	18	17	18	18
Number Responding to at Least One Activity	384,361	391,153	372,486	386,283	421,451	427,691	426,081	425,877	422,599	408,620
FEMALE										
Athletics, Intramural and Community	44	44	45	44	44	45	46	45	46	46
Ethnic Organizations	15	10	10	8	8	7	7	7	7	7
Journalism, Debating, Dramatics	35	32	34	31	30	30	30	30	30	30
Music, Band, Orchestra, Chorus*	30	28	29	41	46	47	46	46	46	45
Departmental or Professional Clubs	29	24	24	21	19	18	18	18	19	19
Religious Organizations	32	28	28	27	25	25	25	25	26	26
Social or Community Clubs	58	54	55	52	51	52	52	51	53	55
Student Government	32	26	26	24	23	23	23	23	23	24
Number Responding to at Least One Activity	407,664	416,571	403,701	425,210	466,850	479,241	480,263	480,826	475,875	459,249
TOTAL										
Athletics, Intramural and Community	55	55	56	55	56	56	56	55	56	56
Ethnic Organizations	13	8	9	7	7	6	6	6	6	6
Journalism, Debating, Dramatics	30	27	29	27	26	26	26	26	26	25
Music, Band, Orchestra, Chorus*	25	23	24	33	37	37	37	36	36	36
Departmental or Professional Clubs	26	21	22	19	18	18	18	18	19	19
Religious Organizations	28	24	25	24	23	22	22	23	23	23
Social or Community Clubs	51	47	48	45	45	45	44	44	46	47
Student Government	29	23	23	22	21	20	21	20	21	21
Number Responding to at Least One Activity	792,025	807,724	776,169	811,493	888,301	906,932	906,344	906,703	898,474	867,869

*Item changed to "Artistic," including "Art and Dance" in 1977.

given college may be used in numerous ways. For some questions and in some categories, it may be useful for a college to compare its individual results with the national data such as those in Tables 6.3 and 6.4. Doing so may reveal differences between the student body at this college and throughout the nation. The evaluation of such data would focus on the extent to which the presence or absence of any difference is understandable and acceptable. National descriptions are not normative prescriptions, and a given college may be aware that its students will differ from students in general. On the other hand, differences between the college and the national group may not be anticipated, and they may signal that the college's reputation differs from what is desired. This may lead to an examination of college programs or of the dissemination of information concerning them.

The decisions concerning programs that result from the SDQ/SRS descriptions influence the nature of the college and the adequacy of its services to its students. Institutional summaries can give the college administration a signal that certain activity areas are likely to be over- or undersubscribed in a given year, allowing the school to shift resources appropriately.

ATP results often are useful in identifying or clarifying very general trends in American education, and the SDQ has facilitated these applications. For example, sex differences in performance on the mathematical sections of the SAT have been observed since the earliest introduction of mathematical material in the 1930s. There is an average differential in favor of males, and the test norms reflect the separate performance of males and females. But there are obvious problems when comparing all the males who take the mathematical sections of the SAT in a given academic year with all the females. There is a tendency to treat the two groups as equivalent, because each consists of high school juniors and seniors who are interested in college and because each group shows comparable high school achievement. However, the groups differ on a critical variable: the level of mathematical preparation. Before the introduction of the SDQ, it was difficult to examine such phenomena without a special data collection. The SDQ specifically asks about the number of years of study of mathematics in high school. Table 6.5 shows the average SAT-mathematical score for males and females for each category in Question 7 and for the total group of males and the total group of females. Figure 6.2 presents graphically the magnitude of the sex difference for these questionnaire categories.

As the table shows, some of the 51-point average scaled score difference in favor of males in the total population is attributable to the greater average

Figure 6.2

Difference Between Male and Female SAT-Mathematical Average Score as a Function of Years of Study of Mathematics

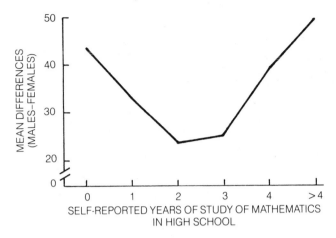

preparation of males. Females show obvious benefits from continued education; they average 345 with one year's work but 530 with more than four. For the groups with two and three years of experience, the differences between the sexes are reduced to approximately 25 points, or only about 50 percent of the overall difference. But the differences persist, even when the sex-defined groups show nominally equivalent years of study, and the difference for the group with more than four years experience is virtually as large (49 points) as the difference for the total groups (51 points). This 49-point difference for students with reported extensive mathematics course work may indicate that females take courses that are different from those that males take.

Thus, SDQ data helps clarify the nature of these relationships, underscores the need to consider years of training, and identifies possible areas of further research into self-selection or the precise nature of course work. There is the suggestion of a pattern in the increasing differences from 24 to 49 for the groups with two, three, four, or more than four years of study. This finding requires additional data for its explanation, but the SDQ question has enabled it to emerge.

The Student Search Service

The Student Search Service (SSS) is an outcome of the recommendation by the Commission on Tests that the ATP move toward more symmetrical services benefiting both students and colleges. The SSS is an effective way for students to learn about colleges with the programs and opportunities they want. At the same time, it is an efficient means for colleges,

Table 6.5

Average SAT-Mathematical Scores for Males and Females and Their Difference by Years of Mathematics Study Reported

Years of Study	Males		Females		Difference in Average Score
	N	SAT-M Average	N	SAT-M Average	
>4	60,095	579	43,751	530	49
4	229,952	514	215,828	475	39
3	81,293	439	129,422	414	25
2	27,084	389	51,375	365	24
1	4,255	379	7,213	345	34
0	886	410	1,059	367	43
Total	403,565	499	448,648	448	51

governmental scholarship agencies, and consortiums of colleges to identify college-bound students with the qualifications or characteristics they seek.

Students may indicate their desire to participate in the sss when they take the SAT, the Achievement Tests, or the PSAT/NMSQT. About one and a half million students do so each year. This pool of potential student contacts is made accessible to colleges through five regularly scheduled searches: the Winter ATP Search, the Spring PSAT/NMSQT Search (Early and Late options), the Limited PSAT/NMSQT Search, and the Summer ATP Search. The size of these various searches and their administration dates are as follows:

Search	Processing Period	Composition	Approximate Number of Participating Students
Winter ATP			
Option 1	December–January	Based on students, mostly seniors, who have taken the SAT at any time through the December administration	780,000
Option 2	December–January	Based on same students as in Option 1 but eliminates those reported in the Summer ATP Search	256,000
Option 3	December–January	Based on same students as in Option 1 but eliminates those reported in the Spring PSAT/NMSQT Search	148,000
Spring PSAT/NMSQT			
Early Option	January–March	All PSAT/NMSQT students, mostly juniors	1,265,000
Late Option	February–April	All PSAT/NMSQT students, mostly juniors	1,265,000
Limited PSAT/NMSQT	May–June	Students reported to institutions 0-5 times in the Spring PSAT/NMSQT Search	477,000
Summer ATP			
Option 1	July–September	Based largely on students who have taken the SAT in the junior year	452,000
Option 2	July–September	Based on same students as in Option 1 but eliminates those reported in the Spring PSAT/NMSQT Search	110,000

Students participating in sss constitute about 80 to 90 percent of the students taking the tests. Participants in sss are thus a self-selected subsample of the total group of students participating in the Admissions Testing Program, whose data, upon graduation, are included in the Summary Reporting Service. Because of the extensive overlap, the Summary Reporting Service descriptions of its database are useful predictors of the characteristics of the sss sample. This enables colleges to avoid a fruitless pursuit of unlikely applicants. The results of the Summary Reporting Service are widely available, without cost.

The high level of student participation reflects the general satisfaction of students with the Student Search Service. Table 6.6 shows the results of a spring 1981 survey of high school seniors who had participated in the Spring PSAT/NMSQT Search during their junior year. It indicates that most students who are contacted by colleges through their sss participation react positively to the service.

Table 6.6

Student Responses to Questions Concerning Satisfaction with Student Search Service (1981 Survey)

Question	Percentage of Those Responding
1. How many colleges contacted you?	
None	2.4
Very few colleges (1-5)	15.4
A few colleges (6-15)	17.4
Quite a few colleges (16-25)	14.2
A lot of colleges (25 or more)	50.6
2. What was your reaction to receiving the mailings?	
Pleased to receive them	70.6
Not pleased to receive them	1.9
Had mixed reactions	27.5
3. Did you learn of colleges of the type you hope to attend but didn't know about?	
Yes	57.5
No	32.9
Not sure	9.6
4. Are you considering at least one college you learned about through the Student Search?	
Yes	41.7
No	51.1
Too soon to know	7.1
5. Have you applied or do you plan to apply to at least one college you learned of through the mailings?	
Yes	46.1
No	47.2
Too soon to know	6.7
6. Would you encourage other students to take part in the Search?	
Yes	87.6
No	3.6
Not sure	8.8

As the table shows, nearly one-half of all students had made an application to a college they learned of through sss, or planned to do so. This is strong confirmation of the practical value of the SDQ information in facilitating student-college exchanges. The Student Search Service can yield a sizable number of contacts; over half of the students responding reported contacts by 25 or more colleges. About 50 percent of the students said that the number of contacts was "just about right" or they "had no opinion." The remaining 50 percent expressed belief that there were either "too many" or "too few" contacts. However, nearly 88 percent of these same students would encourage other students to take part, and over 41 percent were considering a college they were introduced to through sss.

Securing student satisfaction is a principal concern for the Admissions Testing Program, but safeguarding a student's privacy is also a paramount interest. Student information reported to sss participants includes name, address, sex, birthdate, social security number, secondary school, and intended college major. Each institution or agency is required to sign a confidentiality pledge stating that the student information provided will be used only for the purposes for which it was intended: to bring admissions and financial aid information to the attention of the students. Further, if the institution or agency avails itself of a commercial firm to handle its mailing, that firm must also execute a confidentiality pledge indicating that it will not release names or other information provided by the ATP to any other party. Any mailing by a college or agency that is based on sss-provided information must clearly state this fact.

Colleges also report satisfaction with the sss. Four times since 1975 the College Board has surveyed participating institutions. The latest questionnaire was mailed in 1982 and about half the institutions reponded. Approximately 80 percent of all respondents gave positive endorsement to sss services, finding them "very effective" or "somewhat effective," and comparing them positively to other avenues for contacting students.

Contributions of the SDQ

The introduction of the sdq and the development of the services based upon its information add a significant dimension to the capability of the ATP in serving institutions and individuals. Although the information has been restricted to basic factual material, it opens the possibility of a more precise exchange between a college and selected students with characteristics that are known to be appropriate for that college. By providing a basis for the analysis of the

results of the sat and the Achievement Tests, it is responsive to the recommendation of the Commission on Tests (College Board 1970, p. 93) that the Board should "expand and refine the information bearing on college entrance that is available both to students and to colleges." In some ways, the current programs fail to realize all of the idealistic goals of the commission. For example, while the Student Search Service constitutes the student-locater service that the commission encouraged, the symmetrical College Locater Service, intended to serve the student directly, failed upon introduction for lack of sufficient interest. But the commission itself foresaw the many problems in these areas, and it urged that (p. 96) "exploration should not be allowed to inhibit the concurrent operation of what is possible now even though it may soon seem to be a relatively primitive system." Although there is still a need to continue to strive toward the commission's goal (p. 94) of "the most comprehensive and sensitive available descriptions of both students on the one hand and of colleges and their programs on the other hand," the sdq, srs, and sss are positive steps in that direction. The ATP, in the decade following the report of the commission, has made a promising beginning.

Appendix

As described in the chapter text, the content of the sdq is reviewed periodically and modified if changes are indicated. For example, the categories used to describe joint parental income (Question 43) are revised from time to time due to the effects of inflation. A systematic review of the sdq by the College Board and Educational Testing Service was recently undertaken, and a new version will be introduced in 1985-86; therefore, the specific set of questions presented here will be slightly outdated. The version of the sdq included in the appendix is adapted from the 1982-83 *Student Bulletin for the SAT and Achievement Tests*. This version, also current in 1983-84, was used in developing the text and data presented in this chapter.

Principal author: Thomas F. Donlon
Contributors or reviewers: William H. Angoff, Irving L. Broudy, John A. Centra, Janet A. Levy, Leonard Ramist, and June Stern.

Student Descriptive Questionnaire (SDQ)

1. The College Board's Student Search Service is an information service for students, colleges, and governmental scholarship programs. It is <u>free</u> to all students who participate in the ATP and works this way:

   If you ask to participate, colleges and scholarship programs interested in students with your characteristics can ask for and receive your name, address, sex, date of birth, high school, and intended major. The answers you give to the questions that follow may be used to determine if you fit the characteristics colleges have requested in the Student Search Service. Different colleges and scholarship programs will be interested in students with specific characteristics, such as place of residence, range of test scores, intended college majors, ethnic background, and income. For example, a state scholarship program may want to identify all students within that state who are eligible for the Pell Grant program in order to notify them of when and how to apply.

   By participating, you may receive information from a variety of colleges and scholarship programs about their programs, admissions procedures, and financial aid opportunities. The mail you receive may include information from a college well known to you or come from one unfamiliar to you but with the academic program and other features you find important. In either case the Student Search Service can provide you with information you might not otherwise discover.

   Your name will be made available to the Student Search Service only if you answer "Yes" to this item.

   (Y) Yes, I want to be included in the Student Search Service.
   (N) No, I do not want to be included in the Student Search Service.

2. What kind of high school are you attending?

   (A) Public   (B) Other than public

3. Which of the following best describes your present high school program?

   (A) Academic or college preparatory   (B) General
   (C) Career-oriented (business, vocational, industrial arts)
   (D) Other

4. About how many students are there in your high school class?

   (A) Fewer than 100   (B) 100-249   (C) 250-499
   (D) 500-749   (E) 750 or more

5. What is your most recent high school class rank? (For example, if you are 15th in a class of 100, you are in the second tenth.) If you do not know your rank or rank is not used in your school, give your best estimate.

   (A) Highest tenth⎫ top fifth   (D) Middle fifth
   (B) Second tenth⎭   (E) Fourth fifth
   (C) Second fifth   (F) Lowest fifth

Questions 6 through 11 ask you to blacken the letter corresponding to the total years of study you expect to complete in certain subject areas. Include in the total only courses you have taken since beginning the ninth grade and those you expect to complete before graduation from high school. Count less than a full year in a subject as a full year. Do not count a repeated year of the same course as an additional year of study.

   (A) One year or the equivalent
   (B) Two years or the equivalent
   (C) Three years or the equivalent
   (D) Four years or the equivalent
   (E) More than four years or the equivalent
   (F) I will not take any courses in the subject area.

6. English

7. Mathematics

8. Foreign Languages

9. Biological Sciences (for example, biology, botany, or zoology)

10. Physical Sciences (for example, chemistry, physics, or earth science)

11. Social Studies (for example, history, government, or geography)

For each of the subject areas in questions 12 through 17, blacken the *latest* year-end or midyear grade you received since beginning the ninth grade. For example, if you are a senior and have not taken biology or any other biological science since your sophomore year, indicate that year-end grade. If you are a junior and have completed the first half of the year in an English course, indicate that midyear grade.

If you received the grade in an advanced, accelerated, or honors course, also blacken the letter H.

   (A) Excellent (usually 90-100 or A)
   (B) Good (usually 80-89 or B)
   (C) Fair (usually 70-79 or C)
   (D) Passing (usually 60-69 or D)
   (F) Failing (usually 59 or below or F)
   (G) Only "pass-fail" grades were assigned and I received a pass.
   (H) The grade reported was in an advanced, accelerated, or honors course.

12. English

13. Mathematics

14. Foreign Languages

15. Biological Sciences

16. Physical Sciences

17. Social Studies

18. Will you have completed advanced high school or college-level work before entering college? If so, mark the letter for each field in which you plan to apply for advanced placement, credit-by-examination, or exemption from required courses.

   (A) English   (E) Physical Sciences
   (B) Mathematics   (F) Social Studies
   (C) Foreign Languages   (G) Art/Music
   (D) Biological Sciences

19. On the average, how many hours per week do you work in a part-time job? (Exclude vacations.)

(A) None
(B) Less than 6 hours
(C) 6 to 10 hours
(D) 11 to 15 hours
(E) 16 to 20 hours
(F) 21 to 25 hours
(G) 26 to 30 hours
(H) More than 30 hours

20. How much have you participated in community or church groups while in high school?

(A) I have not been a member of any community or church group.
(B) I have belonged to one or two groups but have not participated actively.
(C) I have participated actively in one or two groups but have not held any major offices (for example, president, chairman, or treasurer).
(D) I have participated actively in more than two groups but have not held any major offices.
(E) I have participated actively and have held a major office in at least one community or church group.

21. How much have you participated in athletics in or out of high school?

(A) I have not participated in athletics.
(B) I have participated in individual or intramural athletics.
(C) I have been on one or more varsity teams but have not earned a varsity letter.
(D) I have earned one or more varsity letters in a single sport.
(E) I have earned varsity letters in more than one sport.

22. How much have you participated in clubs and organizations in high school?

(A) I have not been a member of any club or organization.
(B) I have belonged to some organizations but have not held any major offices (for example, president, editor, or class or school representative).
(C) I have held one or two major offices.
(D) I have held three or four major offices.
(E) I have held five or more major offices.

23. During your high school years how many honors or awards (for example, essay contest, debating tournament, science fair, music, art or theater competition, or membership in a scholastic honors group) have you received?

(A) None
(B) One or two
(C) Three or four
(D) Five or six
(E) Seven or more

24. What is the highest level of education you plan to complete beyond high school?

(A) A two-year specialized training program (for example, electronics or laboratory technician)
(B) A two-year Associate of Arts degree (A.A.)
(C) Bachelor's degree (B.A. or B.S.)
(D) Master's degree (M.A. or M.S.)
(E) Doctor's or other professional degree (such as M.D. or Ph.D.)
(F) Other or undecided

25. What is the date of your high school graduation? Blacken month and last two digits of year.

26. When do you expect to enter college? Blacken month and last two digits of year.

Your response to question 27 will not be included in the reports that are sent to you, your school, and the colleges you designate.

27. Do you plan to apply for financial aid at any college?

(Y) Yes   (N) No

28. When you enroll, do you expect to attend college

(A) full-time   (B) part-time

29. When you enroll, do you expect to attend college during the

(A) day   (B) evening

30. Where do you prefer to live during your first two years in college?

(A) At home
(B) Single-sex dorm
(C) Coed dorm
(D) Fraternity or sorority house
(E) On-campus apartment
(F) Off-campus apartment

31. Are you a United States citizen?

(Y) Yes   (N) No

32. Are you a veteran of the United States Armed Forces?

(Y) Yes   (N) No

Questions 33 through 36 are for students who have finished high school and have already attended college. If you have not, go on to the paragraph preceding question 37.

33. Please put the code number of the college you are attending or most recently attended in the spaces provided and blacken the corresponding ovals. See the gray-bordered pages for college code numbers.

34. Are you enrolled in that college now?

(Y) Yes   (N) No

35. Approximately what was your grade point average at that college on a scale of 0 (F) to 4 (A)?

(A) 3.5 or above
(B) 3.0–3.4
(C) 2.5–2.9
(D) 2.0–2.4
(E) 1.5–1.9
(F) Below 1.5
(G) Not applicable

36. If you expect to transfer credits, at what level do you expect to enter the new college?

(A) First semester freshman
(B) Second semester freshman
(C) First semester sophomore
(D) Second semester sophomore
(E) Junior
(F) Senior

The College Board wants its tests and services to be fair and useful to all candidates. Research based on responses to questions 37 and 38 will help the College Board evaluate and improve its tests and services. Your responses will also be reported to your school and to those colleges that accept such information in order to make sure their programs are fair and useful to students of all racial and ethnic backgrounds.

119

37. How do you describe yourself?

    (A) American Indian or Alaskan native
    (B) Black or Afro-American or Negro
    (C) Mexican-American or Chicano
    (D) Oriental or Asian-American or Pacific Islander
    (E) Puerto Rican
    (F) White or Caucasian
    (G) Other

38. Is English your best language?

    (Y) Yes   (N) No

Your responses to questions 39 and 40 will be used only for research. They will not be included in the score reports that are sent to you, your school, and the colleges you designate.

39. Indicate the highest level of education completed by your father or male guardian.

    (A) Grade school
    (B) Some high school
    (C) High school diploma
    (D) Business or trade school
    (E) Some college
    (F) Bachelor's degree
    (G) Some graduate or professional school
    (H) Graduate or professional degreee

40. Using the list in question 39, indicate the highest level of education completed by your mother or female guardian.

Questions 41 through 43 ask about your parents' financial situation and should be answered in consultation with them. Your individual responses will not be reported to anyone. Only summary responses for groups of students will be reported to colleges and high schools.

41. How many persons are dependent on your parent(s) or legal guardian for financial support? Be sure to include your parent(s) and yourself.

    (A) Two (B) Three (C) Four (D) Five
    (E) Six (F) Seven (G) Eight (H) Nine or more

42. During your first year in college, how many persons dependent on your parent(s) or legal guardian will be in college? Include yourself.

    (A) One (B) Two (C) Three
    (D) Four (E) Five or more

43. What was the approximate income of your parents before taxes last year? Include taxable and nontaxable income from all sources.

    (A) Less than $3,000 a year (about $57 a week or less)
    (B) Between $3,000 and $5,999 a year (from $58 to $114 a week)
    (C) Between $6,000 and $8,999 a year (from $115 to $173 a week)
    (D) Between $9,000 and $11,999 a year (from $174 to $230 a week)
    (E) Between $12,000 and $14,999 a year (from $231 to $288 a week)
    (F) Between $15,000 and $17,999 a year (from $289 to $346 a week)
    (G) Between $18,000 and $20,999 a year (from $347 to $403 a week)

    (H) Between $21,000 and $23,999 a year
    (I) Between $24,000 and $26,999 a year
    (J) Between $27,000 and $29,999 a year
    (K) Between $30,000 and $34,999 a year
    (L) Between $35,000 and $39,999 a year
    (M) Between $40,000 and $44,999 a year
    (N) Between $45,000 and $49,000 a year
    (O) $50,000 a year or more

44. You may want to receive help outside regular course work from the college you plan to attend. If so, blacken the letter for each area in which you may want help.

    (A) Counseling about educational plans and opportunities
    (B) Counseling about vocational/career plans and opportunities
    (C) Improving mathematical ability
    (D) Finding part-time work
    (E) Counseling about personal problems
    (F) Increasing reading ability
    (G) Developing good study habits
    (H) Improving writing ability

Questions 45 and 46 concern your interests in extracurricular activities in high school and your plans to participate in college.

45. Blacken the letter for each activity in which you participated while in high school.

    (A) Athletics—interscholastic, intramural, or community
    (B) Ethnic or racial activities or organizations
    (C) Journalism, debating, or dramatic activities
    (D) Art, music, or dance
    (E) Preprofessional or departmental clubs—for example, Future Teachers of America, American Society of Civil Engineers
    (F) Religious activities or organizations
    (G) Social clubs or community organizations
    (H) Student government

46. Using the list in question 45, blacken the letter for each activity in which you plan to participate in college.

Questions 47 through 60 concern how you feel you compare with other people your own age in certain areas of ability. For each field, blacken the letter

    (A) if you feel you are in the highest 1 percent in that area of ability
    (B) if you feel you are in the highest 10 percent in that area of ability
    (C) if you feel you are above average in that area of ability
    (D) if you feel you are average in that area of ability
    (E) if you feel you are below average in that area of ability

47. Acting ability

48. Artistic ability

49. Athletic ability

50. Creative writing

51. Getting along with others

52. Leadership ability

53. Mathematical ability

54. Mechanical ability

55. Musical ability

56. Organizing work

57. Sales ability

58. Scientific ability

59. Spoken expression

60. Written expression

61. From the list that follows, choose the field that would be your first choice for your college curriculum. Write the number of that field and blacken the corresponding ovals.

62. From the same list, choose the field that would be your second choice. Write the number of that field and blacken the corresponding ovals.

63. From the same list, choose the career field that you think you will pursue after college. Write the number of that field and blacken the corresponding ovals. If your exact choice does not appear, select the one most closely related.

Fields of Study in Two- and Four-Year Colleges and Career Choices

100 AGRICULTURE
101 agriculture economics
102 agronomy, field crops
103 animal science
104 dairy science
105 farming, ranching
106 fish and game, wildlife management
107 food science
108 horticulture
109 landscaping
110 soil sciences

125 ARCHITECTURE AND ENVIRONMENTAL DESIGN
126 architecture
127 city planning
128 urban development

150 ART
151 art history
152 commercial
153 design
154 fashion design
155 graphic arts
156 interior decorating
157 museum work
158 photography
159 printing
160 studio art

175 BIOLOGICAL SCIENCES
176 bacteriology
177 biochemistry
178 biology
179 biophysics
180 botany
181 ecology
182 marine biology
183 physiology
184 zoology

200 BUSINESS AND COMMERCE
201 accounting
202 advertising
203 business management and administration
204 court reporting
205 finance and banking
206 hotel and restaurant administration
207 industrial management
208 marketing
209 personnel work
210 real estate
211 sales and retailing
212 secretarial studies
213 transportation and commerce

225 COMMUNICATIONS
226 film
227 journalism
228 radio and television

250 COMPUTER SCIENCE AND SYSTEMS ANALYSIS
251 computer science
252 data processing
253 systems analysis

275 EDUCATION
276 agricultural education
277 art education
278 business education
279 child development and nursery education
280 college teaching
281 educational administration
282 education of exceptional children
283 education of the deaf
284 education of the mentally retarded
285 elementary education
286 general education
287 guidance counseling
288 health education
289 home economics education
290 industrial arts education
291 music education
292 physical education
293 recreation
294 secondary education
295 speech therapy
296 vocational trade and industrial education

325 ENGINEERING
326 aerospace and aeronautical engineering
327 agricultural engineering
328 air-conditioning engineering
329 architectural engineering
330 ceramic engineering
331 chemical engineering
332 civil engineering
333 construction and transportation
334 drafting
335 electrical engineering
336 engineering aide
337 engineering design
338 engineering sciences
339 industrial and management engineering
340 industrial laboratory technology
341 instrumentation technology
342 materials science
343 mechanical engineering
344 metallurgical engineering
345 mining and mineral engineering
346 naval architecture and marine engineering
347 nuclear technology
348 petroleum engineering
349 plastics technology
350 quality control technology
351 surveying
352 textile engineering

375 ENGLISH AND LITERATURE
376 creative writing
377 English
378 literature
379 speech

400 ETHNIC STUDIES
401 American Indian studies
402 Black studies
403 Mexican-American studies
404 Spanish-American studies

425 FOREIGN LANGUAGES
426 Classical languages
427 Eastern languages
428 French
429 German
430 interpreting/translating
431 Italian
432 linguistics
433 Russian
434 Spanish

450 FORESTRY AND CONSERVATION

475 GEOGRAPHY

500 HEALTH AND MEDICAL PROFESSIONS
501 dental assisting
502 dental hygiene
503 dental technology
504 health and safety
505 laboratory technology
506 medical assisting
507 medical records librarian
508 medical technology
509 nursing—practical
510 nursing—registered
511 occupational therapy
512 optometry
513 pharmacy
514 physical therapy
515 predentistry/dentistry
516 premedicine/medicine
517 preveterinary medicine/veterinary medicine
518 radiology and X-ray technology

550 HISTORY AND CULTURES
551 American
552 ancient
553 area and regional
554 European

575 HOME ECONOMICS
576 clothing and textiles
577 family relations
578 food and nutrition
579 infant and child care
580 institution management

600 LIBRARY SCIENCE

625 MATHEMATICS
626 statistics

650 MILITARY SCIENCE
651 air science
652 merchant marine
653 military science—army
654 naval science

675 MUSIC
676 composition and theory
677 instrumental music
678 music history
679 voice

700 PHILOSOPHY AND RELIGION
701 ministry
702 philosophy
703 religion
704 theology

725 PHYSICAL SCIENCES
726 astronomy
727 chemistry
728 earth science
729 geology
730 meteorology
731 oceanography
732 physical sciences
733 physics

750 PSYCHOLOGY
751 child psychology
752 experimental psychology
753 general psychology
754 social psychology

775 SOCIAL SCIENCES
776 anthropology
777 correction administration
778 economics
779 fire science
780 foreign service
781 government service/politics
782 industrial relations
783 international relations
784 law enforcement/police science
785 political science
786 prelaw/law
787 public administration
788 social work
789 sociology

800 THEATER ARTS
801 acting
802 dance
803 drama
804 theater arts

825 TRADE AND VOCATIONAL
826 airline hosting
827 automotive maintenance
828 aviation maintenance
829 building construction
830 carpentry
831 cosmetology
832 mortuary service

900 OTHER

999 UNDECIDED

CHAPTER VII

Construct and Content Validity of the SAT

Introduction

Since the SAT, TSWE, and Achievement Tests are intended to help college officials select and place students, they must relate to success in college, which is usually measured by course grades. Students with high SAT scores should tend to get higher grades than those with low scores; students with high French Achievement Test scores should usually do better when placed directly in second-year or third-year French than when placed in first-year French. In *criterion-related* validity studies, information available at the time of selection or placement—SAT scores, Achievement Test scores, high school record, letters of recommendation, essays, portfolios—is correlated with grades. Many colleges have studied the criterion-related validity of the SAT and other predictors in admissions, and the College Board has provided support for these studies since the introduction of the tests, including, since 1964, the Validity Study Service. Results from the 3,500 studies conducted at 750 colleges through the Validity Study Service are the basis of the reported summaries in Chapter VIII.

Criterion-related validity studies alone cannot evaluate all aspects of validity required for a test. Other analyses are necessary to show that students in most schools are given the opportunity to develop the abilities or learn the subjects being measured. Still other analyses are needed to establish that the abilities or content being measured are themselves important to success in college, and not simply chance correlates. These other analyses are usually considered to be useful in evaluating *content or construct validity;* they will be discussed in this chapter.

The content validity of Achievement Tests is ordinarily evaluated judgmentally. If the tests ask questions that school and college faculties consider important and if the content of the test is covered in high school curriculums, the content of the test is judged to be valid. Such validity may be difficult to achieve, given the diversity of both high schools and

colleges, but the concept of the content validity of an achievement test is not difficult to describe.

Some information about the content and construct validity of the Achievement Tests is provided in Chapter V. Necessarily, the description there is on the general processes by which these validities are obtained, since detailed descriptions of each of the 14 subject-matter tests would create an excessively long chapter. Interested persons may contact the College Board or ETS for additional information. Information about the content and construct validity of the Test of Standard Written English is provided in Chapter IV.

The content and construct validity of the SAT is more complex. Not only is there a need to demonstrate appropriate subject matter, but the validity of *scholastic aptitude* as a concept is equally important. The idea of measuring something as general as scholastic aptitude, as opposed to measuring specific knowledge, came to testing only at the turn of the century. This idea has generated controversy from the beginning, and the psychometric theory it involves has been substantially revised over the years. This chapter presents a discussion of the content and the logic of the SAT, focusing first on the general idea of scholastic aptitude and then on the components of the tests: the individual items, the item types, and then the verbal and mathematical scores they yield.

The Concept of Scholastic Aptitude

There is a long history of interest, both at the College Board and at ETS, in the general properties of the SAT. For example, Coffman (1963, p. 4) observed: "The SAT measures the level of development of the basic learning skills required for college work, skills involving the two primary languages of communication in the academic world . . . English and mathematics. . . ." Similarly, Chauncey (1962, p. 42) called attention to the need to consider the basic nature of the test, and not just its correlational function: "While the interest of most people in the SAT is focused on its ability to predict academic success in college, the significance of the test is really much more basic. It is a test that provides a great deal of information about two important qualities that have wide relevance in our society, verbal and mathematical ability. . . . In the years ahead verbal and mathematical ability will, I think, be recognized in their own right rather than solely for their predictive usefulness." Chauncey's forecast was correct. The concern about the score decline (discussed in Chapter IX) is largely a concern about a decline in the general quality of these skills, and not simply their relationship to college grades.

"Scholastic aptitude" was a convenient label for the test when it was coined over 50 years ago. It is clear, however, that it is not totally satisfactory. "Aptitude" connotes the concept of an innate property of the learner, but the test has never been developed under the assumption that it should (or could) measure innate aptitudes. Rather, a concept of aptitude as a *general readiness* for collegiate work underlies its development. While such readiness is assumed to depend in part on past achievement, the SAT is also distinguished from an achievement test. A good statement of the difference between aptitude and achievement tests is provided by Angoff (1976, p. 3):

> Confusion between the two types of tests arises because tests that measure aptitude for academic performance often contain questions very similar to, and sometimes indistinguishable from, questions in achievement tests. Despite the seeming similarity, however, the two types are fundamentally different, both in purpose and in conception.
>
> Achievement tests are curriculum based; they are designed to measure the educational outcomes of specific subject-matter areas—physics, French, American history, advanced mathematics, for example. They typically assess outcomes of courses that the student has studied recently. Thus, although achievement tests on occasion may be used to predict an individual's future academic performance, they are usually meant to be *retrospective* measures of formal school outcomes and should be evaluated in terms of their relevance to formal course content.
>
> Aptitude tests like the SAT, on the other hand, are designed to sample some of the intellectual abilities needed to perform well in future academic activities; they are more properly thought of as *prospective* measures and should be evaluated in terms of their relevance to those future activities.

The role of the SAT has changed somewhat in response to various social changes, but the fundamental concepts that motivated its introduction have been surprisingly enduring, and the language used

by the committee of psychologists which first met in 1925 to advise the College Board on its introduction is largely current today. The committee wrote (Brigham et al. 1926, p. 46): "To determine who shall go to college is a problem involving all the best available machinery of educational guidance. . . . Comparative studies of [the aptitude test score] seem to indicate that this score is about as good as any other single index. Even the most enthusiastic supporters of such tests, however, do not recommend that admission to college should be granted merely on the basis of a good test score, nor do they recommend that a person should be refused admission to college merely because of a low test score. The facts indicate that this score is best used as a supplement to all other available information concerning any given candidate" (p. 54). In the intervening years, access to college has greatly expanded, but the test itself is still described in much the same way. In a recent version of *Taking the SAT* (College Board 1982c) the student is told, "Your high school record is probably the best evidence of your preparation for college. . . . [S]cores on the SAT are just part of the information used when making an admission decision" (p. 3).

In the 1926 committee report, the SAT was characterized as a supplement to the high school record and to the existing achievement examination program. The following section of the report is as timely today as it was when it was written (Brigham et al. 1926, p. 55): "In some cases, limitation of educational opportunity would seem to be a factor causing low marks in Board [achievement] examinations. This would be expected, since . . . the Board examinations measure specific preparation. On the other hand, [aptitude] tests are so constructed that they put as little premium as possible on specific training, and more emphasis on potential promise as distinguished from prior accomplishment. It cannot be maintained, of course, that the tests measure 'native ability,' irrespective of training, nor is it necessary to prove before adoption exactly what the tests measure. In the particular situation just described, a candidate whose educational opportunity has been limited has a much better chance to show his real capacity in a test which is not a measure of specific preparation, and which is devised so that any person may find increasingly harder and harder problems in which to demonstrate his ability."

In 1926, the members of the committee had clear ideas about the best interpretation of the test (p. 55): "It would seem to be demonstrated that test scores are more certain indices of ability than of disability. A high score on the test is significant. A low score may or may not be significant. A low score, most certainly, should not be taken as significant unless

124

corroborated by other evidence such as low marks in the Board [achievement] examinations and poor school record. On the other hand, high scores may be taken as significant with some degree of confidence." A high SAT score may be approached with some confidence: it is likely that the individual who earns one will have the general intellectual skills to complete a successful college education. But a low score, by itself, is somewhat more ambiguous. It needs the corroboration of other data before the judgment is made that the individual involved is not yet ready for college work.

Similarly, the committee noted that:

> Boards of Admission to colleges, now forced to estimate the future worth of candidates, need all the information which is available and pertinent to reach wise decisions. This additional test now made available through the instrumentality of the College Entrance Examination Board may help to resolve a few perplexing problems, but it should be regarded merely as a supplementary record. To place too great an emphasis on test scores is as dangerous as the failure properly to evaluate any score or mark in conjunction with other measures and estimates which it supplements (p. 44).

The committee uses the term "aptitude" to distinguish such tests from tests of training in school subjects. Any claims that aptitude tests now in use really *measure* "general intelligence" or "general mental ability" may or may not be substantiated. The term "scholastic aptitude" makes no stronger claim for such tests than that there is a tendency for individual differences in scores in these tests to be associated positively with individual differences in subsequent academic attainment (p. 55).

The SAT does not sample directly the content or operations of all the varied curriculums for which it is predictive. Rather than knowledge or skills relating to specific curriculums, the SAT includes tasks that require 1) the recalling or inferring of meaning, 2) the application of reasoning, and 3) the possession of an appropriate standard for judgments of correctness. As these requirements suggest, it is not a narrow assessment of the knowledge of facts. The test requires the derivation of meaning from verbal and mathematical symbols; in Coffman's phrase, the SAT assesses a mastery of "the two primary languages of communication."

The SAT is not intended to include everything that might be considered "scholastic aptitude." As Chauncey wrote (1962, p. 42): ". . . Verbal and mathematical ability are . . . , of course, only two of a number of qualities that are important. Originality, industriousness, thoughtfulness, perseverance, and many other qualities are likewise important and should not be overshadowed by verbal and mathe-

matical ability simply because we know how to measure the last two—and have not learned how to measure the others." Other areas, such as memory and spatial ability, which could be useful in certain contexts as appraisals of scholastic aptitude, are not included. This is because any material included in the test must show usefulness in a wide variety of contexts. This principle, for example, best explains the current exclusion of the measurement of spatial ability from the test. In the past, the Board did offer a measure of spatial ability in conjunction with the ATP, which was moderately useful in selection for certain engineering and science curriculums. However, it was used by too few schools to warrant its continuance.

When Brigham and his fellow psychologists applied the knowledge and principles that they had acquired in the mental testing of military personnel in World War I, the measures they chose were derived from hypotheses about mental processes and not from an analysis of school-based tasks. A student of the work of Binet, the French psychologist who pioneered the assessment of cognitive intellectual functioning in 1905, Brigham together with his fellow workers devised a number of tasks calling for reasoning and judgment, for inferring relations, and for inferring the meaning of symbols. An interest in the test questions as reflections of mental process was evident in Brigham's book, *A Study of Error*, written in 1932, which presented extensive summaries of the results of item analyses. Reflecting upon what could be learned through a systematic consideration of the distributions of answer choices, Brigham (p. 75) characterized these as presenting "a partial symbolic inventory of the college applicant mind."

The Development of Scholastic Aptitude

The concept of scholastic aptitude, as measured by the SAT, is one of general abilities that are developed over a number of years, influenced by experience both in and out of school, and (at least by high school) separable into verbal and mathematical skill areas. This idea of the development of scholastic aptitude is supported by a longitudinal study of verbal and quantitative abilities between grades 5 and 11 reported by Hilton (1979a). The study, which used results from the School and College Ability Test (SCAT), showed that verbal and quantitative abilities improved throughout these grades, although the rate of improvement appeared to diminish for some students by eleventh grade. Because all the students' skills tended to improve, significant changes over time in a student's relative position within the group were not common. In fact, fifth grade scores correlated .70 to .80 with eleventh grade scores.

Although this correlation establishes that the skills measured by the SCAT in fifth grade are closely related to the skills measured by the same test in eleventh grade, it does not prove that the abilities measured remain identical. Some factor analysis studies show that the organization of skills may change with the age of the students. Jones, Burton, and Davenport (1982), after studying the results of the mathematical items in the National Assessment of Educational Progress tests, reported that the ability to do mathematical problems increased from grade 4 through grade 12, but the relationships among various kinds of problems changed. For students in grade school, the ability to work with whole numbers was distinct from the ability to work with fractions. By junior high, these two separate abilities become a single computational ability that is separate from the ability to do word problems. Further, it was shown that by senior high school students exhibit a single mathematical ability including skills that earlier were separate, such as algebra. However, this general mathematical ability is still separable from geometric and, in particular, spatial ability. Thus, the verbal and mathematical skills that are related over fairly long periods of time may function differently as students develop.

Some evidence on the change of verbal and mathematical ability beyond eleventh grade is also available. About half of those students who take the SAT attempt the test more than once. The average change for these students between their junior year and their senior year is a gain of about 12 points each for the verbal and mathematical scores (see Tables 3.17 and 3.18), although 35-40 percent of those who repeat the test receive lower scores. It is very likely that at least some of this gain is attributable to growth in the intervening months. However, this average score gain is not necessarily entirely attributable to growth. For example, those who retake the test are not a representative subgroup of all test takers: those who did better than they had expected the first time they took the test probably will not retake the test, while those who did worse than expected probably will try a second testing (Alderman 1981b). Another possible reason that students may improve their scores on retaking the SAT (besides growth) is that they derive some benefit from the practice of taking the SAT the first time. For whatever reason, there is evidence (Alderman 1981b) of a small average gain (about 15 points) in true score over a six-month interval, supporting the hypothesis

of growth in these abilities.

A study of students repeating the Graduate Record Examinations (GRE) by Rock and Werts (1979a) includes some interesting speculations about growth and score change. The GRE, like the SAT, contains verbal and mathematical sections, but the items are more difficult because the test is designed for students applying to graduate schools. Rock reports that for the GRE, at least over short time spans, by far the largest score gain is realized when the students retake the test the first time. It seems that for the GRE one practice test is sufficient. However, since these findings are based on the scores of students preparing for graduate school, it is not clear that the results can be applied to the younger SAT population.

Rock and Werts (1979a) also analyzed separately the gains of those who retook the GRE after relatively longer time intervals. For the group studied, the size of the gain on the GRE verbal score was positively related to the amount of time between testings. The authors suggested that, while the effect of practice on both verbal and quantitative tests is complete after one experience of the GRE, growth in verbal ability continues after college. No such evidence of growth was found for the GRE quantitative test in the Rock and Werts study, but that might be explained by the fact that relatively few people in their sample were studying mathematics when tested.

To summarize, the Hilton (1979) study indicates that verbal and mathematical abilities grow at least through the eleventh grade; the Alderman (1981b) study of program data supports the concept of growth from junior to senior year; and the Rock and Werts study suggests that growth, at least in verbal skills, continues to occur after college. Although none of these studies proves conclusively that verbal and mathematical abilities continue to grow throughout high school, there is good reason to believe that the abilities measured by the SAT are not static and can be improved.

Coaching. If verbal and mathematical abilities can be improved, is it logical to assume that coaching can improve them and thereby increase students' scores? And if so, is that effect consistent with the concept of developed ability that the SAT is meant to measure? As mentioned above, the average effect of retaking the SAT, based on general program experience, is about 12 scaled score points. The average effect of coaching, as reported in partially controlled studies, has been an additional 15 scaled score points (Messick 1980, Dersimonion and Laird 1983). However, the result of even a 20-point gain (since scores are reported in tens, no individual could receive a 15-point gain) can be no more than an 8-point gain in percentile rank among all college applicants tested. The largest possible gain is from 420 (forth-eighth percentile) to 440 (fifty-sixth percentile) on the verbal test. Students having any other initial verbal or mathematical score and securing a 20-point score gain would achieve smaller gains in percentile rank.*

Two important questions about coaching relate to the validity of the SAT:

1. Does coaching reduce the value of the SAT as a predictor of college success?

2. Does the effect of coaching (as opposed to the claims of coaching schools) call into question the construct of scholastic aptitude?

Coaching is typically claimed to have three possible outcomes: it teaches tricks that may increase students' scores without increasing their ability to do college work; it reduces errors due to anxiety or unfamiliarity with the test; or it genuinely increases verbal or mathematical ability.

The first outcome would clearly reduce both the predictive and construct validity of the SAT. In preparing the test items and assembling the test forms, test development staff and test committees take great pains to avoid such possibilities. In spite of this, there has been widespread effort expended on these techniques. For example, advice to avoid option C, or not to answer any items in section 6, given in magazine articles or by coaching schools, has led a number of students to complain that they received an unfair score: that is, they followed bad advice and did not answer all the questions they could have answered.

The second coaching outcome—the reduction of irrelevant errors—clearly should increase the validity of the SAT as a measure of scholastic ability and improve its construct validity. It might or might not increase the predictive validity of the SAT, since the ability of students to overcome anxiety or deal with unfamiliar situations may be of use in college.

Finally, a real increase in verbal or mathematical ability, the third possible outcome of coaching, should also increase college performance and therefore not affect predictive validity. As for construct validity, if scholastic aptitude were seen as a fixed, perhaps innate, attribute, score changes would seriously damage the construct. But since the concept is

---

*Larger average gains (of 50 or more points) have been reported in coaching studies employing no statistical or experimental controls. See Gilbert, Mosteller and Light (1977) for a discussion of the exaggerated effects usually observed in uncontrolled studies. For additional score gain data, see Tables 3.15 and 3.16 in Chapter III.

of developed ability, changes in SAT scores are not only acceptable, they are required. Changes that are both very large and easily effected over a short period, however, would be difficult to assimilate into the construct, and they could reduce the fairness of the tests.

A reanalysis of coaching data (Messick and Jungeblut 1981) shows that the amount of score gain was related to the amount of time devoted to coaching, but the amount of gain from even extensive coaching was still modest. Sizable amounts of instruction would be needed to raise the verbal score 20 points (57 hours) and the mathematical score 20 points (19 hours). Instruction beyond this level seemed to have diminishing results; the analysis showed that scores increased with the logarithm of the time spent in instruction. Thus, the average gains observed from coaching to date, in relation to the amount of time spent in instruction, are moderate and basically support the concept of slowly developed ability.

Overall Characteristics of SAT Items

Although the SAT is divided into measures of two developed abilities—verbal and mathematical—it is intentionally composed of more than two different item types, and within these major distinctive item formats there is controlled variation both in difficulty and in content. The effect of this variation is to produce complex internal structure in both verbal and mathematical sections. However, the results of factor analysis, such as those of Coffman (1966) indicate that these varied SAT item types basically define only two major factorial dimensions, verbal and mathematical, each of which appears to synthesize a limited number of stable subfactors.

The content of the test has varied somewhat over the years, and research into its development continues. There is no simple formula for this content, but in general, material for the test meets the following criteria:

1. The skills and abilities tapped by the test are ones that develop slowly over time. They begin to emerge many years in advance of the taking of the SAT, and they may continue to grow beyond the point that the SAT is used for college selection. The SAT measures the student's *current* readiness to undertake certain kinds of further education: it is not a fixed quantity.

2. The content of the SAT is broad and varied enough to reflect learning abstracted from many courses of study and life experiences. The test is

designed to avoid, as much as is practically possible, dependence on any specific curriculum. Content is restricted to topics for which most students may be presumed to have had an adequate opportunity for exposure. The reading selections and the vocabulary of the items avoid specialized content, and although it is more difficult to avoid curriculum in the area of mathematics, an effort is made to limit the mathematics required to skills and procedures usually covered well before the end of high school. It is possible to do well on the mathematical section of the SAT without having had courses beyond first-year algebra. Some confirmation of this relative freedom from formal mathematics course work in advanced subjects is provided by the successful use of the mathematical sections of the SAT by Stanley (1978) in selecting mathematically able seventh and eighth graders. Finally, some distance from school subjects is provided for both verbal and mathematical sections by using item formats—analogies, antonyms, quantitative comparisons—not commonly used in school tests.

Many SAT items emphasize process skills. The capacity to reason with specific information, rather than simply to retrieve that information from memory, is stressed. Thus, the analogies, the sentence completions, the reading comprehension passages, and most of the mathematical problems present a considerable amount of context. Although it is necessary to have a store of meanings for words and symbols, the route to an answer is not merely memory.

3. Because a very large number of item types may be developed to reflect the general abilities measured, a number of variations of the general theme of verbal and mathematical ability have been used over the years. Still others were investigated in the course of research studies, and for some of these experimental items, the evidence concerning predictive validity was essentially positive. However, an attempt has been made to limit the test to those types that were most consistently associated with the verbal or mathematical factors. Several item types are necessary to measure complex abilities. The variety of items allows test takers different ways of demonstrating their ability and lessens the possible disadvantage of encountering an unfamiliar item type; furthermore, a number of short items are included so the test is reliable while not being so long that students cannot finish it.

4. SAT items do not require long or complex instructions. The test is intended to be as free as possible of the influence of testwiseness—an ability to infer the correct answer or to get a high score by knowledge of the structure of items or the format of the test. Certain item types, such as those using artificial language, have excellent general potential for measuring verbal abilities. But artificial language requires a relatively large amount of preliminary instruction, and it often appears formidable to the test takers. It demands from the student an initial investment of time to become familiar with the "lexicon" of the artificial test. Although the item type was used operationally several decades ago, experience with it has shown that it is not suitable for the SAT.

5. The item types must be evaluated not only for their relationships within their own section, verbal or mathematical, but across these sections. The practice of reporting separate verbal and mathematical scores was initiated many years ago by Carl Brigham on the strength of the early results of the factor analysis of the test. The choice of item types has a marked effect on the level of correlation between the two scores. The measurement utility of the two scores depends upon their independence of one another.

Vocabulary. The language of the SAT is the language that is used in college education. The vocabulary is not remote from the college experience, nor are the questions based on tricky or minor points of detail. Some evidence on this point is provided by Carroll (1980). Figure 7.1 presents his plots for 15 selected SAT antonym items. The curves are based on five points, derived from the standard item analysis program, which calculates responses for each quintile of the item analysis sample. The figure shows that those in the highest quintile for this administration had an average score of 570 on the verbal section of the SAT; those in the lowest quintile, 262.

The plots indicate that five of these antonyms (CONCEAL, STALE, STIFF, DOUBTFUL, and EQUILIBRIUM) offer discrimination primarily among the lower ability groups; two (VENTURESOME and PARTISAN) differentiate all five groups; and eight of the items offer better discrimination above the mean. It is also evident that for many of the more difficult items the two lowest-scoring groups succeed with a less-than-chance rate, and that, in fact, the lowest scoring group sometimes does slightly better on these items than does the group immediately above it. This phenomenon is probably related to differences in the groups' tendency to guess or omit.

Figure 7.1

Item Characteristic Curves for Vocabulary (Antonyms)
Items from Section 1, Sample SAT
(Carroll 1980)

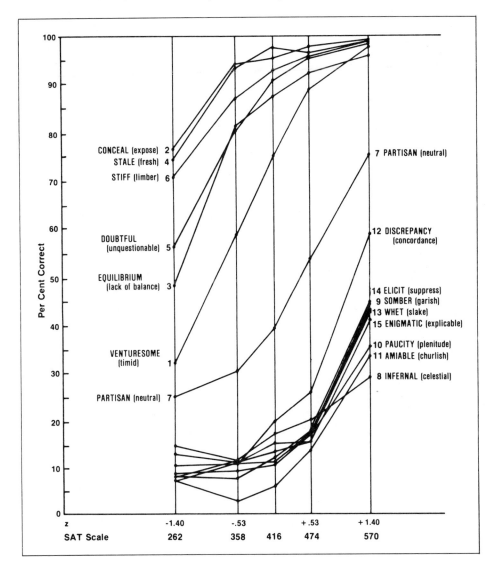

Carroll (1980) related the difficulty values (deltas) for these items to the familiarity of the words as indicated by his Standard Frequency Index (see Table 7.1 on page 130). Table 7.1 shows his data. The SAT antonym item actually has six words, but of these the two that function as stem and key (what Carroll calls "lead" and "choice") are critical, and item difficulty seems logically most related to the difficulty of these two words. As Carroll reported (p. 34):

> Overall the item parameter that was best predicted [by the Standard Frequency Index] was the ETS "delta" . . . . [Standard Frequency Indexes] for the LEAD word (stem) and the *choice* word (key) were in-

tercorrelated .39 with each other, and to the extent of −.643 and −.687, respectively, with ETS delta yielding a multiple R of .799 [F (2,12) = 10.67, p < .01], both variables having significant beta weights. . . .

Quite apart from this, we can use the item analyses data to say something useful about the meaning of different levels of SAT-V scores. . . . [E]xaminees with SAT scores of 570 . . . can be expected to have no trouble with words like CONCEAL, STALE, STIFF, DOUBTFUL, EQUILIBRIUM, and VENTURE-SOME and the keyed correct answers *expose, fresh, limber, unquestionable, lack of balance,* and *timid.* But, I find it rather disturbing that they tend to have trouble with words like PARTISAN, DISCREPANCY, ELICIT, SOMBER, WHET, ENIGMATIC,

Table 7.1

Vocabulary (Antonyms) Items from Sample SAT
in Order of Difficulty
(Carroll 1980)

	b*	p	△	r_{bis}	Estimated SFI values** LEAD	choice
2. CONCEAL: (A) examine (B) recognize (C) expose (D) pronounce (E) arise	-2.70	.92	4.6	.50	41.9	41.9
4. STALE: (A) noticeable (B) fresh (C) dainty (D) moist (E) genuine	-2.50	.92	4.5	.58	42.7	59.9
6. STIFF: (A) limber (B) melted (C) succulent (D) twisted (E) silky	-2.60	.89	5.4	.53	53.7	38.4
5. DOUBTFUL: (A) practical (B) consistent (C) nonexistent (D) impervious (E) unquestionable	-1.65	.82	6.8	.53	47.0	40.4
3. EQUILIBRIUM: (A) opposition (B) insignificance (C) lack of freedom (D) lack of contact (E) lack of balance	-1.35	.83	6.7	.69	37.1	56.4
1. VENTURESOME: (A) lacking agility (B) lethal (C) fragile (D) timid (E) without significance	-0.82	.70	8.7	.66	36.1	45.3
7. PARTISAN: (A) commoner (B) neutral (C) unifier (D) ascetic (E) pacifist	+0.40	.44	11.8	.44	35.8	48.8
12. DISCREPANCY: (A) decision (B) attribute (C) restriction (D) clarification (E) concordance	+1.15	.25	14.2	.54	30.5	20.3
14. ELICIT: (A) leave intact (B) prove false (C) make acceptable (D) suppress (E) expel	+1.52	.20	15.0	.41	20	37.9
9. SOMBER: (A) pale (B) garish (C) fitful (D) extroverted (E) disordered	+1.60	.18	15.3	.46	43.0	30.6
13. WHET: (A) expire (B) heat (C) delay (D) slake (E) revive	+1.60	.20	15.0	.30	30.5	29.0
15. ENIGMATIC: (A) exceptional (B) explicable (C) exportable (D) expedient (E) exorbitant	+1.70	.19	15.1	.35	34.9	20
10. PAUCITY: (A) generosity (B) vacuity (C) excellence (D) variety (E) plenitude	+2.10	.16	15.7	.39	20	20.2
11. AMIABLE: (A) resigned (B) nervous (C) churlish (D) astute (E) obscure	+2.10	.13	16.3	.49	36.7	30.7
8. INFERNAL: (A) exquisite (B) frigid (C) ephemeral (D) mortal (E) celestial	+2.60	.17	15.5	.31	36.2	43.7

*b = value of z at which p = .5 (as estimated from item characteristic curve)
**SFI (Standard Frequency index) is on a logarithmic scale. Values as follows:

60 — 1 per 10,000 words
50 — 1 per 100,000 words
40 — 1 per 1,000,000 words
30 — 1 per 10,000,000 words
20 — 1 per 100,000,000 words

PAUCITY, AMIABLE, and INFERNAL. Most of these words and their paired correct answers are likely to occur in the texts students have to read at the college level.

If we look at the data for people with SAT-V scores of 262, . . . these are people who are totally lost with the more difficult items (that is, with the words contained in them) but they have trouble even with the easier items. The meanings of words like *limber, equilibrium, venturesome,* and *partisan* are unlikely to be familiar to them. These data tell a lot about the deficiencies of people with SAT-V scores as low as 262, and help us characterize the meaning of such a score.

Carroll's study also demonstrated that difficult SAT items are not constructed from verbal obscurities. The easier SAT antonyms tend to be based on words that appear in his samples of text once in a million words; the harder antonyms tend to be based on words that appear once in 10 or 100 million. Carroll urged the application of these item analytic approaches to other tests.

No material is included in the SAT without at least one successful pretesting, and such a pretest requires that there be some reasonable percentage of correct answers. Obscure words usually fail either because too few people know them, or because they do not identify able students, or both. While there does not seem to be any definitive way to demonstrate that the vocabulary of the SAT is the vocabulary of college-level work, a study by Diederich and Palmer (1956, p. 2) used Thorndike-Lorge (1944) word frequency data to identify ''. . . all generally useful, independent words that high school and college students may not know in one of their most common meanings, down to the level at which words occur less than once per million words.'' The resulting list of 4,800 words includes 14 of the 30 critical words involved in the antonym items studied by Carroll. Some of the SAT items are too easy to be included (for example, STALE-FRESH), and quite a few are too hard, invading the ''less than once per million words'' zone. But the comparison does offer some evidence that the words selected for the SAT are drawn from the larger corpus of words that might be designated ''useful for college.''

Readability. The difficulty index and item-test correlation calculated for each item using pretest data are used to assemble each form of the SAT so that it is statistically similar to previous tests. There is a need at times to consider other information as well. In connection with the score decline, Chall (1977) examined the reading comprehension passages and associated questions for one of the several SAT forms in each of six cohort years: 1947, 1955, 1962, 1967, 1972, and 1975. As shown in Table 7.2, the number of passages is fairly constant, while the content coverage of each form showed considerable breadth.

Related tables are shown here as Tables 7.3 (below) and 7.4 (page 132). Table 7.3 displays a number of characteristics of these passages, such as their average length, number of questions, and the number of words in a passage per question asked

about that passage. According to the table, passage length and number of words in the passage referred to by each question rose markedly over the years 1947-1975, but the difficulty of the material, as evaluated by Dale-Chall Readability Formula (1948), declined from 9.0 to 8.3. The corrected grade level for the material was 13-15 in early years, 11-12 in more recent years. However, the difficulty of the SAT material was consistently near college level.

In addition to evaluating the content of the passages, Chall (1977) secured judgments of the level of difficulty of the individual questions, using a system based on Bloom's taxonomy (1956) devised specifically for the study. The scale levels ranged from 1 to 4 (see Table 7.4). The average rating of the questions in a given form ranged from 2.4 to 3.1. Level 2 questions required recall and use of fact: asking *how, why, describe.* Level 3 questions required the acknowledgment of more than one point of view: asking *com-*

Table 7.2

Reading Passages in Certain Content Areas in Six Forms of the SAT (Adapted from Chall 1977)

Content Classification	1947	1955	1962	1967	1972	1975
Philosophy	3	1	2	4	1	
Linguistics	1					1
Literature	2		1	1	2	
Biography	1					2
Travel, geography		1			1	
Music, art		1		1	1	
Biological science		1	1	1	1	2
Physical science		1	2	1	1	1
Economics	1	2				
Political science		2	1	1	1	
Social science					1	1
Total number of passages for test	8	9	7	9	9	7

Table 7.3

Summary Data for Reading Passages and Questions in Six Forms of the SAT (Adapted from Chall 1977)

Year	SAT form	Number of reading passages	Average number of words per passage	Number of questions	Average number of questions per passage	Number of running words in passage per question	Sentence length	Dale score (percent unfamiliar words)	Raw score	Corrected grade level
1947	VSA 3	8	262	45	6	46	31	24	9.0	13-15
1955	DSA 2	9	261	47	5	50	29	28	9.4	13-15
1962	KSA 15	7	362	35	5	72	27	25	8.8	11-12
1967	PSA 13	9	461	45	5	92	28	23	8.7	11-12
1972	USA 25	9	418	45	5	84	28	25	8.9	11-12
1975	XSA 1020	7	442	35	5	88	22	22	8.3	11-12

*The Dale-Chall Formula provides an index of the reading difficulty of prose by considering such factors as the number of uncommon words and the length of sentences.

Table 7.4

Degrees of Knowledge Required by the Questions on the SAT (Adapted from Chall 1977)

Year	1947	1955	1962	1967	1972	1975
Average degree of knowledge required, all questions in test form	2.5	2.7	2.6	3.0	3.1	2.4
Percentage of Degree 1 questions in form	9	0	0	2	0	11
Percentage of Degree 2 questions in form	49	53	46	22	18	57
Percentage of Degree 3 questions in form	20	30	46	51	53	14
Percentage of Degree 4 questions in form	22	17	8	24	29	17
Combined degrees of knowledge:						
Percentage of Degrees 1 and 2 questions in form	58	53	46	24	18	68
Percentage of Degrees 3 and 4 questions in form	42	47	54	76	82	31

*Degrees of knowledge, as defined by Chall (1977), range in increasing difficulty from 1 to 4, defined as follows:

Degree 1: Knowledge of facts; identification of specifics
Degree 2: Knowledge of methods for dealing with specifics; understanding organization, form, structure and style
Degree 3: Knowledge of complex terminology (reading between and beyond the lines); knowledge of the multiple meanings of words
Degree 4: Knowledge of universals and abstractions; ability to use major schemes, principles, theories; knowledge of complex analogous relationships

pare, contrast. No attempt was made to relate these measures of question difficulty to the values determined by ETS item analysis. In general, the consistency of the average of these ratings over the years indicates that the test development processes are quite stable, which confirms the findings of item analysis.

The study made similar analyses of the textbooks used in elementary and secondary schools throughout the years in question. It concluded that the level of difficulty of school reading programs was likely to influence SAT scores. It found that the difficulty of SAT passages declined somewhat over the years, but that the more modern test items seemed to require higher levels of thought.

In general, the study supports the content appropriateness of the test. There has been some variation in the nature of the passages and questions over time due to changes in school and college reading, but the reading passages have consistently covered diverse topics at an appropriate level of difficulty.

Obsolescence. The stability of SAT content was questioned during the analysis of the score decline, and a study by Braswell and Petersen (1977) specifically addressed the rate at which material in the test may become outdated. The study focused on verbal material given at times 3 or 13 years apart, and on mathematical material given at intervals of 4, 8, or 9 years. A number of methods to assess the change were used. Knowledgeable raters were asked to indicate on a five-point scale how the difficulty of each question might be expected to change over the time period. Empirical results were compared with these judgments.

Figure 7.2 shows a plot of item difficulties over a 13-year period. The dashed line shows no change—equal difficulty at both administrations. The solid line shows the overall trend for this test. In general, it is a shift toward greater difficulty across the board, for all items, so that both the 1963 easy items and the 1963 difficult items are found to be more dif-

Figure 7.2

Plot of Item Difficulties for a 13-Year Period
(Braswell and Petersen 1977)

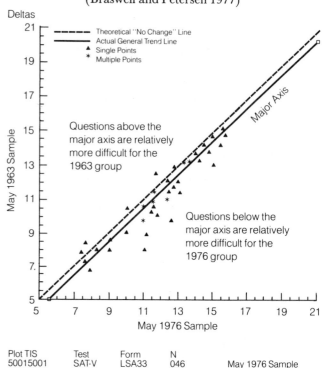

ficult for the 1976 sample, and by approximately the same amount. This overall increase in difficulty reflects the score decline.

A few individual items changed atypically. Some individual items were not more difficult in the later testing, but were in fact easier; others were not only more difficult, but more so than average. Analyses showed that raters were, on the whole, unable to predict the observed change in difficulty level of a question between administrations. The Braswell-Petersen (1977) results confirm that use of knowledgeable external raters would be no more successful in reducing vulnerability to change over time than is the current procedure. As the researchers noted (p. 16), "... while the relative difficulty of some questions changed between administration dates, it was not possible, except for a few mathematical questions, to attribute these changes to curricular or societal factors."

The study reported the specific items that were found to have shifted most severely during the intervals. It is not easy to see common factors in the materials. Why should *hoyden,* a relatively obscure word, be found easier in 1976 than in 1963? Why should *secede* be harder? The report offers no descriptive comment on the subject of *hoyden,* but suggests that there is an absence of the "civil war" era in contemporary social studies, to explain *secede.* In all, there is clear evidence that the 1976 group found the material more difficult than the 1963 group had, but little evidence that SAT items become markedly obsolete. The pattern seems to be one of random fluctuations around an overall increase in difficulty as shown in Figure 7.2.

Cultural Bias. Since the development of language and thought can take place only in the context of a culture, it is inconceivable that the SAT could be culture free. But just as it can be made relatively curriculum free, so it can be made free of obvious bias for or against cultural subgroups such as those defined by sex or minority status. In developing the test, strong efforts are made to ensure such freedom.

These efforts go beyond the psychometric and into the psychological properties of the test. To ensure that no student taking the SAT encounters test content that will be upsetting, a program of "sensitivity" reviews is undertaken. The reviews, conducted by ETS staff prior to the administration of any verbal pretest or final SAT verbal and mathematical material, guard against language that is potentially offensive to subgroups. The procedures for such reviews have become increasingly rigorous in the last decade, as awareness of the potential for bias in language has heightened.

The SAT has been subjected to outlier analyses for item content factors that influence score differences. (See the discussion of this methodology in Chapter X.) In outlier analysis, an item is singled out for attention on the strength of the relative, rather than the absolute, difference between groups in performance on the item. Coffman (1961) analyzed the verbal sections of the SAT and reported that test content was associated with differential performance for the sexes. He wrote (p. 9), "Perhaps it would be fruitful to think of verbal items which are relatively easier for men or for women as words related to 'people' or words related to 'things,'...." Donlon's (1973) study of items with large sex differences supported Coffman's generalization about verbal items and extended the analysis to the mathematical section. His study demonstrated that the sex differences on mathematical items were also related to item content. Women, for example, did relatively better on algebra items and relatively worse on geometry problems.

These findings were confirmed in a later study by Strassberg-Rosenberg and Donlon (1975). This study applied the more formal outlier methodology developed by Angoff (1972), but corroborated the earlier findings: verbal items relating to "Science" and "World of Practical Affairs" categories were relatively easier for males, while verbal items relating to "Aesthetic-Philosophical" or "Human Relations" categories were relatively easier for females. Algebra problems were relatively easier for females, while problems dealing with people and things were relatively easier for males.

Angoff and Ford (1973) conducted a series of analyses on various samples of White students and Black students who took the PSAT/NMSQT, reporting the correlations among item difficulties as a measure of cross-cultural similarity in test performance for these groups. Their study demonstrated that cross-cultural similarity was heightened when ability differences between the groups were controlled. The uncontrolled correlations between performance by Black students and performance by White students, expressed as item difficulties, were in the low-to-middle .90s for the verbal sections of the PSAT and in the upper .80s for the mathematical sections; the correlations controlled for ability were .96 for verbal and .92 for math. These across-group correlations are lower than the within-group correlations, between random samples, of .97-.99, indicating that there are some differences between the groups in item performance. The substantial correlation of item difficulties *between* the groups, however, indicates a high level of psychological similarity for the two groups in spite of their differences.

133

Concern for cultural bias led to a program of fairly frequent outlier analyses by race from 1974 to the present (see Chapter X). As in the Angoff and Ford study, the most persistent result is the demonstrated high correlation between the races with respect to item difficulty. In general, the correlations between item difficulty for White students and item difficulty for Black students are .90-.98 for the verbal sections and .94-.96 for the mathematical sections. These are comparable to the similar cross-group correlations reported by Angoff and Ford, given the relatively small sample of 300 in their study.

Since 1982, a program of item fairness studies using the method of standardization has been instituted. These studies, and their methodology, are described in Chapter X. The predictive validity of the verbal and mathematical sections for various SAT subpopulations is summarized in Chapter VIII.

New Item Types. In 1957, French published an extensive study of "new aptitude tests that might prove to be contributive supplements to the SAT or effective supplements for part of it" (p. 1) and considered 11 special, experimental tests. This set of tests is interesting as evidence of the kinds of material that broadly define the domain of possible SATs. French's criteria for the selection of tests were as follows: 1) they should test some function not apparently tested by the present SAT; 2) they should not be more coachable than current tests; 3) they should not depend to any large extent upon specific school curriculums; and 4) they should appear to measure a quality that is important in some phase of college work. His choices of experimental measures that met these criteria are shown in Table 7.5, together with information on their correlation with SAT-verbal score, SAT-mathematical score, and high school record.

Some of the experimental tests, such as the reading tests, clearly resembled components of the SAT itself. The Inductive Reasoning test (which contained analogy items), the Data Sufficiency, and even, to some extent, the Data Interpretation materials, were similar in content to sections of the SAT. In a sense, then, the study was partly an effort to expand the number of approaches to the measurement of the existing factors. But there were truly different experimental measures as well, in the Visualization and the Memory and Information tests. French did not factor analyze his matrix, but certain broad generalizations seem possible.

The SAT-verbal score correlates best with the experimental Reading; with Information in Art, Literature, and Government; and with the measure of Inductive Reasoning (which was a verbal test). The

Table 7.5

Correlations of the SAT and High School Record with Experimental Tests (Adapted from French 1957)

	SAT-Verbal Sections	SAT-Math. Sections	High School Record
SAT-Verbal Sections	—		
SAT-Mathematical Sections	.42	—	
High School Record	.29	.27	—
Social Studies Reading	.54	.36	.19
Science Reading	.58	.32	.23
Inductive Reasoning	.55	.54	.22
Integration	.35	.43	.27
Sufficiency of Data	.41	.65	.18
Data Interpretation	.41	.42	.17
Visualization	.25	.45	.13
Best Arguments	.30	.20	.16
Perceptual Speed	.14	.23	.19
Carefulness	.04	.10	.06
Picture Memory	.17	.19	.10
Verbal Memory	.32	.22	.18
Number Memory	.08	.23	.20
Art Information	.52	.13	.11
Literature Information	.53	.13	.23
Social Work Information	.42	.14	.23
Government Information	.54	.26	.26
Biology Information	.33	.22	.21
Physical Science Information	.34	.36	.22
Mechanical Information	.12	.22	−.06

highest SAT-mathematical score correlations are with Data Sufficiency, Data Interpretation, Visualization, Inductive Reasoning, and Integration. Virtually every measure demonstrates some positive correlation, but the perceptual and memory tasks show less relation to the SAT than the others. French concluded that the then 150-minute SAT could be replaced with a test consisting of six 25-minute modules, but he decided (p. 37) that "because of the uncertainties introduced by the very different time limits among the tests, it would, in any case, be premature to recommend a specific composite. . . ."

French was concerned about the extent to which the verbal and mathematical scores make independently useful contributions to guidance. As he observed (pp. 41-43), "For maximum usefulness in guidance or in selection for specialized areas, it is desirable to find a very different pattern of test scores associated with each area. . . . The validity of SAT-V is highest for Social Science; that for SAT-M is highest for Science and Mathematics. For Humanities and Languages, the SAT-V validity is dominant over SAT-M as it is for Social Science, but both SAT validities are lower than they were for Social Science. . . . The differences in validity for the SAT are all significant at about the one percent level. . . . A student who stands higher on SAT-M than on SAT-V has a better chance to achieve well in science and mathematics than in other fields. A student who stands higher on SAT-V has a better chance to achieve well in verbal areas. However, the SAT scores cannot distinguish between students best qualified for social science and those best qualified for humanities and languages.''

French returned to some of these measures in a study (French 1963) that examined 15 predictors for high-aptitude students. He remarked (p. 1) on the superiority of the verbal and mathematical model: ''For many years now, the verbal and mathematical sections of the College Board's Scholastic Aptitude Test have been serving well their educational purposes, so well, in fact, that many good ideas for new tests have been rejected since they added nothing to what the SAT was already able to do.'' It was an era, however, of some concern about the adequacy of the tests for high-level students, moved by a strong interest in creativity and divergent thinking and by the attacks of test critic Banesh Hoffman (1962), who charged that the tests were particularly error-laden in their appraisal of high-level learners. Conscious of these concerns, French observed (p. 1) that it seemed ''. . . contrary to common sense that verbal and mathematical tests should reign so supremely as predictors in the complex domain of college work. The thinking required for success at high-level colleges must be particularly complex.''

French envisioned the aptitude domain as very broad (p. 1): ''Important as verbal and mathematical materials may be, their nature is specific rather than general. While it would be impractical for the SAT to measure separately a large number of additional specific aptitudes, it does seem desirable that the College Board's most important aptitude instrument cover as many as possible of the important kinds of ability.'' The difficulties in this approach are reflected in French's attempt to justify information tests as measures of aptitude. Reviewing his prior findings, he wrote (p. 2): ''. . . [G]eneral information' tests containing factual items of a non-academic type considerably improved the prediction of college grades by the SAT. While factual information may not seem to be a suitable content for aptitude tests, or perhaps any college-entrance tests, the findings of the earlier four-year validity study suggest that an important correlate of college work is a student's ability, through the learning of facts or otherwise, to develop an understanding and an appreciation of his intellectual environment. This seems to include such qualities as alertness, curiosity, persistence, and interest, some of which can be called aptitudes. The acquisition of a general understanding of the environment is probably not very different in its essential processes from the acquisition of verbal comprehension as measured by SAT-V, or of reasoning ability as measured by SAT-M. In this sense, it seemed reasonable to consider tests of certain kinds of information to be at least partly measures of aptitudes and therefore suitable tests to try out in this experiment.'' Elsewhere, he wrote (p. 6), ''Whereas present College Board tests are intended to select bright students who have achieved well in their school subjects, these information tests are designed to spot the students who, in addition, are interested in and alert to important happenings in the world around them.''

French felt that possibly the verbal sections of the SAT were failing to capture an important characteristic of the learner (p. 6): ''We all know some young people who quickly understand the things they see. Other young people just do not seem to take very much in. What is this difference? Just as verbal aptitude is assessed by measuring knowledge and understanding of language, this other ability, general alertness, perhaps, can be assessed by measuring knowledge and understanding of a variety of experiences that a student does have or could have.'' French advances a psychological rationale for the kind of material he is interested in exploring. In this, he followed the lead of the committee of psychologists that met to consider the possibility of an SAT in the mid-1920s. To French, information material could be justified if it can be shown to tap basic mental characteristics of alertness or sensitivity to the environment. French was obviously aware, however, that there are many problems in introducing this kind of information material. For one thing, he took care to label his material ''nonacademic'' information; for another, he likened the processes for its acquisition to those that lead to the traditional SAT abilities. With respect to the problem of test items that were susceptible to coaching, French observed (p. 30): ''A recommendation that . . . new tests be substituted for parts of the SAT must take into consideration not only the predictive power of the tests for important criteria but also the likelihood that this predictive power will be maintained in practice (e.g., that the tests are not excessively coachable), that the tests are practical to administer (e.g., that they are machine scorable), and that they will not adversely influence teaching practices.'' In the long run, information items were judged to be inappropriate for the SAT largely because they seemed to penalize minority students and to be too highly susceptible to coaching.

French's findings were based on highly selective

colleges. Flaugher and Rock (1966, p. 1) undertook a follow-up study with the "tests found to be most valuable" in the French study, stressing that the "existing SAT . . . is not employed solely at these high level colleges but is becoming widely used at colleges characterized by significantly lower student aptitude levels." Again, the standard SAT was pitted against the experimental item types. The authors summarized: "The improvement achieved by . . . a drastic change in the content of the SAT . . . is for the most part quite undramatic . . ." (p. 25). "The new battery which was derived from the experimental tests does in fact do a creditable job of predicting academic success . . . [but] the lack of any worthwhile improvement over the existing test content . . . leads to the conclusion that the change would not be worth the trouble. . . . The validities obtained with the existing SAT were already high for the most part, and a significant improvement is less likely under those conditions" (p. 29).

The French and the Flaugher and Rock studies are consistent with each other and with other relevant studies: in the prediction of college work, measures of basic verbal and mathematical skills provide an appraisal suitable for a variety of groups. No more powerful predictors have emerged.

SAT Item Types: Measures of Cognitive Processes

Whitely (1977, p. 725) has observed, "Although literally thousands of studies have accumulated to support the practical utility of measuring aptitude, [its nature] remains unclear after decades of research." She also quoted McNemar (1964, p. 881) to the effect that ". . . studies of individual differences never come to grips with the process or operation by which a given organism achieves an intellectual response" (Whitely, p. 726). Messick (1972) has suggested that understanding intelligence in terms of cognitive processes requires functional-experimental data, and that aptitude tests should be linked to the variables studied in cognitive-experimental psychology.

Brigham (1932, p. 45) wrote that ". . . the ultimate facts with which we are dealing are answers to questions, . . . [which] may be studied in their own right . . . the detailed study of answers to test items provides a completely sound and systematic approach to the study of errors and confusions in thinking." During the 1930s, Brigham built an experimental testing device for recording in greater detail the subject's latency of response to individual items. In general, however, there has been very little work that studied individual responses.

One reason for this lack of research probably lies in the nature of the tasks themselves. Individually, SAT items require relatively little time to complete. The test taker is allowed 40 seconds to process the average SAT verbal item, and about 50 seconds for the average mathematical item. This average time includes the reading of the items and any associated passages, graphs, or figures: the solution process time cannot be neatly carved out of this total. It is probably true that the test taker is actively engaged in trying to answer the question and is carrying out solution processes even as he or she reads along. But obviously not all of the time is devoted to solution processing, for the test taker cannot begin to solve until the problem is understood. The framing of the basic problem and the evaluation of the various distractors is all accomplished in about 30 seconds, on the average. During this time, the test taker moves to a decision through a series of steps so rapid that they may be uncapturable through introspection.

Interview Studies. There has been a small body of work attempting direct observation of one kind of mental process that the SAT taps by asking students to report their thinking as they answer SAT items. Connolly and Wantman (1964), for example, secured oral protocols on 25 items from a sample of nine college sophomores using techniques modeled on Bloom and Broder's 1950 study of the problem-solving process. Judgments of the quality of responses were combined to produce a rank ordering of estimated ability. These ranks correlated with SAT scores approximately .70, which was significant at the .05 level for even this small sample. A good example of a protocol is the following discussion of an antonym item (Connolly and Wantman 1964, p. 62, some editorial changes):

VIGILANT (with choices (A) useless, (B) skeptical, (C) frantic, (D) unwary, and (E) calculating)
It would not be *useless* because that has no meaning at all in connection with it. *Skeptical, frantic, unwary, calculating: Frantic*—no. Vigilant—the word itself implies frantic in certain ways. It's not *skeptical* or *calculating.* There is a relation between vigilant and *calculating,* but it's not that close—it's planning. That's the relation. Vigilance and planning—planning and calculating. So therefore it would be *unwary*—that is the opposite of *vigilant,* because it means *unaware.* When you are *unaware,* you are not vigilant.

The protocol is heavily associative, and substantiates the views of Gentile (1966, p. 7) concerning these processes: "One final idea, which evolved from listening to Connolly and Wantman's taped sessions, was concerned with the frequent statements by students that they had no good reason for choosing (or eliminating) an alternative, but they just had a 'feeling' that it was correct (or incorrect). Little information can be extracted from such a statement. But if the assumption is made that an answer 'feels' correct because the word associations to it converge at some point with the word associations to the item stem, then the mysticism of this phrase partly vanishes. This 'feeling,' in other words, should be traceable to a verbal relatedness, defined as an overlap of word associations. Likewise, if there is a 'feeling' that an alternative is incorrect, then there should be no verbal relatedness.''

Gentile, Kessler, and Gentile (1969) report four studies of the solution processes for analogy items. The first study concerned the extent to which subjects could identify the keyed answer when given a verbalization of the relationship in the item stem either in conjunction with or instead of the two-word stem itself. Subjects did profit significantly from a statement of the relationship provided by an experimenter. The processes used by subjects in generating their own concepts of the relationships, however, were unclear. The second and fourth experiments concerned the extent to which the most frequently chosen responses to analogy items had the greatest perceived ''associative strength'' between stem and response. The third experiment demonstrated that ''priming'' associative strength between the stem and selected responses can be used to alter the attractiveness of responses. As the authors noted (p. 502), ''The converging data [from these experiments] provide convincing evidence . . . that the process that students use in solving analogy items is primarily an associative process. . . . Associative relatedness among the words in the analogy items . . . appears to account for from 28 to 50 percent of the variance in the analogy solution.''

Such studies contribute to the construct validity of the SAT by establishing the kinds of mental process called upon. It is important to realize, however, that the mental processes used may vary from person to person. French observed (1963, p. 1), ''Some tests of higher mental processes are solved in one way by some subjects and in another way by other subjects.'' He pointed to the studies of oral solutions of multiple-choice problems carried out by Bloom and Broder (1950) and by Lucas (1953). It seems possible, he wrote (p. 1): ''. . . that the factorial composition of test problems involving higher mental processes often appears complex not only because they require several different kinds of abilities in their solution, but also because they measure something different for examinees who solve them by using different methods.''

French (1963) carried out an interview study including items similar to those found in the SAT: reading, verbal analogies, and mathematics problems. He concluded that test takers differ in the degree of systematization that they bring to the problems. For example, those approaching reading comprehension passages might systematically begin by examining all the distractors or by reading the passage to note individual points. This systematic approach was contrasted with a more free-form approach which French called ''scanning.'' He felt that both approaches could be used in responding to his items, and that their effects were not always similar. For the reading test, a systematic (versus a scanning) strategy did not seem to change the level of a score, but it did seem to influence its meaning, so that the scores that were the product of the systematic approach showed a reduced capacity to reflect French's Verbal Comprehension factor.

Whitely (1977) studied three major questions about analogy items: Do people apply a single relational concept to several different items? Are these concepts similar across individuals? Is there any psychometric evidence of the semantic structure of relationships? She asked subjects to sort items (analogies, but not from the SAT) into eight major relational categories of similar relationships: Opposites, Functional, Word Pattern, Quantitative, Similarities, Class Membership, Class-Naming, and Conversion. Comparing these classes to systems developed by theorists such as Spearman and Piaget, she concluded that (p. 736) ''. . . the relational categories of the theorists may have little correspondence to the psychological concepts used by subjects to compare analogies.'' Analogy items, she held, indirectly measure higher-order cognitive functioning, despite the belief of other researchers that simple associations govern the solution of analogies. In terms of the implications for construct validity, however, it seems prudent to cite her comment (p. 737) that ''. . . the relational concepts for a culturally-different population may not correspond to those of the population of subjects for whom the test was originally constructed.''

Laboratory Studies of Verbal Ability. Messick's appeal for links between aptitude tests and the variables studied in experimental work on cognitive abilities is met in a study by Hunt, Lunneborg, and Lewis (1975), which considered the question: What does it mean to be a highly verbal person? This research is relevant to the SAT because it offers (p. 195) ''studies of the information processing capabilities of people with varying degrees of verbal ability. . . .'' Verbal ability, in these studies, is measured by the Washington Pre-College Test (WPCT), a standard group-administered test used to evaluate the academic potential of high school juniors. This test is related to the SAT by the authors as follows (p. 195): "For all practical purposes, the WPCT is interchangeable with the . . . more widely used Scholastic Aptitude Test. . . ."

Actually, the WPCT is something like a combination of parts of the SAT-verbal sections, of the Test of Standard Written English, and of a spelling test, for its four subparts include English Usage (EU), Spelling (S), Reading Comprehension (RC), and Vocabulary (V). Accordingly, it is more "analogous to" than "equivalent to" the SAT-verbal sections. Nonetheless, groups identified by the two instruments would be anticipated to overlap considerably.

Hunt et al. concluded that high verbal persons manipulate information in short-term memory more rapidly than persons with low verbal ability. Further, they seem to be exceptionally sensitive to "order" relationships among the elements of information they are processing. Other studies have shown that high verbal persons can access highly overlearned material in long-term memory more rapidly than can persons with low verbal ability.

Comparing the functioning of high verbal and low verbal groups on a variety of cognitive laboratory tasks, Hunt et al. concluded that (p. 223): "University students who obtain high scores on a conventional paper and pencil test of verbal ability do unusually well on a variety of Cognitive Information Processing tasks. [Such tests are] indirectly a way of identifying people who can code and manipulate verbal stimuli rapidly in situations in which knowledge per se is not a major factor."

Other findings were:

1. high verbal persons can more rapidly recognize a particular visual pattern as a word or letter;

2. high verbal persons have a greater ability to retain in short-term memory information about the order of stimulus presentation; and

3. high verbal persons appear, in general, to be more rapid in the manipulation of data in short-term memory.

Hunt et al. then offered some speculations (p. 225): "In our terms, verbal (aptitude tests) directly tap a person's knowledge of the language and indirectly tap Cognitive Information Processing (CIP) Ability. . . . It seems plausible to believe that High Verbal subjects know more about the linguistic aspects of their culture because they are more rapid in CIP tasks, rather than the reverse. . . . [If] two individuals . . . are given the same exposure to linguis-

tic information . . . the high Cognitive Information Processing individual will fix more information in long-term memory. If . . . the initial exposure . . . were individualized . . . then long-term retention should be equated. Indeed, we have previously reported that there is no correlation between verbal ability and retention of information over a period of weeks, providing that individual learning is equated."

Hunt et al. called for continued consideration of the intrinsic nature of the relationships between cognitive abilities and verbal test scores (p. 220): "We believe that the aptitude treatment interactions much sought after by educators are more likely to be found in 'aptitude' as defined by the parameters of the information processing process than if it is defined by one's relative standing in a population." Such developments would do much to confirm the construct validity of the SAT, but they would also perhaps make it possible to improve the test.

SAT Verbal and Mathematical Scores

Factor Analytic Studies. The early development of the SAT took place in the late 1920s, in the years of the emergence of factor analysis as a major psychometric tool. Brigham used Spearman's methods to examine the factor structure of the early forms, and his results caused him to separate the test into its verbal and mathematical components.

In both the verbal and mathematical sections, a single dimension accounts for up to 50 percent of the variance of the score for that section. It is possible to elaborate these dimensions, by varying the factorial methods, and a number of investigators have reported more complex internal structures. Coffman (1966), for example, used a principal-axis factoring to identify six tentative factors in the verbal sections, and Pruzek and Coffman (1966) applied two factoring methods in identifying six possible factors in the mathematical sections. The following lists of tentative factors are based on those studies. They appear in order of their contribution to variance. Such analyses are limited to a single form, and are strongly influenced by the characteristics of that form and of the sample that is used.

Verbal factors

Speed
Vocabulary—unusual words
Verbal reasoning
Reading comprehension—reading detail and
relationships

Vocabulary—general
Reading comprehension—reading for differentiations among options (humanities content)

Mathematical factors

Geometrical interpretation
Computation
Speed
Arithmetic reasoning
Data sufficiency
Rules

A sizable body of factor analytic work on verbal comprehension with other tests has implications for the SAT. Northrup (1977) described a number of studies that have demonstrated a verbal comprehension factor defined by item types very similar to those included in the verbal sections of the SAT, in a variety of contexts reflected in data gathered over 40 years. The verbal comprehension ability, in Northrup's view (p. 1), is defined as "the immediate understanding of the English language" and may be found in "at least 125 published studies."

Northrup's list of the various item types that reflect the factor includes all of the current SAT-verbal items. She points out that the analogy item type, while not always included in the reference tests for the verbal factor, is nonetheless relevant. In Guilford's Structure of Intellect, for example, it appears to be loaded on the factor "Cognition of Semantic Relations" (Guilford 1967).

Some insight into the complex nature of the factor structure of these variables is provided in a study by Ward, Frederiksen, and Carlson (1978). While their study used the verbal and quantitative items of the Graduate Record Examinations, it is included in this review because of the similarity in the two aptitude measures and because of the interesting factor domain within which the aptitude measures were considered. Table 7.6 shows the basic verbal and quantitative aptitude measures in relation to seven factors defined by a variety of tests. The tests were drawn from such sources as the *Kit of Reference Tests for Cognitive Factors* (French, Ekstrom, and Price 1963) and from measures developed by Guilford in his Structure of Intellect research.

These cognitive factors show substantial correlations, and so the pattern of loadings for the GRE aptitude measures tends to be significant across all factors. It is noteworthy, however, that 1) the two GRE aptitude tests, verbal and quantitative, differ in their correlation with the induction tests, which are, in terms of the content and the cognitive operations they appear to demand, quite different from either the verbal or mathematical test; 2) the two GRE apti-

tude tests are about equally correlated with the logical reasoning tests; 3) the quantitative test is more strongly related to the measures of cognitive flexibility, which are intended to gauge the ability to shift among approaches in attempting to solve problems; 4) only one modest correlation (.33) is found between a GRE score and the two divergent thinking factors (Expressional Fluency and Ideational Fluency): that of the verbal measure with Expressional Fluency.

Table 7.6

Factor Loadings of GRE Verbal and Quantitative Aptitude Tests on Seven Factors
(Adapted from Ward, Frederiksen, and Carlson 1978)

Factor	Defining Tests (with Loadings)	Verbal Aptitude Loading	Quantitative Aptitude Loading
Vocabulary	Vocabulary (.93) Word Meanings (.88)	.79	.31
Quantitative Reasoning	Mathematical Aptitude (.78) Necessary Arithmetic Operations (.72)	.56	.80
Induction	Letter Sets (.71) Locations (.66) Figure Classification (.68)	.37	.64
Logical Reasoning	Logical Diagrams (.65) Nonsense Syllogisms (.54) Inferences (.62)	.63	.67
Cognitive Flexibility	Reversed Reading (.84) Sign Changes (.64)	.44	.68
Expressional Fluency	Making Sentences (.54) Arranging Words (.69) Rewriting (.38)	.33	.17
Ideational Fluency	Pattern Interpretation 1 (.62) Different Uses (.77) Unexpected Results (.70)	.16	−.03

An interest in fluency measures as indicators of creative potential was very marked in the early 1960s. These measures are still considered to be related to the ability to solve problems in innovative ways, although the research evidence has been somewhat ambiguous. In general, however, measures of divergent thinking have not proved to be useful in predicting academic attainment in college. The low correlations of the aptitude measures and the divergent thinking measures in the Ward, Frederiksen, and Carlson study, therefore, may be taken as modest discriminant evidence of the appropriateness of the aptitude construct. Although associative processes do figure in the aptitude item types, they are apparently directed more toward a convergent-solution goal than would be the case in a more purely associational divergent thinking test, and, apparently, given the limited predictive validity of association tests, it is this developed capacity for convergent solutions that is stressed in college.

A study of the construct validity of the SAT by Rock and Werts (1979b) used maximum likelihood confirmatory factor analysis to evaluate the stability of an SAT score in various ethnic or racial subgroups of the total test-taking population: Black, Indian, Mexican American, Oriental, Puerto Rican, and White. The method of confirmatory analysis requires a prediction of how items will relate to each other. A chi-square test is then used to compare the predicted structure with the actual data.

Rock and Werts assumed four verbal factors, one for each of the four verbal item types in the content specifications: antonyms, sentence completions, analogies, and reading comprehension. They assumed two mathematical factors also associated with item types: regular mathematics and quantitative comparisons. Because of the large sample sizes being studied (N = 3,000), the chi-square approach was virtually certain to yield significant differences in the comparison among populations, so that the practical value of the fit was better indicated by the root mean square residuals: if the factor model was assumed to hold, these residuals would be uniformly very small. In fact, they ranged from .0120 to .0187 for the verbal sections and from .0000 to .0061 for the mathematical sections, and the authors concluded (p. 13), "The near zero SAT-V and SAT-M residuals confirm that similar factor patterns of zero and non-zero loadings are present in all six populations."

Additional constraints on the model permitted the testing of progressively more stringent hypotheses concerning the equality of units of measurement and of the standard errors of measurement. Again considering the root mean square residuals, the authors found little evidence of population variation (p. 16): "The . . . three sequential tests of progressively stronger models, all of which provide a good fit, suggest that the SAT-V and the SAT-M item types are measuring the same things in the same metric with the same accuracy for all six ethnic populations."

The prediction in the Rock and Werts study was that the aptitude structure of the SAT is the same for all ethnic groups. There was a further comparison of the factor structure across three populations, by determining the answers to three questions: 1) Is the regression of observed score on true score the same in different populations? 2) Are the units of measurement the same? 3) Are the standard errors of measurement of the factors the same across populations? Tests of equality of reliability in the assessment of factors showed that the groups differed. This was to be expected, however, since they differed in the variance of ability. By considering equality of intercept, the authors established that all observed measures had the same zero point.

Various analytical findings concerning the item types were made possible by this method. The analogy item type, for example, seemed somewhat different from the others. This finding supports the review by Northrup (1977), who reported that analogies often related more directly to a reasoning factor than the other item types did.

In sum, these analyses confirm that the SAT has a somewhat complex factorial substructure, derived from the specifications for its construction. The factors are interrelated and consistent across groups.

Principal authors: Thomas F. Donlon and Nancy W. Burton
Contributors or reviewers: Donald L. Alderman, William H. Angoff, John A. Centra, Rex H. Jackson, Samuel J. Messick, June Stern, and Warren W. Willingham

Predictive Validity of the ATP Tests

CHAPTER **VIII**

Introduction

This chapter discusses the predictive validity of the SAT, the Achievement Tests, and the Test of Standard Written English for admission and placement decisions. Predictive validity reflects the degree to which test scores relate to an external criterion, typically information about performance after some period of college attendance. In most cases, the criterion is freshman grade point average. This chapter presents evidence on the contribution of ATP tests to predictions used in admission decisions and provides placement-related information on the prediction of a single course grade. The tests are evaluated singly, in combination, and together with high school record.

The Validity Study Service

The first predictive validity studies of the SAT were made as soon as the students tested in 1926 earned the necessary college grades. Brigham (1932) described studies made in 1927 of nine student groups in six colleges. From 1927 to 1964, most validity studies of College Board tests were conducted by individual colleges. A number of studies, however, were made by the College Board, usually to shed light on some decision about the testing program.

In 1964, the College Board established a free Validity Study Service (VSS) to help colleges perform validity studies, analyze data, and interpret results. In 20 years, approximately 725 colleges have prepared more than 2,000 validity studies through the VSS. In addition, other colleges have been encouraged by the College Board validity study work to conduct their own validity studies.

For all enrolling freshmen and for selected subgroups, three basic statistical outcomes are provided in a VSS analysis: correlations, prediction equations based on multiple linear regression, and measures of the error in prediction. Predictors that can be studied include SAT scores, high school rank, high school average, up to five Achievement Test scores (indi-

vidual or averaged), and up to five additional variables. Among the criteria are college grade point average and up to two additional variables. For each subgroup of students, a college can study up to four sets of variables (for each set, a criterion and some combination of predictors). The college must specify the order in which the predictors are to enter the regression equation. The most frequent specification is the criterion of freshman grade point average against the following predictors: high school rank or grade point average, SAT-verbal score, and SAT-mathematical score. The publication *Guide to the College Board Validity Study Service* (College Board 1982b) explains college participation in the VSS and the contents of a VSS report.

Validity of the SAT and High School Record for Predicting Freshman Grade Point Average

Results of studies carried out in the VSS, the primary source of information about the validity of ATP tests, are presented in this chapter by type of college, by student group, by predictor, by criterion, and by year. Validity evidence is also available from special College Board funded research projects, such as those reported by Wilson (1983) and Breland (1979). While these projects are often not undertaken primarily to demonstrate the general validity of the SAT, they may provide evidence of this in the context of an analysis of special or comparative validities. A third major source of ATP test validity information is the published work of independent researchers, who often include the SAT in institutional or national studies analyzing different student groups, predictors, criteria, or treatments.

Correlations. Although colleges using the VSS can choose a multitude of predictor-criterion analyses, the following discussion is limited to those VSS studies performed on classes entering from 1964 to 1981 that contained a predictor-criterion analysis for all freshmen (males and females combined), predicted

141

freshman grade point average, and included as the first three predictors SAT-verbal and SAT-mathematical scores and high school record (rank or grade point average, school-reported or student-reported) in any order. For colleges with more than one study of this kind, the most recent one was chosen.

Table 8.1 summarizes the results from the 685 colleges with studies that met these specifications, showing both the mean correlation coefficients and the 10th, 25th, 50th, 75th, and 90th percentiles of the distribution of these coefficients.

Table 8.1

Correlation Coefficients for 685 Colleges Predicting Freshman Grade Point Average for All Freshmen (Males and Females Combined) Using SAT-Verbal and SAT-Mathematical Scores and High School Record, Entering Classes 1964 to 1981

| | Correlation Coefficients | | | | | |
| | | Percentiles | | | | |
Predictor(s)	Mean	10	25	50 (Median)	75	90
SAT-Verbal Score	.36	.21	.29	.36	.45	.52
SAT-Mathematical Score	.35	.20	.27	.35	.43	.50
High School Record	.48	.31	.39	.48	.57	.64
SAT-Verbal and Mathematical Scores (SAT Multiple)	.42	.27	.34	.42	.50	.57
SAT-Verbal and Mathematical Scores and High School Record	.55	.40	.47	.55	.64	.70

Clearly, high school record is the best predictor of freshman grade point average, but combined SAT scores are not far behind. In 232 of the 685 studies (34 percent), combined SAT scores contributed more to the prediction than high school record; the reverse was true in the other 453 studies (66 percent). The middle 80 percent of the correlations (between the 10th and 90th percentiles) for high school record are in the range .31 to .64 and the middle 80 percent for the combined SAT scores are in the range .27 to .57.

Because neither SAT scores nor the high school record are used alone, the multiple correlation that includes both SAT scores and high school record is the important correlation. A comparison of either mean or median correlation coefficients shows that, on the average, the use of the SAT adds .07 (.55 − .48) to the correlation obtained using high school record alone. Use of high school record adds .13 (.55 − .42) to the correlation obtained using SAT scores alone.

Proportional Contributions. One way of looking at how SAT scores and high school record contribute to the prediction of freshman grade point average is to examine their proportional contributions in the regression equations. For this purpose, the regression slopes were standardized (stated as beta weights) and the proportion of the total standardized weights attributed to each predictor was determined. The mean and selected percentiles of the distribution of these proportional contributions are shown in Table 8.2.

Table 8.2

Proportional Contributions of SAT Scores and High School Record in Predicting Freshman Grade Point Average for All Freshmen (Males and Females Combined) at 685 Colleges, Entering Classes 1964 to 1981

| | Proportional Contributions | | | | | |
| | | Percentiles | | | | |
Predictor(s)	Mean	10	25	50 (Median)	75	90
SAT-Verbal Score	26%	11%	19%	26%	33%	40%
SAT-Mathematical Score	20%	4%	10%	19%	27%	36%
High School Record	54%	37%	46%	55%	63%	71%
SAT-Verbal and Mathematical Scores (Total Contribution of SAT Scores)	46%	29%	37%	45%	54%	63%

The mean weighting for optimal predictive effectiveness is 26 percent for the SAT-verbal score, 20 percent for the SAT-mathematical score, and 54 percent for high school record. However, the weights do vary quite a bit by college. The middle 80 percent range is 11 to 40 percent for the SAT-verbal score, 4 to 36 percent for the SAT-mathematical score, 37 to 71 percent for high school record, and 29 to 63 percent for the SAT scores combined.

Measures of SAT Scores. In the discussion thus far, SAT-verbal and SAT-mathematical scores have been used as two distinct predictors. The two scores can also be simply summed (or averaged) so that the SAT sum can be treated as a single predictor. The correlation for this single predictor would be identical to that of the multiple correlation for the two scores used separately if the optimal weighting for the verbal and mathematical scores were to be the same. Because the optimal weighting is not usually the same, the multiple correlation is usually slightly higher: a median of .55 compared to .52 for the sum of the SAT scores.

Through vss, a college can either supply student SAT scores for use in the analysis or ask the College Board to retrieve them. If the college chooses to supply the scores and a student has more than one pair, the college must decide whether to use the most recent, the highest, or the average. If scores are retrieved, the latest scores are used. Until recently, there has been little research comparing the effects of these decisions on prediction. A study by Cowen and Abrahams (1982) showed that average SAT scores had a higher validity (.48) than highest scores (.38) at the U.S. Naval Academy. The College Board commissioned a special study of this issue. Preliminary results show little difference in validity among the most recent, highest, and average scores.

Measures of High School Record. In the 685 validity studies, standardized high school rank was used 56 percent of the time and high school grade point average was used 44 percent of the time. However, the trend in recent years has been a shift from rank toward grade point average. For the studies of entering classes prior to 1977, 65 percent used rank and 35 percent used grade point average; for the studies of entering classes 1977 to 1981, only 51 percent used rank and 49 percent used grade point average.

Beginning in 1973, vss gave the colleges the option of utilizing information supplied by students on the Student Descriptive Questionnaire (SDQ) about their high school rank or grade point average (based on the latest grades received in six academic subjects). Between 1977 and 1981, 31 percent of the validity studies have used one of these two student-reported options: rank in 12 percent of the studies and grade point average in 19 percent of the studies.

Table 8.3 compares the validities for the four forms of high school record in studies performed on entering classes 1977 to 1981 (413 of the 685 studies). Although the two college-reported forms are similar in validity, college-reported grade point average has a slightly higher mean validity than college-reported rank, .50 to .48. On the average, the corresponding student-reported forms have validities about .10 below those of the college-reported forms, although there are individual studies where student-reported forms have higher validities.

Comparing the studies from 1977 to 1981 with earlier ones shows that the correlations for high school record have decreased (from an average of .50 to .46). This is partly due to the fact that almost one-third of the newer studies used student-reported rank or grade point average, which tend to have lower correlations. However, the average correlation for college-reported measures has also decreased, from .51 to .49.

Table 8.3

Correlation of Four Measures of High School Record in Predicting Freshman Grade Point Average for All Freshmen for 413 Colleges Performing Validity Studies on 1977 to 1981 Entering Classes

| Predictor | % of Studies | Mean | Correlation Coefficients Percentiles | | | | |
			10	25	50 (Median)	75	90
College-Reported High School Rank	39%	.48	.34	.39	.48	.57	.63
Student-Reported High School Rank	12%	.36	.25	.31	.36	.44	.49
College-Reported High School Grade Point Average	30%	.50	.34	.43	.51	.59	.65
Student-Reported High School Grade Point Average	19%	.42	.28	.35	.42	.50	.59

Differences in validity between rank and grade point average are likely to be specific for each college, depending on how the standards and the student populations of contributing high schools differ. For any given high school, rank and grade point average should be roughly equivalent in validity. The two measures may differ significantly, however, when students from two or more high schools are being compared.

Using rank for selection forces all high schools to be treated in the same way. If, for a given college, the important feeder high schools have students that are of similar ability, then rank is probably the preferable measure to use in selection.

Grade point average, in effect, gives a premium to students from those high schools with the most lenient grading standards. If the high schools with lenient grading standards also have students with high academic ability, then grade point average is the preferable measure for selection. However, differences in grading standards could, to a certain extent, nullify the actual predictive value of the grade point average measure by obscuring differences among schools; in such cases, rank could be preferable for selection because it openly treats all schools the same and preserves most of the within-school differences in performance.

If college-reported high school grade point average is used in a validity study, the college must decide whether to use the full high school grade point average or to recompute it using only academic courses. Table 8.4 shows findings by Goldman and Sexton (1974) that, at the University of California at Riverside, high school course grades in individual academic courses did indeed have a higher correlation with freshman grade point average than high school course grades in nonacademic courses.

Table 8.4

Average Individual High School Course Grade Correlations with Freshman Grade Point Average (Goldman and Sexton 1974)

Academic Subjects		Nonacademic Subjects	
English	.50	Home Economics	.08
Science	.45	Religion	.09
History	.43	Fine Arts	.28
Mathematics	.42	Business/Clerical	.29
Social Science	.41	Mechanical Arts	.30
Foreign Language	.39		
Speech/Journalism	.39		

In the Goldman and Sexton study, however, total high school grade point average and academic subject high school grade point average correlated with freshman grade point average about the same, .47 for the former and .46 for the latter. The authors concluded that while nonacademic courses do not add very much to the validity of the academic course grade point average (because they represent only about 20 percent of the total grade point average), there is little reason to remove them.

Range of Predictor Values

Applicants with low values on the predictors are often not admitted and, therefore, are not included in a college's validity study. In addition, students with either unusually high or low grades or scores may never apply to a particular college. These exclusions tend to restrict the range of predictor values in most validity studies. Criterion restriction is also possible, as students who realize they are likely to fail may withdraw from courses before receiving their grades.

Students excluded from a study for any of these reasons are often the most predictable successes or failures. As Figure 8.1 shows, restrictions from either end of the academic spectrum can reduce the apparent relationship between the predictors and the criterion. As students become more alike, the practical usefulness of a predictor is reduced. In the extreme case, if all students have the same predictor values, no prediction is possible.

Figure 8.1

Effect of Selection and Restriction of Range

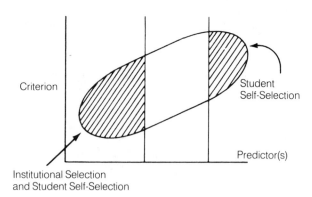

Figure 8.2 shows the relationship between the SAT standard deviation and the SAT correlation with freshman grade point average for 685 colleges performing validity studies on classes entering from 1964 to 1981. Based on their SAT standard deviations, the colleges were grouped into six categories of approximately 100 colleges each. The six groups of colleges were similar in other characteristics. They differed, however, in their correlations of SAT scores with freshman grade point average. Note the almost linear increase in mean correlation from low to high SAT standard deviation.

Figure 8.2

Mean SAT Correlation with Freshman Grade Point Average, by SAT Standard Deviation

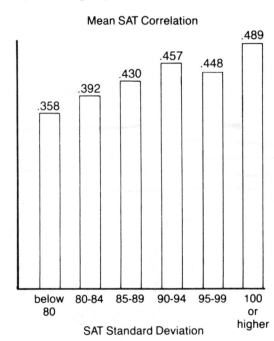

144

Various formulas are available to correct a correlation coefficient from a restricted population. Based on the restricted relationship, these formulas estimate what the relationship would have been in the full population. They assume that the same linear relationship between the predictors and the criterion holds in both the unrestricted and restricted populations and that the standard error of the estimate is consistent throughout the range of the predictors.

In using the correction, researchers define the unrestricted group as either all applicants to a given college or all test takers. Choice of the applicant group may understate the validity of the SAT. As Hartnett and Feldmesser (1980) show, student self-selection is a major factor in the admission process, probably more important than selection by the college, so that the group applying to a given college is already restricted. Part of the validity of a college admission test may be used in informing the student of the appropriate college and course of study. In order to determine the full value of predictors in admissions at the college, a correction defining the entire test-taking group as the unrestricted group will be computed.

The most commonly used formula for correcting one predictor for restriction of range was first presented by Pearson (1903). (See also Guilford and Fruchter 1978, Lord and Novick 1968, and Gulliksen 1950.) The formula assumes that the criterion is linearly related to the predictor (linearity) and that the variability of the criterion is the same for all values of the predictor (homoscedasticity). It requires knowledge of the standard deviation of the predictor in the unrestricted and restricted groups.

The estimated full-range or corrected correlation (in the unrestricted group of all SAT takers) between the SAT sum (the verbal score plus the mathematical score) and freshman grade point average is represented by the following single-predictor correction formula:

$$R_{SF} = \frac{r_{SF}\left(\dfrac{S_S}{s_S}\right)}{\sqrt{1 + r_{SF}^2\left[\left(\dfrac{S_S}{s_S}\right)^2 - 1\right]}}$$

where r_{SF} = the restricted correlation between the SAT sum and freshman grade point average (at the college)

S_S = the full-range standard deviation of the SAT sum (for all SAT takers)

s_S = the restricted standard deviation of the SAT sum (at the college)

R_{SF} = the corrected correlation between the SAT sum and the freshman grade point average (for all SAT takers)

Based on all SAT takers graduating in 1983, S_S is 208. Averaging standard deviations of SAT sums for all colleges doing a validity study on 1977 to 1981 entering classes, s_S equals 151. Since s_S^2 is the variance of the SAT with restriction of range and S_S^2 is the variance of the SAT without restriction of range, the ratio s_S^2/S_S^2 ($151^2/208^2 = 53$ percent) shows the proportion of the variance that remains after restriction of range. Therefore, the process of sorting SAT takers into colleges reduces the SAT variance by almost half (100 − 53 = 47 percent).

For high school grade point average, the College Board publication *National College-Bound Seniors, 1983* shows that the full-range standard deviation (S_S), based on all SAT takers who report grades in each of six subject areas, is .60. The mean restricted standard deviation (s_S), for colleges using high school grade point average in a validity study on 1977 to 1981 entering classes, is .52. For high school grade point average, $.52^2/.60^2 = 75$ percent of the full-range variance. Therefore, while the process of sorting SAT takers into colleges reduces the SAT variance by almost half, the same process reduces the high school grade point average variance by only one-quarter (100 − 75 = 25 percent). This is one way of showing that the range of the SAT for enrolled students is about twice as restricted as the range of high school grade point average.

For all validity studies used to predict freshman grade point average for classes entering from 1977 to 1981, the median correlation for the SAT sum is .40 and the median correlation for high school grade point average is .46. Using the formula above to correct for restriction of range, the SAT correlation becomes .52, an increase of .12. The high school grade point average correlation becomes .51, an increase of .05. This is another way of showing that the range of the SAT is about twice as restricted as the range of high school grade point average.

Figure 8.2 shows the strong relationship between the SAT standard deviation and the SAT correlation with freshman grade point average; the correlation between the two for 485 validity studies on 1977 to 1981 entering classes was .42. A correction formula for individual coefficients should work to reduce this correlation close to zero, so that corrected SAT correlations are not significantly related to the SAT standard deviations of the samples on which they are based. This analysis has been done for the single-predictor correction formula and shows that the correction reduces the correlation between the validity coefficient and the SAT standard deviation from .42 to .02. In other words, the correction formula works empirically in the sense that the resulting corrected SAT correlations are independent of the SAT standard deviations. The mean restricted correlations in Figure 8.2 for six categories of SAT standard deviations are increasing from .36 to .49, but the mean corrected, full-range correlations for these six categories, in the same order, appear to be neither increasing nor decreasing—.50, .49, .53, .53, .51, and .51—and therefore are not related to the magnitude of the SAT standard deviation.

The single-predictor correction formula is appropriate when selection is done explicitly on the one predictor that is being corrected. However, a more accurate model of the true admission process is that SAT scores and high school grade point average are used together, both in student self-selection and in college admission selection. The precise manner in which this is carried out is not known. Therefore, no single statistical model can be confirmed.

If one assumes that there is explicit selection (that is, the use of a fixed cut score) both on the SAT sum and on high school record (see Gulliksen 1950, pp. 158-172), then the corrected validities would be .56 for the SAT sum (versus .52 for the single-predictor correction) and .57 for high school record (versus .51 for the single-predictor correction).* The corrected validities then appear to be about equal for the SAT sum and high school record, .16 and .11, respectively, greater than the uncorrected empirical values. The multiple correlation inferred from the values of .56 for the SAT sum and .57 for high school record would be .64. An alternate approach, assuming explicit selection on an optimally weighted composite of the SAT sum and the high school grade point average,** and using the single-predictor correction formula, leads to a corrected estimate of the multiple correlation of .66.

In the remainder of the chapter, typical SAT correlations are given for various categories of colleges and for various student groups. Differences in these correlations may well be attributed to restriction of range. Therefore, corrected correlations are also reported. Based on its ease of use and apparent empirical effectiveness, the single-predictor formula is used to determine these corrected correlations, which, according to Linn, Harnish, and Dunbar

---

*For this computation, the correlation between the SAT sum and high school grade point average is needed for the unrestricted group (stated as .56 in Educational Testing Service 1980b, p. 22) and for the restricted group (averaging .36 for all validity studies on entering classes 1977 through 1981).

**The average weights and constant for 191 colleges using SAT scores and high school grade point average in validity studies for entering classes 1977 to 1981 were (.12280) (SAT sum) + (.51611) (high school grade point average) − .101825.

(1981), are conservative estimates of what the validity would be for a student body as heterogeneous with respect to SAT scores as the total group of SAT takers. To identify readily which specific college types or student groups have relatively high or low validity after correcting for restriction of range, the differences between the corrected correlations and .52 (the corrected SAT-sum correlation for the average validity study for all colleges and all students) are also shown.

Validity Without Restriction of Range

The full SAT-taking population has a standard deviation for the simple SAT sum of 208. To determine whether there is any empirical evidence of validity in colleges where restriction of range does not occur, a search of the VSS data base for colleges with enrolling freshmen who have an SAT sum standard deviation of at least 200 was undertaken. The search revealed 21 colleges where the variability of SAT scores is similar to that of the full test-taking population. Validity data for these colleges are summarized in Table 8.5.

The average SAT-sum standard deviation for these 21 colleges is exactly 208, the same as that of the full SAT-taking population. In addition, for 11 colleges that used high school rank on a 20-to-80 scale (normalized with a mean of 50 and a standard deviation of 10 for all high school graduates), the average high school rank standard deviation is 7.3, almost the same as the 7.1 for the full SAT-taking population. Also, for the 6 colleges that used high school grade point average on a 0 to 4 scale, the average high school grade point average standard deviation is .59, almost the same as the .60 for the full SAT-taking population. Therefore, these colleges appear to enroll students with an unrestricted range of high school records as well as of SAT scores.

The means of SAT and high school record for these colleges are also approximately the same as those of the full SAT-taking population. The SAT-sum mean of 936 is between the mean of 958 in 1967 and the mean of 890 in 1980, the approximate range of years of the 21 studies. The high school rank and grade point average means of 57 and 3.02, respectively, are almost identical to the full SAT-taking means of 57 and 3.06.

Of the 21 colleges, 18 have a religious affiliation. It is possible that because of this students may have selected these colleges predominantly for reasons other than academic level, usually measured by the high school performance or SAT scores of the enrolled students. The result is that these colleges have distri-

Table 8.5

Average Validity Data for Colleges with
No Observable Restriction of Range

Number of Colleges	21
SAT Means	
SAT-Verbal Score	459
SAT-Mathematical Score	477
SAT-Sum*	936
SAT Standard Deviations	
SAT-Verbal Score	111
SAT-Mathematical Score	114
SAT-Sum*	208
High School Record Means	
High School Rank (20-80 scale, 11 colleges)	57
High School GPA (0-4 scale, 6 colleges)	3.02
High School Record Standard Deviations	
High School Rank (20-80 scale, 11 colleges)	7.3
High School GPA (0-4 scale, 6 colleges)	.59
Freshman Grade Point Average	
Mean	2.64
Standard Deviation	.76
Proportional Contributions	
SAT-Verbal Score	31%
SAT-Mathematical Score	20%
High School Record	48%
Correlations with Freshman Grade Point Average	
SAT-Verbal Score	.53
SAT-Mathematical Score	.50
SAT-Sum*	.56
SAT-Multiple*	.57
High School Record (HSR)	.55
SAT-V, SAT-M, HSR Multiple (Optimally Weighted)	.65
SAT Increment	.10

*The SAT sum is a simple sum of the SAT verbal and mathematical scores. Therefore, the SAT-sum correlation with freshman grade point average is based on an equal weighting of the two scores, while the SAT-multiple correlation with freshman grade point average is based on the optimal weighting of the two scores.

butions of SAT scores that are almost identical to those of the full SAT-taking population.

In this environment of unrestricted range for high school record and SAT scores, both the average SAT multiple and the average SAT-sum correlations with freshman grade point average (.57 and .56, respectively) are higher than the average high school record correlation (.55). The optimal prediction equations place more weight on the SAT (52 percent) than on high school record (48 percent). The incremental effectiveness of the SAT is .10 (the SAT/high school record multiple correlation of .65 minus the high school record correlation of .55). The average SAT-sum and high school record correlations of .56 and .55, respectively, are almost identical to the average correlations for all colleges that were corrected on page 146 for restriction of range using the method that assumes explicit selection both on the SAT sum and on high school record: .56 and .57, respectively.

Improvement in Prediction Attributable to the SAT

It is a common practice to take the multiple correlation with freshman grade point average, including both the SAT and high school record as predictors, and to subtract from it the high school record correlation with freshman grade point average. This difference is considered to be the improvement in prediction or incremental effectiveness attributable to the SAT over high school record.

Despite the simplicity of this concept, there has been a fair amount of disagreement about its application. Ford and Campos (1977) summarized validity studies performed by colleges through VSS for entering classes 1964 to 1974, and concluded that the multiple correlation averaged about .58; the high school record correlation averaged about .50, and the difference or improvement in prediction was .58 − .50 = .08. Slack and Porter (1980) considered the same data, but concluded that the high school record correlation averaged about .52, instead of .50, and that the improvement was .58 − .52 = .06.

Instead of using averages of validity studies performed at a large number of colleges, Trusheim and Crouse (1982) used National Longitudinal Study data on the entering class of 1972. For the study, freshman grade point average from all colleges served as one overall performance criterion, despite obvious differences among colleges. This source of potential error probably explains the relatively low correlations they reported: .462 for the multiple correlation, .407 for the high school record correlation, and .462 − .407 = .055 for the improvement. Willingham and Ramist (1982) questioned the use of the same criterion for all colleges, and reported median validities first published in *Guide to the College Board Validity Study Service* (College Board 1982b, p. 19) for 387 individual college validity studies performed through the VSS for entering classes 1974 to 1978: .551 for the multiple correlation, .465 for the high school record correlation, and .551 − .465 = .086 for the improvement. There is certain to be variation in such results, given the number of factors that could alter them:

1. *Unit of analysis.* One validity study using a single criterion of freshman performance across colleges results in different and lower correlations than the use of an average of validity studies for a number of individual colleges.

2. *Time period.* Validity results vary over time.

3. *Type of average.* Sometimes the mean is used, and sometimes the median is used.

4. *Type of SAT measure.* Use of separate SAT-verbal and SAT-mathematical scores yields a higher multiple correlation than does use of the sum of the SAT-verbal and SAT-mathematical scores. If there are multiple student scores, sometimes the highest is used, sometimes the average is used, but in the majority of the most recent validity studies the latest is used.

5. *Type of high school record measure.* College-reported measures are better predictors than student-reported measures, and grade point average is slightly better than rank.

6. *Correlation correction.* Correction for restriction of range could affect the amount of improvement.

7. *Difference of averages or average of differences.* Each of the published descriptions of the SAT increment for individual colleges has been in terms of the difference between the average multiple correlation and the average high school record correlation. Another possibility is the average of college-by-college differences between the multiple correlation and the high school record correlation. These two are the same for means but different for medians.

8. *Number of significant digits.* Up to .01 of a difference of .05 to .10 can be altered due to rounding three digits to two digits.

Table 8.6 displays the distributions of differences between the multiple correlation and the high school record correlation that are available from VSS studies. The first distribution is based on all 685 colleges that used SAT scores and high school record to predict freshman grade point average in the VSS for any entering class up to 1981, including only the latest study if a given college did more than one. The second distribution is based on the subset of 413 colleges that had such studies for at least one of the entering classes 1977 to 1981, again using the latest of multiple studies for a given college. The third distribution is based on the 21 colleges described in this chapter, for which the variability of the SAT scores and high school record of their enrolling freshmen approximates that of the full SAT-taking group.

The mean, median, and other percentiles for the colleges studying entering classes 1977 to 1981 are slightly higher than for colleges in all years. There is great variability among the colleges in the size of the improvement: the range of the middle 80 percent is .01 to .15. One-quarter of the improvements are less than .04, but one-quarter are greater than .10. Because there is typically two times more restriction of range for the SAT than for high school record, the 21

Table 8.6

Improvement in Prediction Attributable to the SAT: Selected Points on Distributions of Differences Between Multiple Correlations (SAT Scores and High School Record) and Correlations Using Only High School Record, for All Years Through 1981, for 1977 to 1981, and for Colleges with No Observable Restriction of Range

	All Years (685 Colleges)	Entering Classes 1977-1981 (413 Colleges)	Colleges with No Observable Restriction of Range (21 Colleges)
Mean	.076	.077	.093
10th percentile	.014	.014	.043
25th percentile	.034	.036	.068
50th percentile (median)	.067	.069	.084
75th percentile	.099	.102	.108
90th percentile	.145	.148	.156

colleges with no observable restriction of range have a higher average SAT increment (mean of .093).

Recent articles present a variety of interpretations of the SAT increment. The mean correlations for the 21 colleges with no observable restriction of range, .65 for the multiple correlation using SAT scores and high school record and .55 for the correlation using high school record only, will be used to illustrate three interpretations.

1. *Index of forecasting efficiency.* If there is no predictor information available, the smallest expected average squared error would be obtained by predicting the mean of the criterion for all students. The average squared error of this procedure is the variance of the criterion (Sy^2). Its square root, the standard deviation of the criterion (Sy), could be considered the base prediction error.

The standard error ($Sy \sqrt{1-r^2}$) represents the error after the predictors are used. Therefore, $\sqrt{1-r^2}$ (called the coefficient of alienation) represents the proportion of the original error that remains. It follows that $1-\sqrt{1-r^2}$ represents the proportion of the original error that is eliminated by using the predictors. The latter is often used as an index (or coefficient) of forecasting (or predictive) efficiency.

A correlation coefficient of .55 for high school record yields an index of $1-\sqrt{1-(.55)^2} = .16$, which means that high school record alone reduces the error by 16 percent. A correlation coefficient of .65 for high school record and the SAT yields an index of $1-\sqrt{1-(.65)^2} = .24$, which means that high school record and the SAT reduce the error by 24 percent. Therefore, the error reduction due to the combination of high school record and the SAT is 50 percent greater than the error reduction due to use of high school record alone: .24/.16 = 1.50.

2. *Correlation coefficient squared.* The formula for the standard error, $S_e = Sy\sqrt{1-r^2}$, can be solved for r^2:

$$r^2 = \frac{(Sy^2 - S_e^2)}{Sy^2}$$

where Sy^2 = the total variance in the criterion

S_e^2 = the unexplained variance

$(Sy^2 - S_e^2)$ = the explained variance.

Therefore, r^2 = the explained variance/the total variance, the proportion of variance explained by the predictor(s). A correlation of .55 for high school record means that high school record explains $(.55)^2$ = 30 percent of the total variance. A correlation of .65 for high school record and the SAT means that they explain $(.65)^2$ = 42 percent of the total variance. Therefore, the variance explained by the combination of high school record and the SAT is 40 percent greater than the variance explained by high school record alone: .42/.30 = 1.40.

3. *Correlation coefficient.* Brogden (1946) showed that for any given number of students the correlation coefficient (r) is the expected proportional improvement in the criterion mean from random selection (no predictors) to perfect selection (based on the criterion itself). If the top N students based on prior knowledge of the criterion are selected, presumably a class would be obtained that would be B units above the mean on the criterion. If the predictors are used instead, the resultant class probably would be r times B units above the mean on the criterion.

A correlation of .55 for high school record means that use of high school record would be expected to produce a freshman grade point average that is .55B units above the mean for all SAT takers. A correlation of .65 for high school record and the SAT means that use of high school record and the SAT would be expected to produce a freshman grade point average that is .65B units above the mean for all SAT takers. Therefore, use of the SAT increases the average freshman grade point average an additional 18 percent over the mean that would be observed for all SAT takers: .65B/.55B = 1.18. This approach to evaluating

the correlation coefficient is described in Beaton and Barone (1981).

Validity by College Type

SAT Level. In Table 8.7 on page 150, colleges are categorized into 11 groups based on the average sum of the SAT verbal and mathematical scores for their students. As might be expected, colleges with either particularly high or particularly low average SAT scores have lower SAT standard deviations, and, for the most part, SAT correlations (and high school record correlations) are also lower for these extreme groups. They are the only groups defined in terms of SAT level for which the SAT-multiple correlation exceeds the high school record correlation and for which the SAT increment exceeds .10. Surprisingly, the largest average increment of .13 is for the five colleges with an average SAT sum (verbal plus mathematical scores) below 600.

To determine whether there are any effects in addition to a general restriction of range effect, the correlation of the SAT sum is corrected for each category. If the only effect is that of general restriction of range, using the single-predictor correction formula would yield a corrected SAT-sum correlation of .52, the same as for all colleges and all students. The differences between the corrected correlations and .52 are also displayed to highlight the effect of factors other than restriction of range. In Table 8.7 and in subsequent tables, these observed and corrected correlations for the *sum* of SAT verbal and mathematical scores should not be confused with the observed SAT-*multiple* correlation (using optimally weighted SAT verbal and mathematical scores), which is also presented, and is usually slightly higher than the observed SAT-sum correlation. Table 8.7 shows that colleges with higher average SAT scores have lower corrected correlations and colleges with lower SAT scores have higher corrected correlations. Although the SAT is apparently slightly less successful in prediction at colleges with higher average SAT scores, the SAT increment over high school record is relatively large at these colleges.

Size. Colleges using VSS were also grouped into three categories based on the size of their freshman class: large (over 1,000 students), medium (501–1,000); and small (500 or fewer). Table 8.8 on page 151 shows that small colleges have a lower SAT-mathematical mean than the others, but the same SAT-verbal mean as large colleges.

Although the average SAT-sum standard deviations of the large and small colleges are the same,

149

Table 8.7

Average Validity Data by SAT Level (Sum of Verbal and Mathematical Scores)*

	1,200 or Greater	1,100-1,199	1,050-1,099	1,000-1,049	950-999	900-949	850-899	800-849	700-799	600-699	Below 600
Number of Colleges	22	51	51	79	107	117	113	70	55	15	5
SAT Means											
SAT-Verbal Score	607	550	520	490	472	446	423	402	371	309	269
SAT-Mathematical Score	643	592	551	531	504	477	452	426	397	335	304
SAT-Sum‡	1250	1142	1071	1021	976	923	875	828	769	644	573
SAT Standard Deviations											
SAT-Verbal Score	81	83	87	87	88	89	87	86	82	70	58
SAT-Mathematical Score	79	81	88	91	92	94	92	89	85	67	54
SAT-Sum‡	134	136	150	153	156	161	158	154	147	119	93
Proportional Contributions											
SAT-Verbal Score	28%	26%	26%	26%	26%	26%	24%	27%	27%	22%	36%
SAT-Mathematical Score	27%	24%	16%	19%	16%	18%	22%	19%	21%	30%	21%
High School Record	45%	50%	58%	55%	57%	56%	55%	54%	53%	48%	43%
Correlations with Freshman GPA											
SAT-Verbal Score	.28	.30	.36	.37	.38	.38	.38	.37	.34	.30	.37
SAT-Mathematical Score	.29	.30	.32	.35	.35	.37	.37	.37	.33	.33	.31
SAT-Sum‡	.33	.35	.40	.42	.42	.43	.43	.42	.38	.36	.41
Corrected SAT-Sum	.48	.50	.52	.53	.53	.52	.53	.53	.50	.56	.71
Corrected SAT-Sum − .52†	−.04	−.02	.00	+.01	+.01	.00	+.01	+.01	−.02	+.04	+.19
SAT-Multiple‡	.35	.37	.41	.43	.42	.44	.43	.43	.39	.36	.42
High School Record (HSR)	.33	.40	.49	.50	.50	.50	.49	.49	.43	.39	.38
SAT-V, SAT-M, HSR Multiple	.44	.50	.56	.57	.57	.57	.57	.56	.52	.48	.51
SAT Increment	.11	.10	.07	.07	.07	.07	.08	.07	.09	.09	.13

*Tables 8.7 through 8.15 contain one validity study per college, the most recent study for the entering classes 1964 through 1981.
†Subtraction of .52 (the corrected SAT-sum correlation for all colleges and all students) highlights the effects of factors other than restriction of range.
‡The SAT sum is a simple sum of the SAT verbal and mathematical scores. Therefore, the SAT-sum correlation with freshman grade point average is based on an equal weighting of the two scores, while the SAT-multiple correlation with freshman grade point average is based on the optimal weighting of the two scores.

the average SAT-multiple correlation is only .39 for the large colleges compared to .45 for the small colleges. This negative relationship between college size and SAT correlation is consistent with the study by Baird (1983). The same pattern holds for the average high school record correlation (.44 for the large colleges and .51 for the small colleges), and therefore the SAT increment is almost the same for each size category. An explanation of the lower correlations for both predictors at large colleges may be that the greater variety of courses usually offered or the greater variety of standards within a large faculty makes freshman grade point average less comparable from student to student than in a small college, and, therefore, less predictable.

Type and Control. The colleges using VSS were categorized by type and control as four-year public, four-year private, two-year public, and two-year private. More than 90 percent were four-year colleges, and the majority of these were four-year private colleges. The SAT sum is the highest (965) for the four-year private colleges and the lowest (813) for two-year private colleges.

Table 8.9 shows that the SAT-sum standard deviations are fairly similar—all within the 150-154 range. However, the corrected SAT-sum correlations are lower for both types of public colleges, .07 below average for two-year public colleges and .05 below for four-year public colleges. The high school record correlations are also lower for the public colleges, .44 and .45, compared to .49 and .47 for private colleges. Such findings are not limited to College Board scores; similar patterns emerge in work with other college admissions tests (Sawyer and Maxey 1982). Like the large colleges discussed above, perhaps most public colleges offer a broader course selection and have a larger faculty than most private colleges, and thereby comparability of grades among courses and instructors is reduced.

Table 8.10 on page 152 classifies colleges as doctorate-granting, four-year liberal arts, two-year liberal arts, and specialized non-liberal arts. Most of the colleges were four-year liberal arts colleges. The doctorate-granting institutions have the highest SAT sum, 1,032, and two-year liberal arts colleges have the lowest SAT sum, 818. However, both of these types of college have lower corrected SAT-sum corre-

Table 8.8

Average Validity Data of Colleges Classified
by Freshman Class Size*

	Large (Over 1,000)	Medium (501- 1,000)	Small (500 or Fewer)
Number of Colleges	168	151	312
SAT Means			
SAT-Verbal Score	458	462	458
SAT-Mathematical Score	500	499	481
SAT-Sum‡	959	960	939
SAT Standard Deviations			
SAT-Verbal Score	87	85	88
SAT-Mathematical Score	91	88	90
SAT-Sum‡	154	150	154
Proportional Contributions			
SAT-Verbal Score	26%	27%	26%
SAT-Mathematical Score	21%	20%	20%
High School Record	53%	53%	55%
Correlations with Freshman GPA			
SAT-Verbal Score	.34	.36	.39
SAT-Mathematical Score	.33	.35	.37
SAT-Sum ‡	.38	.40	.44
Corrected SAT-Sum	.49	.52	.55
Corrected SAT-Sum −.52†	−.03	.00	+.03
SAT-Multiple‡	.39	.41	.45
High School Record (HSR)	.44	.46	.51
SAT-V, SAT-M, HSR Multiple	.51	.54	.59
SAT Increment	.07	.08	.08

*Fifty-four of the 685 colleges could not be categorized for this analysis.
†Subtraction of .52 (the corrected SAT-sum correlation for all colleges and all students) highlights the effects of factors other than restriction of range.
‡The SAT sum is a simple sum of the SAT verbal and mathematical scores. Therefore, the SAT-sum correlation with freshman grade point average is based on an equal weighting of the two scores, while the SAT-multiple correlation with freshman grade point average is based on the optimal weighting of the two scores.

Table 8.9

Average Validity Data by Public/Private and
Two-Year/Four-Year Contrasts*

	Four-Year Public	Four-Year Private	Two-Year Public	Two-Year Private
Number of Colleges	201	428	25	22
SAT Means				
SAT-Verbal Score	439	469	401	395
SAT-Mathematical Score	480	497	437	418
SAT-Sum‡	919	965	837	813
SAT Standard Deviations				
SAT-Verbal Score	85	87	84	84
SAT-Mathematical Score	89	89	90	86
SAT-Sum‡	151	153	154	150
Proportional Contributions				
SAT-Verbal Score	25%	26%	26%	26%
SAT-Mathematical Score	20%	19%	17%	20%
High School Record	55%	54%	57%	54%
Correlations with Freshman GPA				
SAT-Verbal Score	.32	.38	.32	.36
SAT-Mathematical Score	.32	.37	.30	.34
SAT-Sum‡	.36	.43	.35	.40
Corrected SAT-Sum	.47	.54	.45	.52
Corrected SAT-Sum −.52†	−.05	+.02	−.07	.00
SAT-Multiple‡	.38	.44	.37	.41
High School Record (HSR)	.44	.49	.45	.47
SAT-V, SAT-M, HSR Multiple	.51	.57	.51	.55
SAT Increment	.07	.08	.06	.08

*Nine of the 685 colleges could not be categorized for this analysis.
†Subtraction of .52 (the corrected SAT-sum correlation for all colleges and all students) highlights the effects of factors other than restriction of range.
‡The SAT sum is a simple sum of the SAT verbal and mathematical scores. Therefore, the SAT-sum correlation with freshman grade point average is based on an equal weighting of the two scores, while the SAT-multiple correlation with freshman grade point average is based on the optimal weighting of the two scores.

lations than average. For the doctorate-granting institutions, the high school record correlation is also low, contributing to a low multiple correlation of .49.

For specialized non-liberal arts colleges, the average SAT-verbal correlation is .30, compared to .36 for all colleges, while the average SAT-mathematical correlation of .35 is the same as that for all colleges. As a result, much more weight is placed on the SAT-mathematical score (30 percent) and less on the SAT-verbal score (18 percent).

Regional Differences. Table 8.11 on page 153 shows that there are marked regional differences on all variables. The VSS user colleges in the West and the Midwest have the highest average SAT sums of 982 and 978, respectively, while those in the South have the lowest average SAT sum of 879.

The students at colleges in the West, Southwest, and Midwest are more heterogeneous, with average

SAT-sum standard deviations of 167, 166, and 165 respectively. On the other hand, the students at colleges in New England, the South, and the Middle Atlantic States are relatively homogeneous, with average SAT-sum standard deviations of 141, 143, and 145, respectively, indicating relatively more restriction of range.

One might expect these regional differences to be reflected in the average correlations, and this is partially true. Of the colleges in the three regions with more heterogeneity, the Midwestern and Southwestern colleges have high SAT correlations. The Midwestern colleges also have a particularly high average correlation of .54 for high school record, yielding an SAT and high school record multiple of .60, the highest for any region. For colleges in the West, both the observed and corrected SAT correlations are low.

Although the SAT sum standard deviation for New England colleges is approximately equal to that of

Table 8.10

Average Validity Data by Type of College*

	Doctorate-Granting	Four-Year Liberal Arts	Two-Year Liberal Arts	Specialized Non-Liberal Arts
Number of Colleges	92	487	49	33
SAT Means				
SAT-Verbal Score	492	453	394	461
SAT-Mathematical Score	539	481	425	521
SAT-Sum‡	1032	935	818	982
SAT Standard Deviations				
SAT-Verbal Score	89	86	83	83
SAT-Mathematical Score	92	89	88	84
SAT-Sum‡	156	152	151	143
Proportional Contributions				
SAT-Verbal Score	28%	26%	26%	18%
SAT-Mathematical Score	21%	19%	19%	30%
High School Record	52%	55%	55%	52%
Correlations with Freshman GPA				
SAT-Verbal Score	.33	.38	.34	.30
SAT-Mathematical Score	.32	.36	.32	.35
SAT-Sum‡	.38	.42	.37	.37
Corrected SAT-Sum	.48	.54	.48	.50
Corrected SAT-Sum −.52†	−.04	+.02	−.04	−.02
SAT-Multiple‡	.38	.43	.39	.39
High School Record (HSR)	.42	.49	.45	.44
SAT-V, SAT-M, HSR Multiple	.49	.57	.52	.53
SAT Increment	.07	.08	.07	.09

*Twenty-four of the 685 colleges could not be categorized for this analysis.
†Subtraction of .52 (the corrected SAT-sum correlation for all colleges and all students) highlights the effects of factors other than restriction of range.
‡The SAT sum is a simple sum of the SAT verbal and mathematical scores. Therefore, the SAT-sum correlation with freshman grade point average is based on an equal weighting of the two scores, while the SAT-multiple correlation with freshman grade point average is based on the optimal weighting of the two scores.

Southern colleges, the observed SAT sum correlation for New England colleges is only .35, compared to .41 for Southern colleges. The New England high school record correlation is also lower, resulting in a multiple correlation of only .49, compared to .57 for Southern colleges.

Proportion of Students Who Are Ethnic Minorities. Table 8.12 on page 154 groups colleges into four categories based on the proportion of their students who are ethnic minorities: less than 10 percent, 10-49 percent, 50-89 percent, and 90 percent or over. The great majority of the colleges participating in the VSS are in one of the first two groups.

As the proportion of students who are ethnic minorities increases, the SAT-multiple correlations decrease (from .43 to .36). However, the high school record correlations decrease even more (from .51 to .37).

Perhaps the most interesting group is the 90-100 percent group, comprising what are often referred to as traditionally Black colleges. The SAT-sum standard deviation at these colleges is an extremely low 116, reflecting a very homogeneous group with respect to SAT scores. Although the observed SAT-sum correlation of .35 is below average, the corrected correlation is .04 above average. The SAT increment of .11 is comparatively large.

Validity by Student Group

In order to evaluate the predictive effectiveness of the SAT for various groups of students, a college can subgroup its students however it chooses for separate validity study analyses. The considerations for doing so are discussed in the *Guide to the College Board Validity Study Service.*

Area of Study. Separation of results by area of study is useful because grade point averages of students within the same area of study are more comparable and thus are a more reliable criterion than grade point averages in courses taken by students in

Table 8.11

Average Validity Data by Region*

	New England	Middle Atlantic	South	Midwest	Southwest	West
Number of Colleges	91	168	151	154	40	72
SAT Means						
SAT-Verbal Score	455	460	425	473	451	472
SAT-Mathematical Score	487	492	454	505	480	510
SAT-Sum‡	942	952	879	978	931	982
SAT Standard Deviations						
SAT-Verbal Score	81	83	82	91	92	94
SAT-Mathematical Score	84	85	83	97	96	97
SAT-Sum‡	141	145	143	165	166	167
Proportional Contributions						
SAT-Verbal Score	26%	25%	25%	26%	28%	28%
SAT-Mathematical Score	23%	21%	20%	17%	20%	18%
High School Record	52%	54%	55%	57%	52%	55%
Correlations with Freshman GPA						
SAT-Verbal Score	.30	.33	.36	.42	.41	.36
SAT-Mathematical Score	.30	.33	.35	.39	.40	.34
SAT-Sum‡	.35	.38	.41	.46	.45	.40
Corrected SAT-Sum	.48	.51	.55	.55	.53	.45
Corrected SAT-Sum − .52†	− .04	− .01	+ .03	+ .03	+ .01	− .07
SAT-Multiple‡	.36	.39	.42	.47	.46	.42
High School Record (HSR)	.40	.44	.49	.54	.49	.47
SAT-V, SAT-M, HSR Multiple	.49	.52	.57	.60	.58	.55
SAT Increment	.09	.08	.08	.06	.09	.08

*Nine of the 685 colleges could not be categorized for this analysis.

†Subtraction of .52 (the corrected SAT-sum correlation for all colleges and all students) highlights the effects of factors other than restriction of range.

‡The SAT sum is a simple sum of the SAT verbal and mathematical scores. Therefore, the SAT-sum correlation with freshman grade point average is based on an equal weighting of the two scores, while the SAT-multiple correlation with freshman grade point average is based on the optimal weighting of the two scores.

different areas of study. Higher observed correlations do not necessarily result, however, because more severe restriction of range is also likely in these relatively homogeneous groups of students.

Table 8.13 on page 155 includes validity data for six groups: business, liberal arts, engineering, science, education, and nursing. The highest SAT scores are observed for engineering and science, and the lowest for education. The SAT standard deviations for all of the groups are low, compared to all enrolled freshmen, indicating that subgrouping by area of study results in relatively homogeneous groups with respect to SAT scores. The most homogeneous group in terms of SAT scores is education (average SAT-sum standard deviation of only 129, compared to 152 for all students*), and the least homogeneous are liberal arts (142) and science (139).

Despite the fact that the average standard deviation of the SAT sum for education majors is so low, the mean correlation of the SAT sum is .41 and the corrected correlation is a high .59. The high school

*See Table 8.15 on page 157.

record correlation of .49 for this group is slightly above average, resulting in an above-average multiple of .57.

The highest correlations are for nursing, well above average for the SAT multiple (.46), high school record (.50), the SAT and high school record multiple (.60), and the corrected SAT sum (.61). Nursing also has a slightly larger SAT increment (.10) than other areas of study.

Liberal arts has the lowest correlation for the SAT-mathematical score (.29) and the smallest SAT increment (.07). Possibly because of its very high proportion of males, whose freshman grade point average is less predictable, engineering has the lowest correlations for the SAT-verbal score (.25), high school record (.42), the multiple of the two SAT scores (.37), and the SAT and high school record multiple (.51).

The average proportional contributions of SAT scores and high school record in the prediction equations are also presented in Table 8.13. Liberal arts has the highest contribution for high school record (58 percent) and the lowest for the SAT-mathematical score (15 percent). Reflecting their quanti-

Table 8.12

Average Validity Data by Ethnic Minority Proportion*

| | Ethnic Minority Proportion | | | |
	0-9%	10-49%	50-89%	90-100%
Number of Colleges	353	261	7	22
SAT Means				
SAT-Verbal Score	466	458	368	327
SAT-Mathematical Score	500	488	404	351
SAT-Sum‡	966	946	772	678
SAT Standard Deviations				
SAT-Verbal Score	85	90	93	67
SAT-Mathematical Score	89	92	88	68
SAT-Sum‡	150	159	163	116
Proportional Contributions				
SAT-Verbal Score	24%	28%	27%	28%
SAT-Mathematical Score	19%	20%	21%	24%
High School Record	57%	52%	52%	48%
Correlations with Freshman GPA				
SAT-Verbal Score	.37	.36	.32	.31
SAT-Mathematical Score	.36	.34	.33	.30
SAT-Sum‡	.42	.40	.37	.35
Corrected SAT-Sum	.54	.50	.45	.56
Corrected SAT-Sum −.52†	+.02	−.02	−.07	+.04
SAT-Multiple‡	.43	.41	.40	.36
High School Record (HSR)	.51	.45	.45	.37
SAT-V, SAT-M, HSR Multiple	.57	.53	.52	.48
SAT Increment	.06	.08	.07	.11

*Forty-two of the 685 colleges could not be categorized for this analysis.
†Subtraction of .52 (the corrected SAT-sum correlation for all colleges and all students) highlights the effects of factors other than restriction of range.
‡The SAT sum is a simple sum of the SAT verbal and mathematical scores. Therefore, the SAT-sum correlation with freshman grade point average is based on an equal weighting of the two scores, while the SAT-multiple correlation with freshman grade point average is based on the optimal weighting of the two scores.

tative nature, engineering and science both have high contributions for the SAT-mathematical score (33 percent and 31 percent, respectively) and low contributions for the SAT-verbal score (14 percent and 15 percent).

Sex. Among the 685 colleges that studied SAT and high school record prediction of freshman grade point average for males and females combined, 511 colleges also studied males separately and 574 colleges also studied females separately. Table 8.14 on page 156 presents average validity data by sex for entering class years 1964 to 1981 and for the last five entering years of this period, 1977 to 1981. The female groups have a slightly higher SAT-verbal mean. The male groups have a distinctly higher SAT-mathematical mean and standard deviation.

Table 8.14 shows that women's freshman grade point average is better predicted, using the standard predictors, than men's freshman grade point average is; the SAT correlation, the high school record

correlation, and the SAT and high school record multiple correlation are higher for women than for men. The SAT increment is also slightly higher for women. Optimal predictions typically place more weight on the SAT-verbal score for women and more weight on high school record for men.

Comparing more recent validity studies with older ones (not shown separately in Table 8.14), the differences in correlations between the sexes appear to be getting smaller, particularly for the high school record correlation. The high school record correlation for males remained the same (.44), but decreased for females from .51 (for the 319 studies based on entering classes from 1964 to 1976) to .47 (for the 255 studies studies performed more recently).

Linn (1973) and Wild (1977) report that women usually obtain higher freshman grade point averages for given levels of SAT and high school record. Therefore, the use of one regression equation for both sexes tends to make predictions that are too low for women and too high for men.

This result could possibly be due to differences in the selection of courses by women and men. The College Board's *National College-Bound Seniors, 1984* indicates that more men intend to major in the more quantitative areas of study, such as engineering or the physical sciences, and that more women intend to major in the less quantitative areas of study. Requirements to achieve a given grade tend to be stricter in the more quantitative areas of study and more lenient in the less quantitative areas of study. (See Goldman and Widawski 1976; Goldman and Hewitt 1975; and Goldman, Schmidt, Hewitt, and Fisher 1974.) Thus, women may tend to obtain higher college grades because of factors relating to differences in course selection patterns.

The studies in Table 8.14 offered little opportunity for evaluating the differential effects of course selection. However, studies that used a single course grade (six in English courses and three in mathematics courses) as the criterion and identified male and female students were analyzed for underprediction. In seven of the nine courses, grades for women were noticeably higher than predicted when a single prediction equation was used. Therefore, because underprediction also occurs within courses, underprediction of women's course grades cannot be explained entirely by course selection.

Additional evidence of this was given earlier by Caldwell and Hartnett (1967). For 24 courses at the University of South Florida, the authors administered standardized common final examinations and compared the examination grades with the grades given by instructors. Women tended to receive sig-

Table 8.13

Average Validity Data by Area of Study

	Business	Liberal Arts	Engineering	Science	Education	Nursing
Number of Colleges	100	96	77	64	61	27
SAT Means						
SAT-Verbal Score	460	482	505	500	446	468
SAT-Mathematical Score	515	502	600	558	469	489
SAT-Sum†	975	984	1105	1058	914	957
SAT Standard Deviations						
SAT-Verbal Score	76	83	83	82	76	78
SAT-Mathematical Score	81	84	75	80	76	78
SAT-Sum†	134	142	133	139	129	132
Proportional Contributions						
SAT-Verbal Score	21%	27%	14%	15%	25%	23%
SAT-Mathematical Score	25%	15%	33%	31%	22%	24%
High School Record	54%	58%	53%	54%	54%	54%
Correlations with Freshman GPA						
SAT-Verbal Score	.30	.35	.25	.32	.36	.37
SAT-Mathematical Score	.32	.29	.34	.36	.34	.39
SAT-Sum†	.36	.38	.35	.40	.41	.44
Corrected SAT-Sum	.51	.52	.50	.55	.59	.61
Corrected SAT-Sum − .52*	− .01	.00	− .02	+ .03	+ .07	+ .09
SAT-Multiple†	.37	.39	.37	.41	.42	.46
High School Record (HSR)	.43	.48	.42	.46	.49	.50
SAT-V, SAT-M, HSR Multiple	.52	.55	.51	.55	.57	.60
SAT Increment	.09	.07	.09	.09	.08	.10

*Subtraction of .52 (the corrected SAT-sum correlation for all colleges and all students) highlights the effects of factors other than restriction of range.

†The SAT sum is a simple sum of the SAT verbal and mathematical scores. Therefore, the SAT-sum correlation with freshman grade point average is based on an equal weighting of the two scores, while the SAT-multiple correlation with freshman grade point average is based on the optimal weighting of the two scores.

nificantly higher grades and men significantly lower grades by instructors than would be indicated by their common examination grades. The authors speculate on the possible effects of such qualities as punctuality in turning in assignments, neatness of work, attendance, and attitude.

Moreover, Breland and Griswold (1982) found that women obtain higher scores on an essay placement test than predicted by standardized tests. They conclude ''. . . that women achieve higher than multiple-choice tests predict because they write better and because writing skill is an important aspect of achievement'' (p. 720).

Ethnic Group. In recent years, measurement specialists, educators, courts, and the general public have given considerable attention to the validity of tests for various ethnic groups. Breland (1979) summarized the results of 35 different ethnic group studies, yielding approximately 120 different regression and correlation analyses for minority ethnic groups, most of which were further subdivided by sex.

Table 8.15 on page 157 presents vss evidence about the validity of the SAT for *students at predom-*

inantly Black colleges (colleges with a minority proportion of at least 90 percent). Of the 22 predominantly Black colleges that did validity studies to date, 11 did a study for an entering class from 1977 to 1981, and data for these colleges are displayed separately from earlier data. The old and new validity results for predominantly Black colleges are compared against old and new results for all colleges.

For all 685 colleges doing validity studies, the average contribution of SAT scores is 46 percent, while 54 percent is contributed by high school record. For the 22 predominantly Black colleges, more weight was assigned to the SAT (52 percent) than to high school record (48 percent). In other words, to make the best predictions possible, these colleges should give an average of 52 percent of the weight to the SAT and 48 percent to high school record.

For the 11 predominantly Black colleges that did a study for an entering class from 1977 to 1981, the average optimal weight is even higher for the SAT (56 percent) and lower for high school record (44 percent). The reason for this is that the weight for the SAT-mathematical score rose from 17 percent in the older studies to 31 percent in the newer studies,

Table 8.14

Average Validity Data by Sex for Years 1964 to 1981 and 1977 to 1981

	1964-1981			1977-1981		
	Females	Males	Female-Male Difference	Females	Males	Female-Male Difference
Number of Colleges	574	511	—	255	243	—
SAT Means						
SAT-Verbal Score	473	467	+ 6	460	456	+ 4
SAT-Mathematical Score	485	520	− 35	482	517	− 35
SAT-Sum†	959	986	− 27	942	974	− 32
SAT Standard Deviations						
SAT-Verbal Score	85	85	0	87	85	+ 2
SAT-Mathematical Score	85	88	− 3	86	90	− 4
SAT-Sum†	148	149	− 1	151	151	0
Proportional Contributions						
SAT-Verbal Score	27%	25%	+ 2%	27%	24%	+ 3%
SAT-Mathematical Score	22%	22%	0%	23%	23%	0%
High School Record	51%	54%	− 3%	50%	53%	− 3%
Correlations with Freshman GPA						
SAT-Verbal Score	.39	.32	+ .07	.38	.31	+ .07
SAT-Mathematical Score	.39	.33	+ .06	.40	.34	+ .06
SAT-Sum†	.45	.37	.08	.44	.38	+ .06
Corrected SAT-Sum	.58	.49	+ .09	.56	.49	+ .07
Corrected SAT-Sum − .52*	+ .06	− .03	+ .09	+ .04	− .03	+ .07
SAT-Multiple†	.46	.38	+ .08	.45	.39	+ .06
High School Record (HSR)	.49	.44	+ .05	.47	.44	+ .03
SAT-V, SAT-M, HSR Multiple	.57	.51	+ .06	.56	.51	+ .05
SAT Increment	.08	.07	+ .01	.09	.07	+ .02

*Subtraction of .52 (the corrected SAT-sum correlation for all colleges and all students) highlights the effects of factors other than restriction of range.

‡The SAT sum is a simple sum of the SAT verbal and mathematical scores. Therefore, the SAT-sum correlation with freshman grade point average is based on an equal weighting of the two scores, while the SAT-multiple correlation with freshman grade point average is based on the optimal weighting of the two scores.

compared with an increase from 18 to 21 percent for all colleges. The SAT-multiple correlation (.38) is also slightly higher than the high school record correlation (.36) for the newer studies.

In general, the correlations are somewhat lower for the predominantly Black colleges. However, the SAT increment is .11 (.48–.37) for these colleges, compared to .07 (.55–.48) for all colleges.

The range of SAT scores for predominantly Black colleges is severely restricted compared to that of all colleges that have done validity studies; the average SAT-sum standard deviation is only 119 in the newer studies, compared to 151 for all colleges. However, the corrected SAT-sum correlation of .57 is .05 higher than average.

Table 8.16 on page 158 presents evidence about the validity of the SAT for *Black students at predominantly White colleges.* For the entering freshman class years 1977 to 1981, 11 predominantly White colleges identified Black students as a subgroup in their validity studies. The colleges were of average selec-

tivity. The average SAT-verbal mean was 458; only 2 of the 11 colleges had means above 480 and only 2 had means below 440. The proportion of students who were Black ranged from 3 percent to 18 percent, with a mean of 8 percent. The resulting groups ranged in size from 59 to 401 students, with an average of 180.

The average Black student at these colleges had almost the same high school record (a mean rank of 56, on a 20-to-80 scale and a mean grade point average of 3.0) as other students (rank of 57 and grade point average of 3.2). However, in all 11 colleges, the SAT scores of Black students were lower: a difference of means of 73 points for the SAT-verbal score (390 compared to 463 for other students) and 93 points for the SAT-mathematical score (416 compared to 509 for other students). Like the SAT scores, freshman grade point average was also lower for the Black students in all 11 colleges: a difference of means of more than half of a grade point (2.03 grade point average compared to 2.60 overall).

Table 8.15

Average Validity Data for Predominantly Black Colleges and All Colleges

	Predominantly Black Colleges				All Colleges			
	Older Studies 1964-76	Newer Studies 1977-81	Change (Older to Newer)	All Studies 1964-81	Older Studies 1964-76	Newer Studies 1977-81	Change (Older to Newer)	All Studies 1964-81
Number of Colleges	11	11	—	22	272	413	—	685
SAT Means								
SAT-Verbal Score	340	314	− 26	327	464	449	− 15	455
SAT-Mathematical Score	360	343	− 17	351	488	486	− 2	487
SAT-Sum†	699	657	− 42	678	952	935	− 17	942
SAT Standard Deviations								
SAT-Verbal Score	65	70	+ 5	67	86	86	0	86
SAT-Mathematical Score	67	68	+ 1	68	89	89	0	89
SAT-Sum†	113	119	+ 6	116	153	151	− 2	152
Proportional Contributions								
SAT-Verbal Score	31%	25%	− 6%	28%	27%	25%	− 2%	26%
SAT-Mathematical Score	17%	31%	+14%	24%	18%	21%	+ 3%	20%
High School Record	52%	44%	− 8%	48%	55%	54%	− 1%	54%
Correlations with Freshman GPA								
SAT-Verbal Score	.30	.31	+ .01	.31	.38	.35	− .03	.36
SAT-Mathematical Score	.27	.32	+ .05	.30	.35	.35	.00	.35
SAT-Sum†	.34	.37	+ .03	.35	.41	.40	− .01	.41
Corrected SAT-Sum	.55	.57	+ .02	.56	.52	.52	.00	.52
Corrected SAT-Sum − .52*	+ .03	+ .05	+ .02	+ .04	.00	.00	.00	.00
SAT-Multiple†	.34	.38	+ .04	.36	.43	.41	− .02	.42
High School Record (HSR)	.39	.36	− .03	.37	.49	.46	− .03	.48
SAT-V, SAT-M, HSR Multiple	.48	.47	− .01	.48	.57	.54	− .03	.55
SAT Increment	.09	.11	+ .02	.11	.08	.08	.00	.07

*Subtraction of .52 (the corrected SAT-sum correlation for all colleges and all students) highlights the effects of factors other than restriction of range.

†The SAT sum is a simple sum of the SAT verbal and mathematical scores. Therefore, the SAT-sum correlation with freshman grade point average is based on an equal weighting of the two scores, while the SAT-multiple correlation with freshman grade point average is based on the optimal weighting of the two scores.

The variability in SAT scores was lower for Black students (mean SAT-sum standard deviation of 147) than for other students (169), thereby restricting the observed SAT correlations more for Black students. The variability in high school record (not reported in Table 8.16) was slightly higher for Black students (mean standard deviations of 7.8 for high school rank and .57 for high school grade point average) than for other students (7.4 and .55, respectively).

In 10 out of the 11 colleges, the SAT correlation was lower for Black students than for other students. The observed SAT-sum correlation was .27, .11 below the observed correlation for other students at the same predominantly White colleges, and .10 below the observed correlation for students at predominantly Black colleges. Correcting the SAT-sum correlation increased it to .37, but it was still .08 below the corrected correlation for other students at the same predominantly White colleges, and a full .20 below the corrected correlation for students at predominantly Black colleges.

Thus, as a single predictor, the SAT does not predict as well for Black students who are attending predominantly White colleges as it does for other students. However, it is a more useful predictor for Black students at predominantly White colleges than for other students when compared to or used with high school record. For Black students at these colleges, the mean correlation of high school record with freshman grade point average was only .25, compared to .42 for non-Black students. Despite greater restriction in range for the SAT, in 7 of the 11 colleges the optimal combination of the SAT-verbal and mathematical scores for Black students (mean correlation of .30) was a better predictor than high school record (mean correlation of .25).

As shown in Table 8.16 on page 158, the average weight attributable to the SAT-mathematical score in the equations that optimally predict freshman grade point average was 24 percent for both Black and other students at these predominantly White colleges. However, for Black students, there was an average 12-percentage-point shift in weight toward the SAT-verbal score and away from high school record. Thus, for Black students, more predictive weight was attributed to SAT scores (58 percent) than

Table 8.16

Average Validity Data for Black Students at Predominantly White Colleges,
Compared to Data for Other Students at the Same Colleges and Students
at Predominantly Black Colleges

	11 Recent Studies (1977-1981) for Predominantly White Colleges		11 Recent Studies (1977-1981) for Predominantly Black Colleges
	Black Students	Other Students	
Number of Colleges	11	11	11
SAT Means			
SAT-Verbal Score	390	463	314
SAT-Mathematical Score	416	509	343
SAT-Sum†	806	972	657
SAT Standard Deviations			
SAT-Verbal Score	83	94	70
SAT-Mathematical Score	86	100	68
SAT-Sum†	147	169	119
Proportional Contributions			
SAT-Verbal Score	34%	22%	25%
SAT-Mathematical Score	24%	24%	31%
High School Record	42%	54%	44%
Correlations with Freshman GPA			
SAT-Verbal Score	.24	.33	.31
SAT-Mathematical Score	.23	.34	.32
SAT-Sum†	.27	.38	.37
Corrected SAT-Sum	.37	.45	.57
Corrected SAT-Sum −.52*	−.15	−.07	+.05
SAT-Multiple†	.30	.39	.38
High School Record (HSR)	.25	.42	.36
SAT-V, SAT-M, HSR Multiple	.37	.49	.47
SAT Increment	.12	.07	.11
Freshman Grade Point Average			
Actual Mean	2.03	2.60	2.19
Predicted Mean Using Total Group Equation	2.28	—	—
Difference	−0.25	—	—

*Subtraction of .52 (the corrected SAT-sum correlation for all colleges and all students) highlights the effects of factors other than restriction of range.

†The SAT sum is a simple sum of the SAT verbal and mathematical scores. Therefore, the SAT-sum correlation with freshman grade point average is based on an equal weighting of the two scores, while the SAT-multiple correlation with freshman grade point average is based on the optimal weighting of the two scores.

high school record (42 percent). The average weights were: sat-verbal score, 34 percent; sat-mathematical score, 24 percent; and high school record, 42 percent.

The sat increment was much larger for Black students: .12 (.37–.25), compared to .07 (.49–.42) for the other students at the 11 predominantly White colleges. Thus, the incremental effectiveness of the sat for Black students at predominantly White colleges (.12) was higher than for all colleges (.08) and even higher than for students at predominantly Black colleges (.11).

Breland (1979) reports that in studies where direct comparisons were possible, White students have higher correlations than Black students for high school record in 21 out of 32 cases (66 percent), for sat scores (verbal, mathematical, or multiple) in 79 out of 116 cases (68 percent), and for the sat and high school record multiple in 37 out of 63 cases (59 percent). However, the variability of the groups is not reported, so that the possible effects of restriction of range cannot be assessed. Overall, median correlations for minority group students and White students differ by very little. In the studies reported by Breland, as in the vss studies, the SAT increment is larger for Black students than for White students.

In vss, using SAT scores and high school record in a total group equation to predict freshman grade point average, the predicted freshman grade point average for the average Black student at a predominantly White college (substituting mean SAT scores and high school record for Black students in the equation determined for all students at the college) was computed and compared to the actual average freshman grade point average for Black students. In 9 out of the 11 cases, the prediction was higher than the actual average freshman grade point average; in one case it was the same, and in only one case was it lower. The combination of SAT scores and high school record that is optimal for the total student group consistently tends to give most Black students at a predominantly White college a *higher prediction* of freshman grade point average than the students attain. The average difference for Black students was one-quarter of a grade on a 0 to 4 scale (2.28 predicted and 2.03 actual). In two cases, the average difference was more than one-half of a grade.

This finding is neither new nor limited to the Validity Study Service. Breland (1979) reviewed the literature and reported overprediction for minority students in 26 out of 29 equations based on SAT-verbal score only, in 24 out of 27 equations based on SAT-mathematical score only, in 25 out of 25 equations based on high school record only, and in 25 out of 33 equations based on SAT scores and high school record.

Linn (1983a, 1983b) points out that overprediction for Black students may be the statistical artifact of affirmative action. He shows that when any group of applicants is selected with less emphasis on predictors or at higher rates than the majority of applicants, the result is a pattern of overprediction. The regression line for the group selected with affirmative action is lower and steeper throughout the range of relevant predictor values than are the lines for the majority of selected students or for all students.

Hispanic students were identified in four vss studies, all of them for campuses of large state universities: one in the West, one in the East, and two in the Southwest. The average SAT sum of verbal and mathematical scores was within 40 points of 970 for all four campuses. The proportion of students who were identified as Hispanic was 2 percent (94 students) at the Western campus, 14 percent (92 students) at the Eastern campus, and 8 percent (421 students) and 27 percent (133 students) at the Southwestern campuses.

Although the average Hispanic student had a similar high school record to other students on each campus, for all four campuses, the Hispanic SAT scores were lower. For three of the campuses, the SAT sum of verbal and mathematical scores was 80 to 95 points lower; for the Eastern campus, it was a sizable 223 points lower. Whereas one might expect that the SAT-mathematical score means for Hispanic students would be relatively higher than their SAT-verbal score means (because they may be less hampered by language difficulties in the mathematical part than in the verbal part), for three campuses both were approximately the same amount below the means for other students. For the Western campus, the difference between the mean for the other students and the mean for the Hispanic students was 40 points *greater* for the SAT-mathematical score than it was for the SAT-verbal score. Freshman grade point average was also lower for the Hispanic students at all four campuses: only .04 to .19 lower for three of the campuses, but .55 lower for the Eastern campus.

These results are essentially similar to those of Black students, except overprediction for Black students is larger than for Hispanic students. The average overprediction for Hispanic students was .05 of a grade, compared to .25 of a grade for Black students. There was slight overprediction for three of the campuses and slight underprediction for one.

In terms of predictive validity, correlations with freshman grade point average were generally lower for Hispanic students for both SAT scores and high school record. The proportional contribution of the SAT-verbal score to predictive effectiveness was 15 percent lower for Hispanic students than for other students; the offsetting increases were 10 percent for the SAT-mathematical score and 5 percent for high school record.

After reviewing all published validity studies for Hispanic students, both Breland (1979) and Durán (1983) concluded that there do not seem to be large differences between Hispanic and White students in correlations of the SAT or high school record with grades. However, they both find a tendency for somewhat lower correlations for Hispanic students.

Age. Through vss, Casserly (1982) reported on results of three validity studies in which "older" entering freshmen, defined as 21 years or over, and "younger" entering freshmen, defined as below 21 years, were identified. The average age for the older students was 23 and the average for the younger students was 19.

The mean SAT sums for older and younger students were about the same (939 and 935, respectively). Although younger students had a higher SAT-mathematical mean (490 to 469), the reverse was true for the SAT-verbal mean (445 to 470). Whereas younger males outperformed younger females on the SAT-verbal part of the test, as well as on the SAT-mathematical part, older females outperformed older males on the SAT-verbal part (but not on the SAT-mathematical part). For both males and females, SAT-verbal scores were more variable for older students; the variability in SAT-mathematical scores was similar for older and younger students.

Older students had consistently lower high school grades than the younger students. This difference may be due to recent grade inflation. On the other hand, many of the older students interviewed reported problems or lack of interest in high school as reasons why they did not enter college immediately. Females in both age groups had consistently higher high school grades than males.

Average freshman grade point averages for older and younger males were almost identical (2.36 versus 2.37). However, older females had a somewhat higher average freshman grade point average (2.68) than younger females (2.56) and a much higher average grade point average than older males (2.36). Older students, both male and female, had wider variance in their college grades than did younger students. In college, as in high school, females obtained higher grade point averages. The mean freshman grade point average difference between younger females (2.56) and younger males (2.37) was similar to the average difference for all colleges.

Using high school grade point average and SAT scores to predict freshman grade point average, the older students were somewhat less predictable (mean multiple correlation of .47) than the younger students (.52). However, as one might expect, the difference is primarily because high school grade point average is less valid for older students (.33) than for younger students (.42). SAT scores are approximately equally valid for older and younger students (both have a .39 SAT-sum correlation). Older students had substantially more predictive weight on the SAT-verbal score and less weight on the SAT-mathematical score and high school grade point average.

For older females, both high school record and SAT correlations are much lower than for younger females. The high school record correlation for older females is only .24, and only 28 percent of the predictive weight is on high school record. The SAT correlational increment is an especially high .21 (bringing the high school grade point average and SAT multiple to .45), and 72 percent of the predictive weight is on the SAT.

Only for older females was age significantly correlated with freshman grade point average (average correlation of .24); it provided 26 percent of the predictive effectiveness when used with SAT scores and high school grade point average. The older the woman, the higher the freshman grade point average, even for given SAT scores and high school grade point average.

As is typically the case, the freshman grade point average of females was underpredicted and the freshman grade point average of males was overpredicted. The underprediction was larger for older females than for younger females, but the overprediction was smaller for older males than for younger males.

Handicap. Jones and Ragosta (1982) reported results of two studies assessing the validity of the SAT and high school record for two different groups of handicapped students. One study compared data for 60 deaf students and 140 hearing students at a college that provides special support services to mainstreamed deaf students. The other study compared data for 55 learning disabled and 110 non-learning disabled students at a college where learning disabled students attend regular classes and participate in a special program of learning assistance. Conclusions about these results should be tempered because there is only one study for deaf students and one for learning disabled students, and the numbers of students are small. Additional studies are currently being undertaken.

The deaf students have lower SAT scores (particularly SAT-verbal scores) and freshman grade point average than the hearing students, but the deaf and hearing high school grade point average means differ little. The SAT-verbal correlation for the deaf students is a very low .14, compared to .38 for the hearing students, but the SAT-mathematical correlation for deaf students is .41, compared to .32 for the hearing students. Because the contribution of the SAT-mathematical score is high, the SAT increment is higher for deaf students (.06) than for hearing students (.03) at the college where the study was performed.

Like the deaf students, the learning disabled students also have lower SAT scores, particularly SAT-verbal scores, but the learning disabled and non-learning disabled SAT differences at the college specializing in learning disabled students are about half as large as the deaf and hearing SAT differences at the college specializing in deaf students. However, both the high school rank and the freshman grade point average for the learning disabled students are more discrepant than are high school and college performance of the deaf students. Although the SAT-verbal

160

and SAT-mathematical correlations for the learning and non-learning disabled students are similar, the high school rank correlation for the learning disabled students (.29) is below that of the non-learning disabled students (.39). Because of this, the SAT increment for the learning disabled students is .13 (compared to .06 for the non-learning disabled students).

Trends

SAT Means and Standard Deviations. One of the most publicized changes in testing during the last two decades was the continuous decline in SAT-verbal and SAT-mathematical scores. From 1963 to 1980, the decline in the mean for all SAT takers was 54

points for the verbal sections of the SAT (from 478 to 424) and 36 points for the mathematical sections (from 502 to 466). A brief discussion of the phenomenon is provided in Chapter IX. For a more complete discussion of the issues related to this decline, see *On Further Examination* (College Board 1977) and Breland (1977b). From 1980 to 1984, there have been slight increases in both of the scores: two points for the SAT-verbal score and five points for the SAT-mathematical score.

Figure 8.3 shows SAT means for VSS-user colleges, compared with those of all SAT takers. Over the period encompassing entering freshman classes from 1964 to 1982, the SAT means for VSS-user colleges have experienced irregular changes, but have mostly shown decreases since 1972. These changes may reflect those of colleges in general or they may be

Figure 8.3

SAT Means for 1964 to 1982 Entering Classes

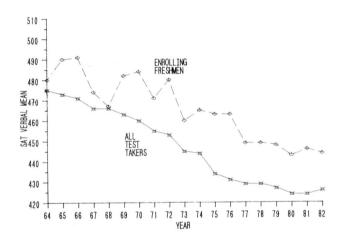
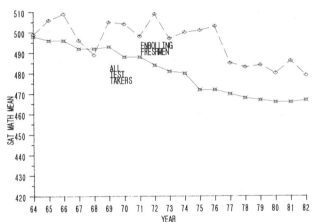

Figure 8.4

Mean SAT Standard Deviations for 1964 to 1982 Entering Classes

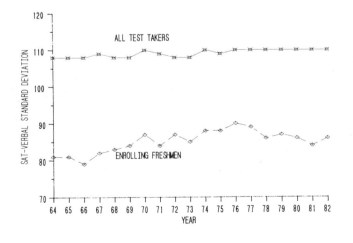
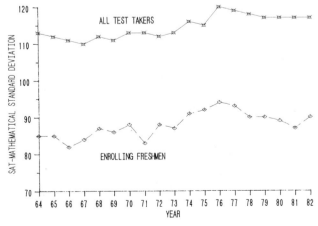

merely artifacts of college self-selection in performing a validity study. (Validity-related data for the 1982 entering freshman class were obtained specially for this section on trends. They were not available for inclusion in the overall validity summaries of earlier sections.) The number of colleges performing a validity study in a year ranged from 32 (in 1971) to 185 (in 1979).

Figure 8.4 (see previous page) shows the average standard deviations of SAT scores for all SAT takers and students enrolled in VSS-user colleges over the period encompassing entering freshman classes from 1964 to 1982. The average standard deviations of students enrolled in a college have been consistently and markedly lower than the average standard deviations of all test takers, about 30 points each for SAT-verbal and SAT-mathematical scores.

Freshman Grade Point Average. Despite declining SAT means, Figure 8.5 shows that the average fresh-

man grade point average of colleges using the VSS increased steadily from 2.20 for the 1968 entering freshman class to 2.65 for the 1976 entering freshman class. This apparent grade inflation was approximately the same for males and females. From 1976 to 1982, however, there has been a moderate decline from 2.65 to 2.54.

Correlations. Figure 8.6 (page 164) and Table 8.17 show the average multiple correlation of the SAT-verbal and SAT-mathematical scores with freshman grade point average, which fluctuated between .38 and .47 during the years 1964 to 1982, and the corrected average SAT-sum correlation with freshman grade point average, which fluctuated between .49 and .57 during this period. The low points were in 1970 and 1971 and the high point was in 1974.

A comparison of more recent studies with older ones, as in Table 8.18 (page 164), shows that the difference between the sexes in the SAT-multiple corre-

Table 8.17

Average Validity Trends*
Part I. 1964 to 1972 Entering Classes

	1964	1965	1966	1967	1968	1969	1970	1971	1972
Number of Colleges	46	74	65	55	36	42	112	32	100
SAT Means									
SAT-Verbal Score	480	490	491	474	467	482	484	471	480
SAT-Mathematical Score	499	506	509	496	489	505	504	498	509
SAT-Sum‡	978	996	1000	970	956	987	988	969	989
SAT Standard Deviations									
SAT-Verbal Score	81	81	79	82	83	84	87	84	87
SAT-Mathematical Score	85	85	82	84	87	86	88	83	88
SAT-Sum‡	140	141	136	142	148	147	150	144	152
Proportional Contributions									
SAT-Verbal Score	29%	25%	26%	26%	27%	27%	27%	27%	26%
SAT-Mathematical Score	16%	13%	13%	14%	14%	14%	14%	13%	17%
High School Record	55%	62%	61%	60%	59%	59%	60%	60%	57%
Correlations with Freshman GPA									
SAT-Verbal Score	.40	.36	.36	.36	.39	.38	.36	.35	.36
SAT-Mathematical Score	.33	.30	.28	.30	.32	.32	.30	.30	.33
SAT-Sum‡	.41	.38	.38	.39	.40	.40	.38	.37	.40
Corrected SAT-Sum	.56	.52	.53	.53	.52	.53	.49	.50	.51
Corrected SAT-Sum − .52†	+.04	.00	+.01	+.01	.00	+.01	−.03	−.02	−.01
SAT-Multiple‡	.44	.40	.39	.40	.42	.41	.39	.38	.41
High School Record (HSR)	.52	.54	.52	.52	.52	.51	.49	.48	.49
SAT-V, SAT-M, HSR Multiple	.60	.60	.58	.57	.59	.57	.55	.54	.56
SAT Increment	.08	.06	.06	.05	.07	.06	.06	.06	.07
Freshman Grade Point Average									
Mean	2.20	2.27	2.23	2.25	2.20	2.44	2.51	2.43	2.54
Standard Deviation	.64	.63	.65	.63	.65	.62	.64	.66	.66

*This table summarizes many more studies than prior tables because it includes the largest study from any year a college did one, and not just the college's most recent study.
†Subtraction of .52 (the corrected SAT-sum correlation for all colleges and all students) highlights the effects of factors other than restriction of range.
‡The SAT sum is a simple sum of the SAT verbal and mathematical scores. Therefore, the SAT-sum correlation with freshman grade point average is based on an equal weighting of the two scores, while the SAT-multiple correlation with freshman grade point average is based on the optimal weighting of the two scores.

lation with freshman grade point average is narrowing: from .10 in favor of females for the older studies to .06 in favor of females for the newer studies. The difference between the correlation for verbal and mathematical scores has also narrowed, from .03 in favor of SAT-verbal scores for the older combined-sex studies to no difference for the newer studies. However, the proportional contribution of the SAT-verbal score is still slightly greater.

Table 8.18 and Figure 8.7 (page 164) show that combined-sex high school record correlations have been decreasing from .49 for the older studies to .46 for the newer studies. The decrease is almost solely due to a decrease for females. The high school record correlation for older and newer male studies has stayed the same, at .44. However, for females, there has been a decline from .51 to .47.

Figure 8.8 (page 165) shows the SAT contribution over high school record for the years 1964 to 1982. After 1964, the overall trend of the SAT increment

Figure 8.5

Mean Freshman Grade Point Average for VSS College Users for 1964 to 1982 Entering Classes

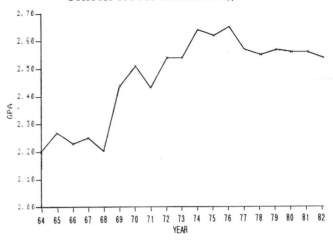

Table 8.17 (continued)

Average Validity Trends*
Part II. 1973 to 1982 Entering Classes

	1973	1974	1975	1976	1977	1978	1979	1980	1981	1982
Number of Colleges	88	111	130	139	151	173	185	181	162	173
SAT Means										
SAT-Verbal Score	460	465	463	463	449	449	448	443	446	444
SAT-Mathematical Score	497	500	501	503	485	483	484	480	486	479
SAT-Sum‡	957	965	964	965	934	932	932	923	933	923
SAT Standard Deviations										
SAT-Verbal Score	85	88	88	90	89	86	87	86	84	86
SAT-Mathematical Score	87	91	92	94	93	90	90	89	87	90
SAT-Sum‡	151	157	156	160	158	153	154	152	148	152
Proportional Contributions										
SAT-Verbal Score	27%	25%	26%	27%	25%	24%	26%	25%	24%	25%
SAT-Mathematical Score	19%	23%	22%	22%	21%	23%	21%	22%	19%	19%
High School Record	55%	52%	52%	51%	54%	53%	54%	52%	57%	56%
Correlations with Freshman GPA										
SAT-Verbal Score	.38	.41	.38	.39	.38	.36	.36	.35	.33	.35
SAT-Mathematical Score	.36	.40	.38	.38	.37	.36	.35	.36	.33	.35
SAT-Sum‡	.42	.46	.44	.44	.43	.41	.41	.41	.38	.40
Corrected SAT-Sum	.54	.57	.55	.54	.53	.52	.52	.52	.50	.51
Corrected SAT-Sum −.52†	+.02	+.05	+.03	+.02	+.01	.00	.00	.00	−.02	−.01
SAT-Multiple‡	.43	.47	.44	.45	.44	.42	.42	.42	.39	.40
High School Record (HSR)	.49	.50	.48	.47	.49	.46	.47	.46	.47	.47
SAT-V, SAT-M, HSR Multiple	.57	.58	.56	.56	.56	.54	.55	.54	.54	.54
SAT Increment	.08	.08	.08	.09	.07	.08	.08	.08	.07	.07
Freshman Grade Point Average										
Mean	2.54	2.64	2.62	2.65	2.57	2.55	2.57	2.56	2.56	2.54
Standard Deviation	.69	.67	.68	.69	.71	.70	NA	NA	.72	.70

*This table summarizes many more studies than prior tables because it includes the largest study from any year a college did one, and not just the college's most recent study.

†Subtraction of .52 (the corrected SAT-sum correlation for all colleges and all students) highlights the effects of factors other than restriction of range.

‡The SAT sum is a simple sum of the SAT verbal and mathematical scores. Therefore, the SAT-sum correlation with freshman grade point average is based on an equal weighting of the two scores, while the SAT-multiple correlation with freshman grade point average is based on the optimal weighting of the two scores.

Figure 8.6

Mean sAT-Multiple Correlation and Corrected sAT-Sum Correlation for vss College Users for 1964 to 1982 Entering Classes

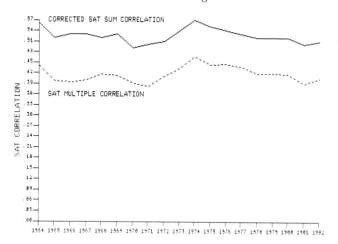

Figure 8.7

Mean High School Record Correlation by Sex for vss College Users for 1964 to 1982 Entering Classes

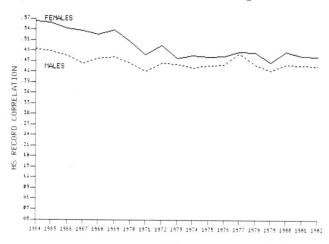

Table 8.18

Average Validity for Older and Newer Studies by Sex

	Male Studies			Female Studies			Combined Sex Studies		
	1964-1976	1977-1981	Total	1964-1976	1977-1981	Total	1964-1976	1977-1981	Total
Number of Colleges	268	243	511	319	255	574	272	413	685
SAT Means									
SAT-Verbal Score	477	456	467	483	460	473	464	449	455
SAT-Mathematical Score	523	517	520	487	482	485	488	486	487
SAT-Sum†	1000	974	986	970	942	959	952	935	942
SAT Standard Deviations									
SAT-Verbal Score	85	85	85	83	87	85	86	86	86
SAT-Mathematical Score	86	90	88	84	86	85	89	89	89
SAT-Sum†	147	151	149	146	151	148	153	151	152
Proportional Contributions									
SAT-Verbal Score	26%	24%	25%	27%	27%	27%	27%	25%	26%
SAT-Mathematical Score	21%	23%	22%	21%	23%	22%	18%	21%	20%
High School Record	55%	53%	54%	52%	50%	51%	55%	54%	54%
Correlations with Freshman GPA									
SAT-Verbal Score	.33	.31	.32	.40	.38	.39	.38	.35	.36
SAT-Mathematical Score	.32	.34	.33	.38	.40	.39	.35	.35	.35
SAT-Sum†	.36	.38	.37	.46	.44	.45	.41	.40	.41
Corrected SAT-Sum	.48	.49	.49	.59	.56	.58	.52	.52	.52
Corrected SAT-Sum − .52*	− .04	− .03	− .03	+ .07	+ .04	+ .06	.00	.00	.00
SAT Multiple†	.37	.39	.38	.47	.45	.46	.43	.41	.42
High School Record (HSR)	.44	.44	.44	.51	.47	.49	.49	.46	.48
SAT-V, SAT-M, HSR Multiple	.51	.51	.51	.58	.56	.57	.57	.54	.55
SAT Increment	.07	.07	.07	.07	.09	.08	.08	.08	.07

*Subtraction of .52 (the corrected SAT-sum correlation for all colleges and all students) highlights the effects of factors other than restriction of range.
‡The SAT sum is a simple sum of the SAT verbal and mathematical scores. Therefore, the SAT-sum correlation with freshman grade point average is based on an equal weighting of the two scores, while the SAT-multiple correlation with freshman grade point average is based on the optimal weighting of the two scores.

164

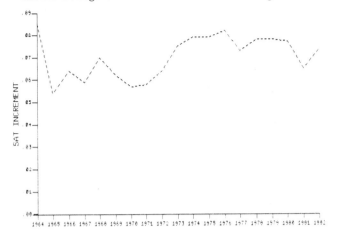

Figure 8.8

Improvement in Prediction Attributable to the SAT
over High School Record (the SAT Increment)
for VSS College Users for 1964 to 1982 Entering Classes

was an increase until 1976, a slight decline until 1981, and a slight increase in 1982 (the 1982 increase is shown in Figure 8.8, but not in Table 8.17, because data in the table are rounded to two digits).

Validity of Achievement Tests for Predicting Freshman Grade Point Average

Table 8.19 on page 166 summarizes validity data from the VSS for all colleges that have undertaken studies using scores on College Board Achievement Tests to predict freshman grade point average. As in other summaries of the VSS (except Table 8.17), only the most recent study per college is included in the combined-sex, male, and female summaries. Since 1964, combined-sex Achievement Test studies have been completed at 140 colleges, while 132 and 159 colleges have done Achievement Test studies separately on males and females, respectively.

Some studies include an average of all Achievement Tests, others up to three specific Achievement Tests, and others a combination of one or more specific tests and an average of all others. For additive effects of Achievement Tests on the correlation, the variables that were used in a study are included in Table 8.19. However, average zero-order correlations are shown only for Achievement Test average, the English Composition Test, and the Mathematics Level I Test, because these are the only predictors used by a sufficient number of colleges.

Because colleges using Achievement Tests are relatively selective, restriction of range has a marked effect on validity study results. Whereas

average SAT-verbal and SAT-mathematical standard deviations for all VSS-user colleges are in the upper 80s, SAT standard deviations for users of Achievement Tests are typically in the middle 70s.

In validity studies that include Achievement Tests, there is apparently more restriction of range for the SAT than for high school record (rank or grade point average, whichever was used). Comparing the average correlations for all VSS studies and those for users of Achievement Tests for all years, the SAT correlation averages are approximately .04 lower for users of Achievement Tests while those for high school record are about .02 lower.

Achievement Test correlations with freshman grade point average are comparable to those of the SAT for Achievement Test users. The Achievement Test average correlation tends to be slightly higher than the English Composition and Mathematics Level I correlations (but for males the latter has the highest correlation). The correlations are higher for females than for males.

In terms of proportional contributions to the regression equation, the SAT and the Achievement Tests each contribute somewhat more than one-quarter to the prediction, so that ATP test scores contribute somewhat more than half and high school record contributes somewhat less than half.

The correlation increment of Achievement Tests, above high school record and SAT scores, averaged about .02, slightly higher in more recent studies. The correlation increment of Achievement Tests and SAT scores, above high school record, averaged about .10 for all years, .11 for recent combined-sex studies, and .12 to .13 for recent single-sex studies.

Validity of ATP Tests for Predicting a Single Course Grade

The *Guide to the College Board Validity Study Service* (College Board 1982b) provides information on the use of VSS for choosing and evaluating a placement test, evaluating the effectiveness of a remedial course, and placing students into the appropriate course. This section presents available information on how well ATP tests predict a single course grade in English, mathematics, science, and foreign language.

English. The ATP includes three tests that could be used for predicting an English course grade: the Test of Standard Written English (TSWE), the verbal sections of the SAT, and the English Composition Achievement Test. The first is a test of writing with greater discriminating power at the lower ability

Table 8.19

Average Validity Data for Achievement Test Prediction of Freshman Grade Point Average by Sex, 1964 to 1981

| | Correlations and Contributions | | | | | | Corresponding Numbers of Colleges | | | | | |
| | 1964-1981 | | | 1977-1981 | | | 1964-1981 | | | 1977-1981 | | |
	Male	Female	Total	Male	Female	Total	Male	Female	Total	Male	Female	Total
Single-Predictor Correlations												
Achievement Test Average	.32	.41	.37	.31	.33	.30	33	28	25	6	6	7
English Composition Test	.30	.36	.36	.30	.33	.32	100	123	118	30	31	50
Mathematics Level I Test	.34	.37	.35	.29	.32	.33	26	25	27	10	11	10
SAT-Verbal Score	.28	.35	.32	.26	.30	.27	131	157	138	33	35	52
SAT-Mathematical Score	.27	.34	.30	.28	.32	.29	132	159	139	34	36	53
High School Record	.42	.47	.45	.35	.37	.38	131	158	140	34	35	54
Multiple Correlations												
SAT Multiple	.34	.42	.38	.34	.39	.35	131	157	138	33	35	52
SAT and High School Record	.50	.55	.52	.45	.47	.47	119	141	125	28	29	47
SAT, High School Record, Achievement Tests	.51	.57	.55	.47	.50	.49	125	151	133	28	30	47
Correlation Increments												
SAT and Achievement Tests Over High School Record	.09	.10	.10	.12	.13	.11	125	151	133	28	30	47
Achievement Tests Over SAT, High School Record	.015	.013	.023	.025	.023	.025	125	151	133	28	30	47
Proportional Contributions												
SAT-Verbal Score	16%	16%	13%	17%	17%	12%	123	148	132	28	30	47
SAT-Mathematical Score	10%	13%	11%	12%	17%	14%	123	148	132	28	30	47
High School Record	47%	46%	47%	39%	37%	44%	123	148	132	28	30	47
Achievement Tests	26%	24%	29%	32%	29%	30%	123	148	132	28	30	47
Total SAT	26%	29%	24%	29%	34%	26%	123	148	132	28	30	47
Total SAT and Achievement Tests	53%	54%	53%	61%	63%	56%	123	148	132	28	30	47

levels, the second is a general verbal aptitude test, and the third is a test of writing with greater discriminating power at the higher ability levels.

Table 8.20 summarizes results from studies in VSS on the effectiveness of each of the three tests in predicting a freshman English course grade. The mean correlations for the English Composition Achievement Test and for TSWE are both .37, and the mean for the SAT-verbal score is .34. Despite the fact that the criterion is only one course grade, the mean correlation for use of the SAT-verbal score to predict freshman English grade is almost as high as for predicting freshman grade point average (.34 versus .36), and the mean correlation for use of the English Composition Achievement Test score to predict freshman English grade is higher than for predicting freshman grade point average (.37 versus .36). For comparison purposes, the mean correlation for use of the SAT-mathematical score to predict freshman English grade, .25, is also shown.

To predict freshman English course grade, 54 colleges have analyzed high school record (grade point average or rank). As shown in Table 8.20, the correlations average .37, the same as that of the English Composition Achievement Test and TSWE, but below the .48 mean for prediction of freshman grade point average (see Table 8.1).

Also, 14 colleges have analyzed high school English course grade prediction of freshman English course grade. The correlations averaged .41, higher than that of the full high school grade point average or rank (.37).

In addition to the zero-order correlations so far mentioned for the prediction of freshman English course grade, Table 8.20 summarizes results of a small number of studies that called for multiple correlations. On the average, the addition of the SAT-verbal score to TSWE raised the mean correlation from .37 to .40 and its addition to the English Composition Achievement Test raised the mean correla-

Table 8.20

Validity Data for Predicting English Course Grade

Predictor	Number of Colleges	Mean	Correlations Percentiles				
			10	25	50 (Median)	75	90
TSWE Score	25	.37	.21	.26	.39	.45	.54
SAT-Verbal Score	68	.34	.14	.25	.35	.44	.50
English Composition Test Score	20	.37	.20	.29	.40	.45	.50
SAT-Mathematical Score	26	.25	.16	.19	.24	.31	.37
High School Record (Grade Point Average or Rank)	54	.37	—	—	—	—	—
High School English Grade	14	.41	—	—	—	—	—
SAT-Verbal Score, TSWE	4	.40	—	—	—	—	—
SAT-Verbal Score, English Composition Test	7	.38	—	—	—	—	—

Table 8.21

Validity Data for Predicting Mathematics Course Grade

Predictors	Number of Colleges	Mean	Correlations Percentiles				
			10	25	50 (Median)	75	90
SAT-Mathematical Score	29	.35	.22	.27	.33	.44	.53
SAT-Verbal Score	16	.24	.06	.12	.23	.37	.42
Mathematics Level I Score	6	.30	—	—	.32	—	—
High School Record (Grade Point Average or Rank)	23	.32	—	—	—	—	—
High School Mathematics Grade	9	.41	—	—	—	—	—

tion only from .37 to .38. The former correlation is about the same as for high school English grade (.41) and the latter is about the same as for high school grade point average or rank (.37).

There are some published studies of the validity of the SAT, TSWE, high school record, high school English grade, and a specially graded essay for predicting freshman English course grade. See, for example: Brown and Lightsey (1970); Breland, Conlan, and Rogosa (1976); Breland (1977c); Michael and Shaffer (1979); and Breland and Griswold (1981, 1982). Some of these results are described in Chapter IV.

Mathematics. Table 8.21 shows that through the VSS 29 colleges have studied the relationship between the mathematical sections of the SAT and a freshman mathematics course grade. The mean correlation is .35, which is identical to that for SAT-mathematical score prediction of freshman grade point average and very slightly higher than the .34 mean for SAT-verbal score prediction of freshman English course grade, but is significantly higher than for SAT-verbal score prediction of freshman mathematics course grade (.24) and for SAT-mathematical score prediction of freshman English course grade (.25). Eighty percent of the correlations for SAT-mathematical score prediction of a freshman mathematics course grade are between .22 and .53. See Gussett (1974), Troutman (1978), and Bridgeman (1982) for published studies.

Only six colleges have studied the relationship be-

tween the current Mathematics Achievement Tests and freshman mathematics grade. The mean correlation for these studies is .30, below the .35 SAT-mathematical score mean for predicting freshman mathematics grade and the .35 mean for Mathematics Level I Achievement Test prediction of freshman grade point average. Thus, this small sample shows different results from Schrader (1971), who reported a median correlation of .47 for 15 validity studies using the older Intermediate and Advanced Mathematics Achievement Tests, compared to .32 for the mathematical sections of the SAT, and concluded that there was ". . . substantial evidence of the superiority of the Mathematics Achievement Tests over SAT-M in predicting mathematics grades" (p. 139).

High school grade point average or rank prediction of freshman mathematics course grade was studied by 23 colleges. The correlations average .32, lower than the mean of .35 for SAT-mathematical score prediction of freshman mathematics course grade.

High school mathematics course grade prediction of freshman mathematics course grade was studied through VSS by nine colleges. The mean correlation is .41, higher than that of total high school record (.32) and of the SAT-mathematical score (.35) prediction of freshman mathematics course grade and identical to that of high school English course grade prediction of freshman English course grade (.41).

Mean correlations for English and mathematical placement are summarized in Table 8.22 (page 168).

Science. Table 8.23 on page 168 displays the handful of validity studies that were conducted through VSS to predict a freshman science course grade.

The SAT-verbal and SAT-mathematical mean correlations for predicting freshman science grade are .43

Table 8.22

Summary of Mean Correlations for Predicting
English and Mathematics Course Grades,
Compared to Mean Correlations for Predicting
Freshman Grade Point Average

	Criterion		
Predictor	Freshman Grade Point Average	Freshman English	Freshman Mathematics
SAT-Verbal Score	.36	.34	.24
SAT-Mathematical Score	.35	.25	.35
High School Record (Grade Point Average or Rank)	.47	.37	.32
High School English Grade	.39	.41	—
High School Mathematics Grade	.24	—	.41
Test of Standard Written English	—	.37	—
Achievement Test Average	.37	.32	—
English Composition Achievement Test	.36	.37	.32
Mathematics Achievement Test	.35	—	.30

Table 8.23

Validity Data for the Prediction of Freshman
Science Course Grade

Predictor	Number of Colleges	Mean Correlation
SAT-Verbal Score	5	.43
SAT-Mathematical Score	6	.42
High School Record	6	.47
High School Science Grade	1	.40
Achievement Tests		
English Composition	2	.30
Mathematics	2	.40
Chemistry	1	.45
Biology	1	.55
Any Combination of Above	8	.42
Average	2	.30

and .42, respectively. The high school record (grade point average or rank) mean correlation for predicting freshman science is .47. The one study using a high school science grade for predicting freshman science grade has a correlation of .40. The Achievement Test correlations for predicting freshman

science grade vary quite a bit, but the average is on about the same level as those of the SAT scores. See Schrader (1971) and Pedersen (1975) for published studies.

Foreign Language. Only four recent validity studies were designed to predict a freshman foreign language course grade. For three Spanish courses, the Spanish Achievement Test has an average correlation with the Spanish course grade of .33. The other study related the German Achievement Test with a German course grade, and the correlation is .39.

Schrader (1971) reports on studies for 12 student groups, mostly for the prediction of a grade in a French course. The mean correlation for the foreign language Achievement Tests (mostly French) is .34, compared to only .18 for the SAT-verbal score. For the four groups for which high school record was included, the mean correlation is a slightly higher .39.

Validity for Other Predictors

Willingham and Breland (1982) report on a study of personal qualities in admissions at nine colleges. A personal achievement composite of extracurricular and employment achievements and personal statement and reference valuations had a correlation with freshman grade point average of only .13, and added only .01 over use of high school rank and SAT scores. A full range of 23 achievement and background measures added .04. The measures that most consistently improved prediction over rank and SAT scores were academic honors, either the content or quality of the writing in the student's personal statement, sex (lower grades for males), and ethnic group (lower grades for minority students). Measures of personal achievements and ratings were more related to freshman peer ratings than to grades.

Breland (1981) and Willingham and Breland (1982) reviewed the literature for studies that evaluate the effectiveness of any of a variety of measures of student characteristics for the prediction of college performance. They found relatively high reported reliability (over .80) and validity (.40-.50) for biographical data and high school student peer ratings. However, almost all of the predictive effectiveness was due to the relationship with rank and SAT scores. Other measures, such as recommendations, interviews, interest measures, personality measures, personal statements, and creativity measures tended to have much lower reported reliability and validity.

Validity for Other Criteria

Long-Term Grade Point Average. Wilson (1983) reports results from a comprehensive review of research on the prediction of grade point average after the freshman year. For the 21 studies reviewed, Wilson reports substantial support for the following four findings:

1. Preadmissions measures of test scores and high school record are as valid for predicting cumulative grade point average (through the sophomore, junior, or senior year), as for freshman grade point average. Correlations between freshman grade point average and cumulative grade point average are .80 and higher; for admissions, they are essentially interchangeable as the criterion.

2. Preadmissions measures have declining validity for each successive year of grade point average. That is, they predict freshman grade point average better than sophomore grade point average (for courses taken only in the sophomore year), which in turn they predict better than junior grade point average, which in turn they predict better than senior grade point average.

3. Freshman grade point average also has declining validity for predicting each successive year of grade point average, but on a higher level than preadmissions measures. Because student ranking on grade point average does not change very much from one year to the next and because tests given to students over two or more years are highly correlated, the decreasing validity of preadmissions measures and freshman grade point average for successive years is at least partially due to changes in the criterion over time (the senior grade point average is a different kind of measure than, for example, the sophomore grade point average) and is not solely due to student changes over time. The best prediction of grade point average in a given semester is the cumulative grade point average up to that point; the next best is the prior semester's grade point average.

4. Preadmissions measures do not add significantly to freshman grade point average in predicting post-freshman grade point average at the same institution.

Wilson concludes that use of freshman grade point average in validity studies for admissions is reasonable because freshman grade point average is an excellent surrogate for long-term cumulative grade point average, is more complete, is available after only one year, and is critical for advancement in good standing toward program completion.

Persistence. The relationship between standard preadmissions measures and persistence is difficult to ascertain because it depends on the length of time of persistence (some studies are for one year and others are for four years); there are great differences in dropout rates among colleges; and additive effects highly depend on which other variables are included in the analysis.

Through the College Board's Admissions Testing Program Summary Reporting Service, colleges can obtain freshman-year persistence data for a variety of student characteristics. For the 1977 entering class, a summary of data for 237 colleges was compiled. By size, control, and academic level of the college, the average freshman year dropout rate ranged from 8 percent for 23 medium-sized (200 to 499 enrolling freshmen) private colleges with a high SAT average (at least 480 for the SAT-verbal score) to 21 percent for 22 large (at least 500 enrolling freshmen) public colleges with a low SAT average (below 435 for the SAT-verbal score). By high school rank, the dropout rate ranged from 11 percent for students in the top tenth, to 13 percent for students in the second tenth, to 14 percent for students in the second fifth, to 18 percent for students below the second fifth. By SAT-mathematical score (the rates by SAT-verbal score are similar), the dropout rate ranged from 9 percent for students scoring in the 700s, to 11 percent for the 600s, to 13 percent for the 500s, to 15 percent for the 400s, to 17 percent for the 300s, to 24 percent for the 200s. These differences are for freshman-year dropout rates defined in the summer after the freshman year, before knowing who returns for the sophomore year, and probably would be greater for sophomore-year nonreturns or for four-year dropout rates.

Willingham and Breland (1982) studied nine colleges, defining persistence as returning in the fall of the sophomore year. The correlation between high school rank and persistence was .03 for all colleges combined, averaging .01 within college. The correlation between the SAT score and persistence was .08 for all colleges combined and averaged .03 within college. These two measures plus eight other personal quality measures of achievement, background, and educational goals correlated .15 for all colleges combined and averaged .08 within college. However, the correlation between an overall college academic composite of rank and SAT means and college persistence rate was .77. The authors concluded that the likelihood of persistence depends on the college attended, but is not predicted well by standard or personal quality measures for the nine colleges they studied.

Astin (1977) analyzed multicollege longitudinal data compiled by the American Council on Education. He reports a correlation between high school grade point average and four-year persistence of .29 and a multiple correlation for a variety of variables of .42. Although no correlation for the SAT is reported, in Astin (1975), when the SAT is used as one of 64 variables in a multiple regression equation, 200 SAT-sum points (approximately one standard deviation for all SAT takers) add about .04 to the probability of persistence, given all other variables stay the same. However, one of these variables is the student's academic rating of his or her high school, which is very highly correlated with SAT scores, and thereby, reduces the SAT increment to the probability of persistence.

Manski and Wise (1983) performed an analysis of 1972 National Longitudinal Study data to determine predictors of four-year persistence in college. In the analysis based only on high school rank and SAT scores, they found that one SAT-sum standard deviation (200 SAT-sum points for all SAT takers) adds about as much to the probability of persistence as does one high school rank standard deviation (25 percentile points); they both add approximately .11 to the probability of persistence and thereby reduce the probability of dropping out by .11. For a high school percentile rank of 100 (the top of the class), the probability of dropping out increases five times, from .10 for an SAT sum of 1,300 to .49 for an SAT sum of 500 (intermediate probabilities are .17 for 1,100, .26 for 900, and .37 for 700). For a percentile rank of 75, the probability of dropping out increases four times, from .16 for an SAT sum of 1,300 to .60 for an SAT sum of 500 (intermediate probabilities are .25 for 1,100, .36 for 900, and .48 for 700). For a percentile rank of 50, the probability of dropping out increases three times, from .24 for an SAT sum of 1,300 to .70 for an SAT sum of 500 (intermediate probabilities are .35 for 1,100, .47 for 900, and .59 for 700).

After College. There has been limited research to relate post-college factors with test, high school performance, or other college predictors, and the results have been mixed. Relevant studies include:

1. Zeleznik, Hojat, and Veloski (1983) analyzed the relationship of the SAT to scores on the Medical College Admission Test (MCAT), to grades in medical school, and to grades on both the basic science and clinical science parts of the National Board of Medical Examiners (NBME) examination.

2. A study by Schrader (1978) investigated SAT scores and quantity of citations of doctorates in psychology 8 to 12 years after receipt of the doctorate.

3. A longitudinal study of Haverford College graduates 10 to 15 years after graduation by Heath (1977) reviewed the SAT and other measures in relation to adult competence.

4. Nicholson (1970) used multiple discriminant analysis to study how well both the traditional academic measures (high school record and the SAT) and nonacademic measures predicted the attainment of an advanced degree and a rating of success 15 to 17 years after graduation from Brown University.

5. Baird (1982) and Crouse (1979) conducted extensive evaluations of the effects of measures of academic ability on after-college accomplishment.

Principal author: Leonard Ramist
Contributors or reviewers: William H. Angoff, Irving L. Broudy, Nancy W. Burton, Thomas F. Donlon, June Stern, and Peggy A. Thorne.

CHAPTER IX

Descriptive Statistics on College Board Test Takers and Other Reference Groups

Introduction

Appropriate information about the distribution of test scores is fundamental to the use of tests. In this context, it is useful to know how many students actually take the College Board's tests, what kinds of score distributions they yield, and what else can be said about the students who take the tests, in terms of such social characteristics as ethnic identity and income level. Information about test performance for different groups of students is widely useful for both the interpretation of scores and for educational planning. The Board, therefore, has regularly provided a large body of information concerning its tests and the students who take them. This chapter provides a selective sample of such information.

Initially, data of this type were simply presented in the annual reports, which gave distributions of test scores. During the 1950s, substantial normative data were provided by Henry S. Dyer and others in *College Board Scores (No. 1)* and two subsequent editions (Dyer 1953, Dyer and King 1955, Fisherman 1957). Beginning in 1962, performance data were reported in *College Board Score Reports*. Currently, the Summary Reporting Service, described in Chapter VI, is the basic reporting channel. This chapter provides information on the principal ways the data are summarized in the current test descriptive materials and on the nature of the test takers.

Since the first edition of this handbook, three major developments have influenced the topics covered in this chapter: 1) the introduction of the Student Descriptive Questionnaire (SDQ), which expanded the quality and quantity of the statistical descriptions; 2) the impact of the SAT score decline and the questions it raised for the appropriate uses of College Board program information in the evaluation of educational outcomes; and 3) the emergence in measurement of a strong interest in criterion-referenced tests, instead of norm-referenced tests, with the need to understand the similarities and differences between these two approaches.

Normative Descriptions of Test Performance

The roles of norms and norm-like descriptive statistics in the Admissions Testing Program are complex. These roles were discussed by Schrader and Stewart (1971) in the first edition of this handbook. The following brief review is largely adapted from their more complete presentation.

For the practical use of a test, the determination of a student's relative standing within some appropriate reference group is often useful information. The most appropriate reference groups for a given college are generally its own applicants and students, summarized in local norms. The College Board encourages the development of local norms. In addition, the Board offers a variety of general norms, useful in providing a wider basis of comparison for a particular college or secondary school, to be used in conjunction with local norms or to be substituted (with care) for local norms, when these are not available.

There is a general need to consider self-selection in interpreting Admissions Testing Program results. This self-selection produces complex variation in the groups that take the tests, such as 1) variation across the tests, with many more students taking the SAT than any given Achievement Test; 2) variation across administrations of a single test, so that students taking the SAT in May of their junior year are more able than those at other administrations; and 3) variations in student tendencies to *repeat* a test. These and other sources of variations require an awareness that descriptive statistics are useful and norm-like in appearance, but they are not norms.

Despite their limitations, descriptive statistics based on program data have a number of advantages. For one thing, they describe the performance of college-bound students tested under realistic conditions. The flow of data is sustained in volume, rapidly sensitive to changes over time, and easy to keep current. The populations involved are relatively large. For these reasons, the descriptive statistics are of significant value in score interpretation. However, attempts to draw more general inferences (such as the meaning of changes over long periods of time) are less justifiable because there is no satisfactory way to assess the effect of self-selection on the results. This same limitation applies, of course, to any comparisons based on nonrandom subgroups of test takers. Comparisons of test performance from one high school to another, for example, and even from one year to another within the same high school, must be interpreted in the light of possible differences in the nature and extent of self-selection.

National Norms

As a supplement to program descriptive data, there have been four major studies that yielded normative data based on random national samples: one in the fall of 1960, one in the fall of 1966, one in the fall of 1974, and one in the fall of 1983 (Braun, Centra, and King 1985, in press; Jackson and Schrader 1976; Seibel 1965a, 1965b). The first two studies involved both juniors and seniors; the third and fourth studies were restricted to juniors only. For convenience in sampling, all of the studies used the Preliminary Scholastic Aptitude Test/National Merit Scholarship Qualifying Test (PSAT/NMSQT) rather than the SAT. The PSAT/NMSQT requires less than two hours of testing time, is parallel in form and content to the SAT, and its score scale is directly related to the score scale for the SAT (multiplication of a PSAT/NMSQT score by 10 yields the comparable SAT score).

For seniors, the mean scores in 1960 and in 1966 were as follows:

	SAT-Verbal Means (Based on PSAT/NMSQT administrations)			SAT-Mathematical Means		
	Males	Females	Total	Males	Females	Total
1960	372	376	374	438	385	410
1966	390	393	392	422	382	401

These data indicate that there was a rise in the average ability on the verbal scale and a decline on the mathematical scale. The patterns observed are consistent for both boys and girls.

For the juniors, the comparable mean scores were as follows:

	SAT-Verbal Means (Based on PSAT/NMSQT administrations)			SAT-Mathematical Means		
Study	Males	Females	Total	Males	Females	Total
1960	336	348	342	404	371	387
1966	353	362	358	392	365	378
1974	344	343	343	395	377	386
1983	350	353	352	391	377	384

The data for juniors for 1960 and 1966 are consistent with those for seniors in those years in that they show an increase in verbal ability and a decline in mathematical ability. Clearly, however, the means for these national samples shift upward and downward over time by small amounts in response to a variety of factors. The score decline phenomenon concerns a *consistent* pattern of decline for a nonrandom sample, and magnitudes much greater than those presented here. But it should be noted that the 1974 study and the 1983 study, carried out after a period of noticeable decline in the annual program data, showed levels of performance for a national random sample of *juniors* that were not greatly different from those for the 1960 study. The test score of the average high school junior in 1974 or 1983 closely resembled his or her predecessor of 1960. The implications of this finding for national samples, in an era of decline within the program, are paradoxical. They may underscore the need to temper any pessimism concerning the quality of American education with some sense that it may not be declining appreciably.

Selected Distributions for the SAT

Tables 9.1 and 9.2 (pages 173 and 174) present data concerning SAT performance for juniors and seniors, for males and females, and for all students who took the test during the academic years 1967-68 through 1982-83. These distributions are based on all students who take the tests during a given academic year, continuing the practice used in tables in the first edition of this handbook. The data for seniors, therefore, will differ somewhat from the data for "college-bound seniors" presented in certain later distributions. Data for "college-bound seniors" consists of reports generated in several different academic years. The college-bound senior distribution is based on the latest test records for all high school seniors who registered for the ATP at any point during secondary school. Thus, it is data *associated* with seniors, but not necessarily obtained by testing in the senior year.

Table 9.1 shows an essential parity in the average performance of the sexes on the SAT-verbal sections, regardless of the year of testing, junior or senior. For the SAT-mathematical sections, Table 9.2 shows that male average performance is greater by approximately 40-50 points in all years, again with no clear association to junior year or senior year status. The data in both tables show that the average SAT scores of those taking the test as juniors are higher than those of students taking the test as seniors, a phenomenon that parallels similar patterns for a number of the Achievement Tests. The self-selection that leads students to take the test in the junior year attracts a more able group, on the average. In contrast to the difference in average junior and senior year performance on the Achievement Tests, the difference between average junior year and senior year groups on the SAT is widening. In the first three years listed in Table 9.1, the observed junior-senior differences average about 7 points for the SAT-verbal

Table 9.1

Means, Standard Deviations, and Numbers of Scholastic Aptitude Test Verbal Scores, Classified by Student's Sex and Educational Level, 1967-68 Through 1982-83

Educational Level	Testing Year	Males			Females			Total*		
		Mean	SD	N	Mean	SD	N	Mean	SD	N
JUNIORS	1967-68	468	108	307,493	473	103	282,382	470	105	589,879
	1968-69	465	106	314,223	469	105	293,667	467	105	607,896
	1969-70	464	109	310,715	466	105	297,908	465	107	608,629
	1970-71	461	108	307,109	462	104	302,493	461	106	609,606
	1971-72	456	105	293,458	454	103	292,302	455	104	585,774
	1972-73	450	105	280,566	448	102	285,738	449	104	570,066
	1973-74	444	104	276,934	437	101	279,294	441	103	556,602
	1974-75	446	104	274,049	448	103	274,135	447	104	548,702
	1975-76	440	106	278,654	440	105	285,665	440	105	564,790
	1976-77	443	105	271,569	437	105	282,276	440	105	553,848
	1977-78	445	105	269,216	440	104	286,214	442	104	555,432
	1978-79	444	107	274,589	439	105	291,639	442	106	566,229
	1979-80	443	105	281,321	435	103	299,658	439	104	580,981
	1980-81	448	105	284,807	436	103	307,215	442	104	592,026
	1981-82	447	103	290,899	438	102	312,509	442	103	603,410
	1982-83	448	106	287,839	437	102	308,920	442	104	596,760
SENIORS	1967-68	463	111	490,737	464	109	399,977	463	110	890,721
	1968-69	457	110	498,462	464	110	415,925	460	110	914,395
	1969-70	457	112	504,588	458	111	429,712	458	112	934,324
	1970-71	449	110	460,715	452	109	403,251	450	110	863,981
	1971-72	447	111	430,208	444	110	390,534	446	110	820,763
	1972-73	441	110	400,108	437	107	373,242	439	108	779,205
	1973-74	443	111	369,627	437	109	360,272	440	110	730,434
	1974-75	432	111	379,095	428	108	373,183	430	110	753,180
	1975-76	426	110	386,896	420	110	387,597	423	110	775,348
	1976-77	424	108	382,856	419	109	388,944	421	109	771,897
	1977-78	424	108	383,657	417	109	406,143	420	109	789,813
	1978-79	420	109	386,322	413	108	408,997	417	108	795,320
	1979-80	418	107	386,043	410	107	413,818	414	107	799,861
	1980-81	420	107	367,359	409	108	403,099	414	108	770,470
	1981-82	419	106	372,451	411	108	405,651	415	107	778,106
	1982-83	417	106	358,444	409	106	389,912	413	106	748,360
ALL GRADES	1967-68	464	110	837,315	467	106	706,511	466	108	1,543,839
	1968-69	460	108	852,105	466	108	733,439	462	108	1,585,560
	1969-70	459	111	854,275	461	109	751,539	460	110	1,605,851
	1970-71	453	110	805,706	456	107	731,456	454	109	1,537,186
	1971-72	451	109	754,404	448	108	705,484	450	108	1,459,924
	1972-73	445	108	708,006	442	105	679,905	443	107	1,398,354
	1973-74	443	109	682,870	437	106	670,044	440	107	1,353,971
	1974-75	437	109	690,984	436	107	678,651	437	108	1,371,232
	1975-76	431	109	705,519	428	109	707,977	429	109	1,414,961
	1976-77	431	108	694,974	426	109	706,819	429	108	1,401,913
	1977-78	432	108	690,498	426	108	726,719	429	108	1,417,232
	1978-79	429	109	700,374	423	108	735,577	426	108	1,435,953
	1979-80	428	107	711,341	419	106	753,083	423	107	1,464,426
	1980-81	431	108	701,955	419	107	756,477	425	107	1,458,449
	1981-82	428	106	732,081	420	107	781,009	424	107	1,513,099
	1982-83	427	107	719,784	419	105	767,939	423	106	1,487,729

*Includes test takers who did not indicate sex.

score, and in Table 9.2 about 9 for the SAT-mathematical score. For 1980-81 to 1982-83, these averages had risen to about 28 and 34 respectively. This apparently reflects trends in self-selection that have sharpened the distinctions between groups, so that more able students take the tests earlier. The proportion of SAT tests taken each year by juniors rose slightly during the interval, from 38 to 40 percent, indicating a possible tendency for students to take the test earlier.

Table 9.2

Means, Standard Deviations, and Numbers of Scholastic Aptitude Test Mathematical Scores, Classified by Student's Sex and Educational Level, 1967-68 Through 1982-83

Educational Level	Testing Year	Males			Females			Total*		
		Mean	SD	N	Mean	SD	N	Mean	SD	N
JUNIORS	1967-68	522	110	307,493	483	100	282,382	504	107	589,879
	1968-69	515	110	314,223	474	98	293,667	495	106	607,896
	1969-70	514	112	310,715	476	100	297,908	495	108	608,629
	1970-71	513	114	307,109	474	102	302,493	494	110	609,606
	1971-72	510	110	293,458	472	100	292,302	491	107	585,774
	1972-73	511	112	280,566	468	101	285,738	489	109	570,066
	1973-74	508	116	276,934	467	104	279,294	487	112	556,602
	1974-75	510	114	274,049	464	105	274,135	487	112	548,702
	1975-76	507	114	278,654	459	105	285,665	483	112	564,790
	1976-77	511	114	271,569	463	103	282,276	487	111	553,848
	1977-78	513	116	269,216	466	105	286,214	489	113	555,432
	1978-79	506	113	274,589	461	104	291,639	483	111	566,229
	1979-80	507	113	281,321	462	104	299,658	484	111	580,981
	1980-81	513	113	284,807	466	105	307,215	489	111	592,026
	1981-82	515	116	290,899	469	106	312,509	491	113	603,410
	1982-83	514	117	287,839	469	108	308,920	491	115	596,760
SENIORS	1967-68	509	117	490,737	466	107	399,977	490	115	890,721
	1968-69	510	116	498,462	465	105	415,925	490	114	914,395
	1969-70	506	118	504,588	462	108	429,712	486	116	934,324
	1970-71	503	117	460,715	462	106	403,251	484	114	863,981
	1971-72	498	118	430,208	453	107	390,534	477	115	820,763
	1972-73	498	117	400,108	455	106	373,242	477	114	779,205
	1973-74	495	120	369,627	454	110	360,272	474	117	730,434
	1974-75	489	118	379,095	442	106	373,183	466	114	753,180
	1975-76	490	124	386,896	438	111	387,597	464	120	775,348
	1976-77	489	121	382,856	437	110	388,944	463	119	771,897
	1977-78	483	120	383,657	434	109	406,143	458	117	789,813
	1978-79	481	118	386,322	433	107	408,997	456	115	795,320
	1979-80	481	118	386,043	435	108	413,818	457	115	799,861
	1980-81	481	117	367,359	434	107	403,099	457	115	770,470
	1981-82	481	118	372,451	433	107	405,651	456	115	778,106
	1982-83	480	118	358,444	433	108	389,912	455	115	748,360
ALL GRADES	1967-68	513	115	837,315	471	105	706,511	494	112	1,543,839
	1968-69	511	114	852,105	468	103	733,439	491	111	1,585,560
	1969-70	508	116	854,275	466	105	751,539	488	113	1,605,851
	1970-71	505	116	805,706	466	105	731,456	487	113	1,537,186
	1971-72	502	115	754,404	460	105	705,484	482	112	1,459,924
	1972-73	503	116	708,006	460	105	679,905	481	112	1,398,354
	1973-74	498	119	682,870	458	108	670,044	478	115	1,353,971
	1974-75	496	117	690,984	450	106	678,651	473	114	1,371,232
	1975-76	496	120	705,519	445	109	707,977	470	118	1,414,961
	1976-77	496	119	694,974	446	108	706,819	471	117	1,401,913
	1977-78	494	120	690,498	445	109	726,719	469	117	1,417,232
	1978-79	490	117	700,374	443	106	735,577	466	114	1,435,953
	1979-80	490	117	711,341	444	107	753,083	467	114	1,464,426
	1980-81	493	117	701,955	445	108	756,477	468	115	1,458,449
	1981-82	492	119	732,081	445	108	781,009	468	116	1,513,099
	1982-83	491	120	719,784	444	109	767,939	467	117	1,487,729

*Includes test takers who did not indicate sex.

Tables 9.1 and 9.2 further indicate that the number of Scholastic Aptitude Tests taken by males declined, over the period considered, by about 14 percent, while the number of tests taken by females increased by 9 percent. As a result, female records accounted for 52 percent of test outcomes in 1982-83 as opposed to 46 percent in 1967-68. Some of the trends in sex differences are undoubtedly due to these shifts in test-taking patterns between the sexes.

Figure 9.1

Number of ATP College-Bound Seniors,
Males and Females, 1972-1983

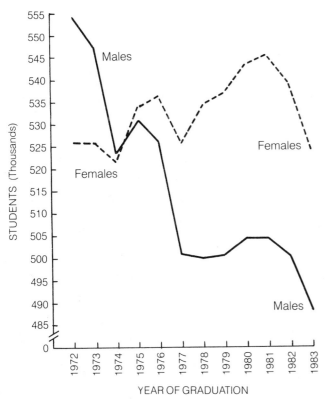

Figure 9.1 confirms these shifts. It shows the frequencies of individual males and females in the college-bound senior distributions over the period from 1972-1983. Because of the difference in the definition of the distribution, these frequencies are lower than those from Tables 9.1 and 9.2. Nonetheless, the pattern also shows a rise in the total number of females, a decline in the total number of males, and a greater proportion of female registrants overall since 1975.

Tables 9.1 and 9.2 may also be used to establish that the score decline occurred for juniors and seniors, males and females. Because of the shifting patterns of self-selection, the amount of decline may appear to vary for different subgroups, but it appears in all cases. Such evidence supports the view that the decline was a consequence of major and pervasive shifts in education and society, rather than a simple change in the test or in curriculum.

Selected Distributions for the Achievement Tests

The numbers of students taking Achievement Tests are fewer than the total number of ATP test takers; most students take only the Scholastic Aptitude Test. The number of students who take any Achievement Test has decreased over the years, reflecting a number of factors, such as a wider variety of course offerings available to students and fewer requirements concerning the Achievement Tests by the colleges. Table 9.3 (see next page) shows the numbers of students taking the various tests in each year from 1967-68 through 1982-83, together with their means and standard deviations. As Table 9.3 indicates, the Achievement Tests are not all equally popular. Table 9.4 (page 177) shows the percentage of 1983 college-bound seniors taking *any* Achievement Test, who elected to take the indicated Achievement Test at least once during their high school years. The table shows that virtually all students who take any Achievement Test take the English Composition Test, and that a substantial block of such Achievement Test takers choose the Mathematics Level I Test. However, the distribution over the remainder of tests ranges from the very few students who elect such languages as Latin and Hebrew up to American History and Social Studies and Biology, which attract about a quarter of the group. The relative popularity of the different fields, as reflected in Table 9.4, has had a fairly stable pattern for some years. The percentages of students among college-bound seniors in 1983 may be contrasted in Table 9.4 with the comparable choices for students tested in 1962-64, as reported in the last edition of this handbook. There are some obvious shifts in the patterns separated by nearly 20 years, but a similarity emerges: more students take the English Composition Test and the Mathematics Level I Test than any of the other Achievement Tests.

The students who take the Achievement Tests are more able, on the average, than those who do not. This is established in Table 9.5 (page 177), which shows the Achievement Test means and the Scholastic Aptitude Test means for the college-bound seniors who take the various Achievement Tests at some time during their high school years. Each of these means is substantially above the average of all the students taking the SAT, and in all cases but

175

Table 9.3

Means, Standard Deviations, and Number of Cases* (in Thousands) for All Students
Taking Achievement Tests by Year, 1967-68 Through 1982-83

Testing Year	English Composition			Literature			French			German			Hebrew		
	Mean	S.D.	N	Mean	S.D.	N	Mean	S.D.	N	Mean	S.D.	N	Mean	S.D.	N
1967-68	514	106	455.9	526	110	8.6	535	108	98.2	524	114	18.1	586	98	1.1
1968-69	514	106	473.8	522	112	22.3	525	107	105.0	518	109	18.8	570	99	1.2
1969-70	512	106	464.6	523	110	22.1	524	106	96.4	525	117	18.5	573	104	1.2
1970-71	513	105	397.0	531	109	21.8	537	102	64.8	527	105	11.7	569	106	1.2
1971-72	516	108	355.9	530	111	19.9	546	106	52.5	544	117	9.7	565	102	1.1
1972-73	512	106	312.0	525	112	13.5	547	108	49.4	542	114	10.0	568	105	1.0
1973-74	511	106	264.1	528	111	23.5	554	105	42.4	552	120	8.8	574	99	0.9
1974-75	518	107	257.0	520	112	24.4	546	111	38.1	544	122	7.9	576	99	0.9
1975-76	527	109	237.9	525	112	22.8	553	107	32.5	551	120	6.7	576	96	0.7
1976-77	514	105	229.3	529	110	20.2	549	109	29.3	549	124	6.2	577	103	0.7
1977-78	511	104	215.1	518	110	18.6	545	105	26.0	539	118	5.8	580	107	0.6
1978-79	512	104	207.6	522	111	17.8	547	107	24.6	545	122	5.5	584	108	0.6
1979-80	515	104	197.4	520	110	17.0	541	104	23.9	537	116	4.9	588	116	0.4
1980-81	512	102	192.7	516	108	15.6	538	103	22.7	541	113	4.8	600	120	0.4
1981-82	517	103	199.3	519	108	15.1	544	105	24.3	552	116	3.0	622	125	0.4
1982-83	516	101	183.8	520	106	16.2	544	106	22.8	558	116	2.9	617	118	0.4

Testing Year	Latin			Russian			Spanish			American History and Social Studies			European History and World Cultures		
1967-68	531	102	18.5	536	130	1.4	511	122	51.4	497	107	138.4	534	109	10.7
1968-69	526	102	15.9	532	133	1.3	513	120	59.0	494	106	135.9	522	109	10.7
1969-70	520	107	12.8	528	135	1.3	513	121	59.3	486	106	126.3	520	107	9.3
1970-71	532	106	7.5	532	133	0.9	525	117	38.8	494	103	114.8	526	106	7.6
1971-72	530	104	5.4	539	136	0.6	533	119	33.8	487	104	108.9	530	110	6.3
1972-73	527	106	4.2	545	136	0.5	545	125	34.8	498	105	89.7	521	107	5.9
1973-74	510	100	3.0	557	142	0.4	548	123	32.1	495	105	73.0	522	106	6.3
1974-75	515	105	1.4	543	148	0.4	539	122	30.3	493	105	71.6	524	104	2.9
1975-76	524	97	1.6	557	145	0.5	541	122	28.1	491	102	67.5	533	113	3.0
1976-77	516	98	1.7	576	148	0.5	534	121	26.6	494	106	66.8	520	103	3.1
1977-78	502	96	1.7	586	150	0.4	536	118	25.7	486	103	62.7	509	103	3.9
1978-79	532	102	1.6	616	169	0.4	534	118	24.9	487	105	59.0	521	109	3.6
1979-80	536	106	2.1	614	170	0.3	518	116	25.8	500	101	57.1	542	103	3.2
1980-81	554	107	2.3	635	161	0.4	530	118	25.6	510	101	53.8	543	100	2.9
1981-82	549	108	2.6	†	†	†	525	118	26.5	504	98	55.5	543	102	3.0
1982-83	553	107	2.5	†	†	†	529	116	25.7	517	100	40.9	547	104	2.3

Testing Year	Mathematics Level I			Mathematics Level II			Biology			Chemistry			Physics		
1967-68	544	102	335.2	675	93	26.8	513	112	62.0	565	105	68.4	579	102	29.1
1968-69	538	99	344.9	668	98	29.5	514	113	63.6	561	109	63.7	587	106	28.1
1969-70	543	104	331.0	668	101	29.8	524	114	53.7	575	111	60.2	587	106	25.3
1970-71	538	99	295.7	662	99	30.9	526	114	56.7	569	105	53.8	590	107	21.9
1971-72	539	100	264.0	658	101	31.3	537	114	57.0	568	112	49.6	599	105	19.0
1972-73	536	101	232.0	664	97	30.1	542	116	58.0	573	106	44.9	601	106	17.1
1973-74	540	101	189.6	661	100	32.1	545	110	50.1	567	109	36.1	599	102	14.4
1974-75	539	103	184.1	658	103	35.8	544	115	52.0	568	101	36.9	598	104	15.2
1975-76	545	100	172.9	662	100	35.7	546	111	54.7	571	103	39.5	594	103	18.2
1976-77	545	100	166.4	667	97	33.4	541	109	53.1	572	105	35.8	593	102	17.8
1977-78	538	96	158.3	657	96	36.3	549	109	49.2	577	103	35.2	583	104	15.9
1978-79	535	94	158.7	650	94	37.9	544	106	45.9	576	102	35.0	580	100	16.3
1979-80	535	94	155.0	651	95	38.2	544	107	41.3	572	99	34.5	593	101	15.1
1980-81	537	93	150.7	646	95	39.3	539	104	40.2	569	99	33.4	592	99	15.6
1981-82	542	93	156.8	654	92	52.3	548	102	39.0	570	96	34.6	590	98	17.7
1982-83	539	92	144.8	656	94	41.4	560	108	40.6	573	100	34.9	596	97	16.8

*The term "case" is used here to denote the taking of a specific Achievement Test. Thus, if a student took the same Achievement Test at two administrations, he or she is counted as two cases.
†No longer offered.

Table 9.4

Percentages of All Achievement Test Takers
Among 1983 and 1964 ATP College-Bound Seniors
Who Elected Specific Achievement Tests*

| | | Percentage of Group** | |
Achievement Test	Number of 1983 Seniors	1983 Seniors	1964 Seniors
English Composition	177,359	92.1	86.3
Literature	16,977	8.8	†
French	22,863	11.9	18.5
German	3,095	1.6	3.3
Hebrew	426	0.2	0.1
Latin	2,411	1.3	5.6
Spanish	25,383	13.2	8.1
American History and Social Studies	43,572	22.6	29.8
European History and and World Cultures	2,624	1.4	2.8
Mathematics Level I	142,306	73.9	56.2
Mathematics Level II	39,093	20.3	21.8
Biology	42,544	22.1	11.1
Chemistry	35,728	18.6	18.6
Physics	16,507	8.6	9.4
Any Achievement Test	192,500	(base for percentages)	

*The 1983 sample contained all seniors who were tested at, or prior to, the March 1983 administration.

**The percentages do not add to 100 because each test taker is included in the percentage for each test that he or she took.

† This test was not introduced until 1968.

Spanish, above the scaled score level of 500. There is some variation in the SAT means themselves, both verbal and mathematical, from one subject-matter area to another, so that those tested in Physics or in Mathematics Level II are more able, on the average, than those tested in English Composition or in Literature. It is precisely these disparities in ability that justify the scaling and equating procedures for the Achievement Tests described in Chapter II. As reported there, the scales for the Achievement Tests are anchored in estimates of the performance of a hypothetical population with mean SAT-verbal and SAT-mathematical scores of 500, standard deviations on these variables of 100, and a correlation between them of .60. In scaling the foreign language tests, information concerning years of study is also taken into account.

The effects of these procedures can be perceived in the Achievement Test averages described in the first column of Table 9.5. In general, the more able a group is, in terms of both the SAT-verbal and SAT-mathematical scores, the higher their average Achievement Test scaled scores will be. The Achievement Test scales also take into account the correlations between the test and the two aptitude measures, so that the average Achievement Test scaled score is not simply a function of the average

Scholastic Aptitude Test scores. Thus, similar Scholastic Aptitude Test means for two groups will not dictate similar Achievement Test results. In Table 9.5, for example, the group taking the American History and Social Studies Test and the group taking the Mathematics Level I Test are reasonably comparable in terms of aptitude means: The Level I group is only 13 points lower on the SAT-verbal score and only 6 points higher on the SAT-mathematical score. The scaled score means, however, for the two Achievement Tests are 27 points apart, reflecting the different patterns of intercorrelation for these tests.

As Table 9.5 indicates, Chemistry, Physics, and Mathematics Level II attract groups with somewhat greater verbal and mathematical differences than the other tests, and with higher mathematical scores. Conversely, students who take the Literature and European History Achievement Tests show smaller differences between verbal and mathematical scores. The general level and pattern of the means reported in Table 9.5 is reasonably close to that of the means reported for the Achievement Tests and the Scholastic Aptitude Test in Tables 3.8 and 3.9 in the first edition of this handbook, which used data based upon the 1968-69 test takers. This stability, in an era of generally declining SAT scores, indicates that the diminishing number of students who take the Achievement Tests reflects a process of self-selection that is related to ability. Smaller and more select groups are taking the tests.

Consistent with this, the Achievement Test means presented in Table 9.3 do not indicate a decline dur-

Table 9.5

Achievement Test and Scholastic Aptitude Test
Means for 1983 ATP College-Bound Seniors
Taking Achievement Tests

Achievement Test	Achievement Test Score Mean	SAT-Verbal Score Mean	SAT-Math. Score Mean
English Composition	518	512	566
Literature	523	524	528
American History and Social Studies	516	513	550
European History and World Cultures	549	563	557
French	548	541	571
German	567	542	586
Hebrew	627	551	588
Latin	550	562	591
Spanish	533	498	542
Biology	544	523	570
Chemistry	569	536	624
Physics	595	536	647
Mathematics Level I	543	500	556
Mathematics Level II	655	550	649

ing this period comparable to that experienced by the SAT. It must be noted, however, that shifts in Achievement Test means reflect not only student performance but the operations that synthesize equating and scaling results; by design, the Achievement Test scales are not as stable over time as the SAT scales, and, while it is evident that the decline experienced with the SAT is not repeated here, this is partially a reflection of redefinition of these scales in the intervening years.

Table 9.6 presents the differences between means for juniors and seniors (also separated by sex) taking each Achievement Test, excluding Hebrew and Russian. As these differences indicate, the average junior taking an Achievement Test in a given academic year does better than the average senior during that year. (Modest exceptions to this pattern are seen in the means for the Literature Achievement

Test, on which seniors do better in some years, and for Spanish in 1978-79.) Such patterns reflect the typical timing of course work and test taking in high school. The data suggest a sizable year-to-year variation in these differences, and some field-to-field variation as well. Thus, for the English Composition Test, differences between juniors and seniors range over the years from –3 to 28 points, and for English Literature from –21 to 25. For the Chemistry and Physics Tests, the median differences in means for males and females are 34 and 46, respectively, while for Mathematics Level I and Level II, they are much less, 24 and 22. These patterns underscore the difficulty in the interpretation of individual records through program statistics. While the fluctuations reflect a complex set of causal factors, the predominant cause can probably be stated as self-selection by the students. Those taking the

Table 9.6

Mean Differences in Achievement Test Scores Earned by Juniors and Seniors, 1967-68 Through 1982-83

Achievement Test	*Junior Mean Minus Senior Mean*															
	1967-68	*1968-69*	*1969-70*	*1970-71*	*1971-72*	*1972-73*	*1973-74*	*1974-75*	*1975-76*	*1976-77*	*1977-78*	*1978-79*	*1979-80*	*1980-81*	*1981-82*	*1982-83*
MALES																
English Composition	19	19	16	11	19	13	1	24	– 2	22	28	24	11	21	17	17
Literature	25	5	–10	–11	– 9	–10	–20	–21	–17	7	5	15	– 1	15	10	0
French	50	60	64	35	45	50	33	38	34	39	34	31	33	33	34	39
German	53	38	64	32	32	36	35	62	29	38	27	40	32	45	54	58
Latin	49	52	48	39	46	48	13	67	5	32	45	53	52	46	21	54
Spanish	55	49	64	32	30	25	– 3	17	– 2	14	– 3	– 7	12	32	29	23
American History and Social Studies	25	33	41	40	36	34	36	38	32	51	22	70	46	56	48	46
European History and World Cultures	11	25	26	9	– 9	– 2	– 4	37	37*	– 4	8	24	27	3	10	7
Mathematics Level I	27	32	26	18	20	24	12	6	7	12	20	25	27	26	22	12
Mathematics Level II	24	29	34	27	15	17	17	29	20	31	25	18	34	31	23	45
Biology	39	20	48	31	22	25	28	36	28	32	40	32	43	46	38	68
Chemistry	27	24	32	34	36	32	8	18	21	12	12	23	24	28	13	29
Physics	41	53	62	54	51	42	25	31	45	49	42	53	54	49	48	49
FEMALES																
English Composition	11	12	7	3	19	6	1	22	– 3	14	20	13	2	15	11	12
Literature	23	10	– 4	1	– 9	– 6	–15	– 2	– 3	10	10	8	– 4	0	7	8
French	30	40	49	27	39	41	29	31	31	30	30	29	29	36	37	41
German	44	32	60	31	15	32	34	49	34	38	41	53	36	48	69	50
Latin	38	45	48	47	51	38	9	60*	28	47	59	50	59	58	43	48
Spanish	38	33	57	21	24	29	0	13	1	24	12	8	21	39	32	31
American History and Social Studies	29	34	45	39	37	32	38	38	47	56	30	70	52	57	50	54
European History and World Cultures	24	14	17	3	16	– 1	0	30*	16*	3	43	47	14	11	30	11
Mathematics Level I	29	35	35	19	20	26	13	7	12	14	16	25	33	27	26	23
Mathematics Level II	19	21	21	24	7	12	– 2	32	23	33	25	16	42	37	19	45
Biology	39	22	53	29	20	27	32	36	32	27	47	38	47	55	51	71
Chemistry	53	44	55	43	53	46	20	31	39	24	25	23	35	31	14	33
Physics	32	47	44	49	46	42	15	10	40	47	40	45	52	58	48	54

*Comparison involving a group of fewer than 100 students.

tests in their junior year are, on the average, more able than those deferring the tests until their senior year. The sequencing and timing of course work by the individual is in part determined by ability, as is the timing of application to college, so that the complexity of the factors reflected in this table should not be underestimated. In general, while the pattern of higher junior-year performance is known and demonstrated in tables such as Table 9.6, the descriptive

information that is offered to assist in interpretation does not separate the two groups since the score is a record of achievement generated at the end of the term in which the relevant course work was completed.

The changes over the years in the timing of applications to colleges, and in the expanded opportunity to take Board tests, has resulted in earlier Achievement Test-taking patterns for students. Table 9.7

Table 9.7

Attendance at Achievement Test Sessions, Classified by Student's Educational Level
for 1956-57, 1968-69, 1977-78, and 1982-83

Student Group	1956-57		1968-69		1977-78		1982-83	
	Number	Percentage	Number	Percentage	Number	Percentage	Number	Percentage
Juniors	17,708	19.9	157,482	26.1	66,777	22.8	69,910	24.9
Seniors tested in:								
November	—	—	—	—	26,991	9.2	26,232	9.3
December	4,993	5.6	171,085	28.4	90,442	30.9	87,761	31.3
January	—	—	131,276	21.8	48,594	16.6	43,281	15.4
March	55,308	62.3	51,515	8.5	12,371	4.2	—	—
May	4,406	5.0	43,208	7.2	8,476	2.9	10,475	3.7
June	—	—	—	—	4,662	1.6	4,612	1.6
July	—	—	12,822	2.1	—	—	—	—
August	1,133	1.3	—	—	—	—	—	—
Total Seniors	65,840	74.1	409,906	68.0	191,536	65.4	172,423*	61.4
All Others	5,283	5.9	35,609	5.9	34,358	11.7	38,320	13.7
Total Attendance (base for percentages)	88,831	—	602,997	—	292,671	—	280,653	—

*Total includes students who were tested at special administrations.

Table 9.8

Volumes for Specific Achievement Tests Expressed as Percentages of
Total Achievement Test Volumes by Year, 1967-68 Through 1982-83

Testing Year	English Composition	Literature	French	German	Hebrew	Italian	Latin	Russian	Spanish	American History and Social Studies	European History and World Cultures	Mathematics Level I	Mathematics Level II	Biology	Chemistry	Physics	Total Number of Tests (base for percents)
1967-68	33.4	0.6	7.4	1.4	0.1	—	1.4	0.1	3.9	10.5	0.8	25.3	2.0	4.7	5.2	2.2	1,323,643
1968-69	34.5	1.6	7.6	1.4	0.1	—	1.2	0.1	4.3	9.9	0.8	25.1	2.1	4.6	4.6	2.0	1,373,650
1969-70	35.4	1.7	7.4	1.4	0.1	—	1.0	0.1	4.5	9.6	0.7	25.2	2.3	4.1	4.6	1.9	1,311,788
1970-71	35.3	1.9	5.8	1.0	0.1	0.03	0.7	0.1	3.5	10.2	0.7	26.3	2.7	5.0	4.8	1.9	1,125,524
1971-72	35.1	2.0	5.2	1.0	0.1	0.03	0.5	0.1	3.3	10.7	0.6	26.0	3.1	5.6	4.9	1.9	1,015,367
1972-73	34.5	1.5	5.5	1.1	0.1	—	0.5	0.1	3.8	9.9	0.7	25.7	3.3	6.4	5.0	1.9	903,057
1973-74	34.0	3.0	5.5	1.1	0.1	—	0.4	0.1	4.1	9.4	0.8	24.4	4.1	6.5	4.7	1.9	776,907
1974-75	33.9	3.2	5.0	1.0	0.1	—	0.2	0.1	4.0	9.4	0.4	24.3	4.7	6.9	4.9	2.0	759,056
1975-76	32.9	3.2	4.5	0.9	0.1	—	0.2	0.1	3.9	9.3	0.4	23.9	4.9	7.6	5.5	2.5	722,312
1976-77	33.2	2.9	4.2	0.9	0.1	—	0.3	0.1	3.8	9.7	0.4	24.1	4.8	7.7	5.2	2.6	691,048
1977-78	32.8	2.8	4.0	0.9	0.1	—	0.3	0.1	3.9	9.6	0.6	24.2	5.5	7.5	5.4	2.4	655,307
1978-79	32.5	2.8	3.8	0.9	0.1	—	0.3	0.1	3.9	9.2	0.6	24.8	5.9	7.2	5.5	2.5	639,490
1979-80	32.0	2.8	3.9	0.8	0.1	—	0.3	0.1	4.2	9.3	0.5	25.2	6.2	6.7	5.6	2.4	616,207
1980-81	32.1	2.6	3.8	0.8	0.1	—	0.4	0.1	4.3	9.0	0.5	25.1	6.6	6.7	5.6	2.6	600,447
1981-82	31.6	2.4	3.9	0.5	0.1	—	0.4	—	4.2	2.4	8.8	24.9	8.3	6.2	5.5	2.8	630,030
1982-83	31.9	2.8	4.0	0.5	0.1	—	0.4	—	4.5	7.1	0.4	25.1	7.2	7.0	6.1	2.9	576,041

Table 9.9

Percentages of Achievement Tests Administered in Five Subject-Matter Categories
by Year, 1967-68 Through 1982-83

Testing Year	English	Foreign Languages	History and Social Studies	Mathematics	Sciences	Total Number of Tests (Base for Percentages)
1967-68	35.1	14.2	11.3	27.4	12.0	1,323,643
1968-69	36.1	14.7	10.7	27.3	11.3	1,373,650
1969-70	37.1	14.5	10.3	27.5	10.6	1,311,788
1970-71	37.2	11.1	10.9	29.0	11.8	1,125,524
1971-72	37.0	10.2	11.3	29.1	12.4	1,015,367
1972-73	36.0	11.1	10.6	29.0	13.3	903,057
1973-74	37.0	11.3	10.2	28.5	13.0	776,907
1974-75	37.1	10.4	9.8	29.0	13.7	759,056
1975-76	36.1	9.7	9.8	28.9	15.6	722,312
1976-77	36.1	9.4	10.1	28.9	15.4	691,048
1977-78	35.7	9.2	10.2	29.7	15.3	655,307
1978-79	35.3	9.0	9.8	30.8	15.2	639,490
1979-80	34.8	9.3	9.8	31.4	14.7	616,207
1980-81	34.7	9.4	9.4	31.7	14.9	600,447
1981-82	34.0	9.0	9.3	33.2	14.5	630,030
1982-83	34.7	9.4	7.5	32.3	16.0	576,041

shows the frequencies of students tested as juniors (almost entirely in May, June, or July) and as seniors at various ATP administrations in 1956-57, 1968-69, 1977-78, and 1982-83. While the proportion of junior year tests has varied slightly (.20, .26, .23, and .25 respectively), the advancement of senior year test dates is reflected in the declining percentage of March tests (62 to 4), their eventual discontinuance, and in the increasing percentage of December tests (6 to 31). Students who choose to take these tests take them earlier than their predecessors did. In some cases, such as Biology, increasing numbers of sophomores take the tests.

The data on the relative popularity of the Achievement Tests presented in Table 9.4 (page 177) may be supplemented by the data in Table 9.8 (page 179), which shows the percentage of specific Achievement Test volumes in relation to total Achievement Test volumes. In combination, these tables indicate that most Achievement Test takers take three tests. This also reflects the testing fee structure, which provides one, two, or three Achievement Tests at the same cost. (There is a modest amount of repeating of the same test.) Thus, each percentage for 1977-78 in Table 9.8 is approximately one-third the corresponding percentage in Table 9.4.

The data in Table 9.8 may be recast into broader curriculum groups as in Table 9.9, which defines five areas and presents the percentage of total test-taking activity that occurs in each area. Table 9.9 reveals 1) a basic stability in the proportions of Achievement Tests devoted to assessment in English, 2) modest increases for tests of science and mathematics, 3) a modest decline for tests of history and social studies, and 4) a somewhat greater decline for tests of foreign languages. Such changes and trends over years are typical of ATP testing, reflecting forces that change the content of high school courses and the relative attractiveness of college major fields.

Selected Distributions Defined by SDQ Responses

The introduction of the Student Descriptive Questionnaire (SDQ) into the ATP in 1972 provided an expanded opportunity for descriptive statistics on the College Board populations. Basically, analyses to date of SDQ-related data have focused on the annual cohort of college-bound seniors. College-bound senior data are computed from the records of self-reported year of graduation and include the most recent information only, which may be results obtained in the junior year or earlier. The group of students responding to the SDQ represents a very large portion of all ATP registrants indicating they will graduate from high school in a particular year, and responses to the SDQ are summarized annually. Each annual summary, then, describes characteristics of substantial numbers of college-bound seniors who have registered for either the SAT, the Achievement Tests, or both at *some* point in their high school career. However, there are two limitations on the interpretation of descriptive statistics yielded by the SDQ that must be emphasized:

1. The group on which data are collected is only representative of college-bound seniors who have taken the College Board admissions tests. The group is *not* representative of *all* college-bound seniors, nor is it representative of all high school seniors.

2. The questionnaire is not completed at a uniform time. In a given group of college-bound seniors, different students have responded to the SDQ at different times during their high school career. Large numbers of students take the SAT twice or take Achievement Tests. Such students have several opportunities to complete the SDQ, because students may fill it out when registering for a particular administration. Some questions will probably be answered more accurately the later the student responds. Examples of such questions are those that ask for high school class rank and number of years of study in particular subject areas.

3. The proportion of SDQ responders who answer individual questions, while typically high, varies somewhat from question to question, as described in Chapter VI.

Table 9.10 indicates the percentages of ATP senior year registrants who also responded to the SDQ (at same point in their high school career) for the annual cohorts of 1973, 1978, and 1983. As shown in the table, the response rate for the total group (males and females combined) rose dramatically between 1973 and 1978 (from 76 percent to 90 percent) and has remained high. Increasingly, therefore, the responses to Student Descriptive Questionnaires are representative of the total group of ATP test takers, as fewer and fewer students fail to provide information. Interestingly, a slightly larger percentage of females consistently responded to at least one SDQ question during each of the three years shown.

Socioeconomic Characteristics of the Groups. Table 9.11 indicates the percentages of all SDQ respondents in 1973, 1978, and 1983 who described themselves as being in one of seven ethnic group categories. These data are based on a question that asked the respondent, ''How do you describe yourself?'' The response options are given in the table. Clearly, the percentage of ATP registrants who classify themselves as belonging to an ethnic group other than White has increased from 1973 to 1983. In fact, about 60 percent of the absolute increase between 1973 and 1978 in the total number of college-bound seniors responding to the SDQ was directly attributable to the increase in the number of minority participants. Virtually all of the increase in minority participation since 1978 is attributable to increases in self-reports of Oriental or Asian American status.

Table 9.10

Number and Percentages of ATP College-Bound Seniors for 1973, 1978, and 1983 Responding to SDQ

1973	Male	Female	Total
Number of College-Bound Seniors	547,018	525,917	1,072,935
Number Responding to SDQ	401,095	413,263	814,358
Percent Responding to SDQ	73	79	76
1978	Male	Female	Total
Number of College-Bound Seniors	500,089	534,007	1,034,096
Number Responding to SDQ	443,116	487,194	930,310
Percent Responding to SDQ	89	91	90
1983	Male	Female	Total
Number of College-Bound Seniors	488,247	524,290	1,012,537
Number Responding to SDQ	430,036	477,663	907,699
Percent Responding to SDQ	88	91	90

Table 9.11

Ethnic Background of ATP College-Bound Seniors for 1973, 1978, and 1983 Expressed as Percentage of Total SDQ Respondents

Response Option	1973 Percentage	1978 Percentage	1983 Percentage
American Indian	0	.4	.5
Black or Afro-American	7	9.0	8.8
Mexican-American or Chicano	1	1.7	1.9
Oriental or Asian American	2	2.6	4.2
Puerto Rican	0	1.0	1.2
White or Caucasian	87	83.0	81.1
Other	1	2.3	2.2
Number Responding	784,848	893,767	875,475
Percent Minority	11	17	18.9

Table 9.12 (page 182) presents student-reported parental income distributions for the 1983 college-bound seniors. The Admissions Testing Program has reported analogous information since the SDQ

Table 9.12

Annual Parental Income by Ethnic Group (1982-83 sdq Questions 37 and 43)

Income	American Indian %	Black %	Mexican-American %	Oriental %	Puerto Rican %	White %	Other %	No Ethnic Response %	All Students %
Under $6,000	9.8	14.3	7.4	7.6	14.6	1.9	9.2	5.0	3.7
$6,000-11,999	16.1	25.2	18.9	13.5	23.5	6.3	17.9	11.7	9.1
12,000-17,999	15.3	19.4	18.6	13.6	17.9	10.3	16.1	13.4	11.7
18,000-23,999	14.3	14.6	17.8	13.8	13.4	14.2	15.1	15.2	14.3
24,000-29,999	12.0	8.6	12.0	10.9	8.8	14.3	10.2	12.7	13.5
30,000-39,999	13.8	8.9	13.5	15.3	9.4	20.7	12.3	17.2	18.9
40,000-49,999	8.3	5.2	6.4	10.4	5.3	12.8	7.3	9.9	11.6
50,000 or over	10.3	3.8	5.5	14.9	7.1	19.5	11.8	14.9	17.2
Total	100.0	100.0	100.0	100.0	100.0	100.0	100.0	100.0	100.0
Mean Income	$27,900	$19,800	$24,000	$32,500	$22,400	$39,200	$28,300	$33,500	$36,400
Median Income	$21,400	$15,000	$19,600	$24,800	$15,800	$31,200	$20,400	$26,200	$29,000

was instituted. Comparisons of cohorts over time, however, in terms of unadjusted dollars are seriously distorted by inflation. In general, as Table 9.12 shows, there is considerable variation among ethnic/racial groups with respect to median income level.

The relationship of test scores to family income is questioned by some, and it is charged that tests may preserve the status quo by denying opportunity to students from low-income families. Since 1971-72 the Board has published statistics relating test scores to family income. The relationship between test scores and family income is far more moderate than has been claimed by critics of the SAT; the correlation between these variables is about .30 (Educational Testing Service 1980a).

Table 9.13 is a partial confirmation of this. It shows the median SAT scores achieved in 1982-83 for eight groups defined by SDQ-reported family income. There is approximately a 120-point range in these SAT medians on both the verbal and mathematical sections, and typical score level is fairly systematically related to income. But the relationship is somewhat curvilinear, with increases in income above about $18,000 associated with smaller increments in the SAT average, and the differences in average SAT scores between adjacent income categories are quite small.

The data in Table 9.13 offer the important advantage of demonstrating both the degree of the relationship and the wide variation in SAT performance within income level. As the data indicate, significant numbers of low-income test takers score well on the SAT, while not all high-income candidates do so. Over 25 percent of students in the lowest income category earn SAT-verbal scores that are greater than the average SAT-verbal score for students whose parents' income is in the $24,000 to $29,999 category.

High School Experience: Achievement and Curriculum. Table 9.14 presents data related to the level of academic achievement for college-bound seniors in 1973, 1978, and 1983 who responded to the SDQ. Several aspects of these data stand out. First, the majority of these college-bound seniors rank themselves in the top two-fifths of their high school class for each year reported: 74 percent in 1973, 72 percent in 1978, and 70 percent in 1983. Virtually no students described themselves as being in the fourth fifth or lowest fifth of their class.

In addition, for each year reported, females on the average report a higher class rank than males. There is some evidence that both males and females are reporting very slightly lower class ranks in 1983 than in 1973. Since the percentage of females tested has consistently risen during this period, it is possible that the female college-bound senior group responding to the SDQ in 1973 was more able and homogeneous than the comparable female group responding in 1983. The issue is complicated by the fact that, in 1973, the response rate to the SDQ was considerably lower than in 1983 for *both* males and females. Thus, there also exists the possibility that in earlier years, the sample of female college-bound seniors responding to the SDQ was a higher scoring and more select group than the group that tended not to fill out the questionnaire. Furthermore, as mentioned previously, it is difficult to interpret variations in self-reported class rank (either over time or for particular groups), because to an unknown extent, such variations are due to uncontrolled sources, such as the point in the student's high school career at which this question was answered.

When estimated high school grade point average is considered in Table 9.15, over 50 percent of each

Table 9.13

Annual Parental Income, Number of Dependents in Family, and Plans to Apply for Financial Aid (1982-83 SDQ Questions 27, 41-43) (Ramist and Arbeiter 1983)

	Male	Percentages Female	Total	SAT-V Percentile Scores 25th	50th	75th	SAT-M Percentile Scores 25th	50th	75th
Income									
Under $6,000	3.2	4.2	3.7	265	340	427	310	380	479
$6,000-$11,999	8.1	10.0	9.1	298	374	452	332	409	502
$12,000-$17,999	11.1	12.2	11.7	329	401	473	355	436	526
$18,000-$23,999	14.2	14.4	14.3	346	414	487	373	453	537
$24,000-$29,999	13.9	13.1	13.5	358	425	496	388	469	552
$30,000-$39,999	19.3	18.5	18.9	367	434	506	398	480	564
$40,000-$49,999	12.0	11.2	11.6	378	445	519	411	494	578
$50,000 or Over	18.2	16.4	17.2	390	460	533	425	512	596
Number Responding (Income)[a]	375,620	407,548	783,168						
Median Contribution	$1,490	$1,260	$1,370						
Median Income	$29,800	$28,200	$29,000						
Dependents[b]									
Two	6.8	6.7	6.8	323	396	473	342	418	508
Three	18.2	18.9	18.6	348	419	493	368	449	536
Four	31.3	31.1	31.2	361	432	507	389	474	561
Five	24.7	24.2	24.4	358	429	504	392	479	566
More than Five	19.0	19.1	19.0	346	418	494	387	474	561
Median Number of Dependents	4.3	4.3	4.3						
Number Responding[c]	412,094	460,682	872,776						
Financial Aid									
% Planning to Apply for Financial Aid	74.6	77.1	75.9	352	426	503	381	468	557
Number Responding[d]	414,249	462,937	877,186						

[b]Number who responded to SDQ Question 43.
[b]The number of dependents includes all dependents (parents, children, others living with the family, etc.).
[c]Number who responded to SDQ Question 41.
[d]Number who responded to SDQ Question 27.

Table 9.14

Self-Reported Class Rank for ATP College-Bound Seniors in 1973, 1978, and 1983

	1973 Percentages Male	Female	Total	1978 Percentages Male	Female	Total	1983 Percentages Male	Female	Total
Top Tenth	21	26	23	21	23	22	21	23	22
Second Tenth	23	26	24	22	23	23	21	22	22
Second Fifth	27	26	27	27	26	27	27	26	26
Third Fifth	24	20	22	25	25	25	26	26	26
Fourth Fifth	3	2	3	3	3	3	4	3	3
Lowest Fifth	1	0	0	1	0	1	1	0	1
Number Responding	341,903	337,239	679,142	420,509	451,969	872,478	406,751	444,619	851,370
Median Percentile Rank	75.6	80.8	77.8	75.2	76.9	76.0	74.2	75.8	75.0

Table 9.15

Estimated High School Grade Point Average* for ATP College-Bound Seniors in 1973, 1978, and 1983

| | 1973 Percentages | | | 1978 Percentages | | | 1983 Percentages | | |
	Male	Female	Total	Male	Female	Total	Male	Female	Total
3.50-4.00	23	32	27	26	32	29	24	30	27
3.00-3.49	29	32	30	30	32	31	29	31	30
2.50-2.99	25	22	23	25	23	24	26	24	25
2.00-2.49	18	12	14	16	10	12	16	12	14
Less than 2.00	6	3	4	4	3	3	5	3	4
Number Responding	383,877	399,202	783,079	430,210	474,985	905,195	417,488	466,790	884,278
Mean	2.95	3.13	3.04	3.03	3.15	3.09	3.00	3.11	3.06
S.D.	.64	.59	.62	.61	.58	.60	.62	.59	.60

*A weighted high school grade point average is computed for each student who reported both his or her latest grade received and the number of years of study for at least one of five subject areas listed in Table 9.9. The method of computation is: multiply the numerical value of the latest grade received (4, 3, 2, 1, or 0) by the number of years of study in each subject area for which both are reported; add these subject-area products and divide the sum of the products by the sum of the years of study for all subject areas included in the product.

of the 1973, 1978, and 1983 groups report that they have averages *above* 3.00, (that is, grade B or better): 57 percent in 1973, 60 percent in 1978, and 57 percent in 1983. Mean grade point averages for the total group are correspondingly above 3.00 for each year. Grade point averages reported in 1978 were higher than those in the other years.

Also of interest is the trend for females to report higher grades and thus higher estimated grade point averages than males. The differences in the latter for these three years are .18, .12, and .11, respectively. As is true for the differences between sexes in self-reported class rank, the discrepancies are small but consistent, and may be affected to an unknown extent by variation in the time when the student responded to the question (that is, as a sophomore, junior, or senior).

The data in Table 9.16 suggest some consistencies in the typical high school curriculum for the total group of ATP registrants over a ten-year period. For the years 1973 and 1983, the table shows the mean number of years of study and the mean latest grade reported for courses taken in six subject areas, for both sexes and for the total group of respondents to the SDQ.

There is relatively little difference between 1973 and 1983 college-bound seniors in the mean number of years of study of English and Social Studies. In each case, approximately four years of English and three years of social studies are reported. By 1983, however, there is evidence of a decrease in the number of years of study reported for foreign languages and an increase in years of study in both mathematics and physical sciences for the total group. These trends are observed for both males and females. The average increases for females in mathematics and in physical sciences, .36 years and .44 years, respectively, are greater than the related increases for males, .22 and .33, but males continue to report more course work in these areas. The consistent dif-

Table 9.16

Mean Number of Years of Study and Mean Latest Self-Reported Grade in Six Subject Areas by Sex for ATP College-Bound Seniors in 1973 and 1983

| | Years of Study | | | | | | Latest Grade | | | | | |
| | 1973 | | | 1983 | | | 1973 | | | 1983 | | |
Subject	Male	Female	Total	Male	Female	Total	Male	Female	Total	Male	Female	Total
English	3.95	3.98	3.97	3.97	4.02	3.99	3.01	3.31	3.16	2.98	3.22	3.11
Foreign Language	2.23	2.61	2.42	2.07	2.23	2.23	2.74	3.11	2.93	2.88	3.16	3.03
Mathematics	3.54	3.14	3.34	3.76	3.50	3.62	2.78	2.81	2.80	2.87	2.85	2.86
Biological Sciences	1.35	1.36	1.36	1.38	1.41	1.40	2.99	3.08	3.04	3.01	3.07	3.04
Physical Sciences	1.72	1.23	1.47	2.05	1.67	1.85	2.87	2.90	2.89	2.94	2.94	2.94
Social Studies	3.32	3.25	3.28	3.25	3.21	3.23	3.16	3.25	3.21	3.18	3.21	3.19

ferences in years of study in various courses reported by males and females make the interpretation of differences in mean grade point averages difficult. Table 9.16 shows that females tend to report higher grades, on the average, than males in all subjects except mathematics and physical sciences in 1983. The most significant differences are shown in English and foreign languages.

Future Aspirations and Plans. A number of questions in the SDQ ask the students about their future aspirations and plans. Table 9.17 presents responses to the question that concerns the level of education the students intended to complete. Data are presented for the 1973, 1978, and 1983 college-bound seniors. For both males and females, there appears to be a trend for a smaller percentage of each group to be undecided. For males, the three percentages were 28, 21, and 18 in 1973, 1978, and 1983, respectively; for females, 27, 23, and 19. A larger percentage of both males and females plan on attending graduate school (either for a master's degree, M.D., or Ph.D.). For males, the three percentages were 42, 45, and 47; for females, 30, 37, and 42. Thus, the increased interest in graduate school is somewhat greater for females (42 percent in 1983 versus 30 percent in 1973) than for males (47 percent in 1983 versus 42 percent in 1973).

For each of the three years, a greater percentage of females plan to terminate their education after a bachelor's degree, while a correspondingly larger percentage of males plan to pursue graduate study. These sex differences, however, appear to be lessening over time, with diminishing differences of 8, 4, and 2 in 1973, 1978, and 1983, respectively, in the percentage seeking a baccalaureate degree and of

12, 8, and 5 in those seeking graduate training.

Students are also asked to indicate their first choice of intended field of study in college. Table 9.18 (page 186) presents the percentages of males, females, and the total group (based on 1983 data) choosing each of 27 fields of study together with the percentages indicating some other field of study or that they are undecided. Most of the 27 fields represent an aggregation of related specific subfields from which the student is asked to choose. For example, the field of Architecture and Environmental Design includes these additional specific subfields: 1) architecture, 2) city planning, and 3) urban development. History and Cultures includes 1) American, 2) ancient, 3) area and regional, and 4) European history. Some fields have a larger number of subfields: Engineering has 27, while Education has 21. The median number of subfields is approximately four. Also presented in Table 9.18 are the SAT-verbal and SAT-mathematical means for the males, females, and total group choosing each field. The five most popular fields of study for the total group in 1983 were as follows:

Top Five Choices for Intended Field of Study

Rank	Field	Percent Choosing
1	Business and Commerce	18.5
2	Health and Medical	14.7
3	Engineering	12.5
4	Computer Science/Systems Analysis	10.1
5	Social Sciences	7.2

The most popular intended fields of study for men are Engineering (22.2 percent), Business and Com-

---

Table 9.17

Educational Goals by Sex for College-Bound Seniors in 1973, 1978, and 1983

	1973 Percentages			1978 Percentages			1983 Percentages		
	Male	*Female*	*Total*	*Male*	*Female*	*Total*	*Male*	*Female*	*Total*
Two-Year Training	3	7	5	3	4	4	3	3	3
Associate of Arts Degree	1	3	2	2	4	3	1	3	2
B.A. or B.S. Degree	25	33	29	29	33	31	32	34	33
M.A. or M.S. Degree	19	19	19	24	22	23	28	25	26
Doctoral Degrees	23	11	17	21	15	18	19	17	18
Undecided	28	27	27	21	23	22	18	19	18

Table 9.18

Percentage of 1983 ATP College-Bound Seniors Indicating Intended Field of Study and
Associated SAT Mean Scores for Males, Females, and Total Groups

	Percentage Choosing Field of Study*			SAT-Verbal Mean			SAT-Mathematical Mean		
	Males	Females	Total	Males	Females	Total	Male	Female	Total
Agriculture	1.7	0.8	1.2	388	424	400	436	433	435
Architecture/ Environmental Design	2.7	0.7	1.6	406	431	412	484	489	485
Art	2.1	4.6	3.4	406	405	405	429	416	420
Biological Sciences	3.1	3.1	3.1	470	476	473	520	498	508
Business and Commerce	17.0	19.8	18.5	407	398	402	468	428	445
Communications	3.3	4.0	3.7	441	448	445	460	434	445
Computer Science/ Systems Analysis	11.8	8.5	10.1	425	397	413	508	454	484
Education	2.0	6.7	4.5	372	400	384	415	419	418
Engineering	22.2	3.9	12.5	444	471	448	573	543	539
English/Literature	0.9	1.8	1.4	526	510	515	516	478	490
Ethnic Studies	0.0	0.0	0.0	380	386	384	377	396	388
Foreign Languages	0.3	1.3	0.8	487	478	480	506	475	481
Forestry/Conservation	0.9	0.2	0.5	409	444	417	447	452	448
Geography	0.1	0.0	0.0	416	433	420	456	461	457
Health and Medical	8.6	20.1	14.7	457	415	427	524	443	465
History and Culture	0.7	0.4	0.5	478	509	490	478	477	478
Home Economics	0.1	0.8	0.5	357	388	384	392	410	408
Library Science	0.0	0.0	0.0	407	470	462	399	441	435
Mathematics	1.1	1.0	1.1	452	453	453	588	557	572
Military Science	1.4	0.1	0.7	435	418	433	476	446	473
Music	1.5	1.4	1.4	435	440	438	466	446	456
Philosophy and Religion	0.5	0.2	0.4	461	465	462	494	473	487
Physical Sciences	2.7	1.0	1.8	498	491	496	572	531	560
Psychology	1.4	5.1	3.3	451	434	437	477	443	449
Social Studies	7.2	7.1	7.2	466	456	461	496	458	476
Theater Arts	0.6	1.5	1.1	458	438	443	462	432	440
Trade and Vocational	0.9	0.7	0.8	350	346	348	399	368	385
Other	1.0	0.8	0.9	390	402	396	439	417	428
Undecided	4.2	4.3	4.2	434	445	440	490	472	480

*Percentages less than .05 are shown as 0.0.

merce (17.0 percent), Computer Science/Systems Analysis (11.8 percent), and Health and Medical (8.6 percent). For females, the most popular fields are Health and Medical (20.1 percent), Business and Commerce (19.8 percent), Computer Science/ Systems Analysis (8.5 percent), and Social Sciences (7.1 percent). Thus, these choices for males and females are similar, except for the fact that Engineering was one of the four most popular fields for men, but not for women, while Social Sciences was one of the four most popular fields for women, but not for men.

There are differences among the average SAT scores of the groups interested in different areas. Student groups (including both males and females) with the highest SAT-verbal averages are those planning to study English and Literature (515), Physical Sciences (496), and History and Cultures (490). The highest SAT-mathematical averages were earned by students intending to study Mathematics (572),

Physical Sciences (560) and Engineering (539). The groups tend to show higher mathematical scores than verbal scores on the SAT, reflecting the pattern for the total group (on the average, across all fields students score 43 points higher on SAT-mathematical than on SAT-verbal sections). However, there are several fields of study for which the difference between the students' SAT-mathematical score and SAT-verbal score does not follow this pattern. For example, the verbal scores of students intending to study English and Literature exceed their mathematical scores by 25 points, on the average. On the other hand, in some fields the mathematical score is unusually higher. Thus, students expressing interest in Computer Science and Systems Analysis have mathematical scores that are 71 points greater than their verbal scores, while groups interested in Physical Science and Mathematics have mathematical scores which are, on the average, 64 and 119 points, respectively, higher than their verbal scores.

The differences between males and females on the SAT-verbal sections and SAT-mathematical sections for the total 1982-83 cohort are: verbal, 8 points (males 427, females 419) and mathematics 47 points (males 491, females 444). These sex differences for the group as a whole are approximately reflected in Table 9.18 for many of the groups choosing the various fields of study. However, some notable exceptions occur, as, for example, in Agriculture, where females earned SAT-verbal scores 36 points *higher* than males (males 388, females 424), and SAT-mathematical scores only 3 points lower than males (males 436, females 433). Other fields attracting a relatively superior female group, in comparison with the male group, are Architectural and Environmental Design, and Geography.

The interpretation of these sex differences must be somewhat guarded, of course, for there is sufficient breadth to a category that it may include groups of males and females pursuing somewhat different interests. Thus, in the Health and Medical area, males, on the average, score higher than females on both the verbal and mathematical sections. In fact, the difference in this category between the sexes on the SAT-verbal sections is 42 points, favoring males, the largest observed difference. However, this merely reflects the facts that proportionately more of the males choosing this response are interested in becoming physicians, while more of the females are considering nursing. Nursing candidates (male or female) score lower than physician candidates (male or female) on both verbal and mathematical scores.

Students have shown a steadily increasing or decreasing interest in a number of areas of study since 1975. Table 9.19a, b, and c (see below and pages 188-189) presents the percentages of males and females choosing each area for each year. The areas showing fairly steady declines of 2 percent or more are: Education and Health and Medical. Subject areas showing fairly steady gains in popularity are Computer Science and Systems Analysis, Business and Commerce, and Engineering. Fewer students describe themselves as Undecided.

Table 9.19a

Percentage of Males Indicating Selected Fields of Study as First Choice, 1975 through 1983*

Year	1975	1976	1977	1978	1979	1980	1981	1982	1983
Agriculture	3.4	3.3	3.0	2.7	2.4	2.1	2.0	1.9	1.7
Architecture/ Environmental Design	3.4	3.3	3.1	3.1	3.1	3.3	3.2	3.0	2.7
Art	2.0	2.2	2.2	2.3	2.3	2.3	2.3	2.2	2.1
Biological Sciences	N/A	5.2	4.7	4.3	3.9	3.6	3.4	3.3	3.1
Business and Commerce	13.5	14.0	15.4	17.2	18.2	18.5	17.6	17.5	17.0
Communications	3.1	3.2	3.1	3.2	3.4	3.4	3.5	3.4	3.3
Computer Science/ Systems Analysis	2.1	2.3	2.7	3.2	4.0	4.9	6.5	8.8	11.8
Education	4.1	4.2	3.9	3.5	3.1	2.8	2.6	2.2	2.0
Engineering	12.9	15.9	16.6	17.6	18.9	20.4	21.5	22.5	22.2
English/Literature	1.5	1.3	1.1	1.0	1.0	0.9	0.9	0.9	0.9
Ethnic Studies	0.1	0.1	0.0	0.0	0.0	0.0	0.0	0.0	0.0
Foreign Languages	0.4	0.4	0.3	0.3	0.3	0.3	0.3	0.3	0.3
Forestry/Conservation	1.8	2.4	2.4	2.1	1.8	1.6	1.4	1.1	0.9
Geography	0.0	0.1	0.1	0.0	0.1	0.0	0.1	0.1	0.1
Health and Medical	N/A	11.6	11.0	10.1	9.7	9.2	9.0	8.5	8.6
History and Cultures	1.8	1.6	1.2	0.9	0.8	0.8	0.7	0.7	0.7
Home Economics	0.1	0.1	0.1	0.1	0.1	0.1	0.1	0.1	0.1
Library Science	N/A	0.0	0.0	0.0	0.0	0.0	0.0	0.0	0.0
Mathematics	2.8	2.2	1.9	1.7	1.4	1.2	1.2	1.1	1.1
Military Science	N/A	1.8	1.7	1.6	1.4	1.4	1.4	1.4	1.4
Music	2.1	2.0	2.1	2.0	2.0	1.9	1.8	1.6	1.5
Philosophy and Religion	0.9	0.8	0.7	0.6	0.6	0.6	0.6	0.5	0.5
Physical Science	N/A	3.8	3.7	3.6	3.5	3.3	3.1	2.9	2.7
Psychology	2.1	2.0	1.7	1.6	1.5	1.5	1.4	1.3	1.4
Social Sciences	N/A	6.9	8.6	9.3	8.3	7.7	7.4	7.2	7.2
Theater Arts	N/A	0.6	0.7	0.8	0.9	0.9	0.8	0.7	0.6
Trade and Vocational	N/A	1.0	1.1	1.2	1.3	1.3	1.2	1.1	0.9
Other	N/A	2.7	1.6	1.2	1.2	1.2	1.2	1.1	1.0
Undecided	7.2	5.0	5.2	4.8	4.9	4.7	4.8	4.5	4.2

*Percentages less than .05 appear as 0.0.

Table 9.19b

Percentage of Females Indicating Selected Fields of Study as First Choice, 1975 Through 1983*

Year	1975	1976	1977	1978	1979	1980	1981	1982	1983
Agriculture	1.5	2.0	1.6	1.3	1.2	1.1	1.0	0.9	0.8
Architecture/ Environmental Design	0.6	0.7	0.7	0.7	0.8	0.9	0.8	0.8	0.7
Art	5.5	5.5	5.7	5.8	6.2	5.8	5.4	5.0	4.6
Biological Sciences	N/A	4.4	4.0	3.8	3.6	3.3	3.2	3.1	3.1
Business and Commerce	9.6	11.3	13.2	15.6	17.3	18.8	19.4	19.8	19.8
Communications	2.3	2.8	2.9	3.1	3.5	3.8	4.0	3.9	4.0
Computer Science/ Systems Analysis	1.1	1.4	1.6	2.0	2.7	3.5	4.8	6.7	8.5
Education	13.8	12.9	11.9	10.6	9.5	9.0	8.6	7.4	6.7
Engineering	0.9	1.4	1.7	1.9	2.3	2.9	3.2	3.8	3.9
English/Literature	3.3	2.6	2.4	2.2	2.2	2.0	1.9	1.9	1.8
Ethnic Studies	0.1	0.1	0.0	0.0	0.0	0.0	0.0	0.0	0.0
Foreign Languages	2.3	2.0	1.8	1.6	1.5	1.4	1.4	1.3	1.3
Forestry/Conservation	0.5	0.8	0.8	0.7	0.6	0.6	0.4	0.3	0.2
Geography	0.0	0.0	0.0	0.0	0.0	0.0	0.0	0.0	0.0
Health and Medical	N/A	23.7	23.5	22.1	20.7	19.5	19.3	19.3	20.1
History and Cultures	1.1	0.9	0.7	0.5	0.5	0.4	0.4	0.4	0.4
Home Economics	1.8	1.4	1.3	1.3	1.2	1.1	1.0	0.9	0.8
Library Science	N/A	0.2	0.2	0.1	0.1	0.1	0.1	0.0	0.0
Mathematics	1.9	1.6	1.4	1.2	1.1	1.0	1.0	1.0	1.0
Military Science	N/A	0.1	0.1	0.1	0.1	0.1	0.1	0.1	0.1
Music	2.4	2.2	2.1	2.0	2.0	1.8	1.7	1.5	1.4
Philosophy and Religion	0.5	0.4	0.4	0.3	0.3	0.3	0.3	0.3	0.2
Physical Sciences	N/A	1.1	1.1	1.1	1.1	1.1	1.0	1.0	1.0
Psychology	5.0	5.1	4.7	5.0	5.2	5.2	5.2	5.2	5.1
Social Sciences	N/A	6.8	7.9	8.7	8.0	7.8	7.4	7.3	7.1
Theater Arts	N/A	1.6	1.7	1.8	2.0	2.0	1.9	1.7	1.5
Trade and Vocational	N/A	0.8	0.8	0.9	1.0	0.9	0.9	0.8	0.7
Other	N/A	1.9	1.3	0.9	1.0	1.0	0.9	0.9	0.8
Undecided	5.9	4.5	4.5	4.2	4.4	4.5	4.8	4.5	4.3

*Percentages less than .05 appear as 0.0.

The SAT Score Decline

The data in Table 9.20 (page 190) and in Figure 9.2 (page 191) essentially constitute the "score decline," the much discussed gradual decrease in the average score obtained by students taking the College Board SAT over the years from 1963 to 1979, when the scores began leveling off. The phenomenon has been the subject of much concern and intense scrutiny from about 1974.

No brief discussion can review all the hypotheses that have been generated, the data collected, and the complex studies reported in connection with the decline. The reader is invited to read *On Further Examination* (College Board 1977), the report of a select committee chaired by Willard Wirtz, which was convened by the College Board and ETS and charged with the responsibility of evaluating the meaning of the decline. The report is based upon a body of special studies commissioned by the panel during its deliberations. There is a great deal of other relevant material on the subject, some of it in the general press, some in special studies by research centers and educational institutions.

The major findings of the Wirtz panel may be stated as follows:

1) The decline was not an artifact of any changes in the nature or difficulty of the SAT or the result of errors in the scaling and equating processes. It was real, reflecting a decline in the verbal and mathematical abilities of the cohorts of students taking the SAT. It affected not only the SAT but also other major testing programs.

2) The decline was significant. It was not unimportant. The sizable shifts in test performance commanded continuing attention and efforts toward understanding and explanation.

3) The decline did not lessen the usefulness of the SAT for its fundamental purpose of predicting performance in college courses. The test continued to correlate well with college performance.

Table 9.19c

Percentage of Total Group Indicating Selected Fields of Study as First Choice, 1975 Through 1983*

Year	1975	1976	1977	1978	1979	1980	1981	1982	1983
Agriculture	2.4	2.6	2.2	2.0	1.7	1.6	1.5	1.3	1.2
Architecture/ Environmental Design	2.0	1.9	1.9	1.8	1.8	2.0	2.0	1.8	1.6
Art	3.8	3.9	4.0	4.1	4.4	4.1	3.9	3.7	3.4
Biological Sciences	N/A	4.8	4.3	4.0	3.7	3.4	3.3	3.2	3.1
Business and Commerce	11.5	12.6	14.3	16.3	17.8	18.6	18.5	18.7	18.5
Communications	2.7	2.9	3.0	3.1	3.5	3.6	3.7	3.6	3.7
Computer Science/ Systems Analysis	1.6	1.9	2.1	2.6	3.3	4.2	5.6	7.7	10.1
Education	9.1	8.7	8.1	7.2	6.5	6.1	5.7	5.0	4.5
Engineering	6.7	8.4	8.8	9.4	10.1	11.1	11.8	12.6	12.5
English/Literature	2.4	1.9	1.8	1.6	1.6	1.5	1.4	1.4	1.4
Ethnic Studies	0.1	0.1	0.0	0.0	0.0	0.0	0.0	0.0	0.0
Foreign Languages	1.4	1.2	1.1	1.0	1.0	0.9	0.9	0.8	0.8
Forestry/Conservation	1.2	1.6	1.6	1.4	1.1	1.0	0.9	0.7	0.5
Geography	0.0	0.0	0.0	0.0	0.0	0.0	0.0	0.0	0.0
Health and Medical	N/A	17.9	17.6	16.4	15.5	14.7	14.4	14.2	14.7
History and Cultures	1.4	1.2	0.9	0.7	0.7	0.6	0.5	0.5	0.5
Home Economics	1.0	0.8	0.8	0.7	0.7	0.6	0.6	0.5	0.5
Library Science	N/A	0.1	0.1	0.1	0.1	0.0	0.0	0.0	0.0
Mathematics	2.4	1.9	1.7	1.4	1.2	1.1	1.1	1.1	1.1
Military Science	N/A	0.9	0.9	0.8	0.7	0.7	0.7	0.7	0.7
Music	2.2	2.1	2.1	2.0	2.0	1.8	1.7	1.6	1.4
Philosophy and Religion	0.7	0.6	0.5	0.5	0.4	0.4	0.4	0.4	0.4
Physical Sciences	N/A	2.4	2.3	2.3	2.2	2.1	2.0	1.9	1.8
Psychology	3.6	3.6	3.3	3.4	3.4	3.5	3.4	3.4	3.3
Social Sciences	N/A	6.8	8.2	9.0	8.2	7.8	7.4	7.2	7.2
Theater Arts	N/A	1.1	1.2	1.3	1.5	1.5	1.4	1.3	1.1
Trade and Vocational	N/A	0.9	1.0	1.1	1.1	1.1	1.1	0.9	0.8
Other	N/A	2.3	1.4	1.1	1.1	1.1	1.1	1.0	0.9
Undecided	6.5	4.8	4.8	4.5	4.6	4.6	4.8	4.5	4.2

*Percentages less than .05 appear as 0.0.

4) The interpretation of the decline is made very difficult by the fundamental problem with ATP descriptive statistics: they are nonnormative, so that shifts from year to year will almost certainly be due to shifts in self-selection patterns in the taking of the tests. The Wirtz panel saw population shifts as a significant factor in decline from 1963 to 1973.

5) Changes in the schools and in society at large could be responsible for, or be contributing to, the decline on a causal basis. The expansion of television, the changes in family patterns, and the introduction of a wider range of elective courses in the schools may all have been possible factors contributing to the decline. However, no adequate basis for a firm conclusion on these points exists.

The possibility of a decline was noted in the first edition of this handbook (Angoff 1971). Chapter authors Schrader and Stewart observed, however, that over the entire 13-year period they examined, the limited range of changes made these patterns (p. 90), ''relatively subtle trends.''

By 1972 the true scope of the decline was easily recognizable. A number of studies were launched in an effort to establish whether the decline was an outcome of the statistical operations. Of these, the most significant study was undertaken by Modu and Stern (1977) and is entitled, *The Stability of the SAT-Verbal Score Scale*. This study compared the results of using verbal tests developed in 1963 with verbal tests developed in 1973 to assess student competence in samples of students in 1975. The tests were randomly assigned to the samples. If there were no equating errors, the means of the random samples should be equivalent, regardless of the form used. As might be anticipated, there was evidence of some scale drift on the verbal sections. However, these modest changes were in a direction that would mask decline, rather than contribute to it. That is, because of the small shifts, an SAT-verbal score in 1973

Table 9.20

Scholastic Aptitude Scaled Test Score Means
(1951-52 Through 1982-83)

| Academic Year | SAT-Verbal Means | | SAT-Math. Means | |
	All Test Takers*	College-Bound Seniors†	All Test Takers*	College-Bound Seniors†
1951-52	476		494	
1952-53	476		495	
1953-54	472		490	
1954-55	475		496	
1955-56	479		501	
1956-57	473		496	
1957-58	472		496	
1958-59	475		498	
1959-60	477		498	
1960-61	474		495	
1961-62	473		498	
1962-63	478		502	
1963-64	475		498	
1964-65	473		496	
1965-66	471		496	
1966-67	467	466	495	492
1967-68	466	466	494	492
1968-69	462	463	491	493
1969-70	460	460	488	488
1970-71	454	455	487	488
1971-72	450	453	482	484
1972-73	443	445	481	481
1973-74	440	444	478	480
1974-75	437	434	473	472
1975-76	429	431	470	472
1976-77	429	429	471	470
1977-78	429	429	469	468
1978-79	426	427	466	467
1979-80	423	424	467	466
1980-81	425	424	468	466
1981-82	424	426	468	467
1982-83	423	425	467	468

*Student is counted as many times as he or she is tested.

†Each student is counted only once, using the latest score earned (figures for 1967 through 1971 are estimates; figures for 1972 through 1983 are actual).

was about 10 points higher than it would have been had there been no drift. Further support on this topic is given in a study by Beaton, Hilton, and Schrader (1977), *Changes in the Verbal Abilities of High School Seniors, College Entrants and SAT Candidates between 1960 and 1972.*

In addition to the verification of the scaling and equating procedures, the test development procedures were studied. No new item types had been introduced into the SAT-verbal sections during the period of the decline; for the SAT-mathematical sections, the quantitative comparison item type replaced the data sufficiency items in 1974. But studies of the performance of the several item types indicated that the decline affected *all* of them, and about equally. Braswell and Petersen (1977) examined the possible impact on the equating process when items

become obsolete. Because the score decline is a direct result of lower average performance on equating items that are reused over a period of several years, it is important to examine equating test content for possible obsolescence. While there was a considerable fluctuation in the difficulty of individual questions over time, it was not possible to attribute these changes to curricular or societal factors, except in a limited sense and only for a few mathematics items.

The significance or importance of the decline cannot be assessed without a values framework. The Wirtz panel summarized it well (College Board 1977, p. 5): ". . . the decline in score means that only about a third of the 1977 test takers do as well as half of those taking the SAT in 1963 did. . . . [A] decline of this magnitude, continuing over a 14-year period, following a previous period of stable or even slightly rising score averages, is clearly serious business." It then added (p. 5), "Any generalization from the SAT statistics has to be carefully qualified. It should not be extended to cover the situation of American youth as a whole or the overall effectiveness of the learning process." In the introduction to its report, the panel wrote (p. 1): "The public's interest, however, is not in the psychometric technicalities of the SAT score decline but in its implication regarding what is widely perceived as serious deterioration of the learning process in America. More and more high school graduates show up in college classrooms, employers' personnel offices, or at other common checkpoints with barely a speaking acquaintance with the English language and no writing facility at all."

From a technical point of view, of course, the implications of the declining scores for the quality of American education are by no means so simple as the public may believe. The Wirtz panel did not commission any studies of the extent to which the lower SAT scores of students led to poorer performance in college in any absolute sense. Such studies would tend to be equivocal, because the criterion itself, performance in college, is not stable.

In general, however, the evidence for sustained validity on the part of the SAT over the period of score decline (1963-1980) was clear and strong. It led the Wirtz panel to note unequivocally (p. 9), "We have also looked into the question of whether the decline in the SAT scores has affected their validity as predictors of individuals' college performance. It has not."

The panel concluded, after reviewing statistics on the amount of time children spend watching television, that television has contributed to the decline. But they admitted this hypothesis could not be

Figure 9.2

Scholastic Aptitude Test Scaled Score Means, 1952 to 1983

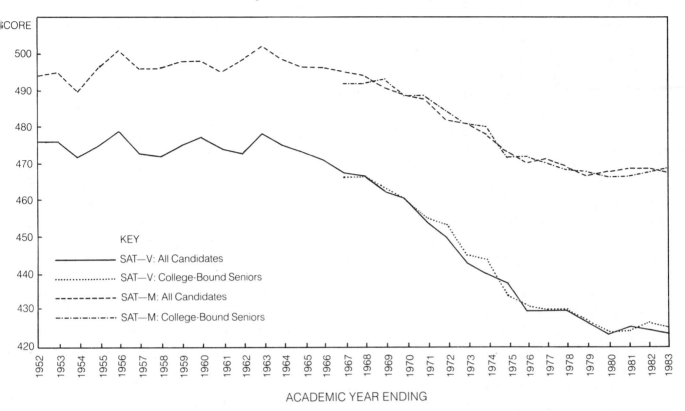

proved. They further cited such changes in education and society as the introduction of the "new math," the growth of the minimum competency movement, and the rising use of drugs and alcohol by youth. They made no special claim to have identified the specific causes of the decline, but they found substantial evidence for a conclusion which may, in the end, be all that can be said. The period covered by the score decline, they wrote (p. 43), ". . . has been an unusually hard one to grow up in."

Criterion-Referenced Testing

Within the last decade, there has been much discussion, within the measurement community, of criterion referencing. No single definition of criterion-referenced testing has won acceptance by all measurement specialists. However, in general, criterion-referenced testing attempts to describe each individual tested with reference to some critical standard or level, while norm-referenced testing offers description with reference to performance by a group. Norm-referenced interpretation has often been discussed in connection with the SAT. The SAT

has two characteristics that lend to its identification with norm referencing: 1) it is reported by means of scaled scores based on an arbitrarily selected reference group and 2) it is interpreted in terms of descriptive statistics, such as those published in the annual *National College-Bound Seniors* (College Board 1983d).

Angoff (1974) pointed out that the function of a scale, particularly the SAT scale, is not essentially normative. The origin of a scale, in the sense of its logical definition (as in the old English measures of yard and foot) does not really determine how it is used to interpret a single given measurement. The fact that the SAT scale is linked to a specific population at a specific time is not really related to norm-referenced testing. A given sample of individuals was used to define the scale, but they simply determine the numbers used as units of measurement, not the interpretation of these numbers.

The descriptive statistics are intentionally developed for essentially normative interpretations, which are often legitimate: the publication of descriptive statistics does not impede the extensive criterion-referenced applications of the tests. Criterion referencing is not really new, and there have always been criterion-referenced interpretations of tests,

191

even of the SAT. As Angoff put it, it is possible to come to "calibrate our own intuitions, . . . to know what the scores mean in terms of the tasks that people at various score levels can accomplish. . ." (Angoff 1974, inside back cover). When an admissions officer translates SAT scores into predictions of performance on a specific campus, this is a criterion-referenced interpretation.

Criterion-referenced applications for the Achievement Tests have been more commonly recognized. The use of the Achievement Tests in placement decisions is implicitly a criterion-referenced application. Although there is also extensive norm-like descriptive information for the Achievement Tests, they have not been criticized in the way that the SAT has been. In part, this reflects the differences in test content, for the Achievement Tests are fundamentally curriculum-based, while the SAT is not. It is easier to sense the underlying criterion-referenced logic for the Achievement Tests than it is for the SAT.

The great benefit derived from criterion-referenced testing lies in its work of defining and defending critical score levels, which produces insights into the nature of the test and its application. A criterion level may serve as an ideal, reflecting a performance level that cannot in fact be achieved by most of those tested. Nonetheless, this ideal standard may be appropriate, as in guidelines for physical fitness, if the goal is to raise the average level of performance. Such standards, then, may not be based on normative considerations. But normative considerations cannot be overlooked, for they are based on descriptions of reality. If the ideal is too remote from reality, it may need to be modified or abandoned. A college seeking a given average level of ability for its entering freshmen may find a steady decline in the number of students who achieve that fixed level. It would be necessary to reexamine the logic that led to the desired average in the first place and to reconsider the nature of student learning strategies. In the long run, the use of both norm-referenced and criterion-referenced approaches is probably superior to a reliance on either one alone.

Principal author: Thomas F. Donlon, with contributions by Janet A. Levy

Contributors or reviewers: William H. Angoff, Irving L. Broudy, Christopher C. Modu, Leonard Ramist, June Stern, and Nancy K. Wright

CHAPTER X

Special Studies

Introduction

The overview of special research studies provided in this chapter has been organized around five central problems to which the studies have been directed: coaching, test fairness, measurement technique, test content, and the score decline. With the exception of the score decline, these topics were also the focus of research reviewed in the first edition of this handbook. This continuity reflects a persistent concern to guide the development of the program so as to avoid inequity and inappropriate material or procedures. Virtually all College Board research on the Admissions Testing Program is aimed at providing the information needed to determine the best way to conduct the program.

As might be expected, much research has been concerned with the nature of the tests, the students tested, and the interactions between the students and the tests. This focus appears to give the research activity an applied quality. However, the Board has supported fundamental research in "true score" theory, in growth, and in the characteristics of colleges, all of which have applications beyond the particular decisions of the moment, and these research studies have contributed to an understanding of the fundamental nature of measurement and education. For example, the development of item response theory at ETS, notably by Lord and Novick (1968), has been significantly advanced by the availability of extensive information about the test score outcomes of the College Board programs.

This chapter by no means provides a description of all relevant work. There is a clear "research" dimension, for example, to certain standard program statistical activity such as test analysis and item analysis. Changes in test specifications or the introduction of new items are hypothesized to yield changes, and the standard statistical summaries confirm or deny these hypotheses. In addition, there are often small *ad hoc* studies of selected aspects of the Board's programs. For example, Swineford (1971) studied the relationship between the item characteristics of various forms of the SAT and the probability that the forms will yield a maximum raw score that scales to 800. While sharply focused on a problem peculiar to the nature of the Board's programs and its score scales, Swineford's study had potential interest for measurement specialists in general. Over the years, the standard Admissions Testing Program activity has been a primary stimulus for the development of measurement models for scaling and equating, and studies such as Swineford's have contributed to knowledge in this specialized area. While not ordinarily published in the professional journals, the results of such studies are often accessible to the measurement community through a series of technical reports. In reviewing research activity, therefore, the number of possible studies is very large, and only a representative sampling of Board-sponsored special studies, illustrating their general nature, has been included in this chapter.

It should be kept in mind that studies of College Board tests are also carried out at colleges and universities, primarily by independent researchers. Such studies are common in connection with the SAT, because SAT scores are widely available as a part of college records, and because these scores are very useful as ability measures in a variety of research efforts concerned with individual ability and institutional functioning. In the six-year span between the development of the 7th and 8th *Mental Measurement Yearbooks,* (Buros 1972, Buros 1978) for example, the editors identified 365 articles that related to the SAT. Only a fraction of these studies were sponsored by the College Board. While such research is rarely applicable to a particular question about the SAT, it provides valuable supplementary evidence concerning the properties of College Board tests.

Coaching and Preparation for Tests

Perhaps no aspect of the Admissions Testing Program has provoked as much controversy as the question of the value of special preparation for tests. Because of the importance of this question in connection with the SAT, discussions of the topic were presented in Chapter III and again in Chapter VII. The discussion here presents a summary of recent related research.

The belief that some effective, relatively short-term treatment would increase test score performance is intrinsically attractive to some students. They are often encouraged by the advertisements of commercial coaching schools, which claim to be able to influence test performance through a brief, intensive course and to ensure higher scores, often without teaching subject matter, by equipping the student with special "testwiseness" techniques that provide a basis for an effective answer even without a knowledge of the material.

The Board has sponsored a number of studies, involving a variety of treatments and conducted by a diverse sampling of coachers. In almost every case, the coachers fully believed in the potential merit of their work, and the student-subjects were reasonably motivated. In fact, most often, the students were planning to take the SAT as a formal part of their college admissions procedure. The aggregate outcome of this body of studies has resulted in College Board statements that assert that short-term coaching, defined as a brief and intensive effort to alter the score by teaching testwiseness and quickly reviewing mathematics and verbal question material, most often fails to yield the level of increases in SAT scores that would warrant the students' investment of time and money.

Over the years the Board has offered a variety of materials to the student to guide preparation, including, where possible, sample test materials. In 1978 a new booklet, *Taking the SAT,* was introduced. The sample test provided in this booklet was a complete recent SAT form, which had been used operationally in the program and was now "retired" from active operational use. At the same time, the related discussion in the booklet was expanded. This practice has been continued in more recent editions.

To evaluate the effectiveness of *Taking the SAT*, the College Board commissioned a special study by Powers and Alderman (1979). The study addressed the question of the extent to which access to the booklet by some students, but not by others, might produce a score benefit. The study did not find a significant score gain by the students using the booklet, in spite of the fact that the booklet contained a complete prior form of the test and suggested strategies for preparing for the tests. In spite of this failure to identify a short-term route to a score increase, the overall response to the booklet more than justified

its introduction by the Board. Students reported numerous benefits from the preparation it provided, and most were extremely pleased with the opportunity to work through a complete form of the test.

Within the period of this review, the Board also investigated the effectiveness of programs of special preparation offered by secondary schools (Alderman and Powers 1979). While the greatest problems with coaching have related to the claims of the commercial coaching schools, some programs offered by secondary schools also claim to increase test scores. Most secondary school test preparation programs focus on familiarizing students with tests and on achieving a relaxed, stress-free testing, but some of them rival the activity of the commercial firms. In view of the importance of the topic, eight different high school verbal test preparation programs were studied.

The results of this study of interventions by high schools corroborated the patterns in earlier studies. The eight high schools examined had all volunteered to participate in the study, and they were responsible for their own test preparation curriculum. Student subjects were randomly assigned to the school-sponsored program, and the control subjects were assured that they would have access to the program after the study and before their own SAT administration. This was done to reduce the anxiety of the control group that the treatment group would have an advantage on actual test taking (if the courses proved effective). The authors found that the effect of the special preparation on the SAT-verbal score was about eight scaled score points, a difference of approximately one raw score point on the test. These results, according to the authors, support the logic of the Board's position, particularly that time for education is a valuable resource and should be devoted to productive study.

An appraisal of coaching for the SAT was undertaken by an office of the Federal Trade Commission (FTC) in 1978. Using score data secured from College Board files at Educational Testing Service, the FTC attempted to compare the performance of students who were coached by commercial organizations with that of students who were not. The FTC report, after pointing to the numerous logical problems with the design and analysis of the study, described an average gain of approximately 25 to 30 points attributable to the efforts of one of the two schools studied. The FTC data were extensively reanalyzed by ETS, in a study reported by Messick (1980). This reanalysis basically confirmed the findings that one coaching school had demonstrated score increments while the other had not, and also yielded similar overall results as to the size of the increment: 20 to 35 points for both the verbal and mathematical sections. The reanalysis pointed out, however, the confounding of coaching with self-selection factors that is inherent in the FTC model, and the limitations on the power of the analysis of covariance to correct this deficiency. Messick concluded (p. 3), "... it is impossible to determine with any confidence whether the effects obtained in the FTC study may be attributable in whole or part to uncontrolled self-selection factors rather than to any impact of the coaching program as such."

Most emphasis in studies on coaching is placed on the possibility of a score gain on the test as a whole, and on the nature of the treatment or intervention. But the coachability of individual item types is an important consideration, particularly from the standpoint of the test construction process. If an item type is unduly susceptible to coaching, it is probably better to select a suitable alternate item type for the test, where available. An inquiry into the coachability of item types was the focus for an important study by Pike and Evans (1972) on the effects of special instruction for three kinds of mathematical aptitude items.

When the study was undertaken, the mathematical section of the SAT consisted of two kinds of items: regular math and data sufficiency. The data sufficiency item type was relatively complicated, but it had important advantages because it required less calculation and could be answered more rapidly. When a new item type, quantitative comparisons, was developed, it was suggested that items of this type replace the data sufficiency items, for quantitative comparison items appeared to secure the advantages of more rapid response but to avoid the complexity. The highly structured nature of the quantitative comparison items, however, led to concern that the item type might be inordinately susceptible to coaching.

In the Pike and Evans study, in contrast to previous studies of coaching, the instruction was highly systematic, with careful controls provided through student workbooks and teacher lesson plans. It was much more comprehensive than the studies considered in the College Board publication *A Statement by the College Board Trustees on Test Coaching* (College Board 1959; College Board 1965, 1968) and included a systematic review of basic geometric principles. It stressed analytic skills, such as simplifying quantitative terms that are being compared, and the use of inference in filling in informational gaps encountered in dealing with inequalities. In short, the instruction was fundamentally a specialized review course in mathematics.

The mean gains obtained by subjects instructed

for the complex item types, data sufficiency and quantitative comparison, were significant. In their evaluation, the authors considered hypothetical gains (p. 29): "If the SAT-M were made up entirely of either of the item formats . . . [quantitative comparison or data sufficiency], the intensive program of instruction described earlier could be expected to produce changes in the scores that could result in different admissions decisions for many of the students." The gains achieved for [regular mathematics] items were seen as "of less practical consequence."

In addition to these hypothetical results, the study permitted a determination of actual gains on the mathematical section of the SAT, and the average gain of a treated subject, pooling across all treatments, was approximately 35 points. But the control subjects also showed an average gain during the same six-week period. Messick (1980) concluded that about 16.5 points could be attributed to coaching. In addition, both the experimental subjects and the control subjects showed SAT-verbal gains even though there was no coaching on verbal material; the experimental subjects, approximately 16 points, the control subjects, 8 points. It seems likely, in view of this general improvement, that the school environment fostered heightened test performance. The experimental group's 16.5-point advantage over the control group on the mathematical section of the SAT is somewhat greater than the 10-point gain reported in previous studies, but the findings do not unequivocally reverse previous generalizations about coaching. For example, in the five-month period following the original coaching, the pattern of additional score changes for the subjects was as follows:

	Additional SAT-Verbal Score Changes	Additional SAT-Mathematical Score Changes
Originally Coached Groups	+ 21	+ 24
Originally Control Groups	+ 20	+ 29

During this time, the (original) control subjects were also coached in mathematics, to balance their preparation for the SAT. Furthermore, this second coaching was not restricted to specific item types as the earlier coaching was, but was aimed at the test as a whole. The pronounced impact in this study on the SAT-verbal score emphasizes the ambiguity of the findings. Coaching specifically aimed at the mathematical sections also produced relatively large gains for the uncoached verbal sections.

In spite of certain ambiguities, however, the Pike and Evans study raised important questions concerning the coachability of specific item types and the value of intensive mathematical refresher courses for the mathematical sections. In a review of prior work in the area of coaching and testwiseness, Pike (1978) suggested three goals for research in this area: 1) to maximize the fairness and validity of the SAT with regard to the effects of short-term and intermediate-term interventions; 2) to avoid discouraging concern and activity regarding test-preparedness *per se* but to "foster realistic understanding and expectations regarding possible outcomes . . ." (p. 72); and 3) to seek "a more basic understanding of the processes involved in test taking and contributing to aptitude test scores" (p. 74).

Particularly troublesome, noted the Pike report, are studies of coaching for the SAT that report large gains, but that lack control subjects and hence cannot establish that the gains were the results of coaching. The report cites as examples the studies by Marron (1965) and Pallone (1961), each of which found large gains in scores after coaching. However, Pike noted (p. 56) that there were shortcomings in both studies and a "need for positive . . . conclusions to be strongly supported by the research design and data." In conclusion, Pike called for further consideration of coaching aimed at specific item types, analogous to the Pike and Evans study.

Messick (1980) also summarized most of the then known research on coaching for ATP tests, concluding with comments on the implications of such research for testing policy and practice. In his discussion, Messick focused on the critical issue of whether score gains through coaching could ever be shown to be predictive of better college performance. If coached gains *are* predictive, adequate educational preparation of this type must be made available for all students. If they are *not* predictive, testing practices must be modified, if at all possible, to stop reflecting an extrinsic source of the variance. Finally, although pointing out that only further research could clarify the relation between special instruction and increments in ability, Messick hypothesized that the relationship was likely to involve the time spent in instruction (p. 67): ". . . it seems very likely that improvement of the comprehension and reasoning skills measured by the SAT, when it occurs, is a function of the time and effort expended. . . . The soundest long-range rule of preparation for the SAT would appear to be a secondary school program emphasizing the development of thought as well as knowledge." (For further discussions of coaching, see Chapters III and VII, and in particular, Tables 3.15 and 3.16.)

Related Studies. The general topic of test preparation continues to receive attention. Powers (1980) studied the various ways in which students use the available forms of preparation for taking the SAT. These preparation strategies are diverse in their intended purpose: some focus on increasing scores, others on decreasing anxiety, and still others on promoting familiarity with the format and general content of the test. The Board itself offers a number of preparation services, primarily through its widespread distribution of information booklets such as *Taking the SAT.* To provide a better understanding of the varied uses of preparation strategies by students, Powers summarized survey data from a sample of 2,024 students who registered to take the SAT at the administration in June 1978. At this time, *Taking the SAT* was just being introduced, replacing an earlier and shorter booklet, *About the SAT.*

Powers' data would seem to indicate that most students do not believe that cramming (intensive, short-term preparation) will improve SAT scores; only 5.8 percent responded that it will. Most students, however, (65.7 percent) saw some form of preparation as likely to improve SAT scores. Of the others, 26.2 percent were uncertain, and only 8.1 percent were in outright disagreement. For most students, preparation consisted of using College Board materials, reviewing a test preparation book, or reviewing course-related books. Only 15.7 percent reported attending a preparation or review session at school, and only 4.8 percent reported attending a review or coaching session outside school. This suggests, of course, that as many as 75,000 students may take out-of-school coaching in the course of a testing year, a not insignificant number. This is, however, a relatively small fraction of the approximately 1,500,000 students who take the SAT each year. Students tended to use several methods in preparing: the modal number of preparations in about 700 responses was two (175 responses). Further, most students did prepare, using some strategy or another.

Lockheed, Holland and Nemceff (1982) studied the special characteristics that might define the subgroup of students who elect to order disclosed materials. To provide some information, a file was prepared containing data for all students who took the SAT in March, May, or June 1980, in New York State, and who subsequently requested materials. These requestors constituted approximately five percent of the total group of students. A random sample of the same size was drawn from the ranks of the nonrequestors, and comparative analyses were made.

Responses to the SDQ and the Registration Form,

plus SAT-verbal and SAT-mathematical scores, were compared, and a very large number of significant differences between the groups were observed. These univariate comparisons were supplemented with multiple regression analyses and with multiple contingency table analysis. The findings indicated that requestors reported higher parental education, higher family income, higher proportion of Asian ethnic identities, less need for financial aid, higher SAT-mathematical scores, higher class standings, and higher levels of doctoral aspirations.

These characteristics were in marked contrast to the predictions by proponents of test disclosure legislation that test disclosure would have socially equalizing consequences. Because requestors were more often eleventh grade students than nonrequestors were, the inference that requesting disclosure materials was intended to facilitate a retest performance was modestly supported. On the other hand, an inference that requesting was intended to facilitate inspection for potential bias was not supported; women and non-Asian minorities were not more likely to request than White males.

Stricker (1982) studied the impact on scores of the special situation created by new practices of disclosure: examinees repeat a test, taking a second form after spending time with the disclosed materials relating to the initial test form. While relatively few students elect to obtain the post-administration SAT Question-and-Answer Service, the issue could ultimately be of considerable practical importance, in view of the substantial proportion of examinees who repeat the test.

Stricker focused on two experimental samples, each consisting of 2,500 students who took the test in May 1981 and who were sent disclosure materials at no cost to themselves. These experimental samples differed in the content of the letter that accompanied the material. The "not encouraged group" merely had the sending of the materials explained to them. The "encouraged" group was given this explanation plus a paragraph asserting that the materials would be useful in taking the test over again. A control group of 2,500 students received nothing.

About 50 percent of each sample chose to repeat the test in October 1981. These decisions could have been affected by the mailings, but the Ns of 1,248 for the control group, 1,229 for the "not encouraged" group and 1,272 for the "encouraged" group suggest very small effects, if any. The samples were not significantly different in initial or in retest performance, suggesting that the disclosed material and the motivating letter failed to have an impact on the level of retest performance. Further analyses established that the materials and letters had at most a

negligible impact on estimates of reliability or of concurrent validity associated with the scores. The author recognized that the study was carried out in a changing information context—all students in the samples had routinely received *Taking the SAT,* many had taken the PSAT, some possibly had purchased disclosed forms other than the one used in the study—and that this changing context created multiple causation patterns that make interpretation difficult, but the results do clearly negate the hypothesis that simple access to and use of disclosure materials will alter retest performance on the test.

Repeated Testings. The phenomenon of score changes upon repeated testings with the SAT is a perennial source of problems in score interpretation. The basic distributions are presented in Chapter III, where the results for a number of repeater patterns (April-November, April-December, etc.) over a number of years are reported. Such gains and losses between test administrations largely reflect the influence of measurement errors, as students with low initial scores stand to gain points upon retesting, while students with high initial scores will tend to lose points.

Because of this large role for measurement error, the observed changes are unreliable measures of individual growth and development for the abilities tapped by the test. But it is difficult for lay persons to understand the changes, particularly the larger ones, in terms of inherent error. It is far simpler for students, parents, and counselors to accept all score increases as a reflection of real growth in academic ability. Often, the increases are seen as the result of some particular event in the interval between testing, such as a test preparation course. Since the course was undertaken in the hope of an increase, the increase is not seen as the outcome of error. Decreases, on the other hand, are seen as indicating either that the administration of the test was faulty or that school instructional programs may not be sufficiently vigorous.

The College Board has supported a number of studies intended to clarify the role of error in the observed changes. Studies by Alderman (1981a, 1981b) examined some of these issues. One facet of these studies centered on regression effects in score change data. Another facet considered the role of student self-selection. Students who elect to repeat the SAT seem to have some knowledge that their initial performance may have been lowered by a sizable, negative error of measurement, as reported in Alderman (1981a). As this study shows, repeating students' initial scores are lower than would be predicted from such associated information as their rank in class, their performance on equating tests, etc. Thus, the students electing to repeat seem to know that this underperformance has occurred and choose to repeat the test. The magnitudes of the underpredictions are not great, perhaps 5-10 SAT verbal or mathematical points, on the average, and there are ambiguities due to positive errors in the scores of students who elect to take only a single testing, but such magnitudes are plausible evidence that self-selection is related to error of measurement. This correlation invalidates a number of important models for studying score change.

Alderman (1981b) also carried out an estimation of average true score change as a function of initial level of SAT scores for both verbal and mathematical tests, and contrasted these estimated results with the observed results. Figure 10.1 presents the findings succinctly. While the observed points conform to the expected pattern of declining gain with increasing initial score, the estimated points yield lines much more unrelated to initial score. The study reveals positive true score changes of 10-20 points for both SAT-verbal and SAT-mathematical, but the average estimated true score change for the lowest scoring students is very little different from the average change for the highest students.

Alderman (1981b) concludes that the common practice of relating score changes on admissions tests to their standard error of measurement is probably inappropriate when there is true change in the relevant abilities over the time between administrations. He suggested as an alternative the use of the standard error of estimate and of the intercept constant as a framework for evaluating score change. Regardless of the basis for comparison, he noted, the inherent unreliability of difference scores suggests that little weight can be given to the observed change in admissions or placement decisions.

Figure 10.1

Observed and Estimated True Score Change by Initial Level of SAT-Verbal and Mathematical Scores (Alderman 1981b)

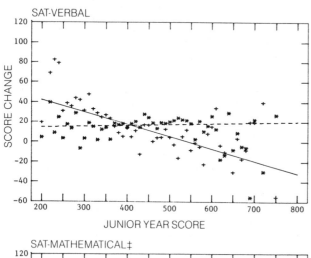

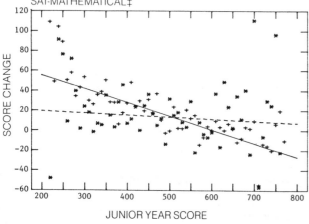

+ Observed Points   ------ Best fitting line, Observed Points
* Estimated Points   ——— Best fitting line, Estimated Points

‡Points for estimated score change at initial score levels of 230 and 770 fall beyond the bounds of the ordinate.

Item and Test Fairness

The first edition of this handbook was published in 1971, at the beginning of an era of intense concern for the fairness of educational and psychological tests and for the problems of providing appropriate access to higher education for minorities. Selective admissions tests do not determine decisions concerning minority admissions, but they do enter into such decisions, and they must be carefully scrutinized for fairness. In the interval from 1971 to 1983, the College Board supported a fairly sizable body of work dealing with the issues of test fairness. No attempt is given here to summarize all of this activity. Instead, attention is focused on work directed at establishing item fairness. Following this discussion, selected other studies carried out during the interval are reviewed.

A number of methods for assessing item fairness have been used at ETS. Reports of eight studies of the SAT, spanning the interval from the administration of November 1974 to the administration of November 1980, have been prepared to date. Descriptive information concerning these studies is summarized in Table 10.1. Brief discussions of the delta-plot, interaction analysis, and standardization methods are provided below.

Delta-Plot Methodology. The delta-plot method is described by Angoff (1972, 1982; Angoff and Ford

Table 10.1

Descriptive Summary of Eight Studies of Item Fairness

Study	SAT Administration	Method	Author(s)	Groups Studied
I	November 1974	Delta-Plot	Stern (1975)	Black Students and White Students
II	December 1974	Delta-Plot	Cook and Stern (1975)	Black Students and White Students
III	April 1975	Delta-Plot	Stern (1978)	Black Males, White Males, Black Females, and White Females
IV	November 1975	Delta-Plot/Interaction Analysis	Blew and Ishizuka (1978)	Black Students and White Students
V	December 1975	Delta-Plot/Interaction Analysis	Blew and Stern (1979)	Black Students and White Students
VI	December 1977	Standardization	Dorans and Kulick (1983)	Males and Females
VII	March 1980	Standardization	Kulick and Dorans (1983a)	Subgroups Defined by Level of Father's Education
VIII	November 1980	Standardization	Kulick and Dorans (1983b)	White Students and Oriental Students

1973). It calls for the calculation of item-difficulty values for different subgroups on the set of items under study. These item-difficulty values are expressed on the delta scale (described in Chapter II), which ranges from 5.0 to 21.0, with a mid-point of 13.0. Very difficult items for a group are represented by deltas of 18-21 (10 percent or fewer pass); very easy items correspond to deltas of 5-8 (90 percent or more pass).

Pairs of deltas, one pair for each item, are plotted on a graph, with the deltas for one group related to the x-axis while the deltas for the other group are read on the y-axis. Typically, this set of points forms a long, cigar-shaped, narrow ellipse. Figure 10.2,

for example, is a delta plot that depicts the performance of White male and female students on the 60 mathematics items in the April 1975 form of the SAT. Note that in this case items that are easy for one group tend to be easy for the other group, while items that are hard for one group tend to be hard for the other. Most items cluster around the major axis of the ellipse, which is the line from which the sum of squared distances of the delta points is a minimum. The distance d_i for the ith item from the major axis line is defined by

$$d_i = \frac{a\triangle_{ji} - \triangle_{ki} + b}{\sqrt{a^2 + 1}}$$

where delta j_i and delta k_i are the deltas for item i in groups j and k, and a and b are the slope and intercept of the major axis of the ellipse.

The correlation between deltas is a useful index, summarizing the degree of relationship between delta values portrayed in the delta plot. The magnitude of the correlation reflects the degree to which a set of items rank in the same order of difficulty for both subgroups of test takers. Very high correlations imply that the rank orders of item difficulties are nearly the same in both subgroups. Low correlations imply the existence of item-by-subgroup interaction, that is, different orderings of item difficulties by different subgroups.

The delta-plot method determines which items are farthest away from the major axis of the ellipse. These items, called "outliers," exhibit differential subgroup performance that is not expected given the delta-plot method's adjustment for differences in group ability. Because "outliers" are farthest from the major axis of the ellipse, they are the items that

Figure 10.2

Comparative Difficulty of SAT-Mathematical Questions (April 1975 Form) for Samples of White Males and Females Approximately Equal in Verbal Ability

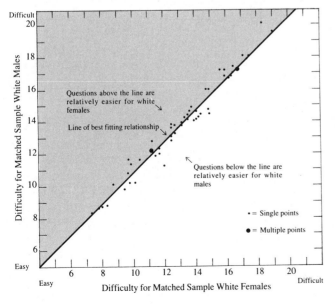

199

are least consistent with the line of relationship suggested by the data in the delta plot. To determine which items are outliers, items are ordered by their d_i values (their distance from the major axis) and an arbitrary cut point is used to classify them.

Given an associated distance from the major axis line for each item, a natural question arises: Do certain item types, for example analogies, tend to lie on one side of the axis or the other? A corollary question is: Are certain item types more likely to be outliers than others? These are questions that the delta-plot method allows researchers to address.

Interaction Analysis. A principal limitation with the delta-plot method of analysis is that it tends to make outliers of items that differ in item discriminating power whenever the subgroups differ in ability as measured by total score.* In an effort to circumvent this problem, a supplementary analysis of the outliers identified by the delta-plot method may be employed. This supplementary analysis, called Item-by-Subgroup Interaction Analysis, or the log-linear method, is a variant of the log-linear methodology for categorical data, described in Bishop, Feinberg and Holland (1975) and in Alderman and Holland (1981). It involves contingency table analyses of group differences in correct *and* incorrect performance at each of a number of score intervals. In applying this procedure at Educational Testing Service, the College Board scale of 200-800 is broken up into 100-point intervals: 200-290, 300-390, etc. Then group differences in correct *and* incorrect item performance within each score interval are assessed via chi-square tests. In particular, these tests are performed on the outliers identified by the delta-plot method to determine whether some factor other than group differences in total score level is producing the apparent item-by-group interaction.

Standardization Methodology. The log-linear method has decided advantages, but when group ability distributions differ, the approximately equal ability subgroups produced by the clustering of test takers into 100-point intervals are not actually equal in ability. More recently the statistical method of standardization has been used to examine whether or not there are "unexpected differences in item performance" across different subpopulations of the test-taking population. An item is exhibiting unexpected differential item performance when the probability of correctly answering the item is lower for test takers at a given score level from one group than for test takers at this same score level from another

group or groups. For example, if male and female students with the same total test scores do not have equal probabilities of successful performance on the item, this difference in probabilities is taken as evidence of unexpected differential item performance for male and female test takers at this score level.

Previous methods used to appraise unexpected differential item performance typically have been hampered by sensitivities to differences in overall subpopulation ability or differences in item quality (discrimination). The standardization methodology, however, controls for differences in both subpopulation ability and in item quality. Standardization means that differences on one variable have been controlled prior to making comparisons between groups on another related variable. A general approach to assessing unexpected differences in item performance via standardization is described in Dorans and Kulick (1983). The essential features of the method as applied to the SAT are as follows: Using the standard College Board 200-to-800 SAT scale one can establish 61 individual ability levels (200, 210, 220, etc.). The probability that a test taker at a given ability level will correctly answer an item can be estimated by the observed percent correct among those with the given scaled score. Studies of unexpected differential item performance focus on differences between two or more groups. One group is arbitrarily designated as the *base* group. The base group is used to estimate the conditional probability of successful item performance at a given score level. Usually the group that provides the most stable estimates of the conditional probabilities across the entire scaled score range is selected as the base group. Typically, but not always, this is the largest group. The remaining groups are study groups, those being compared to the base group.

Several indexes used in the standardization process are defined: P_b is the overall percent correct in the base group for an item. P_{bs} is the percent correct at ability level s in the base group. P_g is the overall percent correct in the study group. P_{gs} is the percent correct at ability level s in the study group. P_b and P_g are not directly comparable when the base group and the study group have different marginal ability distributions. It is necessary to calculate the expected item performance of the study group, $\hat{P}_g$. $\hat{P}_g$ is computed by taking a weighted sum of the 61 conditional probabilities of successful item performance observed in the base group, P_{bs}, where the relative frequencies at each of the 61 scaled score levels in the study group serve as the weights. Use of the study group in this fashion ensures that the most important conditional probabilities are weighted most heavily, that is, conditional probabilities at those

*For related discussions of this problem, see Angoff 1982, Cole 1978, Hunter 1975, Lord 1977, and Shepard 1981.

score levels most frequently attained by the study group. The difference (D_g) between P_g and $\hat{P}_g$, ($D_g = P_g - \hat{P}_g$), is one index of unexpected differential item performance. If there is no unexpected differential item performance between the study group and base group, D_g should equal zero. A positive D_g indicates that the study group exceeds its expected performance, while a negative D_g indicates that the item is harder than expected for this group.

The most precise measure of differential item performance is at the individual scaled score level, $D_{gs} = P_{gs} - P_{bs}$. These differences can be combined across score levels in a variety of ways to obtain a number of summary indexes of unexpected differential item performance. Plots of these differences, as well as plots of P_{gs} and P_{bs} are helpful to visualize the quantification of unexpected differential item performance (see Figure 10.3a and b). One of the

Figure 10.3a

Examples of Conditional Probability Plots for Male and Female Students on Items with Low and High Levels of Unexpected Differential Item Performance (Items from SAT Form 2SA5)

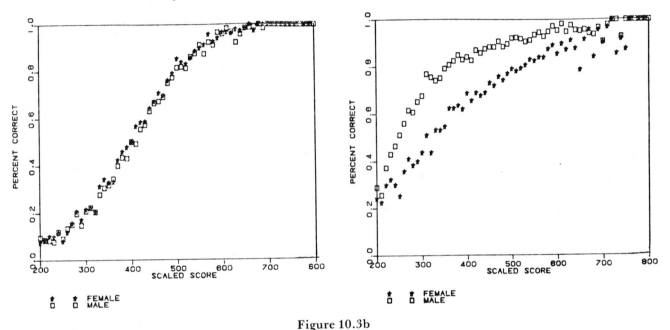

Figure 10.3b

Examples of Difference Plots Corresponding to the Two Items Plotted in 10.3a

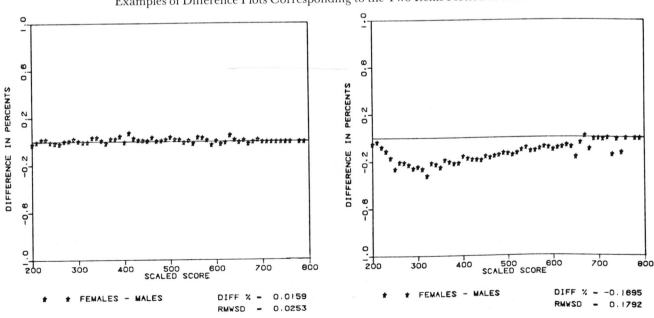

201

most informative of these indexes is the Root Mean Weighted Squared Difference ($RMWSD_g$). The $RMWSD_g$ for an item is obtained by squaring each difference in conditional probabilities of successful item performance between the study and base groups, D_{gs}, taking a weighted sum of these squared differences, and finding the square root of the weighted sum, where the relative frequency distribution of the study group serves as the weighting function. This index is never negative; consequently, every item will have a non-negative value of $RMWSD_g$. An item exhibiting substantial unexpected differential item performance will have a large $RMWSD_g$. An item exhibiting absolutely no unexpected differential item performance will have an $RMWSD_g$ equal to zero.

A problem faced by any investigation that seeks to detect and quantify unexpected differential item performance, regardless of methodology, is the determination of what level of unexpected differential item performance should evoke concern. In answer-

ing this question one must consider the fact that test instruments are always affected, to an unknown extent, by measurement error, and hence a certain indeterminate level of unexpected differential item performance is attributable to the unreliability of the test. In addition, test score is not a perfect measure of ability. In the first report using this approach (Dorans and Kulick 1983), an empirical determination was made concerning the practical cutoff point for values of $RMWSD_g$ using frequency distributions of the $RMWSD_g$ index. According to this determination, an item with an $RMWSD_g$ greater than or equal to .08 merits careful investigation, while an item with an $RMWSD_g$ less than .08 does not require additional study. Items with an $RMWSD_g$ greater than or equal to .16 are exhibiting unacceptable levels of differential performance. Although .08 is used as a cutoff in these studies, it is recognized to be arbitrary. Further investigations of the standardization methodology will provide a better empirical basis for determining an appropriate cutoff value.

Figure 10.4

Plot of Root Mean Weighted Squared Differences (RMWSD)* Between the
Conditional Probabilities of Success for Male and Female Students on
Verbal Items from One Form of the SAT

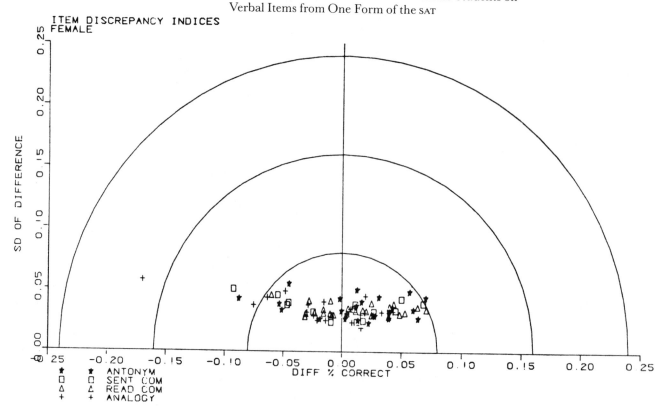

*RMWSD equals the distance from the origin to the point representing the item. Projection of each point on the horizontal axis yields the difference between Pg and $\hat{P}g$, D_f, for that item. Projection of each point on the vertical axis yields the standard deviation of the weighted differences, an index of residual crossover.

An informative graphical display of the principal indexes of unexpected differential item performance is presented in studies employing the standardization methodology. This display permits easy visual identification of outliers, as well as any patterns exhibited by item type groupings (see Figure 10.4).

Findings Using Delta Plots. As indicated in Table 10.1, studies I-V all deal with the differential performance of Black students and White students, while study III also compares male and female students. All five studies indicate that the operational items of the SAT and TSWE, in general, work in fundamentally the same way for both Black and White students. That is, items appeared to be relatively easy or hard for Black and White students (as well as male and female students) in consistent ways, as evidenced by the high correlations between deltas for the subgroups.

The results from these five studies should be approached with the following considerations in mind: the outliers identified by the delta-plot method are *relative* deviates; they are those items that *relative* to all other items in the test tended to deviate the most from the major axis of the ellipse describing the delta plot. In addition, the cutoffs in studies I, II, IV, and V would by definition yield about 20 percent outliers; 17 for the 85-item SAT-verbal and 12 for the 60-item SAT-mathematical. About 50 percent of the outliers of each item type should favor Black students and 50 percent should favor White students. Similar expectations may be developed for TSWE.

Only the verbal results deviate from expectation in terms of the total number of outliers. The studies identified a few (two to three) more verbal outliers per form than expected. But the Black/White student breakdown for outliers was in accord with expected results: for both verbal and mathematical tests, approximately 51 percent of the items identified as outliers favored Black students, while for TSWE the comparable figure was 54 percent.

Some results deviated from expectation, however. For the verbal test, the obtained number of analogy and sentence completion items identified as outliers tended to exceed expectations by two to three items (the observed number of reading passage and antonym items identified as outliers tended to match the expected number). For TSWE, more usage items and fewer sentence completion items than expected were identified as outliers.

In addition, the Black/White student breakdown deviates substantially from the expected 50/50 outcome at the item type level. The analogy and sentence completion outliers from the verbal test tended

to favor White test takers, while the reading passage and antonym outliers tended to favor Black test takers. To a much lesser extent, slight tendencies for item type differences were observed on the mathematical sections and the TSWE. In studies I, II, and IV, the quantitative comparison item type favored the Black test takers, while the regular mathematics items favored the White test takers. But in study V, the finding was reversed. For TSWE, in studies II, IV, and V, the sentence correction item type favored Black students, while the usage item type favored White students. In study I, this finding was reversed.

Study III employed a different approach in an effort to control for ability level differences. Samples of Black male, Black female, White male, and White female students were approximately matched using results on a short verbal test. The matching was incomplete because of the imperfect relationship between scores on the short verbal test and SAT-verbal, TSWE, and (in particular) SAT-mathematical. Consequently, equal ability samples were not obtained. The resulting "matched" samples, however, were closer in ability than the random samples employed in studies I, II, IV, and V. A fifth matched sample of White males was used to develop a cutoff guarding against random results at about the .01 level.

The results of the delta-plot analyses performed in study III exhibited some consistencies with the other four studies. The comparisons of Black students and White students of the same sex indicated that the analogy items were more likely to be outliers, and, as was the case in three of the four other studies, favored White students, on the average, more than any of the other three verbal item types. With respect to the mathematical test, study III revealed that, as in studies I, II, and IV, the quantitative comparison items slightly favored the Black students. However, delta-plot analyses on the matched samples of study III produced only a few mathematics outliers (six percent of the total number of items) in the comparisons of Black students and White students. It is interesting to note in passing that all five outliers in the female analysis favored White students over Black students, and Stern (1978) observed that four of these five outliers dealt with decimals as fractional values. The TSWE analyses in study III showed that in both comparisons of Black students and White students, 10 of the 35 usage items were identified as outliers, and of those, 60 percent favored Black students. In contrast, no sentence correction items were labeled outliers.

The same-race, cross-sex comparisons in study III revealed that female students of either race found analogies and reading passages, as a whole, easier than did male students of the same race, while male students of either race found antonyms and sentence completion items, as a whole, easier than did female students of the same race.

The sex comparison portion of study III produced an average of two more outliers than the race-comparison portion and suggested that outliers which were analogies and reading passage items favored female students, while outliers which were antonyms and sentence completion items favored male students. Earlier studies (Coffman 1961, Donlon 1973, Strassberg-Rosenberg and Donlon 1975) found that items dealing with aesthetic-philosophical and human relationships tend to favor females while items dealing with the world of practical affairs and science tend to favor males. In the White male/female student portion of study III, five of the six analogy outliers tended to deal with aesthetic and philosophical concepts and two of the three reading passage outliers pertained to an argumentative passage dealing with the subject of differences in the psychology of males and females. In contrast, the sentence completion and antonym outliers that favored White males tended to deal with science and the world of practical affairs. In short, the findings of the White male/female student comparison on the verbal test in study V were consistent with earlier research on sex differences and indicate that apparent item type differences may be associated with underlying item content. The number of mathematics and TSWE outliers indicated by study V was very small. The data did not allow any inferences to be drawn concerning male/female comparisons.

Findings Using Interaction Analysis. Studies IV and V attempted to control for ability level differences by applying the log-linear method to the items identified as outliers by the delta-plot method. The most striking features of this analysis are the results obtained for analogy items. In contrast to the other three verbal item types, for which fewer than 10 percent of the items remain outliers after supplementary analysis, 20 percent of the analogy items are still labeled as outliers, an average of four items per form. In addition, 100 percent of the analogy outliers favored White students. In contrast, the use of the supplementary log-linear analysis on mathematics items in studies IV and V removed *any* evidence of favoritism for these items, while application of the log-linear method to TSWE reduced the number of outliers in studies IV and V in half, with the usage items particularly affected. These results show that 10 percent or fewer of each item type on the Test of Standard Written English remained outliers after log-linear analysis and that roughly 50 percent of

them favored each racial subgroup.

Findings Using Standardization Method. The three studies completed thus far employing the standardization approach have focused on different subgroups. Study VI compared male and female performances, study VII analyzed subgroups defined by level of father's education (a variable highly correlated with socioeconomic status), and study VIII examined White and Oriental test takers.

In contrast to delta-plot methodology, where approximately one in five items was arbitrarily identified as an outlier, the standardization methodology identified very few items for more detailed review for possible content bias. Basically this is a function of differences in the cutoff levels that were used. Using the new criteria, only a single analogy item out of 85 verbal items in study VI exhibited a substantial amount of unexpected differential item performance. Four other items exhibited questionable levels, but two of these only slightly surpassed the cutoff. Of these five items two were analogies, two were antonyms, and one was a sentence completion item. Four favored males, including the most extreme item. Inspection of the content of the extreme analogy item revealed some plausible content problems for female students, as it required some knowledge of hunting and fishing, two traditionally male-oriented recreational activities.

Inspection of the doubtful sentence completion item revealed that the subject matter of the item, nuclear power politics, might also be something that males traditionally have shown more interest in than females. None of the content of the other items in question provided any obvious explanations for the observed differences.

None of the item types demonstrated any strong tendencies to favor one group over the other. The analogy items appeared to favor male students, but this was largely due to the presence of a single item, and when this extreme outlier is removed, the apparent advantage of the males is reduced by half. This finding is inconsistent with that of study III by Stern, which determined that females found analogies and reading passages easier than did males.

On the mathematics test there were only three items displaying questionable levels of unexpected differential item performance and none displaying substantial amounts. No generalizations are possible concerning performance on mathematics item type sets.

Similarly on the TSWE test, only two usage items (one each favoring males and females) exhibited enough unexpected differential item performance to merit closer inspection, while most of the items performed as desired. Examination of the content of these two items revealed that the item on which females performed better than expected concerns a female in a professional occupation, while the item on which females fell short of expectation deals with World War II. These content differences, however, would not appear to be sufficient explanations for the discrepancies in the observed and expected performance of females on these items.

In short, study VI uncovered very few items out of a total of 195 items as needing careful review for possible content bias. Of these only one exhibited a clearly unacceptable degree of unexpected differential item performance that could be attributed with some certainty to content bias.

Study VII divided the student population into three subgroups based on reported level of father's education. The education levels defining the groups were: less than high school diploma, high school diploma but less than bachelor's degree, and bachelor's degree or higher. Each item was evaluated twice, using each lower education group in turn as the study group, while maintaining "bachelor's degree or higher" groups as the base group.

Examination of discrepancy index summary statistics revealed little evidence of systematic unexpected differential item performance by either group on SAT-verbal, SAT-mathematical, or TSWE. The same conclusion was reached by inspection of frequency distributions and plots of item discrepancy indexes. The results indicate that the items on these SAT and TSWE forms are equally appropriate for all students regardless of father's level of education.

Study VIII divided the population into two subgroups based on reported answers to a racial/ethnic background question. The Oriental group (including Asian Americans and Pacific Islanders as well) was designated as the study group, while the White or Caucasian group served as the base group. Whereas studies VI and VII had found few or no outliers, this investigation singled out 52 (out of 195) items for consideration.

Although no individual verbal items exhibited clearly unacceptable levels of unexpected differential item performance, 14 verbal items were borderline and were examined more closely. Of these, five were analogies, four were antonyms, three were sentence completion, and only two were reading comprehension item types. Based on their relative proportions in the test, analogies are overrepresented and reading comprehension items are underrepresented among these borderline items. The item most favoring Oriental students and the item most favoring White students are both antonyms. Examination of the content of these 14 items provided no explanations for the observed differences in performance.

No items from SAT-mathematical exhibited clearly unacceptable levels of unexpected differential item performance. Nineteen items, however, displayed borderline levels and were examined individually. Of these 19 items, 12 favored the White students and 7 favored the Oriental students. Of the 12 favoring White students, 8 were regular mathematics types and 4 were quantitative comparison item types. The seven items favoring Oriental students consisted of five regular mathematics types and two quantitative item types. Since there are twice as many regular mathematics items as quantitative comparison types, the observed ratios are approximately equal to expectation. Both categories of item types showed fairly similar distributions of discrepancy indexes.

The TSWE results from study VIII indicate a greater overall level of unexpected differential item performance than any test studied with the standardization approach to date. Three usage items exhibited very high levels and 16 more items displayed borderline levels.

There was a marked difference between the TSWE item types in terms of group performance. Oriental students did much better than expected on sentence correction items, while these students fell short of expectations on the usage item types. All five sentence correction items that fell in the borderline range favored Oriental students. All nine of the borderline items that favored White students were usage items.

Overall, study VIII indicated that unexpected differential item performance between Oriental and White students was rather widespread on this particular test form. Since a substantial percentage of Oriental students ordinarily report that English is not their best language, it may be that some items covered verbal skills that this subgroup had not mastered. This notion was tested informally on the mathematics set of items. A test developer divided the mathematics items into categories of "verbally loaded" mathematics items, "pure" mathematics items, and "neutral" mathematics items. The verbally loaded category had the most unexpectedly difficult items for the Oriental students, while the pure mathematics category had the most unexpectedly easy items for this group. In situations where the test becomes multidimensional for one group but not for others, the scaled score will not be an effective control variable. The results of this study suggest that further investigations of the SAT/TSWE items need to be done where the Oriental group is restricted to those for whom English is the best language. Further, study VIII employed the smallest sample that has yet been used in connection with the standardization procedure, and it may be that a larger sample is needed to accurately estimate conditional percents.

Results from the standardization studies to date indicate that the standardization methodology is a useful and valuable technique for assessing unexpected differential item performance, enabling one to compare subgroups of markedly different abilities. The standardization methodology itself will continue to be improved. A more objectively determined cutoff point for outliers needs to be determined, as do techniques for analyzing relatively small samples. Modifications to the procedure are scheduled in order to determine the most appropriate analyses for pretests, where sample size limitations raise new concerns.

Other Evaluations of Fairness

An important trend in this area is an effort to integrate findings concerning "test bias" into a broader concept of "population validity," as exemplified in a Board-supported report by Breland (1979). Test bias, in most measurement discussions, is focused on differences in the predictions based on specific tests for two samples. Population validity, on the other hand, is an approach more analogous to the concepts of content and construct validity. In assessing population validity, measures are examined from a much broader perspective. Population validity is not to be viewed as a superior method of assessing bias, but as an effort to synthesize the often limited data from individual studies.

While much of the evidence in Breland's review relates to the College Board tests, it was not limited to these sources. The most commonly used college entrance measures were considered, including high school record and a variety of test-based indicators. Studies were grouped by methodology as well as sample. Thus, 35 studies that used a regression analysis and 41 studies that contrasted the correlation coefficients for specific subgroups were considered.

Breland reviewed the models used in a number of test bias studies, and was in agreement with the conclusion of Flaugher (1978), that considerable confusion exists in the area of test bias because there is no universal definition of the term. (Thorndike 1971, Linn 1984.)

Summarizing findings, Breland concluded that:

1. There is a fairly consistent overprediction of college performance for samples of Black students when the regression equation is developed from samples of completely or predominantly White students. An opposite phenomenon occurs for females predicted from male-based equations, where performance is underpredicted.

2. The high school record, used alone, results in the largest overpredictions for Black students. Combining high school record and test scores reduces these overpredictions.

3. When the correlation of test scores and college performance was summarized for different groups across colleges, high school record provided a slightly higher correlation than did test scores for White student samples, regardless of sex. For Black student groups, this general pattern was demonstrated for females and for combined-sex groups, but not for Black males.

4. For all groups, the combination of test scores and other predictors was superior to the use of either alone.

While Hispanic students were considered in Breland's study, a more extensive analysis of population validity for these groups was provided by Durán (1983). Durán synthesized data from a wide variety of sources. He confirmed Breland's view that (p. 92) "there was not convincing evidence that prediction of college grade-point average, by means of regression analysis involving high school grade-point average and college entrance test scores, differed dramatically for Chicano versus Anglo category students within the school sites studied." Nonetheless, he noted, accuracy of college grade-point prediction using equations is still an issue: ". . . the preliminary evidence seems to indicate that Anglos' college grades might be predicted about 9 percent more accurately than Hispanics' (principally Mexican Americans') college grades from high school achievement information and college admissions tests" (p. 93).

Both the Breland and the Durán reports reflect the shift away from a focus on a single study and toward the synthesis of all available information. Further, each exploration is not narrowly concerned with demonstrating the predictive properties of tests, but of the academic performance that is to be predicted. There is a breadth to the evaluations which is often missing in studies that focus primarily on bias more narrowly defined.

Patterns of Development

Minority students may face special problems of

school-to-college transition that adversely affect their first-year performance, after which performance levels may rise, so that later grades will be both higher and better correlated with predictor variables. This is, in effect, a "late bloomer" phenomenon.

A study by Wilson (1978) explored this possibility. At two undergraduate institutions, the cumulative records of cohorts of minority and nonminority students were studied over the years for evidence of a relatively greater improvement in academic performance for minority students. At the same time, the correlational validity of admission tests and school rank for predicting the cumulative grade-point average at the end of each semester in the eight-semester sequence, and persistence to graduation, was also studied.

The two pseudonymous institutions were quite different: Main Campus was a big, central campus of a complex state university system, while College was a selective liberal arts college for men. In each setting, the correlational analyses indicated that the admission variables used were at least as valid for predicting longer term criteria of success as they were for predicting first-year grade point average, for both minority and nonminority students.

The late-blooming hypothesis was definitely not substantiated in the data that provided trends in grade point average at Main Campus. At College, it was not substantiated in the early cohorts considered, but was modestly suggested in the later ones. The interpretation was complicated because at College the grades of *all* students in the later cohorts, both minority and nonminority, were higher than the grades earned by their predecessors. The minority grades simply rose more. Thus, both "inflationary" and "emergent late bloomer" rationales may be offered for the findings, and they cannot be rigorously evaluated from these data. The study points to these unexplained across-cohort increases in average grades and their implications for comparative validity studies generally (p. 78): ". . . limitations of the grade point average as an index of 'academic performance' in comparative validity studies . . . should be given special consideration in future research concerned with . . . minority and nonminority students."

The findings of this study as to the long-range validity of the SAT are consistent with the findings in the study of performance by Mexican American students reported in a study by Warren (1976). Most validation studies are not evaluations of the tests against longer, more cumulative data. Nonetheless, the levels of validation suggested by a correlation with first-year grade point average are reasonably congruent with the levels to be obtained from a longer range study, and may be underestimates, rather than overestimates of the long range values. Wilson observed that the typical college record-keeping process separated the admission descriptors from the indicators developed through study at the college. He advocated a continued effort to apply flow analytic principles to the understanding of academic growth and performance. He also observed that institutional researchers would find this an easier task if the recordkeeping practices were designed with this end in mind.

Failure to persist in higher education often represents a significant loss of potential for earnings and for job satisfaction for the individuals involved. Because of this, there have been a number of efforts by researchers to identify the factors that govern persistence. Such studies, however, commonly share a number of limitations: small samples, after dropout data, a narrow range of factors, and statistical techniques that fail to take spurious correlations or errors of measurement into account.

A study by Hilton (1982) attempted to avoid these limitations. The data source for the study was the approximately 21,000-person sample also studied by the National Longitudinal Study, which surveyed a number of high school seniors in 1972 and, through follow-up activity, in later years. The data analysis used both confirmatory factor analysis and causal modeling techniques. Persistence was defined in a generic sense to refer to all students who are, have been, or plan to be enrolled in college or vocational/technical schools after high school.

Of the sample, about 6,500, or 42 percent, never expressed any intention of attending postsecondary education and never did attend. About 6 percent had, in fact, attended some college by fall 1974 even though they had announced no plans to attend. About 8 percent had *not* attended any college by fall 1974 even though they had announced such plans. About 19 percent expressed plans to attend and did attend, but not continuously. Finally, about 25 percent of the sample expressed plans to attend and did attend continuously following graduation through fall 1974.

The causal modeling analysis indicated that persistence was influenced primarily by previous educational status, by high school curriculum, and by previous academic performance. These findings confirmed most prior work; but the unexpected result was that variables such as race, sex, socioeconomic status, and hours worked did not affect persistence, a finding that was at variance with some earlier reports.

The study contrasted results at two-year and four-year colleges, finding that persistence at two-year colleges was considerably lower than at four-year colleges. This was seen as not necessarily an undesirable career development for an individual; two-year college attendance, it was hypothesized, tends to be viewed as a relatively low-cost exploration by the student.

Measurement Techniques

The Admissions Testing Program confronts a number of difficult measurement problems in its efforts to provide adequate measurement in a variety of fields. To meet these problems, a carefully developed set of program practices has been implemented, as described in Chapter II. These practices are periodically modified where necessary, and research studies are undertaken to guide the changes. Since 1971 a number of such studies have been carried out, many of them centering on the application of IRT methodology. Several of these special studies are described here.

Methods for Pre-Equating. Item response theory (item characteristic curve theory) has a decided advantage for score equating, in that the item parameters have known relationships to the test scores. Thus, item parameters established at pretest can be developed into formulas for converting test raw scores to scaled scores prior to the first administration of the items as an assembled test. In effect, they can be used to "pre-equate" the test scores.

The general idea of such item-based pre-equating is not new; it was studied by Fan (1957) and by Swineford and Fan (1957), using conventional item descriptors of difficulty and discrimination. One clear problem with conventional item descriptors, however, is that they are group-specific; item response theory parameters, on the other hand, are, in theory, invariant from ability group to ability group. Thus, they should be a more satisfactory basis for equating when, as is most often the case, the item statistics from pretesting are based on several different samples.

To demonstrate the general properties of the method, Marco (1977) assembled a miniature verbal section of the SAT, drawing four to seven items from each of eight actual SATS, PSATS, and equating tests. The resulting 40-item test was then pre-equated, using the item-level information from the eight original exposures to the SAT population, and administered as a variant section in the December 1975 national administration of the SAT. This administration permitted the establishment of refer-

ence equating lines with which to compare the pre-equating.

The IRT pre-equating methods were compared with four different post-equatings. The post-equatings that were studied included: 1) equipercentile equating, 2) equating by setting observed score parameters equal, 3) equating by setting true score parameters equal, and 4) a three-parameter logistic post-equating. The fourth, a logistic approach, "probably provide(s) the most adequate criterion for the present study" (p. 23).

The pre-equating line deviated from the criterion line no more than any of the observed score equating lines, over the entire range (when evaluated by the mean square error). In the critical range from 400 to 600, the pre-equating line was as good as the true score line. While urging continued work, particularly with better criteria, such as a self-equated test, the author characterized the results as promising.

To evaluate pre-equating for the TSWE, Bejar and Wingersky (1981) studied two TSWE forms, E7 and E8, that had been equated to a common predecessor form, E5, by conventional linear methods, as part of the operational program activity. The pre-equating of E8 was disappointing, in that large discrepancies were found between the operational conversion line and the IRT-based equatings. These were attributed to the internal structure of E8 rather than to inherent limits in the methods themselves. E8 failed to conform to the factor structure of the other forms (no forms were unidimensional). For E7, results were more favorable, but nonetheless resulted in an overestimation of the mean and the underestimation of the standard deviation of the converted scores. These discrepancies were attributed to various deficiencies in the model, particularly to the use of formula scores. The model assumes a linear relationship between formula scores and rights only scores, but this does not happen in practice. The study concluded with the observation that successful pre-equating seemed assured as better methods for linking parameters are developed.

Equating Tests Across Languages. During the 1960s, the College Board created a test in the Spanish language, modeled on the Scholastic Aptitude Test. The new test was offered as a form of technical assistance to Puerto Rican educators, and to professionals in other Spanish-speaking countries, if appropriate. In time, there was a need for an equation of the scores yielded by the Spanish-language Prueba de Aptitud Académica (PAA) and the English-language SAT, so that a score on the scale would have the same educational and psychological meaning as a score on the other. A study by Angoff and Modu (1973) attempted to develop such an equation.

"Equating" test forms in the same language is not simple. When the model is expanded, so that two languages and cultures are involved, it is much more complex. For example, the concept of test difficulty cannot be dealt with as precisely as is normally expected of equating procedures. The principal methods have centered on the translation of entire tests from one language to another. The translated items are considered to have the same meaning and relative difficulty in both languages. But how is this demonstrated? A conceptually superior method involves administering the two tests to a special population, which is equally bilingual and bicultural, but such special populations are rare. No method is without some major flaw or practical problem.

The Angoff-Modu study focused its attention on a set of common or anchor items specifically assumed from an analysis of the data to represent the same psychological task to individuals of two different languages and cultures. One approach to verification of this assumption was to translate an item from English to Spanish and then back into English again. If the final item result was closely similar to the first version, the item, having survived the double translation essentially intact, was judged to be appropriate. The items were administered to different samples, in both Spanish and English, and difficulty indexes were developed for the items, one based upon its appearance in Spanish, the other on its appearance in English. Plots were prepared, showing the location of each item in a two-dimensional space defined by the two difficulty scales. The degree of correlation demonstrated for such plots is critical for the logic of the equating. In same-language tests, with two groups drawn from the same population, it is not unusual to observe a correlation of .98. In the Angoff and Modu study, initial correlations of .60 for verbal and of .85 for mathematical items were observed.

The authors noted (p. 8), "The fact that these correlations, particularly the correlation for the verbal items, are as low as they are suggests that the items do not have quite the same psychological meaning for the members of these two language groups. In a sense this is one of the most significant findings in the present study, since it reflects in the form of statistical data the very nature of the psychological difficulties that are likely to be encountered in making cross-cultural studies."

While the correlation for the total sample of verbal items was .60, the subset of items actually selected for use as verbal anchor items had a higher level of correlation: .85, and this higher level was sustained for two new samples. For mathematics, an equating subset with inter-language difficulties correlating .97 was obtained; this dropped, however, to .80 for new samples of subjects. Such a drop was not anticipated and resulted from four aberrant items. When these were removed, the equating set showed a correlation of .86 in the new samples. In all, there were 40 verbal and 25 mathematical equating items. These were prepared in the two languages, and administered in the variant sections of the PAA of November 1971 and the SAT of January 1972. This data collection set the stage for the process of equating.

Both linear and curvilinear methods of equating were used. The common items demonstrated a satisfactory parallelism to the operational forms in both Spanish and English for both verbal and mathematical items. While none of the methods demonstrated totally satisfactory properties, a line synthesizing the linear and the curvilinear information was derived. Reviewing the results, the authors commented (p. 27), "In view of possible misinterpretations of the data of this study, it will be useful to restate the limited purpose for which the present investigation was undertaken." Clearly, the accuracy of these conversions is limited by the appropriateness of the method used to derive them.

The complexities of the work are challenging, and the very simplicity of the operations and conclusions could lead to misinterpretation of these data. But the study could also be the basis for conclusions about the cultures as well as the tests and methods. The correlations in the item-difficulty plots could provide a valuable indicator of cross-cultural similarity that might have applications in other contexts.

Modifying Test Content

Change in measurement technique constitutes one major way in which the tests can evolve. Modifications of the content of ATP tests is another. A significant component of Board research over the years has centered on the evaluation of possible new material. Because of the many appropriate characteristics that new material must demonstrate, it is not easy to alter the tests dramatically over a short time, and many proposed modifications are revealed by research to be inappropriate from one standpoint or another. As might be expected, research has a primary role in the processes for evaluating proposed modifications.

New Item Types for the SAT. The first edition of this handbook described three studies that were efforts to develop new kinds of items for the SAT

(French 1957, French 1964, and Flaugher and Rock 1966). These studies considered a number of item types and focused in particular on their effectiveness for more able students. The studies, however, were somewhat contradictory in their import for the SAT, with the result that only a single minor change in the mathematical content specifications was justified.

Since the last handbook, the need to adjust the SAT to permit the introduction of the TSWE has led to the introduction of a new mathematical item type, the quantitative comparison format, which replaced the data sufficiency item type. Examples of this item type are included in Figure 3.4 in Chapter III.

This item type shares with the data sufficiency item type the important characteristic that it is possible to respond correctly to the question without calculating the precise numerical answer. Because two quantities are being compared, it is possible to determine which is the greater or lesser simply by a logical consideration of their mathematical properties. The result is an efficient use of a test taker's time in responding. The quantitative comparison items in this respect became a logical component of the SAT when the TSWE was introduced, because the overall time for the mathematical section of the SAT was reduced from 75 minutes to 60 minutes at that time. Use of quantitative comparison material enabled the test assemblers to preserve important values in test content coverage and in reliability, while not causing undue stress for the test takers with highly pressured timings.

The coaching study by Pike and Evans (1972), described earlier, established that the quantitative comparison items are, like the data sufficiency items, slightly more coachable than regular mathematics items. However, the several advantages they offer offset this disadvantage, and as the use of the booklet *Taking the SAT* has increased, the likelihood that students are unfamiliar with the item type has diminished.

The introduction of the quantitative comparison items required an investigation of their validity, and a number of special administrations were carried out through the Validity Study Service. In all, 16 groups in 12 colleges took a 55-item quantitative comparison test and a 60-item "conventional" mathematical section of the SAT. The results were summarized by Schrader (1973), who reported that there were no systematic differences between the tests with respect to validity coefficients, which were based on the grade point averages of the students. Quantitative Comparison items had a higher validity in six colleges (seven groups), and a lower validity in the remaining six colleges (nine groups), but the combination of high school record, SAT-verbal and the regular mathematical sections of the SAT was on the average no more highly predictive than the combination of high school record, SAT-verbal and the quantitative comparison items. As Schrader observed (p. 3), ". . . the overall validities of the two tests are quite similar."

Schrader also examined the question of systematic differences for specific student groups within the total sample. Considering the ability levels of the groups that demonstrated statistically significant differences in favor of the mathematical section of the SAT, he noted that (p. 4), "The Quantitative Comparison item type may be better suited to students who are relatively high in mathematical sophistication and confidence, and less well suited to students whose mathematical abilities are less well developed."

Evaluating Essay Tests in Social Studies. The College Board, while relying extensively on multiple-choice tests, has maintained a strong interest in the use of essay tests. The English Composition Achievement Test now offers interchangeable forms of the test: some are entirely objective, while others include a 20-minute essay section. English teachers, however, are not the only group of educators who are interested in the possible advantages of including essays in tests. Advocates of this approach for the American History and Social Studies Achievement Test were particularly eager to try the method, and a special study was conducted by Modu (1972).

The study was limited to psychometric considerations. Some of the educational value of including essays in the test could not be evaluated (for example, influences on classroom or individual preparation for the test). One advantage of requiring students to write essays is that they must supply and organize their own data, as opposed to recognizing the correct answer provided by the multiple-choice questions. In addition, students must formulate concise and logical arguments in their essays. This task was considered to be useful preparation for colleges, where essay test questions are invariably required. Lastly, the introduction of the essay in the examination would foster renewed attention to writing skills in high school history and social studies courses.

One criticism of including essays was the concern that literary skill might take precedence over content knowledge. Those who might succeed would be those who wrote well, rather than those who knew the most. Modu surveyed some of the likely issues concerning the problem of evaluating the essay, and concluded that the study could not evaluate such aspects of the essay. Rather, he stated that (p. 3), ''The decision having been taken to give a 20-minute essay as part of the one-hour Achievement Test, the task here is to determine what difference it then made.''

The results of the study demonstrated that the 20-minute essay section in the American History and Social Studies Achievement Test measured a different psychological trait than the 40-minute objective section that accompanied it. Furthermore, the essay test was, in fact, primarily a measure of achievement in the subject rather than one of writing ability. However, the unique contribution of the essay to the total test situation was minimal. The results of the 40-minute objective section, the verbal and the mathematical sections of the SAT, and the all-objective English Composition Achievement Test given at the same administration were considered in the evaluation.

A variety of statistical analyses support the conclusion. First, there was a very high correlation between a composite score based on the weighted combination of the other variables and a combination of this composite score and the essay result. The basic correlation was .997, only minutely different from the 1.000 which would be observed if the two values were identical. Even when the weight for the essay was increased to .3, that of the four-test composite, the correlation remained a very high .957. While the correlation between the essay and objective sections was quite low (.47, or .77 when corrected for attenuation), the overall contribution of the essay test was not large enough to make a difference. Further analyses, based upon factor analysis and discriminant analysis, established that the proportion of unique variance in the essay test was approximately 20 percent. The pattern of factor loadings suggested that this was subject matter knowledge, for the principal loading was on a factor defined by other components of the American History and Social Studies Achievement Test. Because the highest correlation with other parts of this test was with a section measuring factual knowledge, Modu concluded that the essay reflected primarily this dimension. On the strength of these findings, the essay was not introduced into this Achievement Test.

The Score Decline

The research program of the College Board was confronted with a need to develop relatively large amounts of urgently needed information in the years 1973-1977, as the phenomenon of the score decline emerged and caught public attention. The Advisory Panel on the Scholastic Aptitude Test Score Decline ultimately reported some 27 supplemental studies and discussion papers in connection with its summary report, *On Further Examination.* A number of these reports and papers are relevant here, for while undertaken in the special context of the score decline, they are not outside the mainstream of Board activity.

Perhaps one of the most important studies to emerge from the research on the score decline was a study by Beaton, Hilton, and Schrader (1977) which sought to obtain directly comparable data on changes between 1960 and 1972 in reading ability and other characteristics for high school seniors, college entrants, and those who take the SAT. The underlying motivation was to achieve a better understanding of the factors being advanced to explain the score decline. The superiority of the study to the point-in-time data that the Admissions Testing Program generates lay largely in the fact that by using random national samples, Beaton, Hilton, and Schrader avoided the limitations of self-selection on generalization. From one perspective, the study served as a validation of the ''scale-drift'' studies by Modu and Stern in 1975 and 1977 (see Chapter II), but its scope and the importance of its questions move it well beyond concern with just the scale.

The choice of the years 1960 and 1972 was determined by the availability, for each of these years, of extensive data for national probability samples of high school seniors, including such important follow-up data as entrance to college in the year after high school graduation. For 1960, the data had been collected as part of the massive Project TALENT research effort, and for 1972 as part of the National Longitudinal Study of the High School Class of 1972 (NLS). The study demanded a complex equating of the results of the TALENT and NLS scores; not all tests could be used. In a preliminary evaluation study, it was decided that the reading comprehension and the mathematical tests used in the two surveys were sufficiently similar to warrant formal study of their equivalence (Schrader and Hilton 1975). However, further evaluations limited the study to the reading comprehension tests alone.

The major questions and answers that the researchers reported were as follows:

1. *In what ways, if any, did the high school senior population change from 1960 to 1972?*

   The average 1972 senior was slightly older, more likely the child of parents who finished high school, more likely to have parents who were in professional, managerial, or white-collar positions, and less likely to be either an only child or a firstborn. The proportions of males and females was very nearly equal. And, in nearly every subgroup studied, the reading scores were lower for the 1972 group than for the comparable 1960 group. The percentage of high school seniors going on to college increased, however, and the percentage taking the SAT also increased.

2. *In what ways, if any, did the college entrant population change over this period?*

The 1972 entrants were slightly older, included a higher percentage of females, were more likely to have parents who attended college and more likely to have parents who were engaged in professional or managerial occupations. The decline in reading scores was about the same for the college entrants as it was for high school seniors. There was quite a bit of variation across subgroups in the amount of decline. However, no clear causal explanation emerged for a consideration of these variations.

3. *In what ways did the population taking the SAT change?*

In 1972, the SAT population had an increased proportion of women, a decreased proportion of college preparatory students, and more students from large families. The reading score decline for those taking the SAT was approximately *twice as large* as the drop for high school seniors or college entrants in general.

No single factor emerged to explain this difference in the experience of the population taking the SAT. Its implications for the score decline were that if performance changes for those taking the SAT more closely resembled those for college entrants and high school seniors, the pattern of observed decline would be different. The authors noted (p. 20), ". . . changes in the ability level of the high school seniors can account at best for only part of the SAT-verbal score decline."

In an effort to assess the contribution of various factors to the overall magnitude of the SAT decline, a method called partitioning analysis was used. This method separately considered the two kinds of changes occurring between 1960 and 1972: changes in the reading level ability distribution of high school seniors, and changes in the propensity to take the SAT at each reading ability level. Each of these changes could be expected to produce a changed SAT mean if it operated independently. The magnitudes of these changes were estimated. The baseline was 1960, and the questions included:

1. If the seniors in 1960 had elected to take the SAT in the same proportions that seniors in 1972 did, what would have been the effect on their mean? This effect is attributed to the change in SAT-taking patterns.

2. If the seniors in 1960 had had an ability distribution like that of the 1972 seniors, but maintained the same SAT-taking patterns, what would have been the effect on their mean? This effect was attributed to ability distribution changes.

The remaining known change, unaccounted for by these operations, was attributed to scale drift. This estimate of scale drift, analyzed separately, confirmed the Modu-Stern findings, which were that there was a drift of about one scaled score point per year *upward*, in a direction opposite from the course of the decline.

On the basis of the analysis, the authors concluded (p. 5): "We estimate that the change in the high school population by itself would have reduced the 1960 mean by 12 points, . . . whereas, the change in patterns of self-selection by candidates alone would have reduced the mean by 20 points. . . . The effect of scale drift was to *add* 11 points, resulting in the [observed total decline of 21 points]."

As mentioned in the discussion of score decline in Chapter IX, the Beaton, Hilton, and Schrader results seem to confirm the Modu and Stern results with respect to the direction and size of scale drift. Both studies tend to show that the score decline would have been about 10 points *worse* if there had not been a modest scale drift over the interval to counter it. (See the discussion in Chapter II and, in particular, Marco, Petersen, and Stewart 1983.)

Principal author: Thomas F. Donlon with contributions by Neil J. Dorans and Edward M. Kulick

Contributors or reviewers: William H. Angoff, Hunter M. Breland, Gary L. Marco, and June Stern

Bibliography

Abelson, Robert P. "Sex Differences in Predictability of College Grades." *Educational and Psychological Measurement* 12, no. 4 (1952): pp. 638-44.

Alderman, Donald L. *Measurement Error and SAT Score Change.* College Board Report 81-9. New York: College Entrance Examination Board, 1981a. (Also ETS Research Report 81-39).

Alderman, Donald L. *Student Self Selection and Test Repetition.* College Board Report 81-5. New York: College Entrance Examination Board, 1981b. (Also ETS Research Report 81-22).

Alderman, Donald L., and Paul W. Holland. *Item Performance Across Native Language Groups on the Test of English as a Foreign Language.* ETS Research Report 81-16. Princeton, N.J.: Educational Testing Service, 1981.

Alderman, Donald L., and Donald E. Powers. *The Effects of Special Preparation on SAT-Verbal Scores.* College Board Research and Development Report 78-79, No. 4. Princeton, N.J.: Educational Testing Service, 1979. (Also ETS Research Report 79-1).

Alloway, J. Evans, and Gertrude Conlan. "A Proposal for the Development of the Descriptive Tests of Language Skills." Princeton, N.J.: Educational Testing Service, 1974. Unpublished manuscript.

American Association of Collegiate Registrars and Admissions Officers. *A Guide to Postsecondary Institutions for Implementation of the Family Educational Rights and Privacy Act of 1974, as Amended.* Washington, D.C.: American Association of Collegiate Registrars and Admissions Officers, 1976.

American Psychological Association. *Standards for Educational and Psychological Tests.* Washington, D.C.: American Psychological Association, 1974.

Angoff, William H. "Basic Equations in Scaling and Equating College Board Tests." In *Scaling and Equating College Board Tests,* edited by Samuel S. Wilks, pp. 120-29. Princeton, N.J.: Educational Testing Service, 1961.

Angoff, William H. "Criterion-Referencing, Norm-Referencing, and the SAT." *The College Board Review* 92 (Summer 1974): pp. 2-6. (Also ETS Research Memorandum 74-1).

Angoff, William H. "Distinctions Between Aptitude and Achievement Tests." *College Board News* 5, no. 1 (September 1976): p. 3.

Angoff, William H. "A Technique for the Investigation of Cultural Differences." Paper presented at the annual meeting of the American Psychological Association, Honolulu, Hawaii, September 1972.

Angoff, William H. "Test Reliability and Effective Test Length." *Psychometrika* 18, no. 1 (March 1953): pp. 1-14.

Angoff, William H. "Use of Difficulty and Discrimination Indices for Detecting Item Bias." In *Handbook of Methods for Detecting Test Bias,* edited by Ronald A. Berk, pp. 96-116. Baltimore, Md.: Johns Hopkins University Press, 1982.

Angoff, William H. "The Validity of Negative Scores on the Scholastic Aptitude Test." Princeton, N.J.: Educational Testing Service, December 1964. Memo.

Angoff, William H., ed. *The College Board Admissions Testing Program: A Technical Report on Research and Development Activities Relating to the Scholastic Aptitude Test and Achievement Tests.* New York: College Entrance Examination Board, 1971.

Angoff, William H., and Susan F. Ford. "Item-Race Interaction on a Test of Scholastic Aptitude." *Journal of Educational Measurement* 10, no. 2 (Summer 1973): pp. 95-106.

Angoff, William H., and Christopher C. Modu. *Equating the Scales of the Prueba de Aptitud Académica and the Scholastic Aptitude Test.* College Board Research Report No. 3. New York: College Entrance Examination Board, 1973.

Angoff, William H., and William B. Schrader. *A Study of Alternative Methods for Equating Rights Scores to Formula Scores.* ETS Research Report 81-8. Princeton, N.J.: Educational Testing Service, 1981.

Armstrong, R., and J. Jensen. *Report on Massachusetts State College Study of SDQ Student Reported Grades.* Draft report, 1974.

Astin, Alexander W. *Four Critical Years: Effects of College on Beliefs, Attitudes, and Knowledge.* San Francisco, Calif.: Jossey-Bass, 1977.

Astin, Alexander W. *Preventing Students from Dropping Out.* San Francisco, Calif.: Jossey-Bass, 1975.

Bailey, Roger L. "The Test of Standard Written English: Another Look." *Measurement and Evaluation in Guidance* 10 (July 1977): pp. 70-74.

Baird, Leonard L. *Predicting Predictability: The Influence of Student and Institutional Characteristics on the Prediction of Grades.* College Board Report 83-5. New York: College Entrance Examination Board, 1983. (Also ETS Research Report 83-30).

Baird, Leonard L. *The Role of Academic Ability in High-Level Accomplishment and General Success.* College Board Report 82-6. New York: College Entrance Examination Board, 1982. (Also ETS Research Report 82-43).

Baird, Leonard L. *Using Self-Reports to Predict Student Performance.* College Board Research Memorandum 76-7. New York: College Entrance Examination Board, 1976. (Also College Board Research Monograph No. 7).

Beaton, Robert E., and John L. Barone. *The Usefulness of Selection Tests in College Admissions.* ETS Research Report 81-12. Princeton, N.J.: Educational Testing Service, 1981.

Beaton, Albert E., Thomas L. Hilton, and William B. Schrader. "Changes in the Verbal Abilities of High School Seniors, College Entrants, and SAT Candidates between 1960 and 1972." Appendix to *On Further Examination: Report of the Advisory Panel on the Scholastic Aptitude Test Score Decline,* Willard Wirtz, chairman. New York: College Entrance Examination Board, 1977.

Bejar, Isaac I., and Marilyn S. Wingersky. *An Application of Item Response Theory to Equating the Test of Standard Written English.* College Board Report 81-8. New York: College Entrance Examination Board, 1981. (Also ETS Research Report 81-35).

Bishop, Yvonne M. M., Stephen E. Fienberg, and Paul W. Holland. *Discrete Multivariate Analysis: Theory and Practice.* Cambridge, Mass.: MIT Press, 1975.

Blew, Edwin O., and Tomoichi Ishizuka. *College Board Item Bias Study of the Scholastic Aptitude Test and the Test of Standard Written English Form XSA4/E7.* Statistical Report 78-62. Princeton, N.J.: Educational Testing Service, 1978.

Blew, Edwin O., and June Stern. *College Board Item Bias Study of the Scholastic Aptitude Test and the Test of Standard Written English Form XSA5/E8.* Statistical Report 79-37. Princeton, N.J.: Educational Testing Service, 1979.

Bloom, Benjamin S., ed. *Taxonomy of Educational Objectives. Handbook I. The Cognitive Domain.* New York: David McKay, 1956.

Bloom, Benjamin S., and Lois J. Broder. "Problem Solving Processes of College Students." *Supplementary Educational Monograph* 73 (July 1950). Chicago, Ill.: University of Chicago Press.

Boldt, Robert F. "Study of Linearity and Homoscedasticity of Test Scores in the Chance Range." *Educational and Psychological Measurement* 28, no. 1 (Spring 1968): pp. 47-60.

Braswell, James S., and Todd Herman. "Pilot Study of the Impact of Hand-Held Calculator Use on College Board Mathematics Examinations." Princeton, N.J.: Educational Testing Service, 1980. Internal memorandum.

Braswell, James S., and Nancy Petersen. "An Investigation of Item Obsolescence in the Scholastic Aptitude Test." Appendix to *On Further Examination: Report of the Advisory Panel on the Scholastic Aptitude Test Score Decline,* Willard Wirtz, chairman. New York: College Entrance Examination Board, 1977.

Braun, Henry, John Centra, and Benjamin King. *Verbal and Mathematical Ability of High School Juniors and Seniors in 1983: A Norms Study of the psat/nmsqt and the sat.* College Board Research and Development Report. Princeton, N.J.: Educational Testing Service, 1985 (in press).

Breland, Hunter M. *Assessing Student Characteristics in Admissions to Higher Education: A Review of Procedures.* College Board Research Memorandum 81-09. New York: College Entrance Examination Board, 1981. (Also College Board Research Monograph No. 9).

Breland, Hunter M. *Group Comparisons for the Test of Standard Written English.* College Board Research and Development Report 77-78, No. 1. Princeton, N.J.: Educational Testing Service, 1977a. (Also ets Research Bulletin 77-15).

Breland, Hunter M. *Population Validity and College Entrance Measures.* College Board Research Memorandum 79-08. New York: College Entrance Examination Board, 1979. (Also College Board Research Monograph No. 8).

Breland, Hunter M. "The sat Score Decline: A Summary of Related Research." Appendix to *On Further Examination: Report of the Advisory Panel on the Scholastic Aptitude Test Score Decline,* Willard Wirtz, chairman. New York: College Entrance Examination Board, 1977b.

Breland, Hunter M. *A Study of College English Placement and the Test of Standard Written English.* College Board Research and Development Report 76-77, No. 4. Princeton, N.J.: Educational Testing Service, 1977c. (Also ets Project Report 77-01).

Breland, Hunter M., and Philip A. Griswold. *Group Comparisons for Basic Skill Measures.* College Board Report 81-6. New York: College Entrance Examination Board, 1981. (Also ets Research Report 81-21).

Breland, Hunter M., and Philip A. Griswold. "Use of a Performance Test as a Criterion in a Differential Validity Study." *Journal of Educational Psychology* 74, no. 5 (October 1982): pp. 713-21.

Breland, Hunter M., Gertrude C. Conlan, and David Rogosa. *A Preliminary Study of the Test of Standard Written English.* Princeton, N.J.: Educational Testing Service, 1976.

Bridgeman, Brent. "Comparative Validity of the College Board Scholastic Aptitude Test—Mathematics and the Descriptive Tests of Mathematics Skills for Predicting Performance in College Mathematics Courses." *Educational and Psychological Measurement* 42, no. 1 (Spring 1982): pp. 361-66.

Brigham, Carl C. *A Study of Error. A Summary and Evaluation of Methods Used in Six Years of Study of the Scholastic Aptitude Test of the College Entrance Examination Board.* New York: College Entrance Examination Board, 1932.

Brigham, Carl C., et al. "The Scholastic Aptitude Test of the College Entrance Examination Board." In *The Work of the College Entrance Examination Board 1901-1925,* edited by Thomas S. Fiske, pp. 44-63. New York: Ginn and Company, 1926.

Brogden, Hubert E. "On the Interpretation of the Correlation Coefficient as a Measure of Predictive Efficiency." *Journal of Educational Psychology* 37, no. 2 (February 1946): pp. 65-76.

Brown, Jane Lightcap, and Ralph Lightsey. "Differential Predictive Validity of sat Scores for Freshman College English." *Educational and Psychological Measurement* 30, no. 4 (Winter 1970): pp. 961-65.

Buros, Oscar K., ed. *The Eighth Mental Measurements Yearbook, Vol. I.* Highland Park, N.J.: The Gryphon Press, 1978.

Buros, Oscar K., ed. *The Seventh Mental Measurements Yearbook.* Highland Park, N.J.: The Gryphon Press, 1972.

Caldwell, Edward, and Rodney Hartnett. "Sex Bias in College Grading?" *Journal of Educational Measurement* 4, no. 3 (Fall 1967): pp. 129-32.

Carroll, John B. "Measurement of Abilities Constructs." In *Construct Validity in Psychological Measurement.* Proceedings from a Colloquium on Theory and Application in Education and Employment. (ets Microfiche 1939). Princeton, N.J.: Educational Testing Service, 1980.

Casserly, Patricia Lund. *Older Students and the sat.* College Board Report 82-8. New York: College Entrance Examination Board, 1982. (Also ets Research Report 82-49).

Chall, Jeanne S. "An Analysis of Textbooks in Relation to Declining sat Scores." Appendix to *On Further Examination: Report of the Advisory Panel on the Scholastic Aptitude Test Score Decline,* Willard Wirtz, chairman. New York: College Entrance Examination Board, 1977.

Chauncey, Henry. "Report of the President, 1961-62." In ets *Annual Report, 1961-62.* Princeton, N.J.: Educational Testing Service, 1962.

Cliff, Rosemary. "The Predictive Value of Chance-Level Scores." *Educational and Psychological Measurement* 18, no. 3 (Autumn 1958): pp. 607-16.

Coffman, William E. "The Achievement Tests." In *The College Board Admissions Testing Program: A Technical Report on Research and Development Activities Relating to the Scholastic Aptitude Test and Achievement Tests,* edited by William H. Angoff, pp. 49-77. New York: College Entrance Examination Board, 1971.

214

Coffman, William E. *A Factor Analysis of the Verbal Sections of the Scholastic Aptitude Test.* College Board Research and Development Report 65-6, No. 17. Princeton, N.J.: Educational Testing Service, 1966. (Also ETS Research Bulletin 66-30).

Coffman, William E. *The Scholastic Aptitude Test: 1926-1962.* Test Development Report 63-2. Princeton, N.J.: Educational Testing Service, 1963.

Coffman, William E. "Sex Differences in Responses to Items in an Aptitude Test." In *Eighteenth Yearbook,* pp. 117-24. Ames, Iowa: National Council on Measurement in Education, 1961.

Coffman, William E., and Mary E. Parry. "Effects of an Accelerated Reading Course on SAT-V Scores." *Personnel and Guidance Journal* 46, no. 3 (November 1967): pp. 292-96.

Cole, N. S. "Approaches to Examining Bias in Achievement Test Items." Paper presented at the annual meeting of the American Personnel and Guidance Association, Washington, D.C., March 1978.

College Board. *About the Achievement Tests.* New York: College Entrance Examination Board, 1983a.

College Board. *ATP Guide for High Schools and Colleges.* New York: College Entrance Examination Board, 1982a.

College Board. *The College Board Achievement Tests: 14 Tests in 13 Subjects.* New York: College Entrance Examination Board, 1983b.

College Board. *College Guide to the ATP Summary Reports.* New York: College Entrance Examination Board, 1983c.

College Board. *Effects of Coaching on Scholastic Aptitude Test Scores.* New York: College Entrance Examination Board, 1965a, 1968 rev.

College Board. *Freedom and Discipline in English. Report of the Commission on English.* New York: College Entrance Examination Board, 1965b.

College Board. *Guide to the College Board Validity Study Service.* New York: College Entrance Examination Board, 1982b.

College Board. *National College-Bound Seniors, 1983.* New York: College Entrance Examination Board, 1983d.

College Board. *National College-Bound Seniors, 1984.* New York: College Entrance Examination Board, 1984.

College Board. *On Further Examination: Report of the Advisory Panel on the Scholastic Aptitude Score Decline.* Willard Wirtz, chairman. New York: College Entrance Examination Board, 1977.

College Board. *Report of the Commission on Mathematics. Volume 1: Program for College Preparatory Mathematics. Volume 2: Appendices.* New York: College Entrance Examination Board, 1959a.

College Board. *Report of the Commission on Tests.* New York: College Entrance Examination Board, 1970.

College Board. *School Guide to the ATP Summary Reports.* New York: College Entrance Examination Board, 1983e.

College Board. "A Statement by the College Board Trustees on Test 'Coaching'." *The College Board Review* 38 (Spring 1959b): p. 3. New York: College Entrance Examination Board.

College Board. *Taking the SAT.* New York: College Entrance Examination Board, 1981, 1982c, 1983f.

College Board. *10 SATs.* New York: College Entrance Examination Board, 1983g.

College Board. *Your Score Report.* New York: College Entrance Examination Board, 1983h.

Conlan, Gertrude. *How the Essay in the College Board English Composition Test is Scored. An Introduction to the Reading for Readers.* Princeton, N.J.: Educational Testing Service, 1978.

Connolly, John A., and M. J. Wantman. "An Exploration of Oral Reasoning Processes in Responding to Objective Test Items." *Journal of Educational Measurement* 1, no. 1 (June 1964): pp. 59-64.

Cook, Linda, and June Stern. "Item Bias Study of December 1974 SAT for Black and White Candidates." Princeton, N.J.: Educational Testing Service, 1975. Unpublished memorandum.

Cowen, Michael B., and Norman M. Abrahams. *Selecting Qualified Candidates to the United States Naval Academy Using College Aptitude Test Scores.* NPRDC Special Report 82-20. San Diego, Calif.: Navy Personnel Research and Development Center, 1982.

Crouse, James. "The Effects of Academic Ability." In *Who Gets Ahead? The Determinants of Economic Success in America,* edited by Christopher Jencks, pp. 85-121. New York: Basic Books, 1979.

Cureton, Edward E. "The Correction for Guessing." *Journal of Experimental Education* 34, no. 4 (1966): pp. 44-47.

Dale, Edgar, and Jeanne S. Chall. *A Formula for Predicting Readability.* Bureau of Educational Research. Columbus, Ohio: Ohio State University, 1948. Reprinted from *Educational Research Bulletin,* January 21, 1948.

DerSimonian, Rebecca, and Nan M. Laird. "Evaluating the Effect of Coaching on SAT Scores: A Meta-Analysis." *Harvard Educational Review* 53, no. 1 (February 1983): pp. 1-15.

Diamond, James, and William Evans. "The Correction for Guessing." *Review of Educational Research* 43, no. 2 (Spring 1973): pp. 181-91.

Diederich, Paul B., and Osmond E. Palmer. *Difficulty in Grades 11 and 13 of 4,800 Words from 6,000 through 20,000 in Frequency.* ETS Research Bulletin 56-13. Princeton, N.J.: Educational Testing Service, 1956.

Diederich, Paul B., John W. French, and Sydell T. Carlton. *Factors in Judgments of Writing Ability.* ETS Research Bulletin 61-15. Princeton, N.J.: Educational Testing Service, 1961.

Donlon, Thomas F. *Content Factors in Sex Differences on Test Questions.* ETS Research Memorandum 73-28. Princeton, N.J.: Educational Testing Service, 1973.

Dorans, Neil J., and Edward Kulick. *Assessing Unexpected Differential Item Performance of Female Candidates on SAT and TSWE Forms Administered in December 1977: An Application of the Standardization Approach.* ETS Research Report 83-9. Princeton, N.J.: Educational Testing Service, 1983.

Dressel, Paul L. "Some Remarks on the Kuder-Richardson Reliability Coefficient." *Psychometrika* 5, no. 4 (December 1940): pp. 305-10.

Durán, Richard P. *Hispanics' Education and Background: Predictors of College Achievement.* New York: College Entrance Examination Board, 1983.

Dyer, Henry S. *College Board Scores (No. 1): Their Use and Interpretation.* New York: College Entrance Examination Board, 1953.

Dyer, Henry S., and Richard G. King. *College Board Scores (No. 2): Their Use and Interpretation.* New York: College Entrance Examination Board, 1955.

Educational Testing Service (in collaboration with Marjorie Kirrie). *The English Composition Test with Essay.* Princeton, N.J.: College Entrance Examination Board, 1979.

Educational Testing Service. ETS *Standards for Quality and Fairness.* Princeton, N.J.: Educational Testing Service, 1983.

Educational Testing Service. *Test Scores and Family Income: A Response to Charges in the Nader/Nairn Report on* ETS. Princeton, N.J.: Educational Testing Service, 1980a.

Educational Testing Service. *Test Use and Validity: A Response to Charges in the Nader/Nairn Report on* ETS. Princeton, N.J.: Educational Testing Service, 1980b.

Fan, Chung-Teh. "On the Applications of the Method of Absolute Scaling." *Psychometrika* 22, no. 2 (June 1957): pp. 175-83.

Federal Trade Commission, Boston Regional Office. *Staff Memorandum of the Boston Regional Office of the* FTC: *The Effects of Coaching on Standardized Admission Examinations.* Boston, Mass.: Federal Trade Commission, Boston Regional Office, 1978.

Feldt, Leonard S. "Estimation of the Reliability of a Test Divided into Two Parts of Unequal Length." *Psychometrika* 40, no. 4 (December 1975): pp. 557-61.

Fincher, Cameron. "Using Tests Constructively in an Era of Controversy." *The College Board Review* 113 (Fall 1979): pp. 2-7.

Fishman, Joshua A. *1957 Supplement to College Board Scores No. 2.* New York: College Entrance Examination Board, 1957.

Flaugher, Ronald L. "The Many Definitions of Test Bias." *American Psychologist* 33, no. 7 (July 1978): pp. 671-79.

Flaugher, Ronald L., and Donald A. Rock. *The Wide Range Validity of Certain New Aptitude Tests.* College Board Research and Development Report 66-7, No. 8. Princeton, N.J.: Educational Testing Service, 1966. (Also ETS Research Bulletin 66-54).

Ford, Susan F., and Sandy Campos. "Summary of Validity Data from the Admissions Testing Program Validity Study Service." Appendix to *On Further Examination: Report of the Advisory Panel on the* SAT *Score Decline,* Willard Wirtz, chairman. New York: College Entrance Examination Board, 1977.

French, John W. "New Tests for Predicting the Performance of College Students with High-Level Aptitude." *Journal of Educational Psychology* 55, no. 4 (1964): pp. 185-94.

French, John W. *Validation of the* SAT *and New Item Types Against Four-Year Academic Criteria.* ETS Research Bulletin 57-4. Princeton, N.J.: Educational Testing Service, 1957.

French, John W. *The Validity of New Tests for the Performance of College Students with High-Level Aptitude.* ETS Research Bulletin 63-7. Princeton, N.J.: Educational Testing Service, 1963.

French, John W., Ruth Ekstrom, and L. A. Price. *Kit of Reference Tests for Cognitive Factors.* Princeton, N.J.: Educational Testing Service, 1963.

Fuess, Claude M. *The College Board: Its First Fifty Years.* New York: Columbia University Press, 1950.

Gentile, J. Ronald. *Toward an Experimental Analysis of Reasoning on the Scholastic Aptitude Test: A Pilot Study.* ETS Research Memorandum 66-26. Princeton, N.J.: Educational Testing Service, 1966.

Gentile, J. Ronald, Delores K. Kessler, and Patricia K. Gentile. "Process of Solving Analogy Items." *Journal of Educational Psychology* 60, no. 6 (December 1969): pp. 494-502.

Gilbert, John P., Frederick Mosteller, and Richard J. Light. "Assessing Social Innovations: An Empirical Base for Policy." In *Statistics and Public Policy,* edited by William B. Fairley and Frederick Mosteller, pp. 185-241. Reading, Mass.: Addison-Wesley Publishing Co., 1977.

Godshalk, Fred I., Frances Swineford, and William E. Coffman. *The Measurement of Writing Ability.* College Board Research Monograph No. 6. New York: College Entrance Examination Board, 1966.

Goldman, Roy D., and Barbara Newlin Hewitt. "Adaptation-Level as an Explanation for Differential Standards in College Grading." *Journal of Educational Measurement* 12, no. 3 (Fall 1975): pp. 149-61.

Goldman, Roy D., and Dennis W. Sexton. "Archival Experiments with College Admission Policies." *American Educational Research Journal* 11, no. 2 (Spring 1974): pp. 195-201.

Goldman, Roy D., and Mel H. Widawski. "A Within-Subjects Technique for Comparing Grading Standards: Implications in the Validity of the Evaluation of College Achievement." *Educational and Psychological Measurement* 36, no. 2 (Summer 1976): pp. 381-90.

Goldman, Roy D., Donald E. Schmidt, Barbara Newlin Hewitt, and Ronald Fisher. "Grading Practices in Different Major Fields." *American Educational Research Journal* 11, no. 4 (Fall 1974): pp. 343-57.

Guilford, Joy Paul. *The Nature of Human Intelligence.* New York: McGraw-Hill, 1967.

Guilford, Joy Paul, and Benjamin Fruchter. *Fundamental Statistics in Psychology and Education,* 6th ed. New York: McGraw-Hill, 1978.

Gulliksen, Harold. *Theory of Mental Tests.* New York: John Wiley & Sons, 1950.

Gussett, James C. "College Entrance Examination Board Scholastic Aptitude Test Scores as a Predictor for College Freshman Mathematics Grades." *Educational and Psychological Measurement* 34, no. 4 (Winter 1974): pp. 953-55.

Hackman, Judith D., and Paula Johnson. "How Well Do Freshmen Write? Implications for Placement and Pedagogy." *College and University* 53, no. 1 (Fall 1977): pp. 81-99.

Hanford, George H. *Minority Programs and Activities of the College Entrance Examination Board: A Critical Review and a Brief Look Ahead.* New York: College Entrance Examination Board, 1976.

Hartnett, Rodney T., and Robert A. Feldmesser. "College Admissions Testing and the Myth of Selectivity: Unresolved Questions and Needed Research." AAHE *Bulletin* 32, no. 7 (March 1980): pp. 3-6.

Heath, Douglas H. "Academic Predictors of Adult Maturity and Competence." *Journal of Higher Education* 48, no. 6 (November/December 1977): pp. 613-32.

Hecht, Lawrence W., and Frances Swineford. *Item Analysis at Educational Testing Service.* Princeton, N.J.: Educational Testing Service, June 1981.

Hills, John R., and Marilyn B. Gladney. "Predicting Grades from Below Chance Test Scores." *Journal of Educational Measurement* 5, no. 1 (Spring 1968): pp. 45-53.

Hilton, Thomas L. "ETS Study of Academic Prediction and Growth." *New Directions for Testing and Measurement,* No. 2 (1979): pp. 27-44. San Francisco, Calif.: Jossey-Bass, 1979.

Hilton, Thomas L. *Persistence in Higher Education: An Empirical Study.* College Board Report 82-5. New York: College Entrance Examination Board, 1982. (Also ETS Research Report 82-44).

Hoffman, Banesh. *The Tyranny of Testing.* New York: Crowell-Collier Press, 1962.

Hunt, Earl, Clifford Lunneborg, and Joe Lewis. "What Does It Mean to be High Verbal?" *Cognitive Psychology* 7, no. 1 (January 1975): pp. 194-227. New York: Academic Press, 1975.

Hunter, J. E. "A Critical Analysis of the Use of Item Means and Item-Test Correlations to Determine the Presence or Absence of Content Bias in Achievement Test Items." Paper presented at the National Institute of Education Conference on Test Bias, Annapolis, Maryland, December 1975.

Jackson, Rex, and William B. Schrader. *Verbal and Mathematical Ability of High School Juniors in 1974: A Norms Study of PSAT/NMSQT.* College Board Research and Development Report 76-77, No. 2. Princeton, N.J.: Educational Testing Service, 1976. (Also ETS Research Bulletin 76-27).

Jacobs, James N. "Aptitude and Achievement Measures in Predicting High School Academic Success." *Personnel and Guidance Journal* 37 (January 1959): pp. 324-34.

Jones, Douglas H., and Marjorie Ragosta. *Predictive Validity of the SAT on Two Handicapped Groups: the Deaf and the Learning Disabled.* ETS Research Report 82-9. Princeton, N.J.: Educational Testing Service, 1982. (Also Program Statistics Research Technical Report 82-27).

Jones, L. V., Nancy W. Burton, and E. C. Davenport. *Mathematics Achievement Levels of Black and White Youth.* L. L. Thurstone Psychometric Laboratory Report #165. Chapel Hill, N.C.: University of North Carolina, 1982.

Kirk, Barbara A., and Lynn Sereda. "Accuracy of Self-Reported College Grade Averages and Characteristics of Non and Discrepant Reporters." *Educational and Psychological Measurement* 29, no. 1 (1969): pp. 147-55.

Kuder, G. F., and M. W. Richardson. "The Theory of the Estimation of Test Reliability." *Psychometrika* 2, no. 3 (September 1937): pp. 151-60.

Kulick, Edward, and Neil J. Dorans. *Assessing Unexpected Differential Item Performance of Candidates Reporting Different Levels of Father's Education on SAT Form CSA2 and TSWE Form E29.* Statistical Report 83-27. Princeton, N.J.: Educational Testing Service, 1983a.

Kulick, Edward, and Neil J. Dorans. *Assessing Unexpected Differential Item Performance of Oriental Candidates on SAT Form CSA6 and TSWE Form E33.* Statistical Report 83-106. Princeton, N.J.: Educational Testing Service, 1983b.

Levine, Richard S. *Equating the Score Scales of Alternate Forms Administered to Samples of Different Ability.* ETS Research Bulletin 55-23. Princeton, N.J.: Educational Testing Service, 1955.

Levine, Richard S., and Frederic M. Lord. *An Index of the Discriminating Power of a Test at Different Parts of the Score Range.* ETS Research Bulletin 58-13. Princeton, N.J.: Educational Testing Service, 1958.

Linn, Robert L. "Fair Test Use in Selection." *Review of Educational Research* 43, no. 2 (Spring 1973): pp. 139-61.

Linn, Robert L. "Pearson Selection Formulas: Implications for Studies of Predictive Bias and Estimates of Educational Effects in Selected Samples." *Journal of Educational Measurement* 20, no. 1 (Spring): pp. 1-15 (1983a).

Linn, Robert L. "Predictive Bias as an Artifact of Selection Procedures." In *Principles of Modern Psychological Measurement: A Festschrift for Frederic M. Lord,* edited by Howard Wainer and Samuel Messick, pp. 27-40. Hillsdale, N.J.: Lawrence Erlbaum Associates, 1983b.

Linn, Robert L. "Selection Bias: Multiple Meaning." *Journal of Educational Measurement* 21, no. 1 (Spring 1984): pp. 33-47.

Linn, Robert L., Delwyn L. Harnisch, and Stephen B. Dunbar. "Corrections for Range Restriction: An Empirical Investigation of Conditions Resulting in Conservative Corrections." *Journal of Applied Psychology* 66, no. 6 (December 1981): pp. 655-63.

Lockheed, Marlaine E., Paul W. Holland, and William P. Nemceff. *Student Characteristics and the Use of the SAT Disclosure Materials.* College Board Report 82-3. New York: College Entrance Examination Board, 1982. (Also ETS Research Report 82-31).

Lord, Frederic M. *Applications of Item Response Theory.* Hillsdale, N.J.: Lawrence Erlbaum Associates, 1980.

Lord, Frederic M. "Nominally and Rigorously Parallel Test Forms." *Psychometrika* 29, no. 4 (December 1964): pp. 335-45.

Lord, Frederic M. "A Study of Item Bias Using Item Characteristic Curve Theory." In *Basic Problems in Cross-Cultural Psychology,* edited by Ype H. Poortinga. Amsterdam: Swets and Zeitlinger, 1977.

Lord, Frederic M., and Melvin R. Novick. *Statistical Theories of Mental Test Scores.* Reading, Mass.: Addison-Wesley Publishing Co., 1968.

Lucas, Charles M. *Analysis of the Relative Movement Test by a Method of Interviews.* ETS Research Bulletin 53-4. Princeton, N.J.: Educational Testing Service, 1953.

McNemar, Quinn. "Lost: Our Intelligence. Why?" *American Psychologist* 19, no. 12 (1964): pp. 871-82.

Manski, Charles F., and David A. Wise. *College Choice in America.* Cambridge, Mass.: Harvard University Press, 1983.

Marco, Gary L. "Item Characteristic Curve Solutions to Three Intractable Testing Problems." *Journal of Educational Measurement* 14, no. 2 (Summer 1977): pp. 139-60.

Marco, Gary L., Nancy S. Petersen, and E. Elizabeth Stewart. *A Large-Scale Evaluation of Linear and Curvilinear Score Equating Models.* ETS Research Memorandum 83-2. Princeton, N.J.: Educational Testing Service, 1983.

Marron, Joseph E. *Preparatory School Test Preparation. Special Test Preparation, Its Effect on College Board Scores and the Relationship of Effected Scores to Subsequent College Performance.* West Point, N.Y.: United States Military Academy, 1965.

Maxey, E. James., and Victor J. Ormsby. *The Accuracy of Self-Report Information Collected on the ACT Test Battery: High School Grades and Items of Non-academic Achievement.* ACT Research Report No. 45. Iowa City, Iowa: The American College Testing Program, 1971.

Messick, Samuel. "Beyond Structure: In Search of Functional Models of Psychological Process." *Psychometrika* 37, no. 4 (December 1972): pp. 357-75.

Messick, Samuel. *The Effectiveness of Coaching for the SAT: Review and Reanalysis of Research from the Fifties to the FTC.* Princeton, N.J.: Educational Testing Service, 1980.

Messick, Samuel, and Ann Jungeblut. "Time and Method in Coaching for the SAT." *Psychological Bulletin* 89, no. 2 (1981): pp. 191-216.

Michael, William B., and Phyllis Shaffer. "A Comparison of the Validity of the Test of Standard Written English (TSWE) and of the California State University and Colleges English Placement Test (CSUC-EPT) in the Prediction of Grades in a Basic English Composition Course and of Overall Freshman-Year Grade Point Average." *Educational and Psychological Measurement* 39, no. 1 (Spring 1979): pp. 131-45.

Modu, Christopher C. *The Effectiveness of an Essay Section in the American History and Social Studies Test.* College Board Research and Development Report 71-72, No. 6. Princeton, N.J.: Educational Testing Service, February 1972. (Also ETS Research Bulletin 72-5).

Modu, Christopher C., and June Stern. *The Stability of the SAT Score Scale.* College Board Research and Development Report 74-75, No. 3. Princeton, N.J.: Educational Testing Service, 1975. (Also ETS Research Bulletin 75-9).

Modu, Christopher C., and June Stern. "The Stability of the SAT-Verbal Score Scale." Appendix to *On Further Examination: Report of the Advisory Panel on the Scholastic Aptitude Test Score Decline,* Willard Wirtz, chairman. New York: College Entrance Examination Board, 1977.

Munday, Leo. "Predicting Grades Using ACT Data." *Educational and Psychological Measurement* 27, no. 2 (1967): pp. 401-6.

Nelson, G. Lynn. "Toward Teaching English for the Real World." *English Journal* 63 (September 1974): pp. 45-49.

Nicholson, Everard. *Success and Admission Criteria for Potentially Successful Risks.* Providence, R.I.: Brown University, 1970.

Northrup, Lois C. "The Definition and Measurement of Verbal Comprehension." United States Civil Service Commission Technical Memorandum 77-11. Washington, D.C.: United States Civil Service Commission, 1977.

Olsen, Marjorie, and William B. Schrader. *A Comparison of Item Types in the College Board Scholastic Aptitude Test.* Statistical Report 53-43. Princeton, N.J.: Educational Testing Service, 1953.

Osterlund, Blair L., and Kenneth Cheney. "A Holistic Essay-reading Composite as Criterion for the Validity of the Test of Standard Written English." *Measurement and Evaluation in Guidance* 11, no. 3 (1978): pp. 155-58.

Pallone, Nathaniel J. "Effects of Short- and Long-Term Developmental Reading Courses upon SAT Verbal Scores." *Personnel and Guidance Journal* 39, no. 8 (April 1961): pp. 654-57.

Palmer, Orville. "Sixty Years of English Testing." *The College Board Review* 42 (Fall 1960): pp. 8-14.

Pearson, Karl. "Mathematical Contributions to the Theory of Evolution—XI. On the Influence of Natural Selection on the Variability and Correlation of Organs." *Philosophical Transactions of the Royal Society of London:* Series A, 1903, 200: pp. 1-66.

Pedersen, L. G. "The Correlation of Partial and Total Scores of the Scholastic Aptitude Test of the College Entrance Examination Board with Grades in Freshman Chemistry." *Educational and Psychological Measurement* 35, no. 2 (Summer 1975): pp. 509-11.

Petersen, Nancy S., Linda L. Cook, and Martha L. Stocking. "IRT Versus Conventional Equating Methods: A Comparative Study of Scale Stability." *Journal of Educational Statistics* 8, no. 2 (Summer 1983): pp. 137-56.

Pike, Lewis W. *Short-Term Instruction, Testwiseness, and the Scholastic Aptitude Test: A Literature Review with Research Recommendations.* College Board Research and Development Report 77-78, No. 2. Princeton, N.J.: Educational Testing Service, 1978. (Also ETS Research Bulletin 78-2).

Pike, Lewis W., and Franklin R. Evans. *Effects of Special Instruction for Three Kinds of Mathematics Aptitude Items.* College Board Research and Development Report 71-72, No. 7. Princeton, N.J.: Educational Testing Service, 1972. (Also College Board Research Report 72-1 and ETS Research Bulletin 72-19).

Powers, Donald E. *Estimating the Effects of Various Methods of Preparing for the SAT.* College Board Report 82-2. New York: College Entrance Examination Board, 1982. (Also ETS Research Report 82-23).

Powers, Donald E. *Students' Use of and Reactions to Alternative Methods of Preparing for the SAT.* College Board Research and Development Report 80-81, No. 3. Princeton, N.J.: Educational Testing Service, 1980. (Also ETS Research Report 80-30).

Powers, Donald E., and Donald L. Alderman. *The Use, Acceptance, and Impact of "Taking the SAT"—A Test Familiarization Booklet.* College Board Research and Development Report 78-79, No. 6. Princeton, N.J.: Educational Testing Service, February 1979. (Also ETS Research Report 79-3).

Pruzek, Robert M., and William E. Coffman. *A Factor Analysis of the Mathematical Sections of the Scholastic Aptitude Test.* College Board Research and Development Report 65-6, No. 10. Princeton, N.J.: Educational Testing Service, 1966. (Also ETS Research Bulletin 66-12).

Ramist, Leonard, and Solomon Arbeiter. *Profiles, College-Bound Seniors, 1983.* New York: College Entrance Examination Board, 1983.

Response Analysis Corporation. "The College Admission Experience. A Developmental Study Conducted for the College Entrance Examination Board and Educational Testing Service." Princeton, N.J.: Response Analysis Corporation, October 1975. Unpublished manuscript.

Response Analysis Corporation. SAT *Monitor Program. High School Students View the SAT and College Admission Process.* Report on wave of completed questionnaires associated with December 1977 SAT administration. Prepared for the College Board. Princeton, N.J.: Response Analysis Corporation, July 1978.

Rock, Donald A., and Charles E. Werts. *An Analysis of Time-Related Score Increments and/or Decrements for GRE Repeaters Across Ability and Sex Groups.* Graduate Record Examinations Board Report 77-9R. Princeton, N.J.: Educational Testing Service, 1979a.

Rock, Donald A., and Charles E. Werts. *Construct Validity of the SAT across Populations—An Empirical Confirmatory Study.* College Board Research and Development Report 78-79, No. 5. Princeton, N.J.: Educational Testing Service, 1979b. (Also ETS Research Report 79-2).

Sawyer, Richard, and E. James Maxey. *The Relationship Between College Freshman Class Size and Other Institutional Characteristics and the Accuracy of Freshman Grade Predictions.* ACT Research Report No. 82. Iowa City, Iowa: The American College Testing Program, 1982.

Schrader, William B. *Admissions Test Scores as Predictors of Career Achievement in Psychology.* Graduate Record Examinations Board Report 76-1aR. Princeton, N.J.: Educational Testing Service, 1978.

Schrader, William B. "The Predictive Validity of College Board Admissions Tests." In *The College Board Admissions Testing Program: A Technical Report on Research and Development Activities Relating to the Scholastic Aptitude Test and Achievement Tests,* edited by William H. Angoff, pp. 117-45. New York: College Entrance Examination Board, 1971.

Schrader, William B. *Validity of the Quantitative Comparisons Test.* Statistical Report 73-60. Princeton, N.J.: Educational Testing Service, 1973.

Schrader, William B., and Thomas L. Hilton. *Educational Attainment of American High School Seniors in 1960, 1965, and 1972 Feasibility Study.* Project Report No. 75-13. Princeton, N.J.: Educational Testing Service, 1975.

Schrader, William B., and E. Elizabeth Stewart. "Descriptive Statistics on College Board Candidates and Other Reference Groups." In *The College Board Admissions Testing Program: A Technical Report on Research and Development Activities Relating to the Scholastic Aptitude Test and Achievement Tests,* edited by William H. Angoff, pp. 79-115. New York: College Entrance Examination Board, 1971.

Seashore, Harold G. "Women Are More Predictable Than Men." *Journal of Counseling Psychology* 9, no. 3 (1962): pp. 261-70.

Seibel, Dean W. *Follow-Up Study of a National Sample of High School Seniors: Phase 2—One Year After Graduation.* College Board Research and Development Report 65-6, No. 1. Princeton, N.J.: Educational Testing Service, 1965a. (Also Statistical Report 65-62).

Seibel, Dean W. *A Study of the Academic Ability and Performance of Junior College Students.* EAS Field Studies Report 1. Princeton, N.J.: Educational Testing Service, 1965b.

Shepard, Lorrie A. "Identifying Bias in Test Items." *New Directions for Testing and Measurement,* No. 11 (September 1981). San Francisco, Calif.: Jossey-Bass, 1981.

Slack, Warner V., and Douglas Porter. "The Scholastic Aptitude Test: A Critical Appraisal." *Harvard Educational Review* 50, no. 2 (May 1980): pp. 154-75.

Slakter, Malcolm J. "Generality of Risk Taking on Objective Examinations." *Educational and Psychological Measurement* 29, no. 1 (1969): pp. 115-28.

Stanley, Julian C. "The Predictive Value of the SAT for Brilliant Seventh- and Eighth-Graders." *The College Board Review* 106 (Winter 1977-78): pp. 30-37.

Stern, June. *College Board Item Bias Study of the Scholastic Aptitude Test and the Test of Standard Written English Form XSA2/E4.* Statistical Report 78-56. Princeton, N.J.: Educational Testing Service, 1978.

Stern, June. "Item Bias Study of November 1974 SAT for Black and White Candidates." Princeton, N.J.: Educational Testing Service, 1975. Unpublished memorandum.

Stewart, E. Elizabeth. *The Stability of the SAT-Verbal Score Scale.* College Board Research and Development Report 66-7, No. 3. Princeton, N.J.: Educational Testing Service, 1966. (Also ETS Research Bulletin 66-37).

Strassberg-Rosenberg, Barbara, and Thomas F. Donlon. "Content Influences on Sex Differences in Performance on Aptitude Tests." Paper presented at the annual meeting of the National Council on Measurement in Education, Washington, D.C., March 1975.

Stricker, Lawrence J. *Test Disclosure and Retest Performance on the Scholastic Aptitude Test.* College Board Report 82-7. New York: College Entrance Examination Board, 1982. (Also ETS Research Report 82-48).

Swineford, Frances M. *The '800' Score on the Scholastic Aptitude Test.* Statistical Report 71-106. Princeton, N.J.: Educational Testing Service, November 1971.

Swineford, Frances M.. *A Technical Manual for Users of Test Analyses.* Statistical Report 56-42. Princeton, N.J.: Educational Testing Service, 1956.

Swineford, Frances M.. *The Test Analysis Manual.* Statistical Report 74-06. Princeton, N.J.: Educational Testing Service, 1974.

Swineford, Frances M., and Chung-Teh Fan. "A Method of Score Conversion through Item Statistics." *Psychometrika* 22, no. 2 (June 1957): pp. 185-88.

Swineford, Frances M., and Peter M. Miller. "Effects of Directions Regarding Guessing on Item Statistics of a Multiple-Choice Vocabulary Test." *Journal of Educational Psychology* 44, no. 3 (March 1953): pp. 129-39.

Thorndike, Edward L., and Irving Lorge. *The Teacher's Word Book of 30,000 Words.* New York: Columbia University, 1944.

Thorndike, Robert L. "Concepts of Culture-Fairness." *Journal of Educational Measurement* 8, no. 2 (Summer 1971): pp. 63-70.

Thurstone, L. L. "The Calibration of Test Items." *American Psychologist* 2 (1947): pp. 103-4.

Troutman, James G. "Cognitive Predictors of Final Grades in Finite Mathematics." *Educational and Psychological Measurement* 38, no. 2 (Summer 1978): pp. 401-4.

Trusheim, Dale, and James Crouse. "The ETS Admissions Formula: Does the SAT Add Useful Information?" *Phi Delta Kappan* 64, no. 1 (September 1982): pp. 59-61.

Walker, ReLinda C. *A Reader's Guide to Test Analysis Reports.* Princeton, N.J.: Educational Testing Service, March 1981.

Ward, William C., Norman Frederiksen, and Sybil Carlson. *Construct Validity of Free-Response and Machine-Scorable Versions of a Test of Scientific Thinking.* ETS Research Bulletin 78-15. Princeton, N.J.: Educational Testing Service, 1978. (Also GREB-74-8P).

Warren, Jonathan R. *Prediction of College Achievement among Mexican-American Students in California.* College Board Research and Development Report 76-77, No. 1. Princeton, N.J.: Educational Testing Service, 1976. (Also ETS Research Bulletin 76-22).

Whitely, Susan E. "Relationships in Analogy Items: A Semantic Component of a Psychometric Test." *Educational and Psychological Measurement* 37, no. 3 (Autumn 1977): pp. 725-39.

Wild, Cheryl L. "Statistical Issues Raised by Title IX Requirements on Admission Procedures." *Journal of the National Association of Women Deans, Administrators, and Counselors* 40 (Winter 1977): pp. 53-56.

Wilks, Samuel S., ed. *Scaling and Equating College Board Tests.* Princeton, N.J.: Educational Testing Service, 1961.

Willingham, Warren W. *College Placement and Exemption.* New York: College Entrance Examination Board, 1974.

Willingham, Warren W., and Hunter M. Breland. *Personal Qualities and Admissions.* New York: College Entrance Examination Board, 1982.

Willingham, Warren W., and Leonard Ramist. "The SAT Debate: Do Trusheim and Crouse Add Useful Information?" *Phi Delta Kappan* 64, no. 3 (November 1982): pp. 207-8.

Wilson, Kenneth M. *Predicting the Long-term Performance in College of Minority and Nonminority Students: A Comparative Analysis in Two Collegiate Settings.* College Board Research and Development Report 77-78, No. 3. Princeton, N.J.: Educational Testing Service, 1978. (Also ETS Research Bulletin 78-6).

Wilson, Kenneth M. *A Review of Research on the Prediction of Academic Performance After the Freshman Year.* College Board Report 83-2. New York: College Entrance Examination Board, 1983. (Also ETS Research Report 83-11).

Wingersky, Marilyn S. "LOGIST: A Program for Computing Maximum Likelihood Procedures for Logistic Test Models." In *Applications of Item Response Theory,* edited by Ronald K. Hambleton. Vancouver, British Columbia: Educational Research Institute of British Columbia, 1983.

Wingersky, Marilyn S., Mark A. Barton, and Frederic M. Lord. LOGIST *User's Guide.* Princeton, N.J.: Educational Testing Service, 1982.

Zeleznik, Carter, Mohammadreza Hojat, and Jon Veloski. "Long-Range Predictive and Differential Validities of the Scholastic Aptitude Test in Medical School." *Educational and Psychological Measurement* 43, no. 1 (Spring 1983): pp. 223-32.

Index

1104101 • U55P 12 • 001834 • Printed in U.S.A.